RAILWAY
MAN

RAILWAY MAN
AN ENGINEER'S MEMOIR

R.R. JARUHAR

RUPA

Published by
Rupa Publications India Pvt. Ltd 2020
7/16, Ansari Road, Daryaganj
New Delhi 110002

Sales Centres:
Allahabad Bengaluru Chennai
Hyderabad Jaipur Kathmandu
Kolkata Mumbai

Copyright © R.R. Jaruhar, 2020

The views and opinions expressed in this book are the author's own and the facts are as reported by him which have been verified to the extent possible, and the publishers are not in any way liable for the same.

All rights reserved.
No part of this publication may be reproduced, transmitted, or stored in a retrieval system, in any form or by any means, electronic, mechanical, photocopying, recording or otherwise, without the prior permission of the publisher.

ISBN: 978-93-5333-995-1

First impression 2020

10 9 8 7 6 5 4 2 3 1

The moral right of the author has been asserted.

Printed by Parksons Graphics Pvt. Ltd., Mumbai.

This book is sold subject to the condition that it shall not, by way of trade or otherwise, be lent, resold, hired out, or otherwise circulated, without the publisher's prior consent, in any form of binding or cover other than that in which it is published.

*To my supreme Father without whose
help this could not have been written*

CONTENTS

Foreword ix

Preface xi

1. A Way of Life As a Railway Engineer 1
2. Early Impressions of a Railway Engineer 6
3. The Proverbial First Posting 11
4. Construction Engineering 23
5. Open Line Works—for a Change 37
6. Brahmaputra Bridge—New Construction Phase 50
7. The Algerian Experience 102
8. Back to the Indian Railways 123
9. The Great River Gandak Beckons 129
10. Managing the Division—Firozpur 166
11. Return to Wilderness 200
12. Enter the Railway Board 208
13. Secretary Railway Board 226
14. Managing Zonal Railway: Northern Railway 268
15. The Last Post 316

Epilogue 384

Acknowledgements 387

FOREWORD

I was a little surprised when Rajiv approached me to write the foreword to the extremely interesting book he had penned on the life of a railwayman.

I was surprised because throughout his career Rajiv had strenuously tried to avoid even a mention of my relationship with him, much less take advantage of it. However, many pages later in the book, I suddenly came across a personal reference to me where he describes an incident in which the then governor of Chhattisgarh, who was a very close friend of mine, enquired about Rajiv's whereabouts from Nitish Kumar, the then railway minister, when he learnt that Rajiv (who was secretary Railway Board at that time), was also present in the same function. On their way back from the function when Nitish Kumar asked the chairman Railway Board whether he knew that Rajiv Jaruhar was closely related to me (I was then finance minister of India), the chairman said that Rajiv had never told him about that. Nitish ji said that he had also never told him that. As such he was surprised, as anyone in his position would have been because Nitish ji was also my close friend. I was however not surprised because that was the tradition followed by everyone in the family whenever I held an important position in government. Nobody believed in flaunting the connection or taking advantage of it. But that brings me to another issue.

When someone is placed, as Rajiv was placed then, taking advantage of the connection would not occur to him and allowing him any out-of-the-way favour would be unthinkable for me because that is the norm in the family. But what about the punishment he would receive in another government because of that connection? When the then Cabinet secretary B.K. Chaturvedi wrote a book on his years in office he invited me to launch it in Delhi. In the book, he describes a rather sad and sordid episode, which was in fact a blot on the governance standards of those days, when Rajiv's promotion as chairman Railway Board was cancelled—a decision taken at the level of the prime minister—because the railway minister objected to it vociferously, not on the grounds of Rajiv's incompetence but because he was related to me: a member of Parliament in the Opposition then, who was inconvenient to the rulers of the day.

This brings me to the basic issue that I want to raise. All hell will break loose if a politician's relative gets something he richly deserves. It will immediately be broadcast as an undeserved favour. But there is complete silence when a gross injustice is heaped upon someone by a vindictive regime only because he happens to be related to a politician belonging to an Opposition party. I shall forever regret the fact that Rajiv had to pay a huge price because he was related to me.

Be that as it may, Rajiv must have had the satisfaction that he gave his best to the Railways which he served with not only dedication, but also passion. He built an unparalleled expertise in the construction of bridges and in the book, he describes in some detail how he overcame the challenges, technical and other, in the construction of some of the best bridges like Brahmaputra, Gandak in the country. His other major contribution was in the turnaround of the Railways between 2005 and 2007.

I remember that when Nitish ji was the railway minister and I was the finance minister we had agreed on a financial package of ₹17,000 crore as Special Rail Safety Fund for the Railways to strengthen the bridges and the tracks. Once this task was completed, a visionary like Rajiv could immediately realize that the wagons could carry a higher load. This involved altogether an innovative approach. In this book, he has described how a problem defying solution for over twenty-five years could be resolved. This made the turnaround of Railways possible as the Railways started earning more with the same rolling stock. This has been a subject matter of research and discussion in various institutions of repute like the IIMs, ISB, Harvard Business School.

I personally know how busy he was when in service and how he devoted almost all his time to the job in hand, often to the neglect of his family responsibilities. He keeps busy even now because his expertise is much in demand.

This book, *Railwayman: An Engineer's Memoir*, I hope, will be read not only by the members of the fraternity to which he belongs, but also by all others who are interested in the life and times of a dedicated railwayman, a sincere civil servant, an outstanding engineer and, above all, one of the finest human beings.

Yashwant Sinha
Former Union finance minister

PREFACE

Indian Railways is a large government-run organization. A railway engineer in earlier times nearly always meant a civil engineer. In trying to understand why this was so, I soon came to the realization that engineering had originally been developed for its military application. When the application grew more extensive, to improve the standard of living of the general public, it was called Civil Engineering to distinguish it from Military Engineering. In the beginning, it covered all the other disciplines like Mechanical and Electrical Engineering. But in time, the development in the other fields was so much that it could not be contained in one discipline.

A rapid development and industrial growth necessitated a mass or bulk surface transport. The invention of railways for this purpose therefore was a big breakthrough for the Industrial Revolution. Civil engineering which involved construction of new railway lines, tracks, bridges, etc., helped provide this basic framework. This was the cornerstone of development in railways, and the civil engineer was seen as the leader who spearheaded this development. Thus, the engineer was seen as a leader in the development of infrastructure to run the railways. That is why, 'engineer' meant a civil engineer only. Like Military Engineering, disciplines like Mechanical, Electrical, Signalling & Telecommunications were subsequently added as distinctly separate fields. When we joined the Indian Railways, Electrical and Signalling & Telecommunications (S&T) were still called minor departments. Pay scales of the heads of these departments including Stores were a grade lower than those of the major departments like Civil, Traffic and Mechanical Engineering. Today it is no longer so. Vital developments in these fields have led them to command greater importance in the Railways. They have now earned their rightful place in the railway organization.

Civil servants, be it an official district gazetteer recording anecdotes or one writing their memoir, have contributed richly and provided interesting information on how the bureaucracy works. An engineer choosing to reminisce however is rather unusual. There are not many known instances of railway engineers putting their experiences to paper. An engineer is often assumed to be a factual kind of person, unwilling or unable to express their experiences in colourful anecdotes as a civil servant. But there is a story residing in every man, however unadorned or unexaggerated it may be. Some lives are marked by great highs and lows that make it conducive to good storytelling. Importantly, a good story does not only entertain, it instructs. As an engineer, I was actively engaged in construction work in various parts of the country. I came across not only unsurmountable problems but also ingenious solutions to these problems. I met different kinds of people—good, bad and indifferent who led me further down my life's way. I often sensed the gentle, guiding presence of the Divine in my life, in the way it lent me a helping hand again and again. I felt a compulsion, an almost moral obligation, to record my experiences, for I remembered how I had benefitted from the experiences of eminent civil engineers and the urge to share my story grew.

Dr Radhakrishnan mentions in his autobiography that even the most insignificant thing when written sincerely becomes meaningful and receives attention. An autobiography ought to be an honest and sincere description of one's successes and failures. Even though mine is not an autobiography, I do not know what would interest the reader most in my memoir, but I know it has been written with the utmost sincerity of purpose.

I have deliberately held back on the unsavoury details, which may have added spice to the story but nothing to its moral or intellectual slant. I thought it could lead to passing of judgement on others, which is avoidable and without loss of character of the story.

This is an account of my experiences as a railway engineer. The mention of some technical terms and engineering descriptions became unavoidable in my narration. These will surely interest civil engineers and the like but for others, it may be difficult. I advise them to just skip them. They will not miss any important threads in the narration.

Life is a challenge and it provides many lessons. I have attempted to draw these lessons and present them to readers for their understanding and growth. They might appear as management principles but I view them as tools or ideas that have served me very well. The impact of external influences affects all situations, including one's life. It has to be identified and understood to formulate one's response to it. Unless tackled properly, it can ruin all efforts. The capacity to think differently is a powerful tool that can liberate one from the confines of regimented thinking—a must for a leader. Readers will discover how the mind is the sharpest tool available for exploitation. If rightly used it may lead to a meaningful life even if not necessarily an economically rewarding one!

Lastly, like it is said in the Railways, 'Once a railwayman always a railwayman'.

1
A WAY OF LIFE AS A RAILWAY ENGINEER

The early days of my life, as far as my memory can take me, were neither memorable nor pleasant. Growing up among want and pain did not fill my heart with any extraordinary desire to excel or to achieve any particular heights in life. Even today, I wonder how I managed to complete my engineering education. Very often, I did not have enough money either to pay tuition fees or other bills, or for buying books and other course materials. My parents did their best. Of course, my eldest brother would help out in whatever way it was possible. There were also many good friends, even teachers and professors, who helped me financially. The value of money was thus the greatest lesson I learnt. But I do not remember ever having complained. I borrowed technical books from my friends to read. I was just as keen to return these books to their owners and in time, as I did not want them to suffer on my account. This helped me understand the value of time. Often, my friends sought my advice to buy good textbooks. In return, I helped many of them with their studies because I had topped the class throughout the four years. This was a good lesson in optimizing my skills and resources. My mother taught me the value of humility. These attributes became my biggest assets in life.

THE TURNING POINT: CAREER IN THE RAILWAYS

I grew up in these circumstances and background. My sole wish was to earn just enough to pay back my debts and look after myself. My wishes were truly modest. I do not blame or regret not having any urge to achieve something higher. While reading Mario Puzo's *The Godfather*, I was struck by what he wrote about destiny: 'In life, there comes a moment or an event, which changes the course of the entire life. That is destiny!'

I think it happens with everyone. That event in my life occurred when as a young student of Bihar Institute of Technology, Sindri, I was accompanying my mother to Ranchi from Tatanagar (Jamshedpur). The train was around midnight. It was an extremely crowded one. On an impulse, I told my mother that if I joined the Indian Railways (IR), she would not have to suffer travelling in second class. My mother smiled and prayed to God to fulfil my wish I had simply plucked out of thin air. When I was in the third year of my engineering course, my friend's older brother visited him in the college hostel. He was an electrical engineer in the IR but in a temporary cadre. As I was a bright student, he advised me to try for Indian Railway Service of Engineers (IRSE). He told me in great detail about the entire selection procedure. I immediately recalled my mother's words of prayer and decided to apply for it.

As I had practically no information about the UPSC examination, he kindly sent me an old brochure of the Engineering Services Examination published by the Union Public Service Commission (UPSC). I started preparing immediately for the examination. I chose special subjects in my course (for the final year) to suit the UPSC syllabus. I graduated in civil engineering in 1966, but I still did not have the requisite age of twenty years for the competitive examination. I decided to join my alma mater as an assistant professor of civil engineering. This was in the hope that I would receive proper assistance and guidance to clear the examination. And, it proved to be very helpful indeed. There is nothing like teaching to understand a subject. Many of my doubts were actually cleared while teaching subjects like structural engineering, both analysis and design, in the class. I soon became a popular teacher and the students were very happy with my teaching. One of senior professors even told me to give up my pursuit of the IRSE. According to him, only 3 to 5 persons were selected every year in the all India competition. I told him that even if only one person was selected, I would be that person. It may have sounded very arrogant and it was not at all in keeping with my character, but I had my sights set on it and my mother's blessing. Nothing could stop me.

There are a few anecdotes relating to the Engineering Services Examination too. I only recall them because they reinforced my belief in destiny. Firstly, my paper selection for the examination was rather bizarre as I discovered subsequently. I had ignorantly selected a paper like town planning and architecture. I had not read this subject in my graduation. Prof. R.P. Sinha, who taught this subject in the regular degree course, promised to help me. I filled up the application form accordingly. Subsequently, I received the syllabus and also a set of past question papers. When I saw them, I was totally stumped! Even my professor had no clue. My heart sank. Whatever books were available in the college library did not cover the type of questions which were asked or the content in the syllabus. I realized my stupid mistake of trying to play safe by selecting a theoretical subject and thus having unwittingly entered into an unknown territory.

The examination was just three weeks away. I was in Patna. My old college mate, then working as assistant engineer (AEN) in the State Public Works Department (PWD), gave me a copy of the annual publication of the Town Planning and Architecture Association of India. It was an interesting publication. It contained articles on all the famous town planners and architects. I read it from cover to cover, as it was well-written. It also carried good illustrations of their work. I got the biggest surprise of my life when I sat down to answer the paper. The questions were largely based on this very publication of the journal. Well, it turned out that I was able to answer my paper with a lot of authority. I was able to quote extensively from the works of these famous personalities. I scored nearly 70 per cent in the subject. Later, when I mentioned this to my other batchmates in the IRSE, they were completely taken aback. Perhaps, nobody in the IRSE had earlier competed with a subject like town planning and architecture. I had divine help indeed!

The interview for the UPSC

On the basis of the written examination, I was called for the Personality Test on 16 April 1968. I had no idea about such a test at that level. I was advised to be properly dressed and, in particular, to wear a tie. In the month of April, Delhi is blazing hot, but I still wore a tie.

I travelled to New Delhi by chair-car of the air-conditioned *Deluxe Express*. This train had been newly introduced and was reputed to be very fast. I boarded this train at Dhanbad. It was sheer luck that my fellow passenger was a mining engineer posted near Dhanbad. He had graduated in mining engineering from London. In our casual conversation, he gave me a very useful overview of the coal industry and mining technology. This information eventually found its way into my interview for the UPSC. I reached Delhi around 10.30 in the morning, a day in advance of the interview. I had been invited to stay with a cousin, but it so happened that he was away and I had to rely on my own resources to arrange for a modest stay.

INSIDE THE UPSC—A UNIQUE EXPERIENCE

I went to the UPSC's office located in Dholpur House. The building had an aura about it. It is here that all the officers of the Class I services including the Administrative services are finally interviewed. I was made to sit with a group of six. I was the fourth person in waiting. Two of them were from Calcutta (Kolkata now). A third one was attending the interview for the second time. Both of the people from Calcutta were disposed of rather shortly, in about 10 to 15 minutes. They looked very unhappy as they came out. One was asked how many trams he had burnt in college. Calcutta was a political hotbed in those days. The question had rocked him off his balance and he couldn't recover. Just as the third person was called in, I was also taken aside and made to wait just outside the interview board. It was a wait of about twenty minutes. Those were however, tense moments. Imagine a young man from a very small place with very little knowledge of things, waiting outside alone in complete awe of the biggest event in his life. But the blessings of my elders and God were certainly with me. When I entered the boardroom I was totally at ease.

For the Personality Test also, I received divine help in the form of some literature on rural water supply. My co-passenger had already given me very useful information on coal mining. Most of the questions were on these topics. Coal mining probably because I came from a famous coal belt; water supply because I taught that subject. But instead of the usual municipal supply, the emphasis was on rural water supply. I could handle the questions very confidently. I told my brother after the interview that I had done rather well and that I could possibly be among the first four candidates. The final result was to be published in *The Times of India* or *The Indian Express* of 8 June. In our home in Jamshedpur, we received neither of these newspapers. There was, of course, an evening library in the town. I regularly went there in the evenings to read the papers. Curiously, I missed the results in both the newspapers. There was nobody to tell me about the result either. I thought I had not succeeded and simply resigned myself to my fate. My father and brothers probably thought the same, but kindly, nobody even mentioned it.

After the summer vacation, I returned to Sindri to continue my teaching job. At the bus stop, I bumped into R.P. Sinha who congratulated me on my success. I was left speechless! His bus was leaving so he could not give me more details. Back in Sindri, my friend Raman Kumar came to announce that I had stood third in order of merit, in the competitive examination. I was selected!

Imagine, I had suffered agonies for more than a month and a half. My family was, of course, delighted. They said that they had been confident of my success, all along. What had started as mere wishful thinking had come about after a long and tortuous journey. It was not easy, but God had willed it. I loved teaching and my students were also quite happy with me. So, I very seriously contemplated continuing with my teaching job. But my father advised that I could always return to work as a professor if my chosen career disappointed me, but the other way was not possible. Even the state government was very reluctant to release me to join the IRSE. It required a recommendation from the secretary technical education. The dealing clerk in the office of director technical education, Patna, wanted ₹20 to give me the release letter. I queried him about how he could ask for money when I was going to resign! Caught, he looked puzzled and greatly embarrassed.

Despite many twists and turns, on the morning of 12 December 1968, I joined as a railway engineer in the Eastern Railway at their headquarters in Calcutta.

2

EARLY IMPRESSIONS OF A RAILWAY ENGINEER

A PROBATIONER IN THE INDIAN RAILWAY SERVICE OF ENGINEERS

Everything appeared fine when I reported in Calcutta. R.P. Sinha and Binay Prasad—two of my senior professors and conscience keepers, saw me off at Dhanbad from where I boarded the *Bombay Mail* on 12 December 1968. I had a humble beginning and had practically no idea about the organization, society and culture, or any clue about where I had decided to spend my next 35 or 36 years of life. There was an Army couple—Major Sinha in charge of the NCC (the National Cadet Corps) in the college. His wife's father, too, worked in the Railways and lived in Calcutta. They painted an interesting lifestyle of people in the Railways for me. It appeared somewhat mysterious. I was both curious and apprehensive of what was awaiting me in this new life.

I reached Howrah around 11.30 a.m. Leaving my luggage at the station, I reported to the headquarters of the Eastern Railway (ER), known as Fairlie Place, around 12.30 p.m. This was located near the Writers' Building—secretariat of West Bengal government. I had no idea where to go. According to my letter of appointment I had to report to the general manager (GM) of the Railways. Someone had mentioned that he was a very big man. So, on instinct I went to the room of the personal assistant of the chief engineer (PACE), A.K. Guharaja. But, make no mistake, Guharaja was a senior-scale officer and not an ordinary assistant. Well, I had reached the correct place. He was particularly nice and made me feel at ease. After lunch, all the required formalities for the joining were completed quite quickly. It also included the administration of an oath which said, 'I will abide by the Constitution of India and that I will perform my duties of a public servant with sincerity and complete devotion to duty!'

I was given a complete set (about seven in number) of codes and manuals as my personal copies for reference. I was deputed for training for two years, according to a very elaborate schedule and training program. I was given a choice among Dhanbad, Asansol or Howrah, and asked to select one division for this purpose. I naturally selected Dhanbad because of my greater familiarity with it. Everything was arranged promptly including a free railway pass, the reservation of a berth in train and a room in the rest house in Dhanbad. Accordingly, I travelled back to Dhanbad overnight. It was a Saturday. No officer was available on that day due to an accident in the Grand Chord section of the division. So immediately after a wash, I slipped off to Sindri.

I was in Sindri by lunch time. Everyone was so surprised to see me just after a day and looked plainly worried. Soon they were put at ease. I had been a very popular student in my college and had strong ties there. Not only was I good in academics, but I also participated in all the extracurricular activities of the college. I played cricket, I was general secretary of the Students' Union, a good teacher and a fairly good public speaker. During my stint in Dhanbad, I often went to Sindri whenever I found time. And finally, I also found my love and life's companion there.

SHOCK AND DESPAIR OF THE EARLY DAYS IN THE RAILWAYS

I was in for a shock when I eventually reported to the divisional engineer (DEN) on Monday morning. He was so busy that he did not speak to me for quite some time. My Bihari origin surprised or disappointed many. I found out soon that I was only the third Bihari to have joined the IRSE. The IRSE was the topmost grade in the Engineering Services Examination in India. In a batch of eight officers, I was the lone Bihari officer selected for the IRSE. There was acute stagnation in the growth and prospects for promotion in the cadre at that time, which prompted some to wonder how the IRSE recruitment was ongoing. Some were forthright in their taunts, 'Is there an engineering college in Bihar?' One lecturer in Pune said, 'I have heard about *open-floating grace marks* being awarded to anyone who might have failed in any subject'. Or, 'Is English taught as a language?' It was very humiliating. I was naturally upset with the open bias and shaming of the poor teaching and general standards of students from Bihar. I faced such humiliation every now and then for a long time. Regardless, I took my job seriously. I wanted to prove myself. Even in the social sphere, I aimed to swim smoothly. I was a fairly good sportsman and bridge player. In those days bridge-playing partners were highly sought after as it was difficult to get a foursome. I was well-read; I had a fondness for English classics and had a large collection of books. I was good in spoken as well as written English. These attributes did not go unnoticed. People outwardly did not seem prejudiced, but unfortunately, it would surface quite often. I was firmly resolved to combat this bias and I kept trying.

THE SECOND CHAPTER OF INDIAN RAILWAYS—A HUMBLE PARTNER

Rajdhani, a high-speed express train with a speed of 130 kmph, was being introduced between Howrah and Delhi. Although a probationer, I was entrusted with the job of realignment of curves to achieve the high speed in the Dhanbad division. The world standard in high-speed operation was 250 kmph plus. In comparison, this exercise by the IR was modest. The engineers had however decided to introduce the train on the Delhi-Howrah route, on the existing track structure. In the Dhanbad division, the track structure comprised of 90R rail with fish plated joints on CST-9 sleeper having (N+4) density. By global standards, this formed the most primitive track structure—unfit to run a high-speed train. The exercise was considered important because of this primitive track structure. Manual curve realignment was an arduous and back-breaking job, but it was completed in two months' time. The high-speed train was introduced in that section in 1969-70. A momentous feat indeed! Much later in the book, I described this event as the second chapter in the glorious history of the IR. The first was of course the construction of the Bombay-Thane railway line and the running of the first train in 1854. Both these chapters were evidently written by engineers.

It was a landmark achievement because anything over 110 kmph was deemed impossible on the existing track structure. I am glad that I played a small role in this historic event. I did not know then that one day I would be at the helm of affairs of the Indian Railways to write the third chapter. The introduction of heavy axle-load operation which would require breaking of barriers, technical as well as mental, ushered in a golden period in the history of Indian Railways.

Such exposures gradually built a strong faith that decisions were there to be taken. When the moment arrives for a decision, you cannot dodge it, or else the chance will escape you forever. As a young player of cricket, our coach taught us a valuable lesson. Ducking a ball never got you anywhere. If you duck, you would only get more of the same. So, when an issue is brought before you, there is no way to skirt it. My experiences with high speed had demonstrated this aspect. It was an important lesson to learn.

Training in the Indian Railways

As part of my training, I would spend the whole day with the gang, working on the track. I also learnt how a clerk dealt with a file in the office. I was not ashamed of asking questions or showing my ignorance. This helped me a great deal. I was lucky to enjoy great scenic beauty out in the field, but I also learnt how people lived. For construction and survey training, I was deputed to the Cuttack-Pardip and Cuttack-Talchar sections. Nature's beauty was at its best in Orissa (Odhisha now). It was however hard on me because of the food. I was a strict vegetarian. It was almost impossible to get that there. But I managed to survive.

I was the lone officer in my batch attached to the Eastern Railway. But during the probation, two officers from NFR (Northeast Frontier Railway)—A.K. Biswas and A.K. Kohli—were also attached to the Eastern Railway. We became good friends. Kohli was attached to Asansol and Biswas to the Howrah division. We had a wonderful time together whenever we had a joint programme. After the probation they both returned to NFR for their posting.

Apart from being the coal belt and a mineral-rich area, the Dhanbad division is very picturesque. It is hilly and forested, particularly, the Central India Coal (CIC) section has a great natural beauty. The division was on top of revenue loading alongside the Asansol division. While there, I also had a chance to witness a professional quarrel between two stalwarts—Divisional Superintendent (DS) Mr Sachdev from Dhanbad and Mr Gujral from Asansol. Their spars and jabs at each other were famous. Wednesday was the regular club day and all officers were required to attend the club in the evening. Participation in social activities was a must. The DS would note their absence and would often point to the offending officer who had failed in his social duties—an important requisite in the annual assessment of an officer's performance.

The training period in the Railway Staff College, Baroda (now Vadodara), or the Indian Railway Institute of Civil Engineering (IRICEN), Pune, was excellent. The training was held in two phases. The first phase in Baroda was called the Induction Course, where officers of all services joined in. Our interaction with officers from different disciplines was an enriching experience, and helped widen our perspectives. The Railway Staff College also had strict dressing regulations for class, dining hall and sports ground. Physical training in the morning was compulsory, which was resented by some. But the overall atmosphere was very impressive. I am reminded of a one-liner, which I continue to quote even today. I was the leader of the batch at the Railway Staff College. In my valedictory speech, I talked about the impending congestion and prevalent stagnation in our careers. Principal Gokhle in his reply mentioned a popular quote, 'Thoroughbreds do not need a whip nor do they cry, if they lose'. It said all. Nothing else remained to be said.

The IRICEN is located in the pleasing city of Pune. The training here included lessons in civil engineering related to the railways. Principal G.H.K. Keshwani was an excellent teacher and an epitome of a dignified railway officer.

I recall that for my final interview after the training, he asked me which chapter of *Way and Works Manual* contained what subject. I refused to answer, saying that it was not expected of me. If I needed to refer to a subject, I could always open the manual for my guidance. He was annoyed but he knew I was correct!

3

THE PROVERBIAL FIRST POSTING

PAIN AND TRIBULATIONS OF THE FIRST POSTING

Seniors of all disciplines unanimously agreed that the probation period was the most enjoyable—perhaps it even was the golden period of service life. After regular posting began, life would become exacting, they warned. I am not sure if this is completely true, but I learnt a lot of valuable lessons then. Not only did I improve professionally, I also grew as a person. The small-town boy transformed into a self-assured young man.

I enjoyed the period not only for the fun it came with but also because it built my confidence. To complete this personal growth, I am grateful to Prof. B. Prasad, my professor of English in the Engineering College who gave me a copy of the Bhagavad Gita, with an excellent commentary by Swami Chidbhavananda. This still remains my most valuable possession. I religiously read a chapter of it every day and discover a new meaning from the wealth of knowledge it contains.

Life also showed me its dark and difficult side, but bad experiences must be taken as a lesson. It is for this that I must write about it. I was to go to Baroda for the final phase of training at the Railway Staff College. My training would then be completed and I would take up my first post. My father was in his hometown of Deo near Gaya. He wrote me a letter saying that he wished to see me. Gaya is on the way to Baroda. I requested my boss, the DEN, to let me go to Gaya for a day. I would return to Baroda from there. He did not like the idea and refused outright. Well, there was nothing that I could do about it. I wrote to my father that I could not come, but I promised to visit him when I returned from Baroda. But sadly, God willed it otherwise. My father suddenly passed away on 10 August 1970. I was very angry with myself. I then decided not to allow this to happen to anyone else, ever. My boss was however unaffected when he heard about my father passing away. He appeared to be prejudiced against me—not for any professional reason though. Later, when I was in a superior post as PACE, he needed my help. I found it in myself to act as if nothing had ever happened between us earlier, and did whatever I could to help him.

But I must return to my first posting, where I was full of inquisitiveness, euphoria and excitement. I was posted as an AEN, Kanchrapara after the final departmental examination on 12 December 1970. Everyone was surprised at the posting. Some were even shocked. West Bengal was passing through one of its worst periods of political turmoil at that time. Bandhs, unrests, gheraos were the general order of the day. There was insecurity in the state. Fear, anxiety and apprehension stalked the life of common people. No one would open a door after dark. The position of Central government officers was particularly pitiable. They were often soft targets of the agitators' ire. West Bengal had a coalition government supported by the Left who were spearheading the agitation. Kanchrapara has a railway workshop and a large railway colony. This station was a breeding ground of trouble. Two AENs preceding me had either reported sick or had gone away on leave. They were unable to handle the situation. They were gheraoed, and illegally confined by the agitating staff. No help would come from the local administration or the police. In such a grave situation, many saw no chance for a greenhorn like me. They thought that it was unfair to post a young officer to Kanchrapara on his very first posting.

I was advised to represent my case to the CE, Mr Kalicharan, against my posting. I went to pay Mr Guharaja a courtesy visit. He was, of course, sympathetic. He told me what to expect there. He also said that I could see the CE, if I wished to. I thanked him and said, 'I look at it differently. I am going to Kanchrapara with an open mind. If I succeed, it will be to my credit. If I do not, well, it was not expected of me anyway. Hence, I am glad for the challenge given to me at the outset of my career. I will come to see the chief engineer if I succeed.'

Most of my well-wishers thought that I was being heroic.

The Sealdah division of the Eastern Railway, where Kanchrapara is located, caters mostly to the suburban traffic. For some reason, the IRSE officers were generally not posted to this division. Before the Partition, this section was part of the Bengal Assam Railway, which ran across East Pakistan (now Bangladesh), right up to the Assam border. Bangladesh had not been born then and thus Kanchrapara was quite close to the border of East Pakistan.

I reached Kanchrapara late in the evening with two trunks and a hold-all, which contained a sleeping mattress and a rajai (quilt). One trunk had my books. An inspector of works (IOW) met me at the station. We walked down to the rest house about a kilometre away. I mention this because the AEN at that time had no vehicle. Later, I found out that the AEN was given a bicycle. My predecessor, Mr Kataria, was not available on that day. So, I was alone on the first day of my office. Just as I sat down in the office and started looking through some papers, a big crowd suddenly gheraoed me, shouting slogans against me. I very politely told them that I had not yet taken over the charge. They were welcome after I had done so. They went away after an hour, threatening and warning me that they would neither let me live in peace nor let me work. This was merely a glimpse of the shape of things that awaited me. The bada-babu (the chief clerk) lamented at the deplorable state of affairs prevailing in those days.

I looked at the incumbency board. It had B.C. Ganguli as one of the occupants. He was chairman Railway Board then. I felt honoured. But the last three had scarcely been there for six months. The present incumbent did not have even his name up on the board. He later told me that he had come for a month only but had to stay put for more than three months! I then realized the wisdom of the words of the PACE while taking his leave. I had to be prepared for anything, in the days to come. But I was not afraid. There were many problems but mostly they had to do with human relationships. Every small thing that affected the staff would trigger an agitation. There were leaders with vested interests waiting to exploit exactly a situation like that!

APPLYING AND ENLARGING MY OWN ZONE OF INFLUENCE

Only after long years of service, I have now realized the importance of one's zone of influence. Many external factors influence one's lifestyle. But by enlarging your own area of influence, that is, a thing which is achievable, it is possible to push other factors aside or at least marginalize their impact to a great extent.

The Labour Union had two main issues for agitation. One was the payment of bonus and the other concerned the regularization of about eight hundred casual labourers in my subdivision. Both were policy issues at the Railway Board level. I had no role in this. However, issues like improvement in the standard of maintenance of staff quarters, water supply, timely supply of uniforms, issue of foreign line privilege passes and privilege ticket orders (PTO), medical attention and leave, etc. affected the staff more acutely. I could do a lot in these areas without worrying about the larger issues like regularization of services of casual labour or grant of annual bonus. I could also improve my own image as a person who was clean, had integrity and was compassionate. About sixteen railwaymen were engaged by my predecessors for looking after various things at their residence. They were shifted and redeployed to their official positions. I engaged one private cook, paying him from my pocket. My trolley man and a gardener—officially engaged to work at the residence—were the only railway employees in my residential establishment.

I rode an official bicycle. I would ask my IOW to sit at the back. And so, we would go for intensive colony inspections, from house to house. My emphasis was on improving maintenance and more importantly on a quicker response to address the residents' grievances. No payment was made to the contractor until the work done was certified by the resident. I inspected all the completed work. The work culture changed dramatically. My inspectors gladly accepted the change because I led from the front and was willing to take responsibility. Furthermore, I asked the workshop officers if I could do anything to improve their working conditions.

A gangman had difficulty in those days, in getting a privilege pass or sanction of leave. During my line inspection, either made alone or in the company of my permanent way inspector (PWI), a literate office boy, who accompanied me. He would get a leave or pass application signed by the gangmen. The sanction of leave, after checking their service records, was communicated through the control phone within a day. A pass would not take more than a week. It had to be issued by the divisional headquarters at Sealdah. An office boy was deputed to go to Calcutta every week to get such passes issued. Earlier, a gangman had to go himself or would have to pay the union office bearers.

Periodical medical examination of gangmen was a nightmare. A gangman booked for medical examination had to travel, pay money. He would spend up to ten days for this purpose, with untold harassment. I spoke to the Railways' doctor at the Central Hospital in Calcutta. The doctor earmarked one day every fortnight for such periodical medical examinations for my sub-division. The doctor also found this arrangement convenient. Usually a gangman would turn up any time, even on a day when the doctor was busy with surgery. The staff now had its medical test on one day without any hassle or need for undue consideration. A satisfactory solution for both sides.

The supply of uniforms was closely monitored. The divisional superintendent (now divisional railway manager or DRM) was pleased to allow a regular tailor to take measurements and alter the uniform to suit a person. This is just to mention that it was possible to do many things within my competence. I did not have to shout at anyone for this. This was simply done through exercising my own influence and enlarging the same with the resources at my command. It brought me goodwill and tremendous satisfaction to the staff. I made sure that people got what they were entitled to, without them having to ask for it.

Appreciation and reaction

The result was extraordinary, and beyond my expectations. The gangmen stopped their union subscription. Their leaders felt threatened. One evening, I was gheraoed in my office. It went on for hours. Most of the men gheraoing me were from the workshop. They were agitated about casual labour regularization and payment of bonus. I told them that their demands were not within my competence. They said, 'We know. But we have gheraoed you on the premise— "pull the ear, and the head will follow"'. This was a famous leftist slogan. They offered me food, but I refused to eat. I could see they were genuinely unhappy at this. I asked them to eat as they were obviously hungry. They could not however do so, as I had refused food. That caused a commotion. The leaders asked me not to take up the staff problems directly without first consulting the union. But I stood my ground. I said that they were my men first. It was my moral duty to do whatever was possible for their welfare. I did not need permission from the union for this purpose.

This led to a heated argument and someone threw a slipper at me. It sailed over my head. That became a turning point. My men were angry with the union leaders. They said that their sahib was a selfless and an honest person who was only trying to help them. They could not tolerate outsiders insulting their sahib. The gherao was lifted but I continued to sit. I told them that I would leave only if my men asked me to. They had tears in their eyes and begged for forgiveness. They promised that henceforth nothing of this sort would be allowed to happen. This was a great moral victory within only three months of my joining.

A moral victory and a great lesson

Honesty, sincerity and keenness to help people are the key factors for a smooth working within a group. It is important not to offer false promises. While interacting with my men, I always gave an honest estimate and assurance of what I could accomplish. This had a profound impact and it always worked. I am glad that I learnt these lessons the hard way at the beginning of my career. It also taught me to be fearless and forthright. During my career, leaders of the staff federations and my officers were sure of my help and they knew that I would never give them any false hope or promise even under duress!

There was no looking back thereafter. I remember, once I had gone to attend a collision accident near Dum Dum station. It was not my section but since the AEN was on leave, I was looking after it on his behalf. The GM, Mr GP Warrior, came to the site. All the officers were lined up for an introduction. As soon as I introduced myself, he caught me by my arm and took me aside. He said, 'I am very glad with what you are doing at Kanchrapara. Please keep it up.' Everyone was surprised. I was subsequently called by my CE, Mr Kalicharan. He told me that he was very happy with my performance. He told me that he felt like a proud father. He told me that the GM, Mr G.P. Warrior, a celebrated engineer who rose to become chairman Railway Board (CRB), also spoke well of me. He said that the way I had handled a very sensitive and hostile work situation should be a lesson to all.

I survive attempts on my life

Well, things went smoothly for a while. But I earned the wrath of the local union leaders because I had upset their plans. Two attempts were made on my life. I survived both through sheer luck.

I had returned from Calcutta around midnight. I was held up because of dislocation of train services. It was winter and I was tired and hungry. I took the overbridge and as I crossed down to the other side, I saw my office peon sitting on the foot of the staircase, dozing. As I passed him, the fellow woke up. He was waiting to get a bill signed by me. I rebuked him for this. I asked him if the contractor had bribed him for this, otherwise it could have waited for the next day. He very politely admitted that the contractor had paid him ₹10 to get the bill signed and to submit the bill to the divisional office with my signature on it. I immediately felt sorry for the fellow. He had actually earned the money by waiting for me in the cold night. I sat beside him on the staircase, coolly signed the bill and walked away briskly ahead of my trolley man.

I decided to take a different route to my house. There was a culvert nearby which I would have normally crossed. About four men came out of it running towards me, saying that I was going the wrong way. Sensing danger, I started running towards my office. There was a lot of commotion. People came out on hearing the noise. Upon seeing a lot of people around me, my assailants ran away. My sudden change of route probably had upset their plan. But I took things calmly. I was offered personal security by the DS, but I refused.

The second time, I was conducting a trolley inspection in my subdivision. I was on the trolley on another line when a local train just passed us. Seeing me, some people shouted from the train. Before I could make sense of it, a very big bundle of frames from a wooden cot was thrown at me. Alarmed by the shout, I immediately dodged and the frame just missed me. The train must have been running at a speed of nearly 45 kmph as it was entering the station yard. Even the trolley men were saved. People started running towards the station. But the miscreants escaped. It was obviously a deliberate attempt to hit me, but I had survived. There was no doubt that the attempt was crude one, but they were handling a petty officer and must have thought it adequate to scare a person.

The situation had started to improve, notwithstanding the attempts to bump me off. More importantly, the political climate had also improved in the state. That helped too. I think it was my destiny. It reinforced my will to try and attempt to put into practice new ideas and thoughts. I learnt to be proactive. I also started to learn to play the guitar and I made it a point to play it every day. That was my greatest means of relaxation.

BANGLADESH WAR AND THE MISERY OF THE REFUGEES

I distinctly remember the month of March 1971. Across the border in East Pakistan (now Bangladesh), Mujibur Rahman had won the General Election. But the government in Islamabad did not want him to head East Pakistan. There was a great deal of political development after 26 March 1971. Mujibur Rahman was arrested and detained in West Pakistan. He was not allowed to come to Dacca (Dhaka now). The Pakistani Army intervened under the martial law, and came down heavily on the people of East Pakistan in order to secure civil peace. The result was an exodus of a large population, comprising children, women and older people, who had abandoned their homes in the East Pakistan. Right from the border to Dum Dum and everywhere else, the refugees tried to find some shelter. The heavy rains made their condition pitiable. We tried to help out but our resources were too limited to deal with the situation. I have neither seen nor read about such a mammoth-like migration of human population. Refugees even swamped my office. I could not enter it and I ordered to close the office. I remember CE Kalicharan called to inquire into how I had closed the office because it was not under my competence. I had not known that. I was able to explain the unprecedented situation and my action was subsequently regularized by the Railway Board. The international community came forward to provide help, and gradually the refugees were shifted to alternative locations.

This led to a war-like situation. As an AEN almost next to the border, I had a crucial role to play. The Army unit needed our help to handle tanks and warfare equipment. We provided our full support. Unloading ramps were constructed at once, using local resources and without waiting for a formal sanction. The Army officers were pleased with my efforts. The Army was ready with ground-level preparations when war broke out on 3 December 1971. As the joint command of Bangladesh Mukti Vahini and the Indian Army advanced, we supplied pre-assembled one-km long railway tracks to the Army. The Pakistani Army had blown away railway tracks while retreating. There were air raid sirens in the night. I was in charge of civil defense and had worked relentlessly for seven months, but just four days before the final victory on 16 December 1971, I fell and was injured. I was admitted in a Railways hospital when the Instrument of Surrender was signed in Dacca.

Major Narang of 44 Cavalry was the Army's co-coordinating officer for dealing with the Railways. He led the assault in Jessore sector. Before joining the front, he had told me that they would throw a big party for me when they returned from the front. They were victorious but alas, Major Narang was killed in the Jessore sector. Subsequently, when I went to Bangladesh, I visited his place in Jessore. My heart bled for all those who had lost their lives in the war and particularly for those with whom I had closely interacted. I salute them for their courage. They taught me to do something for others, whether pleasant or unpleasant, as one's duty. This is in spirit of 'sthithpragya' or being equi-balanced in thought and action as defined in the Bhagavad Gita. I tried to help the Army with the resources at my command. It was in national interest. I did not wait for a formal sanction at a time like that. Before a proper concrete unloading ramp could be built, a temporary ramp with available wooden sleepers was made at Kanchrapara station. This helped the Army unload the entire fleet of tanks and other equipment. This was a timely gesture appreciated by the senior Army officers. In fact, I was able to get the entire encroachments removed from the area that was a serious security threat. It was a big bonus for us.

Such work was also being done elsewhere in the division bordering East Pakistan. Unfortunately, the loading and unloading ramps were in construction even after war was over. It may seem ludicrous now, but an audit objection was later raised against me because I had made sure that the work completed at Kalyani in time, by awarding the contract to the second-lowest bidder. This completed ramp was also used by the Army. The audit objection was promptly withdrawn when I provided them with complete details.

I had seen the sufferings of a large section of helpless humanity for more than a year. I had seen a bitter war and knew friends who had lost their lives in the war for Bangladesh. My own sufferings in comparison were certainly not worth talking about. But the way my perception changed within a year was unimaginable. I found this to my utter disappointment when I went to Bangladesh, three years after their independence. There was no feeling of gratitude. Instead there was a show of hostility for India's contribution in the Bangladesh struggle for independence. It is worth exploring, but a bit later.

BE AFRAID AND GET DOOMED

I need to describe how an unfavourable situation if tackled well can become one's strength. It is illustrative in nature because it had impacted three sets of people, in three different ways.

As an AEN, I was president of the local bodybuilding club run by the

Railways' staff. An open line AEN is commonly inducted in such an institution. An AEN usually has the wherewithal to support the activities of such clubs or institution. In Kanchrapara, the general atmosphere was charged with instances of violence. Under these circumstances, everyone was encouraged to engage in healthy outdoor activities that the club promoted.

The club had planned its annual day with some attractive programmes. I had spoken to M.K. Sinha—the superintendent of workshops about it. He invited S.C. Mishra, the chief mechanical engineer (CME) as the chief guest. I also requested K.K. Das, the divisional superintendent to preside over the function. Mr Das and Mr Mishra were good friends. Mrs Mishra also came down. The Railway Club had hosted a dinner for the party after which they planned to return to Calcutta.

The programme was well organized and everything was going well. I was suddenly informed that the local communist MLA was planning to gherao us just after the function. Their main target was M.K. Sinha. He was known for his strong hold on administration. Many did not like him. I told him that we should leave the venue immediately. We started leaving hurriedly. All boarded the Willey's Station Wagon. But my wife was held up because people were on the way. By the time she was able to board, the car was gheraoed. Amidst cheering, the MLA gave a provocative speech against M.K. Sinha. The crowd was thumping on the car. The crowd chanted, 'Burn all of them along with the car'. That frightened the ladies and Mrs Mishra was almost hysterical. Mr Mishra was trembling. Mr Sinha was laughing. My wife and Mrs Sinha were quite calm. K.K. Das sitting in the front was very collected. I was concerned but not afraid. The ire was against M.K. Sinha. The MLA read out the corruption charges against him and called for stern action against him.

I opened the door of the car and walked down to him. I spoke in a soft tone, 'Sir, I am the AEN. These guests have come from Calcutta, on my invitation. The crowd is surrounding the car and harassing the ladies in the car. It is difficult to control bad elements in the crowd. If something happened to the ladies, Kanchrapara would be blamed for ever. In West Bengal, ladies are held in high esteem. Should anything untoward happen, people will hold you and me responsible for the mishap.'

He was alarmed. I told him that he had already spoken of the allegations. The CME was here and he would be requested to take the memorandum for necessary action. He agreed. I then requested Mr Mishra to come out to receive the memorandum. Mrs Mishra began to hold him back. So far, I had said nothing about my conversation with the leader. But K.K. Das told him not to worry. He came out—almost shaking. I led him to the front of the car. I told the leader, 'Here is Mr Mishra. I assure you that he will take action after proper inquiry. So please give him the memorandum'. He asked Mr Mishra to stand on the bonnet of the car so that people could see him receiving the memorandum. Mr Mishra was stocky and this was not a feasible option. So, I said, 'You can see that he cannot climb the car. Mishra Sahib, please keep one foot on the bumper—here—so that you are visible. And now, Sir, please give him the memorandum.' He hesitated a bit, but I caught hold of his hand and he reluctantly gave the memorandum to the CME. Mr Mishra in turn promised to look into the allegations. Then I led him back into the car. They allowed us to go. We drove to the club in silence.

Mrs Mishra was very upset and angry. She wanted to leave immediately without any dinner. Mr Mishra was equally angry. K.K. Das then took over. He told them bluntly, 'Satish and Madam, you possibly do not know that these people are facing such situations day in and day out. This young man has tried to bring back the old culture of happier days. It was our duty to help him recreate the lost bonhomie amongst the railway employees. He would have succeeded but for the unfortunate intervention by the MLA. No one had any control over him. You probably do not realize how this AEN managed to rescue us with minimum inconvenience. None of us was willing to venture out of the car. He alone bravely went out and tackled the situation. If we now walk away without having dinner, we are going to set a bad example. The Railway community is never going to forgive it.' He then seized Mrs Mishra's shoulders and smilingly said, 'We are not only going to eat but drink too. So, let us enjoy the party and not spoil it.'

Mr Das asked for full details. While commending me on my guts, he also reprimanded me for my failure to gather intelligence about the impending gherao. He advised that it was important to have intelligence about such things when senior officers were scheduled to visit a place in order to avoid embarrassment. I made a mental note of this. I had learnt my lesson well, and had no occasion to cut a sorry figure thereafter.

There were three important factors that became clear to me from this. Mr Sinha was unaffected by the incident. He remained jovial and appeared as if he were enjoying the show. This was an extreme case. Although difficult, it reflected a don't-care-attitude towards a situation. There was very little one could learn from it.

K.K. Das was more objective. He felt concerned but was not afraid. His was a more seasoned response. He had taken a note of a bad event. But he had not allowed it to affect his response. This was the hallmark of a true leader.

S.C. Mishra was simply overwhelmed. He did not know how to tackle the situation. He was concerned about his own safety and that of his family. He thought that what had happened was an act of insult towards him. He held a high position. He could have capitalized on the opportunity. Unfortunately, he succumbed to the situation, and no lessons were learnt. He went on to become member mechanical Railway Board!

As for me, I acted purely on my intuition. I felt that it was my responsibility to provide safety for my guests. More importantly, I was not afraid. Even my wife was not afraid. She said that she had seen rowdy students shouting slogans against her father when he was the principal of an engineering college. For her it was not a new incident, but she felt that I was trying to be adventurous!

I once read an article by Richard Stengel on Nelson Mandela and his lessons on leadership. It is very relevant. I have compiled Mandela Lessons of Leadership recently and I quote from that: 'Courage is not the absence of fear—it is inspiring others to move beyond it'.

Mandela had also said that it would be irrational to suggest that he was not afraid and that he had pretended to be brave. But what is important is that as a leader, you should not let people know that you were afraid. 'You must put up a front.' Through this act of apparent fearlessness, you inspire others. Walking upright and with pride is enough to keep others going for days.

I did not have the benefit of this lesson then, but understood later that this was the natural way to conduct oneself as a leader. It has only strengthened my belief in the maxim 'Be afraid and be damned'.

PREDICAMENT OF A JUNIOR CELEBRITY OR HERO

Whatever had happened, I had turned out to be a sort of a celebrity, which my boss—the DEN J.N. Biswas did not like. He was a Class 1 officer and I had expected him to understand me better. This, however, did not happen. Being forthright was my fault, I still suffer from this. As a boss if you are not able to help, you should have the courage and dignity to acknowledge that. Your stature in the eyes of others will surely rise, if you do so. My boss would constantly find faults in whatever I did. As a boss it was never difficult to do that. He also spread the rumour that to escape the hardship during the war, I had reported sick! People including our divisional superintendent just laughed at this and told me not to worry about him.

My wedding was fixed for 6 March 1972 and I had decided whom to marry. I had asked for three weeks' leave for my marriage. My boss would dodge the issue whenever I raised it. It was 3 March already—when I had to leave for Jamshedpur, where the wedding was to take place. He called and said that I was to come to Calcutta on the 3rd morning. He said that the leave would be sanctioned and I could catch the evening train to Jamshedpur. When I reached Calcutta around 10 in the morning, I found him gone for an inspection without having sanctioned my leave or having left any message for me. Being an open line AEN, I could not leave the station without proper authority. I was perplexed. I tried to contact him but without success. The only information was that he would return in the evening. I had no further clue.

I was standing in front of the DS room, quite undecided about what to do. As I waited for a few minutes, Mr Das came out of his room. I greeted him and he asked if everything was fine. I then told him of my predicament. Mr Das was a confirmed bachelor. He laughed and caught me by my arm and took me to his room. He said, 'It is of course very unfair. Although I am not married, I definitely want an eligible bachelor like you to be happily married.' He wished me well and asked me to go ahead by sanctioning the leave himself. He wrote something nasty about my boss. Well anyway, I could catch the evening train. The episode might seem silly, but it illustrates how an irresponsible act can cause so much damage to a relationship. As a management principle, such an act today would be unpardonable. This brought out in sharp contrast how DS, a super boss, conducted himself. I still remember both of them but in such different ways!

Stephen Covey very aptly described this in his famous book, *The 7 Habits of Highly Effective People*, 'If you want to know how you wish to be remembered after your death, then you must do the same while alive.' Well, I am sure my boss would not have liked to be remembered the way I remember him today.

An anecdote from Mark Twain comes to my mind. He was travelling by train with his friend in France. He met a station master, who was not at all helpful and was rather stupid. Twain was very angry. He told him, 'OK. I will certainly tell the station master Milan about this.' Then he walked away. His companion was puzzled at his statement. He, therefore, asked Twain about the relevance of his statement. Twain smiled and said, 'I had met the Station Master Milan once. I found him very stupid. So, I promised to inform him if I ever met a station master more stupid than he.' Fortunately, in my case, I did not meet anyone like my boss so far! Apart from whatever misery this caused me, it certainly taught me not to be like him. To that extent, thank you very much!

4

CONSTRUCTION ENGINEERING

BLISSFUL MOMENTS OF BEING MARRIED

Marriage changed so many things. The style and the way one was used to living had to change. This was true for both of us. Even as a bachelor, I had rather good habits. (Well, that was what people would say.) The house was quite clean. Before coming to Kanchrapara I had nothing in the name of furniture or any other household stuff. So I picked up a bed, some cheap furniture and a dining table set from the local market. A small kitchen was also set up. We had a kerosene stove and a sigri which served the purpose. I had around ₹1,500 as savings. This went into setting up our home. Thanks to my wife, Anubha, although sparsely furnished, it was tastefully done. Most importantly, it was done with our own money. I made ₹340 those days. I would give ₹100 or so to Kamlesh my nephew for his studies in the Engineering College. We were very content with whatever was left. We were a happy couple, full of love and care. We were also a reasonably social and pleasant couple. My wife loved whatever I did. She was extremely supportive. That has been my greatest strength all my life!

EARLY BAPTISM AS A CONSTRUCTION ENGINEER

For a couple of months after my marriage, life went on well as AEN at Kanchrapara. I normally attended the permanent negotiation machinery (PNM) meetings of the Railway Workshop. It is a permanent committee of Railway officers and trade union office bearers. The union office bearers were quite happy with me, and they urged the DEN to provide more support for the upkeep of the colony.

At their request, the superintendent of workshop (SW), M.K. Sinha requested DS (K.K. Das) to depute the DEN, J.N. Biswas to attend the next PNM meeting. A couple of days before the meeting, Biswas spoke to me about it. I reassured him that there would be no problem. He however did not turn up for the meeting. He did not even inform why he was not coming. This offended the leaders and they walked out of the meeting. The SW reported this matter to the headquarters which viewed it very seriously. The DEN could not explain his absence and was transferred out of the division. But the engineering department officers in the headquarters suspected that the situation was engineered by me.

As a punishment, I was summarily transferred to the construction department and was posted as an AEN—in charge of Tori-Kumandih doubling. I was upset by the development and I asked the PACE about it. He gave me the background and said that the CE, J.C. Mehta, was told that I had let the department down. It had turned into a tussle between the two departments. The SW was also angry. He wanted to tell the GM about it. I was hurt by the accusation but I thanked him. I pleaded that I would rather accept the punishment and try my luck there.

This was in July 1972, only four months after my wedding. My wife had gone to her parents to attend a wedding in the family. Being the new son-in-law, I was expected to attend it as well. I got three days of leave for this purpose. After the marriage, I handed over the charge and reported to the district engineer (construction), Daltonganj. My long journey as construction engineer thus began under a shadow of punishment—a stigma, for which I had done nothing to deserve! The redeeming act was a warm and touching send-off by my staff, which had not happened for long because of the troubled working atmosphere. In contrast to the gherao and agitation at the start, the same people poured their heart out to me, when I was leaving. It was wonderful parting gift indeed.

My headquarters was in Tori, which was about a hundred miles from Daltonganj and did not have any facilities. So I was temporarily accommodated in one room of the Barwadih Railway officers' rest house. It was deep in the forest. Apart from the railway station and a yard, there was nothing in the name of civilization. I was baptized as a construction engineer, possibly in the most ideal situation one could imagine. I did not know then that a punishment posting would soon turn out to be a boon in disguise—very similar to my first posting in Kanchrapara!

I had seen, heard and read about some illustrious construction engineers. Names like Karnail Singh, Braganza, B.C. Ganguli and V.C.A. Padmanabhan were legends of the Indian Railways, and they had constructed some of the most difficult lines and bridges in the country. Their skill, expertise, knowledge and above all, their ability to take decisions by themselves was their hallmark. An engineer was tested in difficult construction. Inspired by such great people, it was my desire to do something similar. I spent the next twenty-four years of my life as a construction engineer in the Railways. God provided me with opportunities which others would rarely get. Mr Padmanabhan once told me, that a difficult job did not usually appear while one is sitting in a comfortable place. You have to avail an opportunity and venture out. You are more likely to win and get rewarded. In my case, an opportunity was thrust upon me. I was more than willing to accept a tough and difficult life for the sheer joy of completing a structure!

INITIAL LESSON—IN TORI-KUMANDIH DOUBLING

The first construction project I was entrusted with was doubling of the Tori-Kumandih line—a stretch of forty-five km. This is a part of the old Central India Coal Section (CIC) of the Eastern Railway's Dhanbad division. It is located in a deep forest of Chhota Nagpur of erstwhile southern Bihar and now Jharkhand state. The famous Betla National Park is situated here. The railway line passes through the forest reserve. When I joined, there was hardly any organization worth its name for the project. The section was divided into six contract sections. All contracts were awarded. The immediate job was to peg the alignment and to take longitudinal and cross-sectional levels throughout, for contractors to start work. I had only one IOW with me. I did not have even a jeep to move. I had one push trolley whose one wheel would often come loose. This had become a joke. To summarize, the logistics to start a big project were non-existent. It was more of an example of how a construction project should not be planned. When CE (construction) H. K. Banerjee was told about this much later, during his inspection, he was very angry with the person in charge of the project at Calcutta headquarters. He had him replaced. But a lot of damage had already been done by that time.

Tough beginnings, but a feast on nature's bounty

Nevertheless, the job had to be done. For want of family accommodation, we stayed in the officers' rest house at Barwadih about forty-five km away from the project site. Soon after joining at Daltonganj, I went back to bring my wife to the jungle station at Barwadih. I had no idea about the route from Patna. I took an express night train from Gaya which goes to Barwadih via Dehri on Sone. The stretch from Dehri on Sone to Barwadih particularly during night is very unsafe. I had no knowledge about this. Neither did anyone warn me about travelling at night. We were in a first-class coupe. Sometime during the night, there was a thumping at the door asking us to open. We initially paid no attention but it was soon clear that if I did not open the door it would be broken. I got up and opened the door to find about 4 or 5 young men. I shouted at them, saying that they should know that I was AEN and asking how they dared to disturb us. Having said this, I shut the door again. My young wife was also up. As it was her wont, she was wearing most of her jewellery. But I do not know whether it was my shout of authority or God's hand but all of them melted away. I then realized that the coach was practically empty. Later, DEN (Con) R.N. Poddar told me that I had been a fool and that my wife should never have worn her jewellery, especially while travelling during the night. It was a close call but thank God, we escaped!

During my posting, I used to catch a morning train from Barwadih at 4.30 a.m. and would normally reach Latehar station at 6. The project section started short of Latehar—it was roughly midway. I had to get up at 3.30 to catch the morning train. My wife would be up around 2.45 a.m. or so. She would prepare some tea, and a breakfast-cum-lunch and pack it in a tiffin carrier. At about 7 a.m., I would eat a few paranthas for breakfast. Then, again I would eat some paranthas for lunch. Having woken up so early, I would usually rest for an hour or so. This was about a hundred miles from Daltonganj. The area was endowed with captivating natural beauty. The view from the top near Richughuta station was breathtaking, particularly in February or March. You could see the existing single line winding down and crossing the Koel River. In these months, Flame of the Forest (Palash trees) would be in full bloom of red and orange hues, with very a sweet fragrance, completely engulfing the whole forest. You could enjoy the sight endlessly.

Latehar itself was a beauty. The Koel River flowed by the side of the station. There was a lot of rocky outcrop with clean sparkling water. One could sit down, dipping one's feet in the running water. On its bank we planned to construct a rest house. Tori Station is on a plateau with gradient moving downwards on either side. We remember that a fellow sold very good and hot samosas at the station. The weekly market was famous for its cheap vegetables—the costliest being nineteen paise a kg. There are so many fond memories which my wife and I recall and enjoy even today.

I had to walk more than 10 to 12 km every day. Climbing high embankments now and then was usual along with the walk for taking levels. The path was usually through dense elephantine grass, as high as six feet or so. This was the ideal habitat for wild animals especially snakes. Hence, we had to tread very cautiously. At intervals, there were small streams with sparkling clean and cool water, which served our drinking purposes. Fixing the alignment and taking levels with the levelling instrument was really a tough job. I would usually return by the 7 p.m. train, which was habitually late.

Exciting experience at the station in night

Chetar station is located on the side of the Chetar River, just after crossing the bridge on tall steel trestles. The river flows into a deep gorge. On one side sits a high hill and a very dense forest all along. It was pitch dark after sunset. The station master once, very vividly, narrated how a tiger often came and sat on the platform or in the verandah of the station. The station master would keep a lighted kerosene lantern on a wooden stool in the verandah. He would then bolt his door. Waiting for the train in this way was certainly adventurous. I could hear the sounds of many jungle animals mingling with the gurgling of the water in the river. There was, above all, absolute silence except for an occasional conversation on the assistant station master's (ASM's) block instrument. The ASM also spoke in low tones to not disturb the friendly tiger sitting outside. The experience was perhaps very well described by Sir Arthur Canon Doyle in his book, *The Adventure of the Speckled Band*. In the story, Sherlock Homes with his friend Dr Watson sat in the dark room during the night to unearth the mystery of a nocturnal killer.

When the train was due to arrive, the ASM would take me out of the room. With the help of a torch or a lantern he would see me board the first-class coach. He would call the passengers to open the door for me. No one would open the door of the coach unless they knew who was calling. After boarding, I would reach Barwadih station around 10 p.m. I would then take a bath because there was a lot of dust along the way. Then I would eat the dinner made by my wife. I would again wake up at 3.30 a.m. to start the next day's routine. A gruelling routine!

I must thank my wife, a young girl of twenty or so at that time. We had been married only six months. She remained alone in the rest house. There was no company at all for her, except a small radio set. But she had so many hobbies that she never complained. The station was of course quite busy. The station dealt with timber loading. During the day, the merchants and labourers kept the place very lively. But after dark there was nothing but only the sounds of trains running. And yet, my wife said that she was never bored. She had accepted me and the type of life I offered her, wholeheartedly. She also shared my sense of adventure and possibly punishment of a posting to this place.

I sharpen my faculties

But I learnt real engineering. There were no telephones, and writing letters was the only means of communication. A reply would take at least three days. Thus, it became essential to develop my own engineering solutions. A huge quantity of earthwork was involved in the work. According to the technical specifications, the borrow pit earth had to be tested first in the laboratory to ascertain its suitability as earth-filling material. This took time. The sample had to be sent to Calcutta for testing. The lab result took a lot of time. It affected our progress and the contractor would complain about the idling away of labour and machinery. Before sending for borrow pit earth sample for tests, I would invariably get the feel of the soil by touching, smelling and tasting it on the tip of my tongue. My senses gradually grew comparable to discern the qualities of the lab test results. The simple feeling of the soil mass getting sticky or becoming plastic would indicate that the sample had more of silt or clay and was thus unfit. Thereafter, I would just pick up a sample and ask the contractor to use the earth for filling—without waiting for test results. Even today, I do not depend upon just the laboratory results for a good concrete or a good soil. It is possible to train and calibrate one's sense organs—all five of them—to determine the basic properties of construction materials. During our probation, we had heard of a CE who could tell by the feel of a jerk in a running train, that the cross level was out by a quarter inch! We were fascinated by this story of such a sharpened faculty. But I realized that it was possible to develop it if we carefully calibrated our sensory faculties.

This was very exciting and the contractors were very happy indeed. There was no avoidable idling of labour and machine for want of a technical decision from the client side. Many offered money as my share. I was not offended. Instead, I would tell them politely that I did not need the money. I often asked them why they were offering me money that I was not officially entitled to. Was it because they were not happy with my management of the work? I advised them to keep the money for more deserving people.

My 'sanskara' is tested

A contractor once asked me if I was related to Mr A.P. Jaruhar. I told him that he was my father. As a young man he had worked with my father as a contractor. He had learnt a great deal from him. He was happy to learn of this relationship. He told me that all the project contractors were happy and a satisfied lot. He told me, 'Whatever I offered was a token of our respect. You will regret it if you do not accept.' Well, there was a good deal of 'sanskara' within me. It paid very handsome dividends later on. Many old contractors even now come and pay their respects. I still enjoy their goodwill and respect. Their respect was a much better reward. Want of money often haunted us, but I never regretted not accepting such favours, when I could have had it in plenty!

ROMANCE IN THE JUNGLE

Romance at the times of Binaca Geetmala

Our hard life spent together, in the initial phase of construction, made my wife and me strong. We spent some beautiful moments together, holding hands while wading through the stream, enjoying jungle life. We were given an old jeep after 5 or 6 months. A new Type II quarters meant for a Class III staff was built at Tori. We shifted there in December 1972. The house was small but for the first time after coming here, we had something of our own. Our only source of entertainment was still the radio. Those days, an annual *Binaca Geetmala* was presented on the last Wednesday of the year by Ameen Sayani who was very popular. I recall it was 26 December 1972 and the first day after we had moved into that house. The radio was playing the program. My wife just laughed, clapped and danced with joy. It made me very happy. Such small pleasures brought real joy. It was truly God's gift! The radio ran on electricity, but the supply was feeble and erratic. If I recall correctly, we could not finish the complete programme. The electric supply was gone!

We hear a tiger's call

Once, in a dense forest near Kumandih, I was caught up with a bridge concreting work. It was quite late around 9 p.m. when I left the site by jeep. There were three of us—the jeep driver, a chainman and I. The entire area was part of the Betla National Park.

We were crossing a stream—a common occurrence on a construction site, when Willy's jeep got stuck and stopped in midstream. The night was very dark. Besides the sound of flowing water, there were only the sounds of the jungle. The driver told us that a tiger often came to drink water nearby. I got out of the jeep. The water was less than knee deep. The attendant and I started to push the jeep. The driver told me that he could hear the growl of a tiger. He was very scared and in turn he was scaring us. I neither heard any growl nor did I see the shine of the eyes of a tiger. My driver had obviously panicked at what he thought was tiger's growl and the red shine of its eyes, while he held the steering wheel. But we kept on pushing till we crossed the stream. The water had entered jeep's distributor box—a common malady while crossing a stream. After cleaning and drying the distributor box, fortunately, the jeep started.

But the driver was too scared to drive. I pushed him back to the rear seat and drove the jeep myself. I knew the forest roads. After an eight-km drive, we reached the main road—a state highway carrying heavy traffic. The forest guard at the check post was quite surprised and suspicious of us. He wanted to know what we were doing in the forest at that hour of the night. He said, 'You men must be crazy. Haven't you heard that tigers, elephants and bisons often crossed the stream?' Our driver thus found good support and was happy. He told the forest guard that he had warned us repeatedly, but that the sahib had very bravely got out and pushed the jeep out of the stream, otherwise they would not have survived. The tiger, or whatever it was that saw us, must have felt compassion for us. It had simply left us alone.

We reached Tori around 11 p.m. My wife was worried. But I did not tell her anything about the incident. She, of course, looked suspiciously at our wet clothes. Next day, my driver and the chainman must have told her the story with a great deal of exaggeration, having found a more attentive audience in my wife. I had to answer for so much, when I came home for lunch. That encounter was the worse—certainly more difficult than the one with the tiger—had there actually been one!

PROMOTED AS BRIDGE ENGINEER

The construction work was progressing very well. My superiors were quite happy. It must have been early in April 1973 when the engineer-in-chief came for inspection. As soon as he saw me at the station, he asked what I was doing at Tori as I had been promoted more than a month ago. I should have joined the new post. I was not aware of any such promotion order. After the inspection, my DEN, Ashok Ganguli—the son of the illustrious B.C. Ganguli—asked me to go to Calcutta to find out about the order.

I met the PACE in Calcutta. He was also surprised that I was still in Tori. He got a copy of the order issued a month and half ago. He fired his staff for not sending a copy of the order to me. Meanwhile, my orders had been further modified. A fresh order promoting and posting me as a bridge engineer in the Construction Department was issued. This was under the CE (construction) with headquarters in Calcutta. It took one more month to release me because I was the only AEN in the project. It was only on 7 May 1973 that I could join as a senior engineer in Bridge & Planning—my first promotion. What a way this had come about! This was not considered unusual in those days. Today, officers assume their charge the same night, the orders are issued! In hindsight, it was good that the orders were somewhat delayed. It gave me an opportunity to come to a more challenging post.

My job involved design, planning and procurement of steel material. The materials were a controlled item in those days. A much older man in a very high position had occupied this post in the past. The news of a person taking over, particularly on his first promotion, caused some scepticism and tongue-wagging.

I first reported to CE (construction) H.K. Banerjee who had the reputation of being tough. He asked me to commit to memory all the bridge rules and other codes, if I had not already done so. I promptly replied that I needed the analytical skills of a structural engineer for this post. These skills I fortunately possessed in abundance, and that, this was something that could never be memorized. Rules and codes could always be referred to, if one required them. I did not know if anyone had ever dared to speak up to Mr Banerjee before this. He just looked at me, obviously fuming, and said that we would soon find out about that.

But one thing was his strong point—being a go-getter and forthright. He gradually grew very fond of me and would say, 'If you have any corners, preserve them. After all, you would be remembered for that—not for being smooth or pleasant.' He would tell others, 'This fella is a true construction engineer—for he doesn't look for precedence but would create one.' He was decorated with Padma Shri for his outstanding performance in Bangladesh.

One of my predecessors—S.K. Sinha—was known as a mobile encyclopaedia on codes and rules. At the drop of a hat, he could rattle off every codal provision on the subject! Strangely, this ability was considered as a qualification for bridge design. Luckily, I did not believe in the acquisition of such attributes. Many people even now compliment me on my photographic memory. One reading of a document was enough for me to remember its contents. Memory is very versatile faculty. I would mentally focus that I had to read it only once. The faculty had developed accordingly. It was perhaps a legacy of my days as a student. I would borrow books from friends and those had to be returned in time. I did not have the luxury of reading it again and again. It must have helped in building up my memory. But memory need not be abused by cluttering up the entire mental disc by memorizing codes.

BRIDGE ENGINEER WITH A DIFFERENCE

The CE was known to brook no nonsense! I very soon demonstrated that design must take everything into consideration—site conditions, availability of skill, cost and rationalization, etc. Above all, design must be functional, backed by good engineering practices. It should conform to ground realities. The design should take into account the material available in the construction unit. It must also rationalize the use of the material readily available in the market. This makes the design cost-effective.

My skill was greatly appreciated by field engineers. Sound application of structural engineering and good engineering practices made the design simpler and cost-effective. Even now, I emphasize this aspect. Sadly, most of us have become prisoner of codes and rules, refusing to look beyond them. My teaching experiences came in very handy here. I boldly applied new concepts and thinking to structural design. Many firsts and memorable designs adopted were: hollow RCC-hinged portal bridge for rail underbridge, folded plate construction for platform covering at Sealdah south station, in-situ bored piles for the Buckland Bridge at Howrah station, the RCC box pushing for the Manicktala Road underbridge in Calcutta, special prestressed road overbridge design at Ballygunj in Calcutta, to name a few.

I was treated as an upstart at the beginning. I also worked in the office—not in the field. It could have been a handicap, as it had been for many others, but I did not think so. I was often consulted on construction or technical problems in the field. I was given the additional charge of CMDA (Calcutta Metropolitan Development Authority) subsequently. It provided a good experience of tenders and contracts. Thus, it turned out to be a great experience. It was a turning point of my career. The point, once again, I learnt was to expand my zone of influence and to make the best use of the available opportunity.

VISIT TO BANGLADESH—BRIDGE AT GANGA (PADMA)

R.K. Banerjee, E-in-C, had developed a special liking for me because of my clear understanding and fresh approach to structural design. He took me to Bangladesh for the launch of 343 feet of steel girder on the Padma River (as the Ganga is known in Bangladesh) at Paksi. This bridge was damaged by the Pakistani Army while retreating during the Bangladesh War. The Indian Railways had offered to restore the bridge at its own expense as a gesture of goodwill. We travelled by road from Calcutta. On the way, we witnessed the devastation that had been caused by the war. People lived in fear. Mujibur Rahman, the hero of Bangladesh liberation and its prime minister, was assassinated in an Army coup. He was replaced by the army general.

The launching of the girder on the Padma River by cantilever method was a great engineering challenge. I was engaged in a serious technical consultation with the field engineers. The bridge pier was of old stone masonry. For cantilever launching, the girder would deflect downwards. It had, thus, to be received on the other pier's end, below the bearing level. From that level, the girder had to be jacked up to its proper place on the bearing. It was difficult to fix up a bracket in the stone masonry. It was necessary to know where the girder would land—a rough estimate of the location—so that the landing bracket could be fixed in advance. It was a problem of theoretical structural analysis. I sat down on a folding chair with a table on the bridge deck. I had read the Williot Mohr method for calculation in engineering college. I had no reference book at the bridge site. My calculations were therefore on the basis of first principles. Mr Ghoshal of BBJ (Braithwaite, Burn & Jessop)—the old and established steel fabricators and erection engineers—was also present. My E-in-C found the exercise interesting. They stood over me and watched my calculations with fascination.

Brush with engineers from Bangladesh

Two Bangladeshi railway engineers ambled over to the site. Mr Banerjee introduced me and explained the exercise to them. They were obviously not interested. The IR had built a beautiful rest house with a folded plate roof, designed by me, on the banks of the river. The Bangladeshi engineers said that they would take over the rest house. The E-in-C politely told them that the rest house would be gifted to the Bangladesh Railway along with the restored Hardinge Bridge. They did not believe him. They were critical of India for constructing the Farakka Barrage over the Ganga River which had robbed them of hilsa fish—a delicacy for the Bengalis. They were loudly argumentative, which disturbed my concentration. I, therefore, mentioned that the barrage had also saved Bangladesh from recurrent floods from the Ganga.

This was perhaps provocation enough. They jumped at me and started shouting at me about how treacherous India was. They shouted and said that after the war, India had taken away all the gold from their country. India had flooded Bangladesh with fake currency notes. (I understand that soon after liberation, currency notes of the country were printed at the Indian government security press in Nasik. The Bangladesh government did not have their own at that time. It was an obvious reference to this special arrangement to help the new country.) This had apparently ruined the economy of their country. They pushed and shoved me around. With great difficulty, the BBJ and other IR engineers rescued me.

I was shocked and dismayed at how ungrateful the people were! I had seen the Bangladesh War as AEN, Kanchrapara. I had seen how many of us suffered. India had offered to help in the reconstruction of the country when it had been left devastated and rampaged by the Pakistani Army. I was shocked to see how supposedly responsible citizens treated us. It left a sad impression on me. I recalled my personal involvement in the war of liberation. The face of the brave Indian Army major, my friend, killed near Jessore in course of the war also haunted me. In Bangladesh, they openly discussed that it was in India's interest to have joined hands with Bangladesh in its fight against Pakistan. True as that may be, it should not take away the gratitude. Perhaps, this is wishful thinking!

I recall that when I was GM, Northern Railway (NR) much later, a Bangladeshi railway delegation had called on me in Delhi. I had asked out of sheer curiosity, who Mr X was (I am not divulging his name to avoid any possible controversy—diplomatic or otherwise), the man who had actually assaulted me. They said that he was, of course, the chief of the Bangladesh Railway!

DIFFERENT AND DARING STRUCTURES

I enjoyed my work as a bridge engineer. I was relatively a junior officer (five years' of service under my belt) to don the mantle of a bridge engineer, usually served by senior officers of over ten years' service. I had come from a nondescript background. Many thought that my credentials were rather dubious for the job. I had survived the most difficult posting, as an open line AEN. Now they were shocked to see me succeed as a bridge engineer. I was different, confident and in many ways, daring—not at all afraid of experimenting.

Although technical in nature, I wish to mention a few structures because they were different. This might interest structural engineers. Someone once said that structural engineering was like poetry. That was why perhaps French called the bridges *'oeuvre des art* (works of art)'.

Unique road underbridge near Tori

The road underbridge (RUB) on the state highway, between Daltonganj and Ranchi near Tori railway station had to be extended to construct the doubled line. The span of the existing bridge was thirty feet, originally a semi-through steel plate girder. According to the new loading design, the depth of the girder had to be higher too. That meant that the rail level of the new line had to be higher because the RUB had to be given the requisite vertical clearance. The existing line between Tori and the RUB was already having a ruling gradient of 1 in 182. This would need heavy and costly yard remodelling of the Tori Yard. The road was on a gradient and had reverse curve on both sides of the bridge. Thus, a solution was to fit a suitable RCC-arched portal bridge to suit the road moving dimensions.

The structural analysis of such a structure was difficult. It called for a complex integration which can be done easily these days with the available computer software, but which was unavailable in those days. But basic principles of theory of structures were applied and complex integration was done using graphical method. This simplified the analysis. The bridge was successfully completed and has served quite satisfactorily on a high-density route of the Indian Railways. This was subsequently declared as one of the unique structures on the Eastern Railway.

The Buckland Bridge—foundation design

Howrah station is the only station on the IR with a cab road. The Buckland Bridge spanned across the entire Howrah yard. This was an old road bridge and required replacement.

This work, not under my charge initially, was awarded to M/S Chanda Engineers, a well-known contractor. They asked for complete traffic and power blocks on line number 8, 9 and 10. These are the busiest platform lines. The contractor had asked for traffic blocks in their tender, which was accepted. This was required for driving 72-feet long pre-cast piles. Although a contractual commitment, it was unthinkable to grant such long traffic blocks. There was a huge furore and rightly so in the Railways! How was such an important aspect overlooked? The CE (construction), H.D. Bhowmick, was very upset. He asked me to take over all the CMDA works forthwith. I was asked to find an immediate solution.

I was then working on the design of bored piles, developed by Rodio Hazarat—now AFCONS. They were ideally suitable for such a situation. This was however yet to be used in the Railways. I approached the Research Designs Standards Organisation (RDSO) for approval but they were reluctant. I was advised to act on my own and then report the outcome to the RDSO.

The design of the pile presented a real problem. Bored pile then had a maximum diameter of 760 mm only (now it is more than 2 m in diameter). The IS code treated the top 1.5 m length of the pile as unsupported cantilever. No lateral pressure could be availed from the adjoining soil. The code also did not permit any tension in the pile. I considered the ground condition carefully. There was no question of 1.5 metre of depth of ground being washed away in the Howrah yard. It was a busy yard, and hence there was no logic to ignore available passive soil pressure. Only partial passive pressure was taken into consideration to bring the resultant of all the forces within the kern of pile section. This eliminated tension in the pile cross section. To my critics, I referred to the provisions in the IS code which enabled field engineers to take decisions to suit the site condition. The structure was built successfully. It was a daring decision and many felt it was outrageous to violate a codal provision. Only prisoners of codes would moan like that!

Ballygunj road overbridge

The Ballygunj road overbridge also had a typical design problem defying solution. This was an unbalanced cantilever with a main supported span of eighty-eight feet and one end cantilever span of twenty-two feet. The contractor's consultants could not finalize the design. When only the cantilever span was loaded, the main span had negative moments causing tension. The IS code did not permit this for prestressed concrete construction.

The consultants were famous designers. They advised us to accept and approve their design by ignoring the tension. They had followed a conventional approach of placing the prestressing cables below the centroid of the girder cross section. This would not work here because of the large overhang. I suggested that we try placing a few cables at the centroid of the girder cross section. This generated a rectangular pressure distribution. This in turn equalized negative moment from a large overhang.

This was a totally new and unconventional approach. All classical textbooks on prestress concrete taught placing prestressing cables below the centroid of the cross section. Thus, this approach had become a general rule. My suggestion solved the problem completely. The structure successfully completed is serving one of the busiest areas in Kolkata even today.

Why we were different

New thoughts and experimentations were the biggest results from this assignment. I was convinced that with good intentions, one can be successful, especially by being different and daring. Most importantly, it made me confident about taking decisions. In management parlance, it is the ability to take such decisions, albeit small ones, which bolsters one's confidence. A person who has not taken small decisions in the past cannot be expected to take bigger decisions—be it in one's personal or professional life.

Many seniors applauded me and encouraged me for this effort. Others cautioned me to be more careful lest troubles overtake me. But somehow, I got away with it. God was definitely kind! Others felt I was lucky. Of course, both were right!

5

OPEN LINE WORKS—FOR A CHANGE

CHANGE AS HUMAN RESOURCE ADMINISTRATOR—DRAMA AND ALL

I found a great deal of satisfaction in my work as a bridge engineer. I was successful in motivating my design engineers. They learnt a great deal and I had their total support. I developed a good rapport with some leading consulting engineers in Calcutta. This association improved my technical knowledge. I discussed the development of new ideas with them. The practice continues even now, to my immense benefit.

I get a call from the GM

I clearly recall one day (26 October 1976, to be precise) after lunch, around 3:30 p.m. or so I was leaving my room to meet S.P. Banerjee—an eminent consultant. Just then, I was told by the Railway Telephone Exchange that the GM, Mr Simoes wanted to speak to me. The GM of Railways had an air of authority about him. I was asked to hold the line for a second as he was speaking to Mr V.S. Vembu, the deputy chief personnel officer (gazetted) on the other phone from his residence. He told Mr Vembu that I was on the other line. He was telling Mr Vembu to issue my orders for PACE.

Mr Vembu perhaps told him something when the GM flared up. He told Mr Vembu not to worry about Mr Joshi—the CE. He would speak to him in Delhi. Mr T.N. Joshi was in Delhi to attend Works Programme meeting held at the Railway Board. The GM told Mr Vembu emphatically that he wanted my charge report before he left by the *Rajdhani Express* at 5 p.m. Then, he asked if I had heard what he had told Mr Vembu. He asked me to straightaway take charge of my new assignment and report to him before he left for Delhi.

I was taken aback. The post of PACE was a senior appointment. Besides assisting the CE in his technical works, he was the chief establishment officer and manpower planner of the engineering department of the Railways. Because of his proximity to the CE, the PACE traditionally enjoyed a lot of authority.

Mr Vembu asked me to come to his office immediately. I told the additional CE (construction), about what had happened as the CE (construction) H. D. Bhowmik, had gone to Delhi to attend the annual works programme meeting. Then I left for Fairlie Place where the offices of GM, CE, etc., were located.

I take over in a dramatic move

The office of CE (construction) is located on Strand Road. By the time I reached Mr Vembu's room, the orders were ready. Neither Mr Vembu nor I was aware of the urgency and circumstances leading to such an important change, made in such great haste and in such a dramatic manner. He asked Mr N.K. Dasgupta, the PACE to hand over the charge to me. I went to Mr Dasgupta, whose office was on the second floor. I told him how sorry I was about the development. He was a senior Group B officer then and appeared to be totally shocked. He however signed the charge report without demurring. I thereafter rushed to Howrah station to report to the GM. He said, 'Very good' and boarded the train. I had no courage to ask him the reason behind such an urgent step.

The news spread like wildfire. After collecting my bags from my Strand Road office, I returned home to tell my wife about the episode. She could not believe it either. It was bizarre development, difficult to comprehend. Only a spate of telephone calls made me realize the eventual reality. It was again a shock to others. They perhaps could not get reconciled to the fact that a person of my background had got such an important staff position. They also wondered what the GM had seen in me for him to select me for the appointment! After a few days, the reasons for this dramatic change came to light. There were complaints against Mr Dasgupta related to the selection and posting of senior subordinates. It is difficult to verify and prove such allegations. He may have been dealt a bad hand.

It was, however, a good lesson for me. *One should not only be honest and transparent but also appear to be so.* It made an indelible mark on my own conduct. I would thoroughly analyse and ask myself the very questions my critics might ask. In any case, if I did not find a possible answer or satisfactorily explanation of my action, I would revisit the problem or course of action. This was a great lesson and much later, particularly, while working in the vigilance department, I could appreciate its import and fuller implications.

It is a different ball game

The PACE had a totally different job profile. The establishment, manpower planning, etc., looked routine and drab from the outside. But I soon realized that it affected not only a person's own life but also one's family. Everyone wanted to receive humane treatment and consideration in service life. But this was not always possible. Everyone expected compassionate treatment. But in organizational interests, an officer had to be trained by exposing him to different fields and areas of working.

In my perception, the PACE had to be an effective medium or interface between the CE and field officers. CE, T.N. Joshi, was a wonderful person and he soon became fond of me. I helped to improve his communication in a top-down manner. I prepared a databank of all the officers and kept a record of their difficulties, problems and preferences. These details were useful in dealing with officers' training, transfer and postings. I also kept data on officers' willingness for foreign postings and kept a good liaison with the Railway Board. Often, there was no time to seek willingness from officers before nominating a person for an overseas assignment in response to the Railway Board, but with the help of a databank such nominations could be sent immediately. Of course, V.C.A. Padmanabhan, GM, who subsequently became member engineering (ME), helped a lot and championed the cause of the Railways.

Suddenly, the morale of officers improved. Traditionally, officers posted in the Eastern region complained of neglect. This was no longer the case. I also introduced this practice later as member engineering. It was thus possible to address officers' personal problems to a great extent. It improved their performance, commitment and dedication, which are crucial factors for any organization. The office of the CE no longer possessed the reputation of being shrouded in any unwarranted secrecy. It was no longer approachable only by those who had power, money or clout. Transparency made my CE, otherwise a reserved person, a popular boss and a great achiever.

GROUP 'B' SELECTION—A TRANSPARENT PROCESS

Testing time—wearing transparency on our sleeve

The selection for Group 'B' officers was testing. The Group B position or cadre is meant for deserving persons in the senior supervisory cadres of works, track and bridges. The persons in senior Group C cadre were in the selection zone. In the past, group 'B' selection was notorious and there were many complaints.

I decided that the process should be as good as possible. The correct assessment of vacancies was the first step. In close coordination with the construction department, the vacancy list was totally updated. It was important to ensure balanced question papers to give a fair chance to all categories of staff. In the past, this was a usual complaint stating that the question papers were biased to the advantage of the open line staff. On my request, Mr Joshi called Mr Ramachandran, the CE (construction) to his room. I put the syllabus and question papers of the past five examinations as a guide, before them. I requested they work together to set the question papers. Mr Joshi loudly protested. Mr Ramachandran however jokingly said that I had cleverly set them up and that there was no way to get out of it. I went out and closed the door. After setting the papers, Mr Joshi called for me to take it away for typing. I said, 'Sorry, Sir! But I will collect this from you only around 8.30 next morning from your residence.' The examination was to be held on Sunday. There was again a protest but I stayed firm.

I collected the manuscript of question papers from his residence at 8.30 a.m. the next day. The examination was scheduled for 10 a.m. The stenographer of the CE typed the question paper on a stencil. It was ready by 9.45 a.m., just before the examination. Immediately after the examination, the answer books were sealed and sent to the examiners within an hour. The entire process of selection was over in a month's time. There were no complaints whatsoever. Everyone was happy with the balanced question paper and smooth conducting of the examination. I got a pat on my back. Most importantly, people's faith in the system was restored. This is a tremendous achievement for any organization.

Later in my role as a vigilance officer, I was disappointed with how officers refused to pay requisite attention to details. Let us not focus on those of deceitful intentions, but even the people with good intentions were not careful about ensuring transparent conduct. It is difficult to answer embarrassing questions if transparency is not ensured. As a public servant, we hold public assets on behalf of the public, hence we have to be answerable. It is, therefore, essential to be prepared for a scrutiny at any time.

V.C. A. PADMANABHAN—A DOYEN

Process to regularize appointment

V.C.A. Padmanabhan, GM, was a versatile personality and he ushered in many changes in work culture. He soon took a fancy for me and often called me directly. Way back in 1957-59, when he was deputy chief engineer of the Ganga Bridge at Mokameh, some technical persons were recruited on an ad hoc basis for the construction project. They were rendered surplus after the completion of the project. They were taken on temporary roll of the Eastern Railway with no lien (or place) in the cadre. A lien, in simpler terms can be explained as follows: every person appointed as a railway servant has a cadre or a position in the list of staff, according to his category. This list contains names of all such persons appointed through a regular selection process. Since these persons were appointed on ad hoc manner to fulfil the temporary needs of a project, they were not eligible for inclusion in the cadre. So, technically they had no lien or place. Thus, even though being seniors, they were ineligible for any selection procedure. They petitioned Mr Padmanabhan as soon as he joined as general manager. He was moved by a sense of guilt as he later told me. He decided to do something. He asked me to find a solution. There were forty such persons with temporary status. They had no lien anywhere in the cadre of the Eastern Railway. They had to be screened and inducted into some cadre by providing lien. There was no other solution. It was a stupendous task. Many persons originally from the Eastern Railway had gone to other Railways on transfer for a long time. The Railway had no information on them: if they were absorbed into other railways or if they had any intention of returning to their parent railway. We were reasonably confident that a thorough probe could yield enough vacancy in the lien, to accommodate the surplus persons.

The GM consented to my plan. Many such persons were unlikely to return. After confirming the position from the other railway, these temporary men were fixed against such vacated liens. In case of a chief draftsman, he was temporarily placed as a Group D staff after screening. He was again screened for Group C as a junior draftsman. It took about a month or so. But all were duly screened and provided with lien. Their status changed from temporary to permanent. They were accordingly eligible for all the future senior selection processes including those for AEN.

When they went to thank Mr Padmanabhan, he told them that I was responsible and that only I deserved compliments. During their discussion, the chief draftsman also told him how he was made a Group D staff on paper before being inducted in his cadre in rather a circuitous way. Mr Padmanabhan had a hearty laugh. He said that he did not know that I could be a devil like that! The CDM worked with me when I was a bridge engineer in the construction department. He eventually became an AEN. This was the quality of Mr Padmanabhan who always backed his staff and ensured justice for them.

Mr Padmanabhan's humane approach—a great lesson

Soon after joining as GM, Mr Padmanabhan went to the Danapur division. He also visited the Ganga Bridge at Mokameh. One IOW (survey), who had worked with him as a river surveyor for the Ganga Bridge, met him. He remembered the IOW. He met him warmly and asked him about his welfare. The IOW was evidently frustrated, so was blunt in his response, 'Sir, you have become GM now. After the project, you went away to your hometown in the South. I am left behind and still doing river survey at this godforsaken place. Sir, I am now going to retire. I will be happy if I am posted in Calcutta area before my retirement'.

The GM was embarrassed. He asked me whether the IOW could be transferred to the Calcutta area before he retired. There were only two Grade I IOW (survey) posts in the Calcutta area. Both incumbents were senior people and due to retire in six months' time. They could not be moved out. Mr Padmanabhan again called me to his room. There was an inland letter in his hand. He said, 'Look, Jaruhar, he has written a long letter virtually accusing me, that I have done nothing.'

I told the GM about the status of available vacancies in the Calcutta area. I told him that it was not possible to displace any of the present incumbents when they were due to retire in six months. I said, 'Sir, let me call him to explain that he will have to wait for six months for the Calcutta posting.' He said, 'No, no. He will think that he was being just put off. You will also fire him and tell him not to bother the GM again. I do not like to leave that sort of impression. He has written a personal letter with basic confidence in human relations. If this faith is damaged, it will ruin everything I have always stood for.' I was stumped by this! I told him, 'The next best option is to issue a prospective transfer order which will take effect six months hence, after the retirement of the present incumbent. I will also record that this order cannot be changed without the personal approval of the CE so that the order is not changed subsequently.' The GM liked this suggestion. He asked me to issue the order and to give him a copy. He also told the CE about it. He then wrote a personal letter to the IOW, enclosing a copy of the prospective order and explaining the entire situation. I think this was a marvellous example in human resource management. It exhibited concern, sincerity and truthfulness. That is why Mr Padmanabhan had no equal. His behaviour enhanced and fortified my own belief in human relationships!

Mr Padmanabhan believed in solving problems. The contract of the Ballygunj Road overbridge was stalled because the cost of cement had gone up from ₹7 a bag to ₹20 in a lump sum contract. He was convinced that it was a force majeure issue and prevailed upon all concerned to approve of a suitable revision in rate. Work could hence be completed successfully. In another instance, the track recording car had recorded deteriorated track parameters of the *Rajdhani Express* route on Grand Chord. Mr Ganguli, ME and CRB, wrote a stinking letter to the CE. Mr Padmanabhan did a quick, special window trailing inspection and promptly replied that barring a few locations, he found that its running was quite good. And that the CE was attending to the matter urgently. The CE was thus protected.

A little known fact about him was that he could dictate to two stenographers at the same time, on two different subjects. He used to speak rapidly and one had to be very attentive to follow and keep pace with him.

A vibrant interaction with Mother Teresa

Mr Padmanabhan helped many charitable societies and was thus keen to help Mother Teresa when she requested for a small piece of railway land at Barrackpore for herMissionaries of Charity , as a home for the destitute and the aged. He got the proposal approved from the Board as a special case, on payment of a nominal licence fee. He prevailed upon the Eastern Railway Women's Welfare Organisation (ERWWO) to donate some money so that out of the interest accrued on the fixed deposit, the annual licence fee could be paid by the Mission.

Shortly after, I got a call from her Mission saying Mother wanted to speak to me. Like many, I was also in awe of her personality and thus when she came on the line, I was significantly moved. She wanted to know what was being done about her request for the railway land. I explained to her the detailed position and how the ERWWO had also decided to help her. Her voice was quick and vibrant, stirring me. I cannot forget the conversation and, in the end, she said, 'God bless you.' I just sat down for a while with her words echoing in me. I can still feel the echoes whenever I recall that conversation. An unforgettable experience of how positive energy is passed on to the recipient. The Mother is no more but her services have made her immortal. Certainly, it was my good fortune to have played had a small role, which gave me an opportunity to receive have her blessings.

INTEGRITY IS IMPORTANT—DO NOT PUSH, SIR

This particular assignment, no doubt, allowed a grand overall view of the Railways. It also allowed an insight into the working of other departments. I lived in Liluah railway colony, about eight km away from Fairlie Place. An office bus took us to the office and back home. I travelled by bus in the morning. The bus ride provided an exchange of important information. In an intensely competitive scenario, it was essential to be alert and look ahead of others.

Derailments in Mughalsarai

Mughalsarai was the biggest marshalling yard in India. The yard had to be in prime condition to maintain the fluidity of the heavy traffic passing through Mughalsarai. Any derailment on the hump yard would upset the operation. A daily incident report bulletin was brought out by the traffic department. This report out at 11 a.m. daily recorded any unusual incidents, during the last twenty-four hours having a bearing on the movement of traffic. The department responsible for the incident had to explain themselves. Once, for three consecutive days the bulletin reported 6 to 8 derailments in Mughalsarai all on the engineering account. A nasty note from the GM, S.N. Sachdev, was on the CE's table by the afternoon. Referring to the derailments, he asked, 'Is this how the engineering department functions?'

The CE was furious. There were, of course, other reasons for the provocation. Mr Sachdev was the chief operating superintendent (COPS) of the Railways, while Mr Joshi was the CE. They were good friends but after becoming GM, Mr Sachdev often enjoyed snubbing Mr Joshi, and at times, for petty reasons. Mr Joshi resented this. I requested that he allow me to handle this. In fact, such minor derailments were a daily occurrence at Mughalsarai. Everyone knew about it and also that they were mostly due to rough shunting. But they were seldom reported by the operating branch. It was, thus, plain that someone intentionally reported them to run down a department for some niggling reason. Very unfair indeed!

The permanent way inspector (PWI), Mughalsarai, was called with a breakdown register. The Accident Relief Train (ART) or the gang was always called to attend to an accident. Their deployments were recorded in the breakdown register. The ART gang claimed their breakdown allowance on this basis. From the register, the details of all accidents in the previous month were picked up. Of the two hundred and odd accidents, the engineering department had accounted for eighteen, a good 70 per cent was on account of the operating branch—attributable to poor or rough shunting.

A note was sent to the GM in response to his note, giving a full account of all the accidents that had occurred during the month. The note underlined that it was time for other departments to be more careful. This directly indicted the operating department as the villain. The note was sent around 11 a.m. Within forty-five minutes, there was a great deal of commotion. The secretary to the GM told me, 'I do not know what you have sent but the general manager is furious.' As an offshoot of this, the station superintendent, Mughalsarai was fired for having parted with the breakdown register. This was uncalled for. The register was not a confidential one. Anyone could access it. But that was the end of the pin-pricking. The GM, however, soon found out who was behind the note. Many in the department had given me credit for the note. But the GM thought it was time I was moved out of the post! I was convinced that integrity was important. You cannot push others around only because you have the authority to do so. It was not fair.

The office of CE had been traditionally known to wield a lot of authority, so, it was only expected that it would respond strongly—always defending the department and its people.

An incident, not very long ago, was related by B.M. Taneja, the then DEN (planning) in the office of CE and now Dy CPO (Gaz). Taneja was in charge of all the works program proposals of the Railways, under ENC (G) Mr Gupta who was very methodical and believed in intense scrutiny before admitting any proposal in the WP. He did not like a proposal for water supply received from the Danapur Division and he told Taneja to call Divisional Superintending Engineer (DSE) R. K. Banerjee to come and explain. It was almost 5 p.m. and the office bus to Liluah where Taneja lived, would leave Fairlie Place at 5.15 p.m. So, he hurried back to his room and asked his PA to write a letter to DS Danapur to depute R. K. Banerjee for the purpose. The PA did not know who was the DS. Taneja told him that he was the same man who was earlier as DS Dhanbad. The letter was brought and he signed it without reading and ran to catch the bus. Next day, late in the evening, R. K. Banerjee rang him up to ask what type of letter he had sent to the DS. Now the DS was none other than the heavyweight, M.S. Gujral. Taneja was aghast to learn that he had signed a letter which began with the address— 'My dear Dhanbad'. Next morning, he went to CE Kalicharan as soon as he arrived and told him about his mistake. The CE fired him for being negligent but just then Gujral called him. Before he could say anything, the CE told him that it was impossible to deal with any WP items of his division. The division has been given an outstanding officer for this and it appeared that he was not being utilized fully. Gujral said that, in that context, he had wanted to refer to a letter which the DEN Planning had written. The CE cut him short and said, 'DEN Planning, what are you saying? Even the peon of this office exercises the authority of the CE. You must know that.' He then slammed the phone down. That was how he disposed of a heavyweight like Gujral.

FLOOD RESTORATION ASSIGNMENT

Well, I came to know about the plan to move me out of the post, much later. Look at the irony of events. One GM wanted me to hastily join the post. The next one felt that I was no longer convenient for the system and had to be replaced. This was how the circle of karma worked. The people remained the same, but only the context had changed. I had learned to take such things in my stride.

The Government of India introduced training programmes for Class I officers. I was selected for ten weeks' Executive Development Program in the National Institute of Training in Industrial Engineering (NITIE), Bombay (Mumbai), a premier institution. The programme started from August 1978. It was different and very educational. The programme had twenty officers drawn from different governmental departments. There were only three officers from the Railways. I received for the first time, formal education in general management which was my introduction to Peter Drucker—the illustrious management wizard—which was sensational. Lessons in organizational behaviour including transactional analysis opened up a new horizon for my personality development. The essence of transactional analysis is so well described in the famous book, *I'm Ok, You're Ok* by Thomas Harris.

Another small episode connected with the NITIE training related to a visit by the additional secretary (AS) of the Department of Personnel & Training (DoPT), in charge of the training visiting the class. The lecture on statistics was going on at that time. The AS told this story about the subject statistics. A normal query was sent by the divisional commissioner to all the deputy commissioners (DCs) in Orissa to enquire about the production of papayas in their district. He was the DC and he replied promptly without referring it to anyone. The Government of India had been assessing the production capacity of papaya in the country as there was a good prospect of its export. In about a year, he became the divisional commissioner himself. In an annual conference of DCs, the office asked all the DCs why it was that only one district had given this information about production of papaya even after a number of reminders. He said that he was amused to know that the reply had come only from his erstwhile district. He says he was amused because his reply that had come more than a year ago was—'the production in the district this year was the same as last year'. That is how the statistics was being used, collected! Laugh, but what could one say.

Unprecedented flood in West Bengal—a great calamity and the damage

There was a heavy cloud burst in October 1978, causing devastating floods in West Bengal. The rainfall was over four hundred mm on a single day. The flood gates of many water-retaining structures like Mayurakhsi Dam, the Bakreshwar Barrage were opened simultaneously to save them. The result was a total deluge and caused great calamity.

I saw the area subsequently. There was clear-cut evidence of a twenty-feet high column of water suddenly sweeping village after village around 7 p.m. Many were inside their homes after dark. Many villagers and cattle were swept away. They never had a chance. This caused heavy damage to Bolpur-Sainthia section of Sahebganj loop, Katwa-Nalhati of BAK loop and Katwa-Ahmedpur NG line. It was befitting to restore these lines on a war footing, on an urgency certificate.

My training in the NIITE was completed on 27 October 1978. My wife came down to Bombay for a week's holiday after the training programme. But the day my wife arrived in Bombay, I was informed by wire that the leave I had requested, could not be sanctioned. I was asked to return to Calcutta immediately because of the floods. After a day in Bombay we returned to Calcutta. It was of course very disappointing for the family.

I move to repair the flood damage

I was posted as DEN (Special), Howrah for the restoration of flood-damaged lines. This was in view of my rich experience in bridges.

It was common to post a person back to the same station and post after such trainings. But in my case, they had decided to entrust me with a very difficult job. The work had to be completed before the next monsoon, within a period of six months. A tall order indeed! But I accepted the challenge. I was not aware that the posting was on purpose and with some design. The CE told me that the GM had asked him to entrust this job to me. He could not resist as the division had not taken any action for the permanent restoration of the damaged lines before I had joined. Not even an organization was in place.

The work was divided into three parts. Two broad gauge sections Sainthia-Ahmedpur and Katwa-Nalhati had been temporarily restored with speed restrictions, but temporary measures had to be replaced by permanent ones before the next rainy season. Monsoon sets in April in West Bengal.

The narrow gauge section between Katwa and Ahmedpur was not even touched. Bridge drawings had to be finalized with detailed estimates. Tenders had to be issued accordingly to execute this work.

I had neither an organization nor any trained manpower. Tender documents were to be prepared and called for. We however worked hard. Technically, I was confident. All documents were, therefore, ready at a fast pace. Tenders were called within a short opening period. They were decided in the span of two days after their opening. All the major bridge drawings were finalized by me. The chief bridge engineer (CBE) was scandalized. He saw a clear-cut usurping of his authority. He complained to the CE that I did not listen to anyone and that I worked as if I was still the PACE. During the inspection of the CE and the CBE, I explained that the span arrangements were based on approved construction drawings. There was very little time and I had to move fast. Mr Joshi appreciated my initiative and asked the CBE to allow me to continue with the work.

The narrow gauge was restored at a fast pace

I was able to find solutions to most of the problems without bothering anyone. The local population was keen on an early restoration of the narrow gauge line. The line however was non-remunerative and therefore was lower on the list of priorities. I had decided to cut down on costs. Thus, rail clusters were used for small culverts. It was a cheap and fast solution. At some places, concrete Hume pipes, suitable for road loading were used. The major bridge on the Saraswati River was damaged. The effect and the fury of the flood must be seen to be believed. Three spans were washed away. One girder was swept away over half a kilometre. One pier was shorn from its base.

The bridge engineer from the headquarters advised that we increase the waterway of the bridge to suit the high flood discharge that was passing at the time. It would have been costly and clearly was not needed. A cloud burst had forced a heavy discharge from the Mayurakhsi Dam reservoir. This was an unprecedented flood and it was not necessary to let it guide the design. Structures need not be designed for such a calamity. This was successfully argued before the additional commissioner of rail safety.

Thus, the existing waterway was retained. The span arrangement was staggered by inserting a new pier to bypass the broken one. Remaining bridge spans were retained saving huge amount of money. The CE appreciated the arrangement. I invited Mr Sachdev, the GM, for the opening function. He was very happy and took a lot of credit for finding the right person to handle the restoration work. Well, his action was justified in a way! My faith that working on a challenging and difficult situation provided greater satisfaction grew stronger. It was like batting on a sticky wicket. Sunil Gavaskar always rated his knock of 101 on a turning wicket at Old Trafford against England as the most treasured and satisfying innings of his illustrious career.

By the end of April 1979, most of the work was close to completion before the deadline, of the rainy season. There was some problem in major bridge No.125 near Sainthia. I suggested a revised arrangement which I could not have executed before I left but it was completed by my successor subsequently.

Move to a yet bigger construction assignment

I was now in a position to move out and take up a much bigger assignment. There was already talk about that. But I thought that it was better to complete the task of flood affected lines. By the end of April 1979, I was ready.

But before moving out, I was asked to pay for the use of one extra set of pass. After the final accounting, I had actually used an extra set over and above my entitlement. This was when I was on training at NITIE. It was an inadvertent error. According to the rules, the GM could condone this by setting it against next year's entitlement. I was called by Mr Parbinder Singh, the GM, to explain. I was nervous. He asked, 'Son, tell me how you managed to use more than six sets? I have never been able to do so. What is the trick?' He smiled and winked at me. I told him, 'Sir, my wife keeps running to Patna every now and then. I was alone in Bombay with three days off, during Durga Pooja. So, I went to meet my wife at Patna'. He laughed and said that he did not really need an explanation. He said, 'Son, I am glad you enjoyed yourself. Compliment your wife on exhausting a privilege. I will also tell my wife to do something like that although it is too late for us.' With that, he condoned the excess use of the pass. It was a kind gesture! Mr Singh was really a warm-hearted person. In the days of Emergency, in an attempt to enforce staff punctuality, GMs were asked to close the main gate and send late-comers away. As the GM, Northern Railway, he refused to shut the gate of Baroda House after 10 a.m. He said that it was against the rule. According to the story, he earned the wrath of the minister and was sent packing to the North Eastern Railway. He was adored by all who knew him for the lessons he taught.

6

BRAHMAPUTRA BRIDGE—A NEW CONSTRUCTION PHASE

POLITICAL TURMOIL IN INDIA

The period from 1974-75 and 1975-78, was a very eventful one in the history of India. It also affected the Indian Railways a great deal. Firstly, there was a country-wide railway strike in 1974, spearheaded by George Fernandes, a prominent trade union leader. The strike paralyzed trains all over the country. But the government came down with a heavy hand and was successful in breaking the strike. The government of that time felt that it was being coerced to concede to demands which would have wider and larger ramifications in industrial relations all over the country. All the same, it was difficult to appreciate the highhandedness of the measures adopted to break down the strike. The unrest, however, affected other walks of life. Jayaprakash Narayan, a famous socialist leader and a renowned freedom fighter called for a 'total revolution'. It called for the right of the people to recall its elected leader. The movement gathered a lot of momentum. Youth and students at the grassroots level participated in the movement in large numbers.

The government reacted swiftly by clamping down an internal emergency. Without going into the rights-and-wrongs of such a step, the performance of the Indian Railways certainly improved a great deal during 1975 to March 1977, when the Emergency was in force. We were often asked to count the advantages of this in official interactions. The Emergency was eventually lifted in 1977, followed by the General Election. It is widely believed that Indira Gandhi, the prime minister (PM), was advised by the astrologers and other intelligence outfits that she would win hands down, if an election was to be held. But apparently the mood of the people was different and the ruling party lost badly in the hustings. A new coalition government, under the leadership of Morarji Desai, came into power. The new government emphasized the development of the Northeastern states. The people of this region had often complained of poor connectivity not only with the rest of India, but also within seven states of the region. This brought about the construction of a bridge across the Brahmaputra River.

Majestic Brahmaputra—a male among rivers

The most striking feature of the picturesque Northeast is the all-pervasive presence of the majestic Brahmaputra. This river is considered masculine because of its size. The only other masculine river in India is Damodar. According to Hindu mythology, both these rivers are sons of Lord Brahma and both are known for their devastating nature, which are rightly dreaded by common people. This led to an interesting interaction with a Malaysian Army delegation, led by a senior general. While explaining various facets of the bridge, I mentioned that the Brahmaputra was a masculine river. It was comparable to the Amazon in Brazil in its size and characteristics. The general jokingly said, 'But the river has typical feminine curves of a river.' I said, 'Well, actually they are its muscles rippling, warning you to keep your hands off.' It is the longest river in Asia at a total length of 2,880 km—920 km of which is in India. It cuts across the seven states of the Northeast.

Brahmaputra had only one bridge

The people of the Northeast had a long-standing grouse. They said that the Ganga had as many as nine bridges, but there was only one across the Brahmaputra. The new government under Morarji Desai was keen on amending that. They initiated major developmental schemes in the region. For this, the North Eastern Council (NEC) was set up to coordinate, initiate and bring about development in the seven states of the region. To improve communication in the region across the Brahmaputra, four bridge locations on the river were selected by the NEC. The first of these was a road bridge in Tezpur, Assam. It was sanctioned with a lot of promise in October 1978, largely due to the initiative of governor of Assam, L.K. Singh, who was also the chairman of the NEC.

ROAD BRIDGE ENTRUSTED TO THE RAILWAYS—A MATTER OF TRUST

There are many versions of how the project was transferred to the Railways. But according to the one that is most prevalent—L.K. Singh called a meeting in Delhi after the project was sanctioned by the government. The purpose was to decide on the agency to execute the work. He asked in the meeting, 'Gentlemen, the project has now been sanctioned. Now the question is as to who will construct the bridge.' The Assam PWD said that they lacked experience of such major bridge construction but they believed that the Central Public Works Department (CPWD) should be able to manage. The representative of the CPWD said that they were confident of handling it although they had no experience.

L.K. Singh was very clear and said, 'I thank all of you but we must bear in mind that the people have placed a lot of hope on this bridge. It is an emotional issue with them. It will not, therefore, be prudent to subject it to experimentation because bridging the mighty Brahmaputra is very challenging. In my opinion, the only organization having expertise of bridging all important rivers in India is the Indian Railways. It will be in fitness of things if the Railways undertake the project in service of the Northeast.'

Indian Railways accept the challenge

The Railways' representative in the meeting was Vijay Singh. Although an eminent bridge engineer, he was not competent enough to take such a decision. He had to consult the Railway Board. The meeting was adjourned to enable Vijay Singh to consult the Railway Board. He rushed hastily to Mr Padmanabhan, member engineering, who attended the meeting in the afternoon. He thanked L.K. Singh for the faith reposed in the Railways for the prestigious project. He offered to construct the bridge on nominal departmental charge of 1 per cent against the normal fees of 12.50 per cent. He also promised to train Assam PWD engineers so that the next bridge could be constructed under their own banner. He however insisted that all technical decisions would be taken by the Railways, which was fully competent in this respect. This gesture was loudly appreciated. A far-sighted decision, and in the time to come, it proved to be an excellent one. It paved the way for a flow of technology to the state while ensuring that the project did not suffer from unnecessary interference.

Mr Padmanabhan was in charge of construction of the rail-cum-road bridge on the Ganga at Mokameh in Bihar. L.K. Singh was the district magistrate (DM) of the area at that time (1956-59). He was greatly impressed with the IR's professional approach and expertise in construction. He accordingly pitched for the IR to construct the Tezpur Bridge. Mr Padmanabhan had also executed the famous and challenging work of construction of the DBK (Dandakaranya-Kiriburu) iron ore line. Till date, this has been one of the greatest engineering challenges.

The project was formally entrusted to the IR in early 1979. The Railway Board took up this project in all seriousness. A special organization under GM (construction) was created in North East Frontier Railway (NF Railway, construction) with headquarters in Maligaon, Guwahati. It was the first of its kind and was done with a view to expedite construction in the Northeastern states. The idea was that a senior person—the rank of a GM—with the power that he held would be able to take all the decisions quickly. N.N. Sarma became the first GM (construction). Soon after that, the hunt was on to select good officers for this project.

Mr Padmanabhan invites me to the project

Mr Padmanabhan knew me and was well aware of my technical expertise and managerial capabilities. He was on his way to Guwahati to inspect the project sometime in April 1979. I was asked to see him in the CE's room at Fairlie Place. As soon as I entered the room, he asked, 'Why are you wasting your time and talent in small works in the Railways? You should go to construct the bridge on the Brahmaputra in the Northeast Frontier Railway. Such an opportunity comes once in a lifetime or in a decade.' The mention of the Northeast Frontier Railway was unnerving in those days. I had to consult my family before taking the decision as the Northeast Frontier Railway was considered a punitive posting. I was not sure how my wife would take that. The ME was to return to Delhi after two days in Guwahati. I was asked to meet him at the Calcutta airport. The proposed posting as deputy CE in the junior administrative grade (JAG) was a promotion. Our CE, T.N. Joshi, of course, requested the ME not to take away good officers from this railway. He told the ME that I would be promoted to the JAG in the ER by July 1979. But the ME dismissed him by saying that the job being offered to me was a prestigious assignment. It could not be compared to the normal and ordinary jobs.

I agree to go to the Northeast Frontier Railway

I returned home in the evening unsure of what I should do. Truly speaking, if the ME had taken a fancy towards me for this job, he could unilaterally issue orders as I was an All India Service officer liable for posting anywhere in India. It was really good of Mr Padmanabhan to have asked in advance. I narrated to my wife about what had happened. She instantaneously said, 'No'. I could not blame her for such a reaction. We were just debating the issue when suddenly my father-in-law came in. He was at that time the director, science and technology, government of Bihar. He had come to Calcutta for a meeting. After settling down, we mentioned about the posting in the Northeast Frontier Railway. After pausing to think for a while, he advised me to accept the prestigious assignment for the sheer value addition that it would cause to my career. He said, 'From the point of view of the family also, it will not be inconvenient. For the next 5 to 6 years, Shravani, my daughter, will need primary education which will not be a problem. In any way, it is better to have an inconvenient posting in early part of the career.' So, the decision was made. Looking back, I must say that the whole affair must have been preordained, like so many more in my life. My father-in-law's arrival was sudden without any prior plan. His logic was explicit. I met Mr Padmanabhan at the airport and conveyed my acceptance. He told me that the orders would be issued on his return to Delhi.

PROMOTION AS DEPUTY CHIEF ENGINEER—SEEKING MY DESTINY

I arrive at Maligaon

My orders were of course issued immediately. I, however, came to know about it much later when N.N. Sarma, GM (construction), called me to find out when I was going to join the Northeast Frontier Railway. The restoration work of the flood affected lines of the Howrah division was expected to be completed by the end of April 1979. I was finally released on 5 May 1979.

I boarded the *Kamrup Express* from Howrah and arrived at Maligaon the next day. I reported to the office of GM (construction). I was asked to wait for two days before I could see the GM. The secretary to the GM was Mr Jund. We soon became very good friends. He told me that the GM was contemplating posting me to Silchar for the construction of a new line. I was very upset because I had come for the Brahmaputra Bridge. Otherwise, there was no point in leaving the Eastern Railway. Better counsel eventually prevailed and I was finally posted as deputy CE (construction) Tezpur, a place 187 km away from Guwahati.

It was a promotion for me. But nobody talked much about it. It was certainly a major milestone in my life and an important event from the point of view of my professional life, as well as our own lives for the next seven and half years! Technically and professionally, this assignment changed my career. On our personal life front, we were blessed with a daughter, Shreya, and a son, Shrimant, to give company to our eldest daughter Shravani, who had just started going to school.

On way to Tezpur—a giant step

While travelling from Howrah, the landscape and the scenic beauty totally changed once we crossed New Jalpaiguri. The sky was deep blue, the likes of which I had not ever seen. A green landscape, rivers and streams made nature look at its best. I was staying in the officers' rest house in Maligaon. After posting orders were issued, I was given a car to travel to Tezpur. Monsoon had started and it was raining heavily in the morning. I was waiting for the rain to abate before I left. Locals told me that it was unlikely. So, I left in the rain. Tezpur is on the north bank of the Brahmaputra River. Leaving Maligaon, one crossed the Brahmaputra. This was the only bridge on the river constructed under the stewardship of the legendary B.C. Ganguli in 1962.

After seventeen years, another humble person much less endowed in technical excellence than B.C. Ganguli was endeavouring to construct the second bridge over the Brahmaputra. Suddenly, what Mr Padmanabhan had told me and what my own father-in-law had advised, dawned on me. I was reminded of what Neil Armstrong had uttered while setting his foot on the Moon. It was a small step for him but a giant leap for mankind. Crossing the Brahmaputra was awe-inspiring at that time. Subsequently, I found the expanse of the river more frightful in Tezpur. I was humbled and I wondered how I was to emulate a feat created by a legend like B.C. Ganguli.

FINAL LANDING IN TEZPUR—A HISTORICAL PLACE

We left the national highway near Rangiya and turned on the state highway, called North Trunk road. The view was majestic around us. The sight of pink flowering trees known as 'April fool', was particularly spectacular. What a bloom! It was an unforgettable experience. We crossed many well-known rivers on the way. The villages in Assam were neat and clean. Particularly impressive was the presence of a large number of school children. The large number of girls dressed in the typical Assamese sari was a sight to behold. The rain had stopped by then. I reached Tezpur railway station around 11.30 a.m. and was met by the executive engineer, an elderly, serious-looking gentleman. He was Mr C.R. Kar, a senior Group B officer. The second was an IOW, an inspector. The first impression that they gave me was that I was not welcome. Luckily, it did not prove to be right.

I land at Tezpur—witness historical surroundings

It was my first visit to Assam. Tezpur was in the news during the Chinese aggression in 1962. I was studying in the engineering college then. The Chinese had entered India through Twang in Arunachal Pradesh about 275 km from Tezpur. The Indian Army was not at all prepared for the assault. The Chinese had thus, entered without any significant resistance up to Bomdila, 105 km from Tezpur. The fall of Tezpur to the advancing Chinese Army looked imminent. Prime Minister Jawaharlal Nehru in fact had given a statement that he felt sorry for the people of the Northeast. This caused widespread scare which forced many to leave the area in panic, seeking safety. The family of the young DC of Tezpur also left. The DC had gone to the airport to see off his family. But the family had strongly persuaded him to leave along with them. The poor fellow must have been emotionally blackmailed; and in fit of emotion, he had boarded the flight, deserting his post. It had a demoralizing effect. Ultimately, the Chinese stopped at Bomdila and a ceasefire was announced. The Chinese eventually vacated the Indian territory. Nothing happened to Tezpur except for the loss of confidence and morale of the people.

Tezpur at the foothills of the Himalayas and bordering the state of Arunachal Pradesh was the district headquarters of Darrang. It was perhaps the only town of fame and importance in northern Assam. A city set in a picturesque location, with a number of tea gardens on the banks of the Brahmaputra, it looked clean and beautiful in the month of May. On clear days, one could see the snow-laden peaks of the Himalayas. It was undoubtedly blessed with a pleasing climate for most of the year.

Even in mythological records, Tezpur is mentioned as Sonitpur—city of blood. According to mythology, Anirudh, son of Lord Krishna, came here and fell in love with Usha, daughter of a local king. A bloody battle was fought in which Lord Krishna and Lord Shiva also participated. The blood which spilled in course of the war, led to its naming as Tezpur or Sonitpur (both Tez and Sonit mean blood). According to the local history, remains of the fort where Anirudh and Usha had lived, are still there. It is known as Usha hill. The hill has a magnificent view of the Brahmaputra and the bridge-site. Darrang district was subsequently divided into two—one known as Darrang with its headquarters as Mangaldoi and another as Sonitpur with its headquarters as Tezpur. It has the biggest Air Force base east of Bagdogra. It is also the headquarters of 4th Corps of the Army, the biggest Army set-up in northern Assam.

REALIZATION OF THE TASK

I suddenly realized what I was in for. There were no logistics available for undertaking such a mega project. The two gentlemen used the waiting room of the railway station as their office. They had a second-hand jeep. All that they could call their office was contained in the briefcase they carried. But contract for a geotechnical investigation was given to the AFCONS on the proposed alignment of the bridge.

Developing a rapport with stakeholders

I had to start from scratch—an unpleasant thought. But nevertheless, this had to be done. I parked myself in a room of the officers' rest house. I started searching for rented accommodation for other officers and our staff. A suitable house for the office was also needed. For the next two weeks, this was done in great speed. Mr Kar was very helpful. I think he found me much better than he had assumed initially.

I was convinced that a project of this nature could succeed, but it would be determined to a large extent by how external influences were generated and managed. For this, a good rapport with the local people, civil administration, military and the Air Force authorities was gradually developed. The Army and the Air Force bases in Tezpur had a large stake in the bridge. This area in Assam produces a large quantity of tea. There are many tea gardens all round, with tea processing industries. They were also keen on the bridge. We quickly developed good networks. I frequently interacted with them to brief them about the progress. Mr Sarma, the GM (construction) told someone that he was glad that he had not actually pursued his initial thought of posting me to Silchar.

Mr Padmanabhan had told me that the time was ripe to develop proper relationships and gather all the details. These included data on distance and time taken from all important places, quarry details, rates of all construction materials and names of the key persons who could deliver them. I was able to develop dossiers on all these. It came in handy when the main bridge contractors came for a site investigation.

The Railways had to supply cement and steel for the project. These were long lead items and had to come from outside Assam. The rail transport called for the transhipment from broad gauge to meter gauge. Advance planning was essential for procurement and collection of these materials. It was not a problem to store steel in advance but cement could not be stored. About 800 to 1,000 metric tons of cement was required per day during the working season. It would have been impossible to procure and carry such large quantities during the working season. Thus, cement had to be stored even during the monsoon. Good storage godowns were made available with special heating and dehumidifying arrangement (industrial silica gel) to keep the godown dry. An imaginative and new idea and that was the only answer to the problem.

IMPORTANCE OF PLANNING—LEARNING PROCESS

Important tasks ahead

Planning plays a very important role in any major project to avoid costly mistakes. Unfortunately, there were no details available on the magnitude and logistics required for a mega project like this.

The river contained a number of major channels whose configuration was quite uncertain, and it changed not only from season to season but also during the working season. The exact location of the channel was crucial for deciding the location of the guide bundh on the south bank. The width of the river at the proposed location was more than eight km. It was not possible to see the other bank. M/S Rail India Technical and Economic Services (RITES) had prepared the project report based on a preliminary survey alone. Clearly, additional studies were required for detailed execution drawings. The estimate prepared by the RITES was also sketchy. It had to be revised, enlarged and updated to account for all the activities. The state government had to acquire land for the project.

The final hydraulic model test was done at Uttar Pradesh River Irrigation Institute (UPRII), Roorkee. After the test, the axis of the bridge was changed from the bearing of 355^0 to 342^0 30' minutes. This required a fresh survey along a revised bridge axis.

Correct alignment was essential for such a long bridge. The base line had to be set up on either side of the river. This called for a geodetic and astronomical survey. This was a specialized job and normally, the services of the department of the Survey of India were requisitioned for this purpose. In short, a great deal of preparatory work was necessary before actual construction could begin.

Giants initiate me into river training

Honestly, my knowledge of river training, key to the construction of the bridge, was almost non-existent. It was limited to the reading of literature available on the subject. I, however, had the benefit of intimate interactions with some of the giants in the field. They included B.C. Ganguli, the retired chairman and member engineering Railway Board. He had extensive knowledge on the subject of rivers in Assam and West Bengal. He was CE (construction) of the Assam Rail Link Project. He had a reputation for possessing the sixth sense in bridge engineering. Mr V.C.A. Padmanabhan was another great bridge engineer. Debes Mukherjee had excelled in the West Bengal Irrigation department. He was credited with the construction of large hydraulic structures like Narmada Dam, Farakka Barrage, Kosi Barrage in Bihar and many more. I was very fortunate to have made their acquaintance. They were unanimous in their advice to me. 'See and observe the river. Try to learn as much as possible from the experience of local boatmen and fishermen. They have generally good practical knowledge and experience of the river.' I followed their advice religiously. While crossing the river in a boat, I used to interact with the boatmen. I recall B.C. Ganguli telling me, 'You should never enter the river unless both your pockets are full—

one with materials and the other with money. And you should talk and listen to all before stepping into the river but once you have entered, stop listening to anyone else. You should become your own master. You will otherwise perish.' How appropriate was the counsel indeed! A general in a war cannot run or look for advice while a battle is on!

Their advice about the suitability of a flexible boulder crated apron on alluvium deposits saved not only crores of rupees, but also a mitigated disaster both in the case of the Brahmaputra and the Gandak bridges. Their advice to understand nature and provide the same in design consideration was religiously followed by me. 'Never use any brute force against nature but try to use nature's force to do your work.'

I preached and followed this for the rest of my life. One's knowledge, skill and ingenuity lay in this realm. I was able to learn because of my approach as a student. I was never afraid of asking even silly questions if something was not clear or if it bothered me. It was God's wish and preordained. Otherwise, it is difficult to explain how and why such giants happened to come to Tezpur as a great constellation. It was unbelievable!

EXAMPLE OF POLITICAL LEADERSHIP IN NATION BUILDING

Much is known or talked about B.C. Ganguli in the Railways. It may be interesting to know that Mr Ganguli and Mr Mukherji were classmates in Bengal Engineering College, Shibpur, West Bengal, which was a premiere institution in the country. Mr Ganguli had topped the class while Mr Mukherjee was second in the order of merit. According to the practice then, Mr Ganguli was offered the post of engineer in Bengal Nagpur Railway (BNR). So, Mr Ganguli came into the Railways, although BNR was a private railway at that time. After the reorganization of railways in India, BNR became a government railway and was called the South Eastern Railway (SER). He thereafter charted an illustrious career in the Railways.

But Mr Mukherjee joined the State Irrigation Department and made a name for himself. In this context, I would like to share what Debes Mukherjee told me about his experience of Kosi Barrage. The Kosi, known as the River of Sorrow of Bihar, had been responsible for untold flood devastation year after year in north Bihar. Entering Bihar from Nepal, the river makes a short detour in the plains before joining the Ganga.

A decision was taken to construct a barrage over the Kosi in its stretch in Nepal to control the river. The construction being tricky, it was decided to entrust it to someone having the requisite experience. Chief Minister (CM) of

Bihar Shri Krishna Singh, a towering personality, was a contemporary of Dr B.C. Roy, CM of West Bengal. Dr Roy was a well-known physician and a freedom fighter of repute. He had fought alongside Jawaharlal Nehru in the campaign for Indian independence. Shri Krishna Singh requested B.C. Roy to lend him the services of a competent engineer for the job. He sent Debes Mukherjee to S.K. Singh for this purpose.

Mr Mukherjee first went to the Kosi site to understand the nature of the work before meeting Shri Krishna Singh. He explained the difficulties involved in the work, to the Bihar CM, when he met him in Patna. He told the CM that it was essential to divert a channel of the Kosi River before the barrage could be constructed. The diversion of the channel would have cost a few crores of rupees (this was a large sum in 1955-56). There was however a risk that the diversion of the channel might not succeed and the expenditure could thus become infructuous. In a government project, such a waste would be treated as criminal and would end with a call for his head on the block. He requested the CM to grant him immunity in such an eventuality. It was a tall order and the request was uncommon indeed. Mr Mukherjee recalled that the CM did not utter a single word but simply nodded before the meeting was over. He thought that his terms were surely not acceptable. Accordingly, he returned to Calcutta, completely forgetting about the project.

After about three weeks, he was again asked to meet the chief minister. Shri Krishna Singh gave him a copy of the resolution of the Bihar Cabinet absolving him of any responsibility in the event of failure to divert the channel of the Kosi River. He was awestruck. He immediately joined the Bihar government. The rest is history. The most difficult work was successfully completed. It however demonstrates the political will. Normally, such a resolve is not common but for a giant like Shri Krishna Singh it was a matter of conviction!

FIRST STEP IN LAND ACQUISITION—A RIGHT CHOICE

The land had to be acquired for the construction of the site office and residential complex. I realized that getting land in Tezpur was not going to be easy on two counts. One, the land was scarce hence costlier; two, there was an inherent resistance or antipathy to part with land to a Central government department. The DC hailed from Nagaland and was a simple person. He smoked beedi, and was fond of alcohol. He suo moto got me a drinking licence. Assam being a dry area, one needed a medical certificate from the civil surgeon—to the effect that a regular intake of alcohol was essential for the upkeep of one's good health! In contrast, it was a striking sight to see his wife smoking India King or 777 and the husband lighting a beedi. His wife was a tall, beautiful lady and spoke English with an impeccable accent.

He advised me to set up office on the outskirts of the town. A piece of land outside Tezpur, on the way to the bridge site, was selected. Meanwhile, the DC was transferred but the gazette notification for the land acquisition had not been issued. I went to meet him on his last day at office. I politely reminded him of his promise to get the land deal settled. It so happened that the district land acquisition officer turned up, at that very moment to get his signature on his travelling allowance bill. The DC asked him, 'I had asked you to issue a gazette notification for a railway land. Please get the paper ready for my approval. Unless it is done, I will not sign your TA journal.' This worked. Before the day was over, all documents for the transfer of the land were ready for publication of a notification in the Gazette.

The cost of land outside Tezpur was much lower and it was hardly two km away. The state government showed a great deal of expedition in transferring the land at Dolabari. Being outside the town, it was virtually away from all disturbances, particularly the long-drawn out agitation in Assam which had started in September 1979.

We were also able to select cheap but elegant specifications for the buildings from the PWD. The intention was to transfer the complex to the state government after the bridge work was over. The Railways had no use for it. Built in a record time of nine months, the office and the residential complex was cited as an example of good engineering as well as one of economic construction.

APPROACH TO MANPOWER

The project needed good and experienced engineers and supporting staff. People from outside Assam were not willing to come to the NF Railway or Assam. It was considered a punishment posting. Many in Maligaon jokingly would ask me, 'You're posted in NF—how come? Did you incur the wrath of your superiors? Or, were you enamoured of the pretty women of this area, to come all the way to this place?' I would always reply 'Well, nothing of the sort had happened. I had come of my own volition.' So, this puzzled many. Since, experienced persons were not available, I had asked for fresh junior engineers just recruited by the Railway Recruitment Board (RRB). It was possible to train and mould them according to our requirements. It was easier to instil proper work culture in them. This was readily agreed to because nobody wanted to part with trained and experienced employees.

Young IRSEs join us

I invited some known officers to join the project. Some of them were willing to come but their departments raised many obstacles in releasing them. This did not prove successful. Eventually, we requested ME to send a batch of IRSE probationers. They could come and complete all the survey work and finalize detailed estimates, etc. Mr Balachandran, the GM, was also the secretary Railway Board in his previous stint. He was full of dynamism and could move the right persons in the Board. He liked the idea very much. He prevailed upon Mr Basrur, ME, to post sixteen IRSE probationers for about two months.

They were young and technically sound engineers. It was difficult to accommodate them as they arrived without much notice. Some of them were married with children too. Our local team quickly found rented accommodations for them. My wife took a lot of initiative to equip them with the bare minimum furnishings including kitchenware. She looked after the families personally and made them feel comfortable. They started enjoying the place as if they were on a picnic. We had a small club, where we hosted pot-luck parties. My wife had a knack of drawing out young ladies and involving them. She became their fond leader. Mr Padmanabhan had also told me about the importance of looking after the staff and their families in a project. We took it as our duty to take care of them, particularly the young ones who had come from far-flung places, away from their homes. We were genuinely interested in their welfare. My wife felt as if she was their bhabhi ji or elder sister and she took that responsibility with natural ease. This paid rich dividends. We came to be known as a kind and considerate couple. Of course, the key was to be sincere and have a genuine concern. It could not be faked.

Some of the IRSEs became the jewels of the Indian Railways

This philosophy became a part of our total personality as a couple all through our life. We were genuinely proud to have earned the love and respect of so many. It has been long and enduring indeed. At the work place, these probationers became willing and enthusiastic workers. We were conducting a geodetic survey for the base line. It involved an astronomical survey also. Although the basic work was being done by the team from the Survey of India, our team was fully associated. This not only helped our own team to pick up first-hand knowledge of survey technique but it also helped the Survey of India team to complete the work in a very short period of time. Some of the probationers became quite interested in the project. They liked the existing working environment. A few IRSE probationers eventually agreed to join our project team after completing their probation. I am very proud of them. They are V.C. Sharma, H.K. Jaggi, M.R. Chowdhary, Pankaj Jain, Singhal and Aditya Mittal. Aditya Mittal rose to become member engineering. All of them excelled in bridge engineering and river training. They turned out to be true assets to the Indian Railways. Of these, V.C. Sharma subsequently succeeded me. He was the leader of the team, which built the third bridge over the Brahmaputra at Jogighopa. He was IR's pride in the Union International of Railways (UIC), Paris—a global body of railways.

ASSAM AGITATION—BEGINNING AND THE BACKGROUND

I cannot avoid mentioning the Assam agitation, which started in September 1979. The outrage was over the vast ingress of foreign nationals, mostly from Bangladesh. It also included issues like utter neglect of not only Assam but also the other states of the Northeast like Meghalaya, Arunachal Pradesh, Nagaland, Mizoram, Manipur and Tripura—the seven sisters. The agitation was headed by students, the All Assam Students' Union (AASU) being the front. They were also supported by the All Assam Gana Sangram Parishad (AAGSP), a group of non-political citizens of repute.

The background of the Assam agitation

The agitation generated a great deal of sympathy and support from all walks of society. They had been complaining about the unabated infiltration of the Bangladeshi nationals since 1960. They alleged that it was being indirectly encouraged by political parties. The infiltration had assumed alarming proportions threatening to upset the very basis of the cultural and demographic pattern of the society. They wanted the identification of all such illegal immigrants and their deportation.

This sounded absolutely correct. We wondered why the government was not doing anything worthwhile. It was an enigma to us. The movement gathered steam as a non-violent and peaceful agitation similar to that by Mahatma Gandhi against the British. Schools, colleges and offices were closed on the call of the agitation leaders. The wife of the DC was seen leading the protest march to the collector's office.

The agitation also targeted non-Assamese

In some places, non-Assamese citizens were also asked to quit Assam. This affected the workforce in tea gardens, where most of the labourers were from outside Assam. We were no exceptions. The protesters came to our office also.

The local staff ran away at the sight of them. They asked me to close down the office. I spoke to them in English or Hindi but they insisted that I speak in Assamese only. I said, 'I have come at the invitation of the Government of Assam to construct a bridge over the Brahmaputra. This work is also part of your demands. Since I have come recently, I need time to pick up your language.' The next time, I started speaking to them in broken Assamese. They found it difficult to understand. But I said that unless I tried speaking to them, I could not learn their language. They finally conceded that I could speak in Hindi or English. They could understand both better than my broken Assamese.

The impact of agitation is profound—its dynamics incisive

The situation in Maligaon, the headquarters office was worse. Nobody was allowed to go to office. All the officers would assemble in the Officers' Club. The agitators soon drove them away from the club. The chairman Railway Board heard of this. He directed the officers to attend to their duties. The government was also firm. They arranged for proper security to be provided by the Central Reserve Police Force (CRPF). As a result, the officers marched in a column flanked by the CRPF jawans, presenting a ludicrous scene.

Such security arrangements were not available to us. We just walked to the office and left when forced by the agitators. The agitation grew from strength to strength. Students participated in large numbers. The academic calendar was totally muddled. Parents were worried of the loss of more than a year of academic work. Many children left Assam for Delhi or for other states to pursue their studies. Despite several dialogues between the government and the agitation leaders, there was no solution for more than two years. It possibly also gathered cross-border encouragement and militant support. The leaders felt that the government was only keen to exploit the resources of the state like oil and coal. So, they disrupted the oil supply line. The disruption of the oil pipeline had serious ramifications.

By the end of the year, the agitation had blown up to assume dangerous proportions. Life was no longer normal. It affected the regular supply of essential goods to the entire Northeastern region. All non-Assamese were held in contempt by Assamese. The most hated community was the Bengali. It was strange, but its origin must have been from the pre-Independence days. The British had administered the Northeast with the help of Indian babus, mostly literate Bengalis. The Assamese recalled how the lower levels of the bureaucracy comprising Bengali babus were apathetic to them. The Bengalis thought they were superior due to their educational advantage and their position under the British.

Surprisingly, the same community did not resent the Muslim immigrants although the agitation was against them. The reason was rather simple. These immigrants from erstwhile East Bengal were actually hard-working agricultural labours. They had augmented agricultural production in the state by transforming many lands hitherto unfit for cultivation, into high yielding ones. Assamese, mostly absentee landlords were the direct beneficiary of this additional revenue. They encouraged the import of farm labourers from outside no matter where they came from. In course of time, these immigrants acquired citizenship and eventually became title holders. They started asserting themselves, as distinct entity for a share of the political power. The Assamese resented the change in their status. It was a highly complex subject and I do not claim to have the best of knowledge. My insight into the problem was based on conversations with the local intelligentsia and agitation leaders. I had to understand the basic dynamics of the agitation to cope with its massive influence, which threatened to disrupt the project.

IMPEDIMENTS AND HOSTILITY CAUSED BY THE AGITATION

The working environment in Assam was seriously vitiated. This further compounded the problem of flow of technical people and high technology to Assam. By mid-1981, we shifted our camp to the newly built complex at Dolabari. This brought about immediate relief from the frequent strikes because Dolabari was located in a minority-dominated area. The inhabitants were mostly migrants from Bangladesh. They were opposed to the agitation because it was aimed to dislodge people like them. Because of their strength and clout, the agitation leaders were afraid to come to this part of the city to enforce strikes there.

Thus, there was virtually no effect of the agitation on our work. This, however, caused some hostility against us in the hearts of agitation leaders. We contacted and convinced the leaders that it was in the best interest of Assam to allow us to continue our work on the bridge. It was after a long time (the first bridge on the Brahmaputra was built in 1962) approximately after eighteen years, that this work was actually taken up. If this was disrupted, it would cause undue delay. People who had come to do this work would simply go away. It was difficult to say when this could be resumed.

This logic was appealing. But it was not possible for them to publicly allow us to attend office. I asked them to let our people work in this area. They suggested that we close the offices from the front to give an impression of a shut office. After which, there was no problem in the site work near the river. The bridge site was free from agitation.

CRPF presence—boosts security confidence

The Central government had sent the CRPF battalions to Assam to reinforce the security of the state. These units were placed under the control of the district administration. However, they had to arrange for their accommodation, which was difficult. I offered to put up one such battalion near the bridge camp site. The main bridge contractor was prevailed upon to provide shelter. Thus, the senior superintendent of the district police was obliged to us. Also, the commandant of the CRPF was happy about the arrangements made for his jawans. In return, they ensured that the bridge site was totally protected.

AGITATION AFFECTED LIFE OF THE PEOPLE IN ASSAM

The agitation was quite long and many were desperate to find a face-saving formula. There were hawks and doves on both sides. But it was also important to understand the unique cultural identity of the Assamese. In years bygone, the Hindu kings had conquered Assam. To sustain their flood-affected kingdom, Brahmins and pundits were brought from the north. They eventually settled down and married the locals, and adapted themselves to the existing culture. This is reflected in many surnames that the Assamese have today.

The Assamese are simple, honest and helpful people. Women are far more forward-thinking and educated. Crimes like thievery, robbery, eve-teasing were unheard of. One could leave the house or car unlocked without fear of any mischief. The people are emotional and place a high value on words and promises made. In such a cultural background, the agitation touched the hearts of the Assamese all across the state. This also, quite naturally, opened up old hostilities.

The long-drawn agitation thus affected the common people a great deal. Uncertainties about the future of young children were particularly disturbing. This brought in violence in general conduct and strained the relationship between the different communities with whom they had lived peacefully for ages.

INITIAL PLANNING GETS A SETBACK

The preparation of detailed estimates and tender documents for the project was the most important activity. M/S RITES had prepared a detailed project report. But it lacked many cardinal details. Obviously, it could not be used for the preparation of either draft tender document or the estimate.

I expected the old documents of the first bridge over the Brahmaputra to be available for our guidance. We looked for them without success. Someone suggested looking for it in the closing cell of the old office of the CE (construction) in New Jalpaiguri. We could not find them there. But there, I happened to come across a retired audit officer. He smiled and told me that I would never find them because they had never been made. I was shocked.

M/S Hindustan Construction Company and M/S BBJ were the main contractors specially invited for this work. They were completing the bridge over the Ganga in 1959 at Mokameh at that time. There were no other agencies with such expertise and resources. There was no question of calling for any tender. They were simply asked to start work and were paid on the basis of rate analysis for the work by a standing committee of the contractors' engineer, a Railways' executive engineer and a senior finance officer. This practice was fine for good old days but not for now. Thus, the exercise began ab initio.

There were two basic components of the work. One was the main bridge with 12-metre diameter well foundations and 120-metre span balanced cantilever box prestressed concrete girders. The second one was a massive 2-km long elliptical guide bundh and an almost 1.7-km long approach bank. There being no precedence of construction of such massive structures, the cost or tender rates for them were not available. The Brahmaputra is known for its ferocity and this called for massive mobilization. It allowed only 135 days in a year for working in the river bed. Costing had to be done taking all these factors into account. Visiting similar construction sites elsewhere was necessary to have an idea of the expenses.

Two works nearby were considered similar in nature. One was a road bridge 5-km long over the Ganga, near Patna, by Bihar PWD. It also had 125-metre prestressed concrete box girder with hinged joint and a 12-metre well foundation. The work had been awarded to Gammon India on a lumpsum contract and was in an advanced stage of construction. Thus it had not given a unit cost of the components separately. The second one was a barrage over the Teesta River with a long guide bundh near New Jalpaiguri by the Irrigation Department of West Bengal being executed by the Hindustan Construction Company. We visited both these works to collect sufficient data for analysis. Based on these details, it was possible to work out the cost of the project. It was, however, difficult to prepare draft tender documents because the design concept was different.

The second bridge on the Hooghly River, named Vidyasagar Setu was also being planned as a second crossing, away from the old Howrah Bridge. Although it was finally built as a cable stayed bridge, at that time, the option of a prestressed concrete box girder was also under consideration. A global consultant had prepared the draft tender documents and technical specifications. This came in very handy. We were able to prepare good tender documents. It almost took two months for me to complete. After considering several drafts, the final document was extremely good. For all important structures thereafter, these documents became a model. The perfection of any tender document was in the final execution of the work, with as few contractual problems as possible. These documents were liked by all. It not only enabled good competitive bidding, but also a smooth execution. In the final reckoning, the detailed estimate of ₹70.50 crore also proved to be very accurate. When the work was completed it only called for an insignificant variation of less than 5 per cent. There is a different story connected with this, which I will narrate subsequently.

AWARD OF TENDER FOR THE MAIN BRIDGE IN RECORD TIME

By June 1981, we were ready to call the bridge tenders. We had already qualified four eligible tenders—Hindustan Construction Company, Gammon India, UP State Bridge Corporation and Continental Construction. The preparation of tender cost-estimate was very important. We had done extensive study of some ongoing works and had carried out the rate analysis for special items of work on that basis. Thus, the tender estimate was worked out as ₹20.80 crore approximately, and everyone approved of it, especially after they had looked at the basis of such elaborate analysis.

Bridge tender awarded in record time

Tenders were opened on 4 August 1981. The lowest offer was from Hindustan Construction Company at ₹20.50 crore—lower than the estimated cost. This was unbelievable. I informed the general manager in the evening, about the bidding. Naturally everyone was quite happy. I got a lot of praise for preparing a very realistic estimate. The speed of processing the tender was the fastest one I have known. It was in the Board's office by the third week of August 1981. Tenders were accepted in September 1981. The acceptance of their tender was telegraphically communicated to Hindustan Construction Company by mid-September 1981. Such a major contract being finalized in span of two months was a record for all time to come and was talked about for a long time. It was due to the teamwork led by the agile and encouraging GM Mr Balachandran. He was keen to get the fieldwork started. He abhorred endless model studies. He, as usual, gave me the entire credit for it. And he remained the same till the last I saw him. His eyes would lit up, telling umpteen anecdotes in his inimitable style. May God rest his soul in peace.

Work commences—people are excited

The contractor was quickly mobilized with the help of our support. We had anticipated the requirements like land for their workshop and camp, electrical substation and back up diesel generating set (although small for the total requirement, but initially, it came in very handy) and had planned accordingly. Some surplus dwelling units were also given, which helped them move their engineers immediately. The first well was pitched in November 1981. Altogether four well foundations were taken up in the first season. The contractor was complimented for this feat. They also acknowledged the excellent support they had received from the Dy CE team. We were happy and satisfied indeed.

The initiation of the actual fieldwork had a salutary effect on all, including the agitation leaders. There was joy in the hearts of the common people. A large number of visitors came to see the bridge work. Controlling the crowd particularly on a holiday was difficult. The civil administration helped us regulate it. The safety of visitors was our prime concern. The police were, of course, more concerned about possible disruptive activity by terrorists. They had some intelligence about this and hence safety precautions were put into place accordingly. The presence of the CRPF at the bridge site had a salutary effect. In short, soon it was on the state's tourist map. Naturally our stature also increased accordingly.

The HCC had taken up four foundations in the first season, P2, P3, P4 and P5. The closest to the north bank was P2 which got stuck in a rocky outcrop about thirty metres below. P3 went ahead well, till just about two metres above the designed founding level. The slope of Bhomoraguri hill extended beyond P2 and perhaps close to P3. It was plugged at that level. P4 and P5 were taken up later. They crossed scouring level but were above the founding level of RL 5.00 when the floods came in. We did not have accurate information of the behaviour of the river. Water levels started rising from 26 March and on 5 April it stopped all work. The contractor made valiant efforts to resume work after the flash flood. But it was to no avail.

LESSONS OF THE FIRST SEASON—LOGISTICS DESIGN FOR THE SECOND SEASON

Important lessons were drawn from our experience of the first season. First, work could not start before November. Withdrawal of equipment had to commence from 26 March and had to be progressively completed by 5 April. Second, the capacity of concreting had to be augmented. Third, the stock of raw materials like sand and aggregates had to be good enough for a month's usage. Fourth, all fabrication, overhauling of various machinery had to be completed during the lean period from May to September.

Supply of cement—a DGS&D rate contract item— was crucial in those days. For 71,000 cum of concrete, 23,800 MT of cement was required. Jogighopa was the broad gauge (BG) rail head and Tezpur was on meter gauge (MG). The Railway Board had banned the transhipment from BG to MG. So, cement had to be carted by road from Jogighopa with a lead of 327 km. As a second option, cement was transported by barges along the Brahmaputra. Planning and strategy for the next season was worked out in detail during the lean season accordingly.

The commitment of the corporate office of the HCC was crucial. They were called to the site, for detailed discussions to finalize the next season's programme. On the GM's approval, the programme was closely monitored. Import of some vital machinery was also planned. The automatic concrete batching plant from Germany, bridge builder, for the superstructure construction from Norway and slip form shuttering from Sweden were to be imported.

TRAVAILS OF IMPORT OF EQUIPMENT

The imports of project equipment had to follow a complex procedure in those days. Foreign exchange was not readily available and hence import had to be regulated. For import licence, the DGTD (director general trade & development) had to clear the import by certifying that indigenous machinery was not available in India. This activity was under the domain of the Ministry of Commerce & Industry. After getting the import license, the Ministry of Finance (MoF) released foreign exchange for imports. Only after this, a letter of credit (LC) in favour of the supplier firm could be opened. The HCC requested the Railways for help in completing these formalities in time. The HCC in their special tender condition had asked for a loan of worth ₹80 lakh in foreign exchange for import of equipment. This was accepted by the Railway Board. The GM deputed me to Delhi for this purpose. The Board had already processed the case and the file had to go to the MoF for foreign exchange sanction. I was told to pursue the MoF and I was accordingly in North Block by 11 a.m.

The section officer marked the files to be sent to three different desk officers. One desk dealt with Deutsche mark for German equipment. It had to come from a specific German loan arrangement. Likewise, for Swedish equipment, Swedish kronar came from a Swedish loan arrangement. For Norway, the funding had to be in US dollars. He said that the process might take a couple of months.

It was utterly disappointing. I told him that I was the deputy CE in Tezpur,

BRAHMAPUTRA BRIDGE—A NEW CONSTRUCTION PHASE

Assam, assigned for the construction of a bridge over the Brahmaputra. He did not know much beyond Guwahati. I showed him its location on a map. I told him, 'I am not an Assamese but I have volunteered for the post'. He said, 'I am sorry but why did you go there? I know the Brahmaputra is a ferocious river and constructing the bridge must be difficult. And there is the Assam agitation too.' I told him that the train took fifty-four hours to reach Delhi and involved three changes. 'If you ask me to come again, I have to undergo this torture once again. We also lose one working season', I said. He was deeply moved. He said, 'Being non-Assamese, you have volunteered for such a difficult task. We must also do something. Please come at 2 p.m. after lunch.' When I met him after lunch, he said, 'Mr Jaruhar, here are the sanctions from all the three desks. We got all the sanction in one hour. I told my colleagues that I have never met a more selfless and motivated person. This is our contribution from the North Block. But please put the files in your briefcase so that you are not stopped at the gate by the security.'

I delivered the files to the Railway Board. They were taken aback. Sanction letters were signed immediately. I was in Guwahati by 10 a.m. Mr Balachandran had talked to the financial commissioner (FC) about this case and he had told him that the case was with the finance ministry and would take time. He was, therefore, not expecting me when I entered his room at 11 a.m. He could not believe his eyes when he saw the letter and heard the story.

I do not now recall the names of the extraordinary persons in the North Block who arranged for the sanction of foreign exchange in two hours' time, but their contribution was duly acknowledged. They were the unsung heroes who also served the cause! Letters of credit were opened in time. Machines arrived at the beginning of 1983. They were the first of their kind to be used in the construction industry in India. They greatly enhanced the productivity and pace of construction in the second season.

SECOND SEASON STARTS BUT IS HINDERED BY AGITATION

We got some good IRSEs as assistant engineers. They were here as probationers earlier. We made a good start in October 1982. The HCC had extensively mobilized. Work had picked up at a good speed and progressed smoothly till January 1983.

The Assam agitation had persisted all along. The government was forced to take the tough decision of holding a General Election. The perpetual run of president's rule had led to a constitutional crisis of sorts. The agitation leaders would not allow the elections to be held without carrying out a revision in electoral rolls. They wanted the names of all illegal immigrants to be deleted from the voters' list. Despite this, the government announced elections in February 1983. The government was forced to do so because it had no other option. The Election Commission issued a notification accordingly.

The agitation leaders reacted strongly by plunging the entire state into an indefinite strike. Thus, everything stopped from 4 February 1983. It included government offices, schools, colleges, post offices, banks, transport system, etc. Only essential services like hospitals functioned. Railway trains were run infrequently. The Indian Airlines flight between Calcutta and Tezpur was allowed to operate. We were in the thick of the working season. Stopping our work had grave consequences. There was a risk of the well foundation getting stuck, short of the scour level. Such a well could tilt in the flood due to scouring action of the river. It would make subsequent construction impossible. We explained the implications and the consequences of stopping the bridge work to the agitation leaders accordingly. We persuaded them not to interfere with the main work. They agreed but they could not permit our offices at Dolabari to open. Thus, construction work at the site continued without much difficulty. Fortunately, we had one month's stock of raw materials. We had to, of course, walk to the site from Dolabari, as vehicles were not allowed to ply.

An unprecedented initiative

But the contractor required money to sustain a large workforce of five hundred persons besides payment to suppliers. I told the GM about the problem. He spoke to the FC who told the GM that we would be authorized to withdraw cash from the station earnings. However, that was not a suitable solution. Tezpur was a small railway station and had meagre station earnings. The agitation had forced very few to travel and thus gate collection was also low.

I requested the senior accounts officer, 'Roy Sahib, let us go to the bridge site. Carry the official cheque book'. We walked the eight-km distance to the site. I was used to doing this, so it was not a problem, but for Mr Roy, an elderly person, it was surely too much. He was, however, quite sportive and excited. Both of us reached the office of the HCC. I asked Assistant Engineer V.C. Sharma and the project engineer of the HCC to calculate the value of the work executed by the HCC. This was checked and verified from the personal records maintained by the AEN.

Railways have elaborate procedures for payments to contractors. The bill is checked at various levels in the executive engineer and accounts officer offices. After checks and cross checks, the amount actually payable is determined in the accounts office. Any recovery, like advances and taxes, is also deducted from the gross amount. The cheque is then signed by the accounts officer after all those checks. The bank is also informed accordingly about the cheque details.

The routine procedure could not be followed as the office was closed. The contractor was unable to sustain the pace of the work without payment. I must admire and salute the courage of Mr Roy. He knew exactly what was being asked of him. He said, 'I trust Mr Jaruhar. If he says it is urgent, it has to be done. I know if I make a mistake, he will take due care of it.' Taking the cheque book out of his breast pocket, he signed it as if it were his personal cheque. It was for ₹50 lakh—a very large amount considering the value of money in 1983. Issuing the cheque was one thing, drawing the money from the bank was another. All the banks in Assam were closed. So, very thoughtfully, the cheque was issued on the Reserve Bank of India (RBI) in Calcutta. The SAO also informed RBI Calcutta by telegram. The HCC sent a person by flight to Calcutta. He returned to Tezpur a day later after withdrawing the money from the RBI. It was as if a magic wand had been waved! The strike continued for twenty-two days. So, after fifteen days, the HCC had to be paid again and the same modus operandi was adopted to overcome the financial crisis. This on account payment was around ₹45 lakh.

Mr Balachandran was shocked when I told him about it later. He thought I was a real devil! He personally appreciated the SAO for his brave action. After things became normal, all transactions were duly regularized. Mr Roy was of course given the GM's annual award during the Railway Week function that year. A well-deserved award. Bravo!

SOME EPISODES CONNECTED WITH THE AGITATION

I must however return once again to some crucial episodes of the Assam agitation in 1982-83. The election was conducted under an extraordinary security cover. All election personnel were brought from outside the state. There was an understandably low turnout all over except in the area dominated by minority communities. But this unleashed violent reactions everywhere.

Minority communities supported the election. The ire was therefore against them. Pockets of their settlements were the main target. In one such incident, the entire Nelly village near Naogaon was burnt down, and the people were brutally killed. This was the most gruesome incident in the history of independent India. It was compared to the Jallianwala Bagh massacre. It sent shockwaves all around. The minority community retaliated by attacking the Assamese. Our colony in Dolabari was thus an ideal soft target for the attack by the people of the minority community. But somehow, we had not anticipated the threat. Not even the local police with whom we had a close liaison had warned us of such a threat.

Dolabari colony seized by attackers

One night, in the month of March 1983, I woke up to a lot of noise at the front door of my residence. I found that all the Assamese staff with their families, crying in alarm. Our entire colony was encircled by thousands of people about two km away. They were beating drums and waving torchlights. I immediately realized that we were in for an immediate attack and a possible massacre. I immediately called a local strongman—a minority community contractor—Muhammad Ali to whom some petty contracts were awarded. He was thus obliged to me. I told him, 'Look Ali, nothing should happen here. You cannot touch our Assamese brethren without killing me. You should not forget that we have helped you and we have lived peacefully with goodwill. I know that this attack has your support. It will be foolish to feign ignorance and hence you must act immediately to stop it.' I was very harsh. He protested loudly about his innocence. He said, 'Sir, I promise that nothing will happen. Give me some time.' He was gone but my people obviously did not trust the contractor. I asked them not to worry. In case they attacked, I promised them that I would be their first victim.

Phones were not working. We could not contact anyone in the district administration. But we waited with patience although it was nerve-wracking. But I tried to comfort the families. They were pleading with me to save their lives, or at least those of their children. But slowly in the distance, we could see torches turning away. The noise levels started to drop. In another half an hour all was clear. The cheer came back on their faces. They fell at my feet for saving their lives. I asked them to only thank God. We could also see the police arriving. Had we waited for them it would have been too late. I asked my senior colleagues to escort the people to their quarters. They were too scared to go back to their houses.

My policy to involve the local people in the fruits of a project had paid off. Hence, Muhammad Ali did not find us hostile. He evidently realized that he could avail the fruits of economic activities and we were not averse to it. He was a local strongman and the community leader. And this had come in handy. Being too tired I went back home to find my wife in deep slumber. I got up early in the morning as usual and left home, as was my routine, at 8.15 a.m. after listening to the 8 a.m. news bulletin on the All India Radio. I returned home as usual to have my lunch at 1.30 p.m.

My wife was furious when I came home for lunch. She asked me why I had not told her about the night's episode. It was usual for the ladies to meet around 11 in the morning. They narrated the entire episode to my wife. Their tale included how I had taken up the entire responsibility and risked my life. My wife obviously did not know anything because she was fast asleep. She asked me, 'Why did you not wake me up? I would have also protected my children. You left the front door open. It was not safe at all. I am sorely indignant because I had to learn all this from others. You should have told me.' My answer was, 'You were in such a deep slumber. It would have been a crime to wake you. Particularly after God resolved things in the best possible manner, there was not much for me to narrate about my own role.' My young friend's father, Mr Jaggi, had come to visit his son. He said that the scene here was similar to those during the riots after the Partition. His narration of the night's episode was quite eloquent. I did not realize what I was doing except that I was not afraid. He saw me running from one person to another, reassuring them, telling them not to worry and that everything would soon be all right.

It earned us a great deal of respect from all quarters, including the leaders of Assam agitation, for my courage and standing by the Assamese. They had possibly thought I was a sympathizer of illegal immigrants. It was an important issue. It enabled us to gain acceptance from both sides, and when they eventually came to power after the Assam Accord in 1986, it gave us a great advantage.

THE WORK GOES ON DESPITE THE AGITATION

The progress of the work during 1982-83 was extraordinary despite the intense Assam agitation. It earned us commendations from many quarters including the national media. I appeared on the national television channel several times to talk about the bridge. Perhaps this was the only work of national importance going on full swing in the Northeast and the Central government lost no chance to garner some sort of glory for initiating development schemes in the state. Home Minister Zail Singh informed the Parliament that the work was in full swing. This boosted our morale.

Two well foundations were in deep water. P8 had forty feet depth where as P9 had eighteen feet depth of water flowing at a velocity of four metre per second. It required floating and launching of steel caissons to construct the foundations. This was a major activity.

The construction of the south guide bundh and approach bank was another major activity. Both these activities called for detailed planning. The caisson work was taken up during the 1983-84 season. The guide bundh was 2,038-metre-long, and of elliptical shape with the connecting south approach bank at about

1,680-metre long. It involved 19 lakh CUM worth of earthwork and 8.20 lakh CUM of stone work. This was the first guide bundh on the Brahmaputra. The work had to be done in 135 days, in one season. The logistics for the mammoth work was surely mind-boggling. The plan was to take up and complete the work in the 1984-85 working season. But the contract had to be fixed during 1983-84 to allow the contractor to have at least six months' of mobilization time. It was a tall order. Meanwhile, the bridge superstructure work also had to be taken up. It was a new activity and it called for an altogether different technique and approach.

Caisson work was challenging and exciting

The caisson launching was a tricky affair. A caisson, in simple words, is a hollow cylindrical steel body in the shape of circular well foundation. Being watertight and hollow, it can float on water. It is securely held by the barge and floating pontoons. When suitable weight is added, it sinks and is placed on the correct location, at the well foundation. This procedure is called grounding. The trick and skill of the engineers lie in accurately grounding the caisson in its correct location. Essentially, the scheme should enable the caisson to be shifted or lifted in case it is incorrectly positioned. In fast-flowing water currents like the Brahmaputra, it is more easily said than done.

According to the launching scheme, two sets of floating pontoons—one on either side of the floating caisson—were planned. These pontoons could help guide the caisson to the location. The final grounding of the caisson was to be done by water ballasting, that is, pumping the water in or out of the pontoons to weigh them down or up with the weight of water. M/S Gammon India had used this scheme earlier for Vidyasagar Setu on the Hooghly River. Under tidal wave conditions, dangerous oscillation developed with resonant frequency, ultimately leading to the overturning and capsizing of the structure.

We were helped by a team of naval architects from IIT Kharagpur to analyse the problem and resolve it. The huge mass of water in a single long pontoon was found to oscillate under the condition of a wave. Thus, smaller rectangular compartments were provided to break dangerous oscillations in the single pontoon. Pumping of water was regulated by a common manifold valve. This ingenuous design was tested successfully in a mock trial before being adopted for our work.

For a successful launch, the caisson has to be accurately positioned in the centre of the well determined by the network of ground baseline stations. Taking rays from three base stations which in an ideal condition should intersect at a point if the location is correct. But if this does not happen, then it will form a triangle known as a triangle of error. B.C. Ganguli in his technical paper had observed that it was futile to attempt a triangle of error of less than three inches (75mm). But hats off to those engineers, who had worked with such primitive survey instruments, like Sextants and Theodolites with a least count of 20". Communication with base stations was by means of a set of flags. On the contrary, we used theodolites of 1" least count and electronic distance measuring devices known as distomats. We had walkie-talkie sets for communication. Because of very good control, the triangle of error was reduced to that of a pin head.

I recall, I was on the pontoon, directing grounding of the caisson for P8 when the chief justice of Assam arrived at the site for a visit. According to the protocol, I had to receive him on the north bank. The district judge kept sending frantic messages to me but I was unable to leave, as the grounding was in progress. I asked the HCC's protocol officer to meet him and explain the seriousness of the situation. Somehow wiser counsel prevailed. I could complete the grounding and escort the dignitaries to the site. He was overwhelmed by the magnitude and complexities of the operation. And I, through luck, escaped a possible contempt of court!

I cannot describe the tense and anxious moments, the entire operation provided. Once, the second caisson weighing 750 metric tonne in the course of towing from the launching jetty to the bridge location approximately two km downstream, lost control of anchors. The huge mass started floating down the river. Anything could have happened. The possible disaster was unthinkable. But luckily, the caisson got stuck on a small sandy shoal from where it was retrieved to our delight. It not only saved us from charges of criminal negligence, but also taught us to check the anchoring of a floating caisson.

As ME, I asked my CAO (construction) about the safety precautions taken for the launch of the caisson for Jubli Bridge over the Hooghly River. He had come to receive me at Calcutta airport at 8 p.m. He looked completely blank! I had read his monthly report that day, before leaving from Delhi. It was fresh in my mind. Very interestingly, M/S Gammons India was executing the work! I told him that caisson launched by Gammons in Vidyasagar Setu had capsized. The next day, he informed that everyone had been called in the night to check the procedure adopted by the contractor. When questioned, Gammons' engineers admitted that the caisson had indeed capsized on the second Hooghly Bridge! The CAO asked them why those checkpoints and calculations were not made in this case. Alas, tragedy did strike! The next CAO did not pursue it. As a result, the caisson capsized. It was retrieved only through great effort. The saving grace was a mild current. Obviously, some lessons are learnt the hard way. In the Ramayana, there is a mention that a fool may never learn even when Lord Brahma is his guru!

CONSTRUCTION OF THE FIRST GUIDE BUNDH

The construction of guide bundh was altogether a different experience. There was a separate deputy CE—an officer on deputation from Assam—posted on the south bank for this purpose. He was older to me and quite good, but had a few basic limitations. I remember once Mr Balachandran asked me something about the guide bundh and I told him that I was not sure since it was under a separate deputy CE. He was upset and admonished me, 'Look, never say that again. I know there is a separate deputy. But for me, you are fully in charge of that work also. You know what I am talking about.'

The initially prepared detailed estimate of the guide bundh and south approach bank was on the lower side. After visiting the Teesta Guide Bundh construction site, I advised them to revise its cost. Somehow this was neither done nor was I informed about it. The tenders were called on the basis of a lower estimated cost and justly, rates tendered were higher than the estimate unlike the bridge tender. It was at that stage, the mistake was realized because the estimate had not taken into account many factors like heavy mobilization of machines, unavoidable wastage, many enabling work required to do the actual work. We prepared detailed justification to support the tendered cost by accounting for these factors. It was brought out because only a short working period was available and it was necessary to deploy more than the normal requirement of machines. Also, the high water current washed away the work before protection work was done, causing heavy wastage and also how much enabling work like temporary bridging, temporary closure and diversion of water channels, etc. were required. Financial Commissioner M. Ram Ji and Member Engineering Mr Ramchandran of the Railway Board visited the bridge site separately between January and February 1984 to have a first-hand experience. I was able to explain and convince them of the proposal by actually showing them the finicky nature of the great Brahmaputra River. What probably struck them most was the fact that the river could change its course even in one day.

In any contract, it was essential to ascertain the known or likely risks. It must be clear who would take them—the contractor or the client. Risks are acute and quite costly in such major contracts. A channel at a particular location may change its course when the work is actually taken up after the flood. Many enabling details, although not paid for separately, are necessary to execute the actual work. All activities have to be factored into the cost. The location of the south channel carrying sizeable discharge was not fixed. In the last two years, it had shifted southward considerably. In short, accounting for such projects called for imagination. Unless the actual operation with full mobilization was taken into account, mistakes were inevitable.

I had the advantage of observing similar preparatory projects for the main bridge. I could demonstrate this to the higher-ups from the Railway Board. They could see the ground realities as well as the operations involved in the work. After updating the cost, the tender offer of M/S Jaiprakash Associates was justified. When I saw Mr Ramachandran, ME, in June 1984 before leaving for London for training, he beamingly informed me, 'The tender of the guide bundh has been accepted in its entirety'. It was really good news!

NOMINATION FOR TRAINING IN ENGLAND

I was initially nominated to go to the UK for a training course in general management in January 1984 under the Colombo Plan. I was supposed to have left on 7 January.

Mr Ramachandran came to visit the bridge site on 22 December 1983. S.M. Kaul, the GM came with the ME in the morning but he was asked to go to Malda to meet the railway minister, Ghani Khan Choudhury. So, he left Tezpur immediately. Thus, the ME was completely alone with me during his inspection. I had known Mr Ramachandran from the Eastern Railway when he was CE (construction) and I was the PACE. So, I told him after the inspection, 'Sir, I do not want to go to the UK for training at present. The working season is on. We have planned to take up superstructure work during this period. The guide bundh tender is also under finalization. At this stage, work might suffer if I go.'

Mr Ramachandran just stopped and looked hard at me. He said, 'You know how many people request me for nomination for such a foreign training programme? They also bring a lot of pressure. I have found the first person in my life, who does not want to go to the UK. It is, of course, easy to pull you out citing administrative exigency but I am not sure if I will be able to nominate you again for the next programme.'

Mr Kaul was unhappy to hear about this. He even requested Mr Ramachandran not to withdraw my name. But it was perhaps late. In early May 1984, Shreya was very sick. We were in the hospital with her. I got a message that the GM wished to speak to me, so I went to the office to call him. He read out the Board's telegraphic message, nominating me for training on 'Managing Large Scale Projects' in URWICK Management Centre London (it is now a part of PriceWaterhouse Coopers, a famous global management consultant). I was to leave on 8 June 1984, barely three weeks after the illness in the family. I thanked Mr Kaul, but I mentioned that I could not even think of going unless Shreya recovered. She was quite sick and struggling then.

Mr Kaul was dismayed but appreciated this. He was kind enough to come down to Tezpur to visit us in the hospital. Luckily, Shreya started to improve and the doctors told us that she would be fine in a week's time. To cut a long story short, everything could be worked out, including the passport and visa. I thus found myself standing before Mr Ramachandran who kept on telling me that he felt morally absolved because he could get me nominated for this programme in the UK during his own tenure. He said that I deserved it the most. It was again ordained. I did not know how to thank all those who thought so much of me and really cared about me. This was the best blessing from God! The programme suited me and the overall schedule of the project.

The superstructure project had a lot of teething problems, but it had begun. It was the rainy season and hence, no fieldwork was in progress. The annual work planning meeting with the HCC was over and the follow-up action could well be taken up by my able lieutenants. The months of June, July and mid-August were generally holidays, when officers would take leaves to visit their homes. Thus, I left in June and was back by 12 August 1984. The timing could not have been fine-tuned any better!

Shadow of Blue Star—as we depart

I had gone to meet Yashwant Sinha (my wife's uncle) who was then the joint secretary, Shipping & Transport on 7th of June in the evening. He had given me a gift to carry to his colleague in the Indian High Commission. He said that his friend would be helpful during my stay in England. He quietly informed us about an Army operation that was going on against militants, who had occupied the Golden Temple in Amritsar. Fingers were crossed but frankly speaking I had no idea about its complexity or significance at that time.

Our British Airways flight from Delhi took off at 6 a.m. on 8 June. The Operation Blue Star aimed to flush out terrorists from the Golden Temple was launched by the Army during the night. When we landed in Kuwait in the morning, local newspapers carried full details of the operation. It evoked strong reactions all over. We finally landed in London in the evening. We reported to the Indian High Commission, the next day. After an introduction and initial briefing, we went to have lunch in the High Commission canteen, which apparently served good Indian food at subsidized rates. It was then that the High Commission was surrounded by Sikh protesters, shouting and burning an effigy of Prime Minister Indira Gandhi. We were quietly whisked away through the back entrance. My first day in London was therefore quite eventful.

About the training programme and the participants

There were seventeen participants in the programme—ten from India and one each from Sri Lanka, Pakistan, Bangladesh, Uganda, Papua New Guinea, Ghana and Kenya. I was the only one from Indian Railways. We were asked to present the projects we had been engaged with. The entire group was impressed by the size and magnitude of the project I had handled. The programme had some good subjects like financing and investment. It lent a good scope to interact at a global level, which broadened our perspectives—a useful gain from the programme. Our visits to countries like France and West Germany provided a good exposure. All said and done, one also learnt a lot of jargon. The only problem for me was Indian vegetarian food, which was not available except on weekends when we went out. Salads, fruits and soup became forced survival food which made me genuinely averse to them.

We also came by an interesting information. The Ugandan participant was a man of about twenty-seven years. The average age of the group was in the range of 35-40. When asked about it, he frankly admitted that Idi Amin, the previous president had liquidated most of the senior persons. Those who had survived got promoted! Well, such things also happened elsewhere in the world. In contrast, living in our democracy is indeed fortunate. A tribute to all of us, common people included.

The Pakistani participant Saeed Ahmad was a fan of Lata Mangeshkar's songs, so he was overjoyed when I gave him all of my collection of Lata ji's audio cassettes. He said that the average Pakistani did not want tension between India and Pakistan. He mentioned that they often listened to reports of imminent attack by India. They had even been told that India was the aggressor in the 1971 war!

Appreciation and interaction with the British

I was the leader of our group of four participants, formed under the programme to study at East Anglia Railway Electrification project at Ipswich. We saw a lot of the English countryside while travelling by road to Ipswich. It was interesting to learn how project implications varied from our country. Many bridges had to be rebuilt under the project. I believed that a better approach was possible and I suggested it to the bridge engineer. But by his look, he was far from convinced.

Freedom of action—'You do not need copies'

We discussed the report with the project director in the project headquarters in Liverpool. He was a nice and receptive gentleman who had been the bridge engineer before he was promoted. I discussed and explained my suggested bridge building technique. He readily agreed with me. I asked, 'Why don't you intervene?' He smiled and said, 'Look he is the bridge engineer responsible for the job. It will be inappropriate if I told him how to do his job. He is not expected to follow the same technique I had once used. He has a task as a manager. It is his responsibility and we must trust him.' I was impressed, and learnt that, it was a cardinal principle to develop a person. It was not necessary to produce a number of copies. That was the reason why many did not mentally develop beyond the level of AE. If one was good, he wanted to go on doing the job in the same old way. Unless forced to quit the old habit, he would find it very easy and convenient to remain in the same old groove! Such people are a nuisance. They retard the growth of any organization. But alas, they are in plenty!

VISIT TO CAMBRIDGE UNIVERSITY

Out of the many places we visited, our Cambridge visit is worth mentioning. It retains its past glory and preserves it with pride. For example, the laboratory where Isaac Newton worked is kept in the same manner. Interestingly, there was a small pocket diary which Newton had maintained. On one page was the entry, '10 p.m.—went to the pub. Had a drink, paid four pence'. Likewise, we were shown the room where Prince Charles had stayed. He had lived like an ordinary student. The guide told us how he would go to a common bathroom for a shower and was found running back to his room in a towel! He and Lady Diana were married recently and that the wedding was discussed with joy—for the first time a commoner was married into a royal family.

Integrity of English society

Another striking aspect of English society is their integrity. I was having a bite while waiting for a train at the Paddington Railway station. I decided to use the weighing scale. The fifty pence coin got stuck and the next one also met the same fate. The loss of one pound was disappointing. I told the person at the desk although I saw no way to retrieve the money. As I was talking, he took one pound out from the drawer and gave it to me with an apology for the inconvenience. Astonished, I asked him, 'What about the machine? How do you know that I am telling the truth?' He said, 'Sir, you are a gentleman. You should not worry about it. The agency which installed the machine shall pay for it'. As simple as that!

Likewise, I posted a letter to my family. After a few days, I received a letter from the Royal Mail saying, 'Your letter was understamped but considering its urgency we have allowed it. We would appreciate if the envelope is properly stamped!' I also once complained to the hotel desk that the telephone bill appeared to be inflated. They apologised and asked me to strike out whatever calls I had not made. They settled the issue then and there. They trusted people and felt that nobody would complain unless it was genuine.

BACK TO TEZPUR FOR THE THIRD SEASON—THE LOGISTICS OF GUIDE BUNDH

I returned to Tezpur after an outing. It was a much needed one. During 1984-85 working season, two most important items of the work—superstructure of the bridge and river training works, involving construction of guide bundh and south approach bank had to be taken up. The work of prestressed concrete cantilever girders was started in a small way during 1983-84 season with the help of the bridge builder—the new imported equipment. It was being used for the first time in the country. We had to learn and assimilate the new technology. There were 24 such spans of 120 metres with a suspended span of 15 metres in between. This was estimated to take more than two seasons.

The challenging task—the guide bundh

But the guide bundh work was totally time bound. It had to start in October 1984 and had to be completed by March 1985. This was the first guide bundh on the Brahmaputra. The contract was awarded to M/S Jaiprakash Associates in June 1984. Their top executives came to the site after being awarded the contract and witnessed the ferocity and fury of the river during the floods. They were naturally frightened and later on shared their concern with me, 'Sahib, I told my people that Indian Railways is stupid. How one can plan to tame the river by constructing a guide bundh? But we are even more stupid to have given a quote and agreed to do this work. Can anyone in his senses think of ever touching such a violent river? British were no fools and hence they kept away from this river.' In my view, awarding a contract in June was in a way good. Observing the might of the river instilled proper concern in the mind of the contractor, and helped them to prepare themselves mentally as well. They had enough time to mobilize their resources.

Main construction machinery had to be taken across the channel to the work area. This was a crucial activity. This was often difficult because small channels were generally quite active in the month of October, and sometimes even in December. It was, therefore, necessary to cross such streams by constructing temporary bridges. Alternatively, some machines could be taken on a barge if a proper draft in the channel was available. In this case, both were done simultaneously. It proved very advantageous. Lighter earth moving equipment and pile driving equipment helped begin some of the work. Even the construction of a temporary bridge could be handled from both ends.

The south channel carried a dry weather discharge of 100 cumec, which had to be closed. It was the most crucial activity because the success of the project depended on this. It was a massive operation that called for sheer courage. The work to close the channel started from both ends and as closure gap gradually reduced, the velocity became very high causing deep scour. The water roared, as if on boil. It easily washed away a man-sized boulder, weighing 60 to 70 kg. Only people with steely nerves and courage could go to place boulder crates with dozers and excavators. But once the channel was closed in a continuous operation of forty hours, the water body became totally placid, as if nothing had happened. Immediately thereafter the closed channel was filled and a road built on the top to transport the entire fleet of machinery.

The scene was unique on 24 October 1984. Mr Balachandran, ME, was personally present to see the operation. I thought this moment was quite memorable for me. He visited my house after to bless my son Shrimant born on 12 October. I was a mere deputy CE at that time. A member of the Railway Board insisting on visiting us and blessing the child was a momentous occasion for us.

My eldest brother and sister-in-law had come all the way for the ceremony to wish my newborn son. A tea party was organized in the evening, after the ME had left for Delhi. I did not have any money at that time for the party. I returned to my office after seeing them off at the airport. My good friend, A.N. Ray, walked in to my room to say, 'Sir, you have been very busy with the ME and the GM so I could not talk to you. But there is a DA arrear of ₹700. Please take it because the cashier has gone away.' It was sweet music and came as a godsend. I immediately gave it to the organizers. God had chosen to bless us in so many ways. On my personal front, the new arrival in the family was a great blessing. On the professional front, the channel was closed to pave way for the construction of the south approach bank and guide bundh. To top it, Mr Balachandran had found time to visit us and bless the mother and the newborn. We were totally overwhelmed!

GUIDE BUNDH—A VERY DIFFICULT CHALLENGE AND MANY LESSONS

After the closure of the channel and establishing direct access, the entire fleet of earth moving equipment could be mobilized in a war-like operation. Things moved according to plan and schedule. The wisdom of B.C. Ganguli and Debes Mukherjee could be appreciated much better now.

The long lead material like boulders and GI wires were procured in advance. The contractor did not have to worry about them or for that matter, about the money. Contractors were paid every week. This was unheard of earlier. Mr Ray was an able associate in this connection. The contractor had to keep his machinery in top condition, working it round the clock, to a plan. There were around 3,000 workmen all eating a single type of food in a common kitchen, equipped with ultra-modern equipment and gadgets. This encouraged unprecedented camaraderie and bonhomie. The site looked like a big village fair with milling visitors.

Quantities of work executed would indicate the magnitude of the operation. The guide bundh was elliptical in shape and 2,038 metres long—1633 metres on the upstream and 405 metres on the downstream side. The south approach bank was 678 metres long mostly on the bed of the river and joining the flood embankment on the south bank from where the PWD had to construct the connecting links to the National Highway 37. Quantum of work would show the type of challenge it was, as given by following targets and achievement:

Items of Work in South Guide Bundh and Approach Bank	Target Quantity
Earth work involved	19 lakh cubic metres
Stone/boulder work involved in apron and slope pitching	8.2 lakh cubic metres
Galvanized wire 8 SWG for boulder crates	5,300 metric ton
Cost of guide bundh & approach bank (1984 prices)	₹29.50 crore
Maximum earthwork done in a single day (1984-85 working season)	16,800 cubic metres
Maximum of stone/boulder work done in one day (1984-85 working season)	9,350 cubic metres
Maximum work value on a day—contractor payment (1984-85 working season)	₹11.60 lakh

Source: Collated by the author from various sources.

For the sheer quantum of work, it was one of the best. The Gandak was perhaps better—I will talk later about it. Hats off to all those who worked very hard to realize the objective! Very few had actually expected the Railways to execute the job. Success, when it came, tasted very sweet indeed!

SUPERSTRUCTURE OF THE BRIDGE—A HISTORICAL FIRST-TIME EVENT

While history was being written by constructing the first ever guide bundh on the Brahmaputra River, another history of sorts was also being written in the construction of prestressed concrete cantilever span with the help of a bridge builder imported from Norway.

The design needed an innovative approach

Although all designs must conform to the standard *Codes & Manuals*, we believed that pragmatism or knowledge of the ground reality formed an important consideration in the design, too. Thus, some account of how a pragmatic approach was applied, is in order to reinforce my belief in common sense. It has also a lesson for pundits, bound by confines of Codal Rules. Our teacher in structural engineering always emphasized the importance of ground conditions and good engineering practice. These had to be taken into consideration in design. This aspect is demonstrated very well in the design of the bridge.

The superstructure was initially designed by the RDSO. However, they issued only provisional drawings. This was unacceptable in a contract. We strongly raised this issue but the RDSO raised their hands and refused to finish it. Director Standards Mr Palit categorically admitted that the RDSO did not have the experience and thus, could not issue approved drawings. In a meeting in the Board, the ME, Mr Basrur, decided that IIT Madras should be asked to check the RDSO design. M/S HCC was asked to associate during the process of proof checking because under the contract, they had to be satisfied about the structural safety of the girder.

Dr Rajagopalan, the head of structural engineering in IIT Madras, formed a research team of post graduate research students for this purpose. The team initially designed the bridge on SAP-IV software. The RDSO had also used the same software. The computer design showed some discrepancy and hence the team undertook manual checking of the design. Even after laborious manual checks the flaw in the RDSO design persisted. For final approval, I went to IIT Madras. Dr Rajagopalan explained in his presentation how the cantilever box developed a tension when it carried two lanes of the IRC Class 'A' tracked vehicles. The structure was safe with single lane Class 'A' load or the heaviest Type AA loading. But the Indian Road Congress (IRC) Code did not permit this. The IIT team advised us to change the girder cross section since it did not meet the stipulations of the IRC Code.

I politely said that we should accept the design without any changes. Dr Rajagopalan naturally reacted strongly. He observed that the Codal provision could not be overruled. Ignoring his reaction, I explained why the violation of the Codal provision in the design, could be accepted. Only a few weeks ago, Assam had suffered from one of the worst floods because of the overflowing of the Brahmaputra. The highest flood level (HFL) recorded in the river was only a foot below the design HFL. This flood had totally inundated all the adjoining areas. All the connecting roads to the bridge were cut off. 'Tell me under these circumstances, can anyone ever visualize that the bridge will have two lanes of type "A" loads? To top it, the highest seismic forces would also act simultaneously. Dr Rajagopalan, how can so many vehicles approach the bridge? It is a totally impractical situation. The single type "A" loading and of type "AA" loading has practically ensured safety. It meets all reasonable and foreseeable situations. The design as provided should therefore suffice.' I asked Dr Rajagopalan, 'Can you ignore such clear-cut ground realities? Also, we should not forget that the Codes let the owner of the structure decide what loading to be taken for design. So, I have the authority, right?' He was completely floored. He complimented me for the clarity I possessed. He said, 'Well, I need a kick on my back.' The design was accordingly approved. Mr Balachandran laughed when I briefed him on my return from Madras. He jokingly said, 'You are a devil!' I had learnt to cross the confines of Codes early in my life especially when it was strongly supported by ground reality; it caused no discomfort at all!

Use of admixture—first in the Railways, must for pump concrete

The concrete pump and bridge builder were used in the superstructure. The concrete pump was being used for the first time in the Railways. It required concrete of high workability—slump of not less than 150 mm. The concrete box girder was deep (8 m) with a narrow web section. The concrete would have to be virtually fluid and made to flow into the slender and deep section of the box girder. It was not possible to manufacture a high strength concrete of this type (M450 kg/sq.cm) without use of suitable admixture. The Code related to concrete in India did not allow the use of admixture.

We decided to use 'LOMAR D' as a super plasticizer after a lot of research. Tests were successful and we were saving in cement as well. Its use however had to be approved. Even the RDSO refused to say anything unless it was tested by them. GM M.N. Prasad had to therefore intervene and approve it. The CE (construction) Mr Jaggi had used it in Iraq but he could not approve its use in India unless cleared by Indian Codes. Typical prisoner of codes and procedures!

But pending formal approval, I had already authorized its use. During one of the presentations before the ME, R.K. Jain, I showed some slides of concreting. This was obviously possible only with super plasticizer. Mr Prasad remarked, 'Oh, so you were already using this product before getting my formal clearance.' He told Mr Jain about the background and commented that we took his approval for granted. I was not defensive. 'Sir, before seeking your approval I had to be convinced about its efficacy. That was not possible without actually using and testing it.' A weak argument certainly, but thankfully it was appreciated for the initiative and the courage of conviction that had been collectively demonstrated by us.

ENTER THE GUINNESS WORLD RECORDS

The use of super plasticizer opened the door for admixtures not only in Indian Railways, but also in other departments. Thankfully, the standard specifications permit its use now. It solved our concreting problem particularly that of pumping. But the major problem was the segmental casting by bridge builder.

Its suppliers had indicated a time-cycle of seven days for a segment. The span had thirteen segments. But instead of 91 days, the first span took 137 days. Disappointing! The superstructure would thus take more than three years, that is, the bridge could not be completed before 1988. The cycle time was unacceptable and discussed at length. The HCC wanted two more bridge builders taking the cycle time of 118 days for a span.

I was alone in my belief that the cycle time could be reduced. Unfortunately, no one was experienced enough in the country to guide us. On my request, Mr Balachandran, ME, called a meeting in the Board, which was attended by Ajit Gulabchand, MD of the HCC. He also saw no way to reduce the cycle time. But there was a known and accepted concept, a learning curve and I was certain of the cycle time coming down being a repetitive process. If it took seven days elsewhere, it should not take more than eight days here. Evidently, we were making some mistakes. We needed guidance from the suppliers' experts. The Railway Board agreed with me to call the expert. It also released US$ 25,000 for this.

Innovative approach—help from Norway

The expert from Norway was a young man. He went through the process very intently and in great detail. He suggested some changes in the erection method and shifting of bridge builder from one position to another. The girder had many prestressing cables which obstructed the movement of the bridge builder. The design was checked. We found that four cables could adequately support the segment. Thus, other cables could be inserted subsequently. The profile and sequence of prestressing were accordingly changed to enable the quick movement of the bridge builder.

The grouting of cable ducts after prestressing became a contentious issue. Full proof arrangements had to be made to prevent concrete ingress into ducts. At that time, a similar bridge at Zuari in Goa had collapsed due to corrosion of the cables. The investigation brought out, that the ducts were not grouted. The additional director general, bridges from the Ministry of Surface Transport came to ensure this aspect. He was unsure of how grouting could be ensured in long prestressed girder. We had a friendly bet of ₹1,000. A thin metal sheath that covered the cables was generally prone to puncturing during concreting. The concrete slurry would thus, invariably, leak into the ducts to block them. We thought of inserting a high density polythene pipe in the duct through which cables were inserted. It formed an exterior cover to protect against the leaking concrete slurry. The pipes were taken out after concreting. Ducts were thus completely free from obstruction. The cables could be threaded subsequently and also the duct could be grouted without any problem. I am glad that the experiment of using the HDPE pipe in a cable duct has now become a standard specification in the country, replacing the use of thin metal sheath, which was prone to puncture allowing ingress of leaking cement grout.

We enter the Guinness World Records

With these changes, the cycle time was brought down progressively to less than six days for a segment and the average time for a span came down to seventy-eight days. In one case, the rising flood had threatened to wash away the temporary arrangements. If not completed during the 1985-86 seasons, another bridge builder would be required. That span was completed in sixty-three days. The last segment was done in three days after stressing the cable, the moment the concrete attained three days of strength amounting to 300 kg/sq.cm. This was done by changing the mix design. It was a good demonstration of ingenuity and innovation.

All the prophets of doom were proved wrong. The ultimate recognition perhaps came from the bridge builder company in form of a letter. It said that this equipment was also being used by a contractor in Malaysia where he was satisfied with a cycle time of seven days. However, by application and ingenuity shown by the project team at Tezpur, a cycle time of less than five days was achieved, which has found a proud place in the Guinness World Records!

Once the basics of a bridge builder operation became clear, the construction cycle was easily improved. We used a simple form with a similar principle for one more span. With this, the deployment of a bridge builder was no longer critical. All but one span was ready which was also completed by December 1986.

We had planned to complete the work by January 1987. By then, a new government led by Prafulla Mahanta, the leader of the Assam agitation, was elected after the famous Assam Accord. Rajiv Gandhi was requested to inaugurate the bridge. Unfortunately, he had no time before April 1987. Assam celebrates New Year festival of Rangoli on 14 April which was chosen for the inauguration as it was naturally more appropriate.

MADHAVRAO SCINDIA VISITS

Minister of Railways Madhavrao Scindia visited Tezpur. Mr Balachandran arrived a day in advance. Mr Scindia arrived in a helicopter in the morning from Guwahati. Mr Scindia was an icon and a young and dynamic minister. He would chat with us as if we were chums. He was greatly impressed with our achievements. I made a presentation in our conference room. I recall that he wanted coffee and when it was served, he asked for it without sugar. Unfortunately, the second time too the coffee was not right. I was unhappy and on checking it out I found that the coffee was prepared with tinned milkmaid which had sugar. I explained to him and apologised but he had a hearty laugh. That was his simplicity.

The cantilever span was being cast with the bridge builder. I felt the minister would appreciate it better from the pier-top but climbing it would have been difficult. The only other way was to hoist him by a crane in an open cage. For the minister, it was risky and the HCC engineers flatly refused because of safety reasons. I took the entire responsibility upon myself by giving them written instructions. Before actually taking him to the top, I told the minister, 'Sir, this is a makeshift lift. I have tested it myself and it is quite safe. It is, however, not certified by any safety regulator. M/S HCC's engineers are unwilling to take you to the top. But I have taken the responsibility on myself. You will not be able to appreciate the work without going to the pier-top. So, Sir, if you do not mind an adventure, you may step in the open lift.' He said enthusiastically, 'Oh! I do not mind and here I am.' He really enjoyed the ride and liked the actual construction work going on the top. He even found someone from Gwalior working on the pier top. He asked him how come he was working so far away from his home. He remarked that they did not work in their own state.

While returning, having persuaded the minister, I was filled with tension. It was with a sigh of relief that we brought him back safely. He wrote a lovely letter to me later, praising the efforts of my team and me in particular. It was a great tribute. His remark in the visitors' book was also very encouraging.

BALACHANDRAN AND M.N. PRASAD—THE EPITOME OF LEADERSHIP

After Mr Scindia's departure, Mr Balachandran announced that I was nominated for the Algerian project and that I would have to leave soon for Algeria. It came as a surprise. Mr Prasad voiced his protest feebly, of course, saying how indispensable I was, as the work was not fully complete. Mr Balachandran was angry and said, 'You are selfish. This boy has shed tears and blood for the project. I know how poor and financially starved the fellow is. The foreign assignment might give him some compensation. All critical work is now over. If all of you cannot complete the work from here on without Jaruhar, you are simply useless.' Well, I was embarrassed.

But that was how Bala conducted himself! Very candid—he never minced words. He was keen to help me and he believed he had told me that I might not get a foreign posting after he left. He supported all the performers to the hilt and would let it be known to all. I once took a proposal to him for installing electrical substation on the project site on a single tender basis. He just signed it. I thought it was not fair and that he should have read the proposal. He said, 'I knew it was urgent and important because you brought it personally. Unless it was correct you would have never done so.' This was one way of his showing trust in me. Actually, it is the hallmark of managerial skill. It makes the people, on whom the confidence is placed doubly responsible. That is the key to good organizational behaviour.

Lapse in realizing freight charge of cement

An anecdote may be in order. Usually, cement was supplied to the BG rail head at Jogighopa. It was carted to Tezpur from there either by road or barge. I was once travelling from Guwahati by train. A CPWD executive engineer posted in Arunachal Pradesh was my co-passenger. He informed me that the road freight incurred to carry cement from Jogighopa could be got reimbursed. This was news to me. Cement was a controlled item, which was allotted on the Director General Supply & Disposal (DGS&D) rate contract. Its rate included rail freight, 'on free on rail up to destination' basis. In this case, the cement was actually carried by rail to Jogighopa, which was 320 km short of Tezpur—the ultimate destination. The freight cost either by road or barge from Jogighopa to Tezpur was reimbursed considering the case where cement was notionally carried by rail to Tezpur, entirely. A reimbursement bill had to be submitted to the central freight pool.

The controller of stores was requested to change all the purchase orders accordingly. But claims older than six months had become time-barred. Thankfully, not only our unit, but also other construction units took advantage of this and got a sizeable reimbursement. Unfortunately, some time-barred claim cases were not pursued. This was considered a lapse causing loss to the Railways and a draft audit para was issued to fix responsibility. I was asked to hold the IOW responsible. Someone from the accounts office brought the file to me when I was having lunch in Maligaon. He said that the FA & CAO had asked me to record and fix the responsibility. I asked him to come after fifteen minutes. I returned the file after recording my views.

Soon the FA & CAO called me and asked, 'What is this? Why have you written that you are responsible? Everyone knows you are not the custodian.' I politely explained that if nobody knew this rule then the IOW could not be responsible. 'Since you insisted, I held myself responsible.' He took me to Mr Balachandran and narrated the whole thing. The GM had a hearty laugh and said, 'Look, it is actually our fault. This young man had the moral courage to tell you what was correct. I think it is time we admitted our responsibility. This young man has shown initiative and found out the rules and taken action as quickly as possible. Jaruhar, you must excuse us for even bothering you for this draft audit para.' That was the end of it. He took up the subject himself and demonstrated that innocent people must be protected. This increased camaraderie.

M.N. Prasad, a sensitive, astute leader

M.N. Prasad was an excellent GM, very competent in administrative matters besides being technically sound and a very capable bridge engineer. He was posted as GM in 1984 September just ahead of the guide bundh construction work. He had a very warm heart and would look after everyone's interest.

He liked me very much. He was a simple person with a frugal lifestyle. The television had just arrived in the market. We recommended the purchase of two television sets—one for the officers' club and another for the staff institute. He however approved of only one set to be kept in the staff institute or the officers' club, where both could watch TV with their families. I did not like the idea. We were not short of any bonhomie or camaraderie but I felt that the club was a place to relax. Besides, I could not ask officers' families to all watch TV together. So, I asked the TV to be installed in the staff institute.

After quite some time, the FA & CAO visited us and asked why the officers did not have a TV. I informed him that only one TV was approved. I thought it was better to provide this facility to the staff first. The FA & CAO said that he had agreed to two television sets, but the GM seemed to have sanctioned only one. He must have had words with Mr Prasad about this because soon enough Mr Prasad asked me why his orders were not complied with. I told him that it was out of question not to comply with his orders. As ordered, one set was installed in the staff institute. But the other half of the order, that the officers and staff should both watch TV together, was not enforceable. He sounded unhappy on the phone. He, however, appreciated my point and approved the purchase of another TV for us. He subsequently told others that their deputy chief was a unique person and that he wished there were more people in the IR like him!

Another time, I had to go to Shillong once and asked for a leave to go there because the visit was private. He told me that I could go and visit the headquarters of the NEC also. I returned from Shillong late in the afternoon. His secretary told me that I could go into his office because he was chatting with the CE. When I stepped into his room, he asked me to wait. I was called in after some time. I briefed him about my discussions with the NEC. I was already delayed so I wanted to leave for Tezpur. He said, 'That is why you were in a hurry to record your attendance?' I was very upset. It was Mr Balachandran, who had legislated that I must see the GM whenever I was in Maligaon. Otherwise, I had no work there that day.

I said, 'It is true that I came here to mark my attendance. Otherwise I had no particular reason to see you. It is late (it was 4 p.m. already and in the Northeast, it becomes dark by 5 p.m. even in summer) already and I have almost three and half hour's drive. My family is with me and it is unsafe to drive late in the evening. Your secretary said that I could go in. Yes, it is true that I am in a hurry.' He was immediately very apologetic and said, 'Look, I was not in good mood because I returned from Calcutta in the afternoon after seeing my sick son. So, I was perhaps upset and hence I reacted. Please do not delay any further and proceed to Tezpur.' I picked up my family and reached Tezpur at about 9 p.m.

My bungalow's peon informed me on my arrival that the GM sahib had called at least twice. He had asked me to speak to him as soon as I had reached. I called him. He said, 'Look, Jaruhar, have you reached safely? Actually, I am very upset with myself for having behaved so rudely with you this afternoon. I was keen to tell you how sorry I am.' What stellar qualities, this man possessed! I was totally embarrassed. This was the hallmark of a great human being—a saintly person.

Many treated his humility as his weakness. As GM, Eastern Railway, he told me that the minister wanted him to go to a different ministry as a secretary, to bring Vijay Singh, his batchmate but his junior, as member engineering. He said that he preferred working under Vijay Singh. Many considered Singh superior but Mr Prasad was equally good, if not better. He eventually became member engineering. I told him that one day he would become the chairman. He said that it was not likely. There was a move to elevate Anoop Singh, the member mechanical by giving him an extension in service. I was in Algeria at that time but I told him that he should not worry. I knew that giving extension in service and promoting both together was not common. Well Mr Prasad finally became the chairman Railway Board. He enjoyed being the most uncontroversial and strong member of the Board!

CARDINAL POINTS IN MANAGING LARGE-SCALE PROJECTS

The Brahmaputra project was proceeding very smoothly. I recall a well-known axiom that good planning would make difficult work look very simple whereas poorly planned work even though simple would look very difficult indeed. While in the UK for training in URWICK School of Management, I presented a paper on 'Managing a Large Major Bridge Project', based on my experience in handling the Tezpur Bridge. Basically, there are three aspects in a project that require proper management. They are:

- Technical management
- Financial management
- Management of external and internal Influences

All project activities followed the S-curve

All projects follow a typical S-curve profile. Projects take time to start and the build-up can be seen on the flatter bottom of the letter 'S'. This is the time for mobilization of resources, design and deployment of manpower. This takes 15 to 20 per cent of the time and the resource and comes with very low, physically measureable yield.

All major factors like actual ground work, construction activity, financial yield or expenses follow the straight-line portion of the letter 'S'. The project is stabilized during this time. This is roughly 60-65 per cent of the total time. Eventually activities in a project taper down like the upper limb-like portion of the S-curve. Winding up takes place during this time. This paper was very much appreciated in the UK. It demonstrated the phenomenon associated with the S-curve syndrome. Our project was cruising in a smooth way because we were in a straight-line portion.

The importance of external and internal influences is also seldom appreciated. External influences can play havoc with a major project. The most important example of external influence in our case was certainly the Assam agitation. We had no role in this factor, but it had threatened to completely destroy this project. Many other projects sponsored by the Central government in the state in other departments suffered incalculable damage. The project managers could not handle the external influences. In contrast, because of good management, the Brahmaputra Bridge project had continued almost smoothly.

Approach towards the management of external influences

Success in dealing with external influences always depends upon:

- Intelligence: Is anything brewing to upset the project schedule? Who is behind it and what is their strength?
- Sharing information: A good information system or PR exercise can kill many such threats or at least mitigate their impact significantly.
- Evaluation: We must evaluate the strength and weakness of such a threat. We should also evaluate our strength. We should also find who are likely to support our cause. Without suitable evaluation, it is sometimes dangerous to take a pre-emptive step. Most important aspect is time.
- Strategy: Good planning and more often multi-level actions with good PR as a backup. It is no use defending an indefensible act. In such cases, we should quickly acknowledge it and come up with good, acceptable responses. We should also solicit for the support of public or stakeholders at large. In all cases, such projects have larger public interest and higher public stakes. We may say that this was the price of development and inconvenience, which although regrettable, was not totally avoidable.
- Response measurement: We must have a response measuring mechanism to enable us to revisit the strategy, if necessary.

Admittedly, these are general guidelines. I benefitted a great deal by following these general principles. Today the media plays a very active role and without good strategy and an intelligence system, one is likely to be bogged down, almost virtually by default. Many successful project leaders, to a large extent, should thank their good PR team and selected executives.

Another instance of the impact of an external influence on us was a big boulder near P1 on Bhomoraguri hill. It had an inscription of a bridge on it. Local historians said that it was the sketch drawn by Ahom General Kalia Bhomora who had attempted to construct the bridge on the Brahmaputra. This was sufficient for some activists to bring an injunction from the court. It had political ramifications and the DC once told me privately to blow it up. But I knew that I had to solve this issue. We brought in specialist rock cutters from South India. In an intricate process, we sliced the rock safely preserving the inscription. The rock mass weighed over six hundred tonnes. The portion was placed alongside and a suitable memorial was raised by the Railways. While it fetched enormous goodwill, it also took the wind out of the sails of the activists. The external influence would have killed the project but by good management we turned the tables on them.

A COMICAL TAKE ON PROJECT MANAGEMENT

A comical take on project management was also circulated while we were in the UK for training at URWICK. It is interesting although it looks comical. According to this, stages in a project are:

- Enthusiasm: People are usually very enthusiastic about the project at the start and everyone talks about it. This is the first stage when the project has just started.
- Confusion: After some time, if the project does not go well, there is a lot of confusion about issues raised against the project. This can be called the second stage in the project.
- Doubts: This is the stage when doubts are raised about the efficacy and advantages of the project. Expert committees or some persons with vested interest raise issues, which cannot be easily answered. This gets encouragement, if no clarity is there or project authorities are not decisive. This is of course the third stage.
- Suspension and punishment: After considerable delay or maybe after the change of a government, work is suspended, based on the report of the expert committee. Scapegoats are hunted for and all who worked hard are found and punished. This is the painful, fourth stage in a project.
- Reward: After considerable time, the project restarts and is eventually

completed. All those, who are available in the end, are rewarded even though their contributions had been inconsequential. This is the finale—when only those who watched the proceedings remain; all actual players have been either shunted out or punished.

AN INTERESTING ANECDOTE—VARIATION IN COST ESTIMATE

Soon after the Assam Accord, Prime Minister Rajiv Gandhi, who was also the chairperson of the NEC decided to attend the annual meeting of the NEC in Shillong.

The original project cost was ₹70.50 crore. Because of the escalation and minor variations, the revised cost was now ₹73.50 crore merely 4.25 per cent more. A variation of less than 5 per cent did not require a fresh sanction from the Railways. Neither the NEC nor the home ministry had such authority. The case was therefore sent to the PMO for approval. Sarla Grewal, the principal secretary to the prime minister, wanted to have this case cleared a day before the scheduled meeting of the NEC.

She was apparently not happy with the papers sent to her. She called the secretary of the NEC who in turn talked to Mr Ranganath. The GM informed me of this development around 3.30 p.m. on phone. I reached Maligaon immediately. The principal secretary directly told me that there was some mistake in the figure—she said that apparently, the decimal point had been incorrectly placed. It took some time for me to understand what was amiss. I politely said, 'Madam, the decimal point is correctly placed. Total variation is only 4.25 per cent and not 425 per cent. This is less than 5 per cent.' She said, 'What is this? The PMO has never dealt a case like this. We normally sanction variations over 700-1000 per cent and even more. Why are you wasting our time on such an insignificant variation? It is unbelievable and most exemplary. Take it as sanctioned.'

It was creditable. I recall a statement made on the floor of the Parliament by Home Minister Zail Singh that the Brahmaputra Bridge was not only being completed according to schedule but also within the estimated cost! It was the ultimate recognition. I thank God for the honour.

DEVELOPMENT OF SUBORDINATE AND SUCCESSOR

The project had many firsts and technical innovations. The project was on course to scheduled completion due to exemplary camaraderie. By June 1986, all important milestones were achieved. The team was fully charged and trained. I started delegating my authorities (the GM had delegated all the financial powers of CE to me) to V.C. Sharma to give him confidence in dealing with major projects. He was also promoted as a JAG.

I asked him to take all the major decisions. I advised him to render me redundant. I discouraged any consultation with me. He gradually gained confidence. I also asked him to give full charge to S.M. Vaidya, who was promoted as a senior scale officer. He was an officer of great intelligence and promise! Sharma would keep on asking and advising him in the beginning. Once while crossing the river, I told him, 'Vipin, you have not kept your promise, whereas I have kept my part of promise.' He looked bewildered. Then I said, 'Why are you constantly advising Shashank? How will he develop if you do not let him do the job in his way?' He immediately understood what I meant. He told me that it would never happen again.

B.C. Ganguli always maintained that no job was complete unless a suitable successor and a new contractor was developed. The IR found two excellent officers out of the project, who not only brought laurels to the Railways in India but also earned it abroad. In many ways, I must admit with great pleasure and satisfaction that Sharma proved to be much better than I. Those who followed the career of Vaidya will agree with my assessment of his technical and managerial acumen.

As GM or ME, I always insisted on the decision being taken at an appropriate level. The development of subordinates is the most important responsibility of a superior.

TIME TO BID GOODBYE

So, once everything was in place I began to miss the challenge of work. I thought that the time had come for me to move out of the project.

R.K. Jain, ME, asked me where I would like to go after the project was over. Mr Balachandran had nominated me for the Algerian project with the IRCON. Somehow the project was not forthcoming. He also nominated me as construction consultant in Iraq, but it was shelved because of the Iran-Iraq war. So, I told Mr Jain that I would like to move to Delhi. He said that there would be no problem about that.

But soon after that, the Algerian project received a clearance. I was asked to join the IRCON in Algeria immediately. I had to leave Tezpur in September 1986. Many friends and well-wishers advised me to stay back and formally complete the project. I had very little to contribute further in the project. If I stayed back, I would be carrying out only the ceremonial duties of organizing inauguration ceremony. But they had a point.

I realized subsequently that people counted completed cakes. Someone mentioned that after all I did not see the completed work. The FC, Mitra, on a visit to Gorakhpur, when I was doing Gandak Bridge, asked me to take some lessons from V.C. Sharma. 'Do you know him?' he asked. I nodded and told, 'Yes, Sir. We worked together in Tezpur.' But as one says: '*Jo jita wahi Sikander* (Only the winner will be called Alexander [The Winner]).'

YOU MUST LEAVE WHEN THE TIME COMES—YOU MUST KNOW WHEN TO LEAVE

Leaving a place or an organization built largely by one's own efforts is always difficult. There is an emotional attachment, an umbilical cord. It has to be cut physically as well as emotionally. The episode describing how Sage Vishwamitra took his leave from King Dasharath comes to my mind. They had returned to Ayodhya after the wedding of Lord Rama. The king said that he had received so much only because of his grace. The sage replied that the company of Lord Rama was a great experience. But this raised attachment or moha. This was not desirable. A wise person should understand and recognize such a moment. If the attachment is not given up in time, it will eventually be taken away because that is nature's law.

About Nelson Mandela, Richard Stengel wrote, 'One day it is necessary to quit. Because [Nelson] Mandela felt his job was to set the course and not to steer the ship. Leaders lead as much by what they choose not to do as what they do. He quit as President after his election in 1994 when he could have remained President for life.'

Thus, there was definitely a time to call it a day. For me, it had arrived.

I had to also protect my young team

I was constantly aware of a large following of young people working relentlessly for the project. After the project, financial closure was due and large procedural irregularities would come to light. Quite certainly, these people would be hounded.

I always tried to look after such people. But after I was gone, many might not recall the circumstances under which this project was executed. So, after recording a usual handing-over note, I also recorded an emotive and a personal note to the GM. I wrote:

> I leave this project after serving for nearly eight years. We took up this

challenging work with practically no experienced hands. We began and carried out the work with the help of probationers and newly recruited IOW. Although we had some experienced people from Assam government, but they were unfortunately not well versed with Railway's rules and procedures. Thus, I was the only person to guide the people doing the work. In such a background, commission of unintended mistakes can be expected.

Today everyone is singing praise for the project. It is being heralded as a technical and managerial marvel. I am being credited with a lot of glory. But as I leave today my heart is full. I am fully conscious of the toil and tear put up by the young men to achieve this result. They did not know the procedures but blindly followed my instructions and direction. It is our moral duty to condone the lapses, discovered subsequently. I without any reservation take full responsibility for them. In any case, it was my moral and official duty to train these people, most of them on their first appointment.

When people congratulate me, I feel a pain inside me. If I am not held accountable for the lapses in the project, I cannot acknowledge the accolades showered on me. Because I will be walking over the bodies of the workmen who have fallen while trying to hold me up for the glory. This note is recorded in full consciousness and faith that it will be taken as a defence for those who have been unwittingly found responsible for lapses, at a future date, when I will not be available to defend them.

Well, many called them words of bravado. But I received an instantaneous response from Mr Rangnath promising me that I need not worry about them. Everyone would be looked after. He of course gave me a lot of credit, for the courage I had shown. He said that it was his personal and moral duty to protect the staff that had shown such an exemplary devotion to their duty.

I had not told anyone about this letter but many found out later. I got many letters expressing their gratitude. The letter was a purely emotional response to my feelings. I realized that it was better to put on record a difficult working situation in time to enable posterity to take a balanced view. Then it was not likely to be considered as an afterthought. I must thank my superiors who did everything possible. As a result, no person had to face any problem. Based on my experience of reimbursement case of cement (described earlier), I was apprehensive that some lower functionary would be sacrificed in a routine manner in order to save the organization. Bravado or not, it was God's grace that my prayers were heard and granted. This gave me a great deal of peace. In my career, I have often stuck my neck out in defence of genuine persons. God has been kind that each time I got away.

On the morning of 22 September 1986, I eventually left Tezpur to catch the *Tinsukia Mail*. When I had first come to Tezpur, our family consisted of my wife and my six-year-old daughter Shravani. While leaving, we had our second daughter, six-year-old Shreya and a two-year-old son, Shrimant. Besides, we had loads of goodwill, the happiest of memories and extremely touching love and the affection of so many. That was certainly the heaviest load we ever carried on transfer. I promised to come to Tezpur for the inauguration which was scheduled to take place about six months later! I did not know what time would change in the short interval. Of course, I did come to attend the ceremony inaugurated by Prime Minister Rajiv Gandhi on 14 April 1987. That journey was very eventful. Full of tears, feeling both pain and pleasure, I came to receive the gold medal given by the prime minister. I will describe the event in just a little while. *Sil vous plait* (in French, it is 'if you please')!

7

THE ALGERIAN EXPERIENCE

We boarded the *Tinsukia Mail* from Guwahati and reached Patna the next day around 2.30 p.m. Our entire household effects also reached Patna simultaneously by truck.

Algeria is a French-speaking country. It did not have any English-medium schools then. Shravani was in Class 7 and obviously could not go to Algeria. Shreya was in Class I and Shrimant had yet to go to school. Shravani was admitted in St Joseph's Convent School in Patna. It was a difficult decision, which we regret even now. A local school in Patna permitted children of Shreya's age to pursue studies in such countries. They provided books and syllabus and parents could homeschool their children. The school had arrangements to examine the child once a year, when they would return to India. If the child passed the test, the school granted a certificate. Well it served the purpose for Shreya and Shrimant. The whole arrangement was painful and if asked again I would flatly refuse. But it was divine will, which I then followed enthusiastically. The foreign assignment had appeared as a remedy for the financial hardship that dogged us, and seemed to be an honourable way into a well-provided life, if not one of extravagance. It was a glorified mirage. I found subsequently that our destiny was different. Maybe, poverty and I had become mates! Poverty had followed me like a shadow and hence this suffering seemed a small price for the promise of a good life.

I ARRIVE IN ALGERIA

We had to make arrangements to store our luggage in Patna besides looking into the schooling arrangements. My father-in-law's house lacked the extra space, so two small rooms were built on the terrace for storing our luggage. We left for Delhi on 27 September 1986. I had to leave the very next day. My family went back to Patna after seeing me off at Delhi. Along with Y.P. Singh and P.S. Kochar, I left for Frankfurt by Lufthansa en route Algiers. We were in Frankfurt for a day, on transit. I had been to the city earlier in 1984. September is a beautiful month, there. We took an Air Algérie flight for Algiers and arrived there by lunchtime. We went directly to the company's guest house, in the beautiful city of Algiers. The view from the aircraft of the Mediterranean Sea was like a glittering jewel on a turquoise background.

We were in a foreign country with great excitement, in search of something new. I was looking forward to contribute a great deal in the IRCON project. We were a contractor now and required to work on the other side of the table. It called for a paradigm shift. For many Railway officers, this shift was difficult. Mr Chelam, project director, asked us to spend a day or two in Algiers. But I wanted to be in Ain Temouchent straight away—the project site six hundred km away. We left by road the next day and were there by 9 p.m.

People were having dinner when we arrived. Meeting old friends was nice. After dinner, we were taken to a house which was taken on lease in the city, about 4 or 5 km away. This house was sparsely furnished. The site authorities had known about our arrival for over a month. A better arrangement was surely possible. Apparently, no thought was given to this!

People were neither treated well nor welcome. Many looked frustrated and wished to get repatriated. The lustre of money that had lured people to come to a foreign country to work was fading due to an apathetic work environment. I was appalled to note that the people managing the team thought that they could hold a person hostage in a foreign country and not allow him to be repatriated. Such coercion is not only foolish but becomes counterproductive as well. As director of works later, I made sure that such a foolish idea was abolished. Instead, an impression that everyone was welcome and needed was created. It was my firm conviction that a person delivered his best when he felt that he was actually needed. The organization has to sincerely make him feel welcome and comfortable. A mindset that believed in buying a person and enslaving him, was a sick one. It would eventually lead to their deserting the ship at the first opportunity, like in the film *Ben-Hur*.

THE ALGERIAN PROJECT—CHALLENGES

Under the project, IRCON had to construct a 22-km railway line from Ain Temouchent to Benisaf—a port city with a huge cement plant. The line, traversing through deep gorges called for the construction of many long and high viaducts. Some bridge piers were eighty metres tall—taller than the Qutub Minar. The SNTF (Societe Nationale Transports Des Ferrovaires) Algerian Government Railways for short, were the clients. Kamel Slaimia, a young man, a hard task-master with a bundle of energy, was the project director. The

SOCOTEC of Paris—a highly respected agency was the client's consultants. They were also consultants for the English Channel underground rail project. The work was awarded to the IRCON in 1984. They had started working but the country soon had some financial problems. This led to a suspension of the contract in 1985. The work recommenced in 1986 after the financial issues were resolved. Bridge works had just begun in September 1986 when we arrived. The earthwork in rail embankment was in good progress. I was posted as a chief of section for planning. I had to replace L.C. Jain who had to go back to India to deal with family problems.

K. Ramakrishna, another very senior railway officer, was the director works. The IRCON had already executed the Saida project in Algeria but its financial closure was in progress. A. Chelam was the project director for both these projects. I met Mr Ramakrishna in the morning. What a disappointment! He had absolutely no time for us and was very curt. Others, however, said that he was just being himself. It was too short a time to judge a person. On the other hand, Mr Chelam was a warm person. He also knew me from Tezpur. I was by then a well-known young engineer, but Mr Ramakrishna chose to ignore me. It is established that a project leader determined the project; a bad one was not only forgettable but would do incalculable damage to the organization and in the process could even jeopardize the project itself.

Launching of girder—a serious difficulty with the SICET girder

A new member of the project team is usually not trusted until he proves himself. Here the problem was more pronounced as the team leader did not take me seriously. Bridge substructures were in the process of being ready but there was no plan to launch the girders. I called for a launching scheme of thirty-metre prestressed precast girders. The IRCON had procured a launching girder from SICET, Italy, but it was lying unused in the yard. Another bright, young engineer, Pradip Kulshrestha, was equally keen. He got the equipment unpacked and tried to read through the available literature. To our horror, there were no launching details with back-up calculations. Somebody had purchased a launching girder for thirty-metre span without considering the type of girders it had to launch. We calculated the factor of safety with the available details. It was hardly 10 per cent.

We summoned the manufacture experts from Italy. They were reluctant because the equipment had been purchased a year ago, and was no longer covered by their warranty clause. From our discussions with the suppliers, we learned that the launching girder was actually suitable for a road girder. The rail girder is usually heavier. The design of the PSC girder was not finalized when the launching truss was purchased. It was obviously presumed to be able to handle the thirty-metre rail girder also. What a goof up! With some modification which was limited, the factor of safety improved to 12 per cent. We crossed our fingers and the trials started. I asked Mr Ramakrishna to approve the scheme but he was evasive and impatient. I insisted on his involvement in the scheme, and persisted with a note to seek his formal approval. He was upset but I did not relent. It was certainly excellent equipment but it did not exactly suit the job. The modification had made it fit for a cautious attempt.

A MAJOR MISHAP AND A PERSONAL TRAGEDY

The trial assembly of the launching girder was taken up in bridge No. 9 known as OA9 (Ouvret des art in French). Its abutment was not high and the first pier was just on the edge of a fairly deep gorge. The first stage of the launch was relatively simple and was successfully executed. In the second stage, the trolley had to carry a trapezoidal frame from the abutment to be placed on the top of the pier next to the abutment. This was the first major operation.

In order to closely observe and guide the operation, I was standing on the pier top. Suddenly, the electric power supply tripped. Not a problem, as the electromagnetic lock should have locked the trolley wheel. But the tripping caused a sudden jerk, which caused the trolley wheels to derail. Once the wheels derailed, nothing could stop the trolley from rolling down with the frame on its tip and at a great speed. The sound unnerved us. The fellow at the other end shouted, 'Sahib, trolley has derailed'. With the stability calculation in my mind, I knew in a flash where it was heading to. Once the trolley moved beyond a point, the entire launching truss would topple, leaving no chance to the workmen to escape. So, I shouted out to them to jump clear. I was the target—being in line of that uncontrolled trolley. So, I jumped down the pier. A big mistake! Had the truss toppled at that stage, I could not have escaped. Luckily, the trapezoidal frame at the girder tip swinging down and it hit the ground. Had it moved another 2 or 3 feet, it would have gone down the gorge. The girder would have certainly toppled then. But as soon as it hit the ground, the stability equation changed. The trolley stopped and nothing more happened. A miracle! The incident made us aware of the derailing tendency which was duly rectified.

But it was at the cost of a terrible personal tragedy. I had jumped because the pier was not very high. But the ground was on a slope and at the edge of the gorge. A lot of materials were lying around including concrete blocks. There was a great cracking sound as I landed and then I passed out.

CRIPPLED—I SUFFER IN A FOREIGN LAND

When I regained consciousness, I was lying on the ground in great pain. Workers were surrounding me. I could see my left ankle turned askew and hanging. Someone said that the ankle was broken. The sardar immediately twisted it straight causing great pain. I lost consciousness again. When I regained it, I was on the floor of our office bus. Rajat Mitra held my head and was asking the driver to drive slowly. Again, I passed out. The next time I came to my senses, I was on the floor of our camp dispensary. R.D. Bhandari, a surgeon, was trying to fix my foot with plaster. He told me that I had suffered a huge fracture of the ankle joint known as Pot Fracture. Some sedative was given to me because I was gone again.

Next time I gained consciousness, I found myself on a bed in the guest room. I was there for a week but in great pain. The doctor told me that the pain would gradually go away. It was not so. I was taken to the local civil hospital. The x-ray report showed that the joint was not fixed properly which is why the pain relentlessly continued. Surgery was necessary to fix it with nails and screws. Dr Carlos, a Cuban Army surgeon, was the only one who could do this. He was to go back to Cuba on a long leave, so he was unwilling to perform the surgery. Dr Bhandari somehow convinced Dr Carlos, assuring him that he would take care of the post-surgery care. I gave my written consent that the surgery was on my request and at my own risk. For any post-surgery complication, I would be taken out of Algeria for further treatment. I trusted Dr Bhandari with whose younger brother I had played cricket in a match when I was in the engineering college in Sindri.

Surgery to fix my ankle

The hospital was well-equipped, particularly the operation theatre. Dr Bhandari assisted Dr Carlos in the surgery. It was unusual for a government hospital to allow a private doctor to assist in the operation theatre. Dr Bhandari was very skilled and we shared an excellent rapport. I recall he smiled at me when I regained consciousness on the operation table. He told me that the operation had been successful. During the complex surgery, the broken pieces of bones were fixed by driving a nail through them and screwing it tightly with a steel cover plate a few inches long. I was in the hospital for three weeks in a general ward. Dr Bhandari told me that it would take nine months to recover. Physiotherapy was essential to enable me to walk again. I had come to Algeria on 30 September 1986 and the accident took place on 16 October 1986. I did not know French and I was alone in my suffering.

I was lucky that we had an Indian doctor friend. Local Indians looked after me including my toilet needs. I was not able to eat much. I was grateful to Mrs Lakshmi Jain (wife of L.C. Jain. They could not go back to India because I was injured and was not in a position to replace him). She came to see me every evening with some home-cooked food. Later, I was asked to return to India for physiotherapy.

I was allowed to travel by the end of November 1986. I was put on Air Algérie flight from Algiers for Frankfurt. After a long wait there, I was put in a Lufthansa flight to Delhi. I landed on 6 December 1986 early in the morning. My brother-in-law Sanjeev picked me up from the airport. I had to leave by an afternoon flight for Patna. I reached late in the evening to greet my wife. It was also her birthday. Shrimant, who was just two, insisted on sitting on my lap. I let him and the fellow would only cry saying, 'Papa, your leg is broken!' My mother had also come to the airport. She caught hold of my hand and would just cry.

When tragedy strikes, it takes you by surprise. I had left with a lot of enthusiasm and the conviction that I would be achieving my goals. But destiny had other plans. In only fifteen days after my arrival in Algeria, the tables had been turned. I was a helpless creature at the mercy of friends, family and other well-wishers. Well-known orthopaedic surgeons in Patna had a look at my injury. They thought that the surgery was not done well. This would give rise to problems in time to come. But at this stage, nothing further could be done about it. My only hope was recovery through physiotherapy. A specially designed shoe was given to me. It was enormously painful at the beginning. My elder brother Madhu bhai took me religiously to the physiotherapist for hourly sessions. After four months of intensive therapy I started to walk with a special boot and a stick. I could not believe it myself because orthopaedic surgeons were extremely doubtful about my recovery.

ANOTHER TRAGEDY—A TERRIBLE AND AN IRREPARABLE LOSS

From the time the accident took place to March 1987, I had only known pain. My appearance had drastically changed and I looked very old. 6th March was our wedding anniversary. My mother came to see me on 5th March. She was with my elder brother. I had been living at my in-laws' residence then. We had planned to go to the temple in the morning after which we planned to visit our mother. It was around 11.30 a.m. and I was waiting for my wife to get ready.

My mother departs—an irreparable loss

Just then, I saw my nephew Shrinjay, barely five years old, standing near the door. I was surprised to see him particularly because we were scheduled to go there ourselves. The sight of the boy puzzled me. I saw another person standing behind him in the doorway. He then came forward to tell me, 'Your brother has sent me. I did not know your house. I have therefore come with Shrinjay. I have to sadly inform you that your mother is no more. She passed away some time ago'. I could not believe my ears. I was looking forward to her blessings after a visit to the temple. The moment had suddenly taken away my priceless possession. My mother had had a profound influence on me. Time did not give me even an hour! I could not see my mother alive, and that left me shocked.

According to our custom, the last rites of mother were usually done by the youngest son. I was a cripple who needed help to do my own chores. With my brother's help, courage and solid emotional support of my wife, I performed the thirteen days of arduous task. My mother had imparted a basic philosophical background and encouraged a spiritual awakening besides giving me life itself. I knew I had failed her in so many ways when she wanted me to hold her. She had never complained and perhaps had forgiven me. But there is nothing to be done for failed karma. One has to undergo the pain associated with it. This was the only way to atone for one's sins. At that time, nothing would console me. It was the final snap of the umbilical cord, which joined a mother and a child both physically and emotionally. Now the latter had to walk along a path, alone in this world, chosen by his destiny. There would be no more tears. There would be no mother to look back to, who would wipe my tears away.

In a true sense, a mother should eventually be relieved of the responsibility towards her offspring. This was 'mukti'—deliverance! In the case of my mother it did not happen as long as she was alive. Only death parted her from us. In the Mahabharata, one day, Ganga, the mother of Bhisma Pitamah, told him how long he would keep running to her for help. He had to learn to face the result of his own karma. After 6 March 1987, I was a different person with an altogether different mission. I had no mother to hide my face in her lap!

FELICITATIONS FOR BRAHMAPUTRA BRIDGE—BEGINNING OF A NEW LIFE

I started living once again just like a child, except this time, it was without a mother. I had to learn to walk again. The inauguration of Brahmaputra Bridge was fixed on 14 April 1987. Prime Minister Rajiv Gandhi was to dedicate the bridge to the nation in an inaugural ceremony in Tezpur. Mr Rangnath, GM, NF Railway (construction), invited me personally for the inaugural ceremony. My physical conditions did not permit me to go there. How could I go up to the prime minister with my foot strapped in a special shoe and with a stick in my hand? When I told Mr Rangnath about this, he said that they could not think of the function without me.

I had promised to be there for the inaugural ceremony, so I decided to go with my wife and children. My sister-in-law, Anuja, assistant editor of *The Hindustan Times* in Patna, also accompanied us. Mr Rangnath had made all the arrangements for our travel. We reached Tezpur on the 13th evening. Our old friends received us and made us comfortable. I was taken to the venue of the function. Important members of the construction team were to be presented to the prime minister. I was given the honour to be at the top of the line for the introduction. Mr M.N. Prasad had also come. He was at that time the GM of Eastern Railway. The prime minister's entourage comprised Madhavrao, the railway minister; Arjun Singh, the minister of communications; Rajesh Pilot, the minister of surface transport; Bhisma Pratap Singh, governor of Assam and head of the NEC and Prafulla Mahanta, the then chief minister of Assam. I was introduced first. This followed a presentation of a gold medal by the prime minister. I had told the SPG security that I could not go to the dais to receive the medal from the prime minister, but he asked me not to worry about it. He promised to carry me personally, if required. In the end, he helped me climb a few steps up to the dais. There was a big applause. The prime minister held both my hands as the citations were read. He asked me, 'How did you do it?' I just blurted, 'I was allowed to do it.' It was a bit curt and a junior officer like me was certainly not expected to speak in such a manner to the prime minister. Mr Scindia came forward and relayed something about me to him. He told him that I had been involved in the project since the beginning and most of the credit should go to me. He also said that I was posted in Algeria currently, where I had met with an accident. The prime minister then said, 'Oh! I am very happy. I wish all projects are completed like this.' It was the ultimate tribute as far as I was concerned. I could not have asked for more!

After the ceremony, the GM told me that the railway minister's medal (the highest in the Railways) had also been awarded to me. This was to be given during the Railway Week function on 16 April in Delhi. I was asked to travel by air for this function. Acknowledging it with the greatest respect and humility, I begged to be excused for two reasons. One was my physical condition. I was with my family and could not go to Delhi, leaving them behind. Secondly, I had to meet my ex-colleagues and associates before leaving Tezpur. It had a greater priority because I did not know if I would meet them again.

A great sense of humility overcame me while leaving Tezpur. Going across the Brahmaputra on the newly opened bridge, I bowed down to the great river, which had honoured me by allowing us to construct the bridge on its bosom.

It also fetched the highest recognition during my professional and personal life. Newton had said that many of his epoch-making discoveries were nothing but a small pebble on the vast shore of the nature. When one has achieved something very rare and good for the larger section of society, it brought humility. It was a divine experience as my mother would often tell me. This was as if God had chosen me for this extraordinary experience, it was His blessings. I can only say that it certainly lessened the pang of my personal tragedy and trauma to a large extent.

We returned to Patna happy. Anuja wrote an article commending my efforts in *The Hindustan Times*. It was well-received. My in-laws threw a party to celebrate the event, after which we had a pooja in the house. We did not know, however, what I was going to do after all the celebrations.

RETURN TO ALGERIA TO RESUME THE ASSIGNMENT

Mr Rane, the MD, called me from Delhi to enquire when I could return to Algeria. I was perplexed. I was unfit for any work on the construction site. He said that I could undertake planning work, which was sedentary. I told him that my family had to go with me. He agreed to all my conditions. Accordingly, I left for Algeria at the end of April 1987. Shravani, who had summer holidays, also joined us.

We travelled to Frankfurt by Lufthansa with a day's stopover. There was an unfortunate delay when we were taking the taxi to the airport. In spite of our best efforts, we missed the Air Algérie flight to Algiers. We did not have enough money and I did not know what to do. The lady at the Lufthansa desk asked me not to worry. She must have taken pity on me. She tried frantically to put me on some alternative flight. Eventually, she succeeded in sending us to Algiers via Vienna. After a short stop there, we eventually reached Algiers by an Air Algerie flight around 4.30 p.m. Since we had come in an unscheduled flight, there was none to receive us at the airport. We couldn't reach the office when we had called. I stood outside the airport, wondering what to do, praying for divine help when I saw Mr Khanna, our accounts officer, outside the airport. He was just getting into his car. I tried to run after him—limping and shouting. Almost as if it were a miracle, he heard me and stopped. He was puzzled to see me. After the accident, my physical appearance had changed quite a bit. It was difficult for a person to recognize me. In any case, he was a godsend. He was surprised and told me that people had arrived to receive me at the airport in the morning. The office telephone number had changed as the Algiers' office had shifted. He had just happened to be passing through the airport, when he stopped for some coffee here. He collected our luggage and happily we were all taken to the guest house.

Algiers is a beautiful city with lovely beaches by the Mediterranean Sea. After a day's stay, we left for Ain-Temouchent by road. The drive, though more than five hundred km long, was very enjoyable. We were greeted on our arrival in the evening. We were put up in the guest house, which had been converted into a residence for our use. Dr Bhandari was happy to see me back. They were of course surprised to see me back when I was not fully fit. I was convinced that the Indian Railways had enough talent available for the job. But somebody thought differently and had gambled for a semi-invalid person like me. I had really no clue! Mr Balachandran thought I was worth my weight in gold even in a sedentary job. As events proved subsequently, I did not disappoint anyone except perhaps my own boss.

I AM IN CHARGE OF PLANNING

I met Mr Ramakrishna in the morning. He asked me to relieve Mr Jain. He also asked me to go to the bridge site in a wheelchair, if necessary, to supervise girder erection. The planning portfolio was of course fine. It would have been humiliating to go in a wheelchair to a bridge site. I told him that I was not fit to do that kind of a job. I also told him that I had made that amply clear to Mr Rane, too, before I had agreed to return to Algeria. If he thought differently, I was ready to pack my bags and go back. It silenced him immediately. The office opened at 8 in the morning and I was there sharp at 8. Nobody except an Algerian colleague was be there at that time. Working was quite different because I had to do everything myself. The only problem was the language. The original documents were in French. Quite frequently, the English translation was not very accurate. Amongst the clients, the project chief knew English fairly well. The main engineers of the consultants had good knowledge of English although their diction and accent were difficult to understand. The IRCON was the main contractor. Besides, it had three subcontractors one each for earthwork, bridges and piling works. They were Indian contractors with back-to-back contract with the IRCON. They were called Earthwork Division, Bridge Division and Piling Division. Their camps were also separately located.

INTRODUCTION OF A FUNCTIONAL APPROACH

I was quick to earn the respect of clients as well as the consultants. The French consultants over-designed the structure. They chose heavier specifications—

totally unwarranted for the function that the structure was expected to perform. I was unable to comprehend the logic behind such stipulations. But slowly it dawned upon me that the consultants wanted the project to be expensive so that their own fee, which was based on a percentage of the total cost, would also go up. I found it diabolical—a professional dishonesty. I took the chief of project into confidence about it. I explained how their country was unnecessarily being made to spend more on the project. I showed him some of the specifications used by the IR, which were meant for much heavier routes. I was successful in convincing him that there was room to cut down the cost. He was, however, unsure about the modality. I thought that the best course was to convince the consultants.

Most of the bridges in the project were across deep gorges with tall piers. These gorges had a history of carrying flash floods, and so the consultants had provided heavy gabions for protection against any flood. It was unwarranted. I suggested a simpler design that was good enough but it was rejected. Slaimia, however, asked Paris office of the consultants to re-examine my design because of larger financial implications. Their chief designer from Paris was asked to discuss the design at Ain Temouchent. I presented my design with calculations to justify it. He refused to accept it. After a long argument, I asked him, 'Please tell me where this design has been used? What is your experience in flood design?' He fumbled and said, 'It was of course used in the French river Seine.' This river had no comparison with any one of our major rivers. I asked how much discharge the river carried. He thought about it a lot and said that it was over 600 to 700 cumecs. I said that I had the experience of working in the Brahmaputra which carried a discharge of 98,000 cumecs! He was dumbstruck. He could not comprehend the enormity of the discharge the Brahmaputra carried although he knew about its ferocity. He slowly but clearly conceded that I had an unparalleled experience in river protection and that his proposal had to be approved.

There was a total silence. The local engineers of the consultants were initially adamant. They could not think of accepting the views of an Indian engineer. Mr Slaimia was the first to react. He said, 'We must thank and compliment Mr Jaruhar for his perseverance with his design. Due to this, we would save a considerable sum of money. It is obviously not in the interest of a contractor but he has shown a greater degree of professional integrity at the cost of his business interest.' This obviously turned the tide.

Naturally my acceptance grew a great deal in the SNTF. The consultants wanted load test of the bridge. I had used theodolites to measure the deflection of a 250-feet steel girder on Feeder Canal in Farakka. My work was also accepted and published in a technical journal. I used the same method for the Algerian 100-feet (30.50 M) girder too. The consultants accepted it because of its simplicity and accuracy. All bridges had identical span of thirty metres but they asked us to test all of them. In India one typical span is tested. Such tests of all the girders were uncalled for. The consultants wondered, 'Why are you protesting? You are being paid for it.' Ridiculous! We took our responsibility not merely as a commercial contractor but also as true professionals. That was enough. Mr Slaimia took a serious view. The services of the SOCOTEC were dispensed with. They accepted my technical advice which was more practical. We were happy and for once Mr Ramakrishna also acknowledged the way I had handled the affairs of the contract!

PROBLEM-SOLVING IN CONTRACT WITH THE ASSOCIATES

Associates Contracts were running in with serious problems. The IRCON had made a back-to-back contract with the Associates. Soon after the award of contract to the IRCON, the SNTF faced serious financial problems in 1985, forcing them to withhold the work and to suspend the contract. The work recommenced in 1986 on the basis of the original contract conditions with a mere extension in time. Factors like cost escalation, idle manpower and machinery cost were not flagged at the time of recommencement. There was no agreement on neutralization of cost escalation. Moreover, in order to expedite the completion of the work within a compressed timeframe, more plants and machinery were inducted. This increased the financial liability of the Associates. Other issues also cropped up in the course of execution of the work. Some of them were forced by the clients. They were clearly beyond the original scope of the work.

The IRCON was a commercial enterprise. Many of the issues could be clearly foreseen as having considerable cost implications and as a commercial enterprise, the project leaders should have flagged them, instead of overlooking them and just continuing with the work. The Associates were contracted on a bid cost, but they had a limited margin and this could not absorb the cost of such extra work without compensation. They were restless as work drew to a close. I prevailed upon Mr Rane to intervene. A committee was formed as suggested by us. I was appointed as its convener. All the associates were asked to file their claims which were examined in detail. The committee held the deliberations in Algiers to avoid interference. We finalized our recommendations in a week's time. I had planned to go to India for a week in February 1988. The report was completed and had a small preface written by me, which became much talked about. The preface was the icing on the cake. After signing off on the unanimous report, I left in the morning for Algiers with my family. The report was submitted to Mr Ramakrishna in the morning. As usual, he thought very little of it. He believed that a report prepared by the committee without seeking his guidance could not be anything but worthless. What disdain!

My experience of contract management had helped me find a possible solution. Quite clearly, the IRCON had in turn to agitate the SNTF for compensation against the justified claims. I had raised this issue in September/October 1987 during Mr Rane's visit to the site. I was ridiculed and told that claims in countries of Islamic belief were not even entertained. Paying of interest on bank deposits also was considered un-Islamic. 'You cannot get even a dollar. Credit will go to you, if you do', they said. But this was a challenge. I genuinely believed that my well-presented arguments would be acceptable in a civilized society. I had no experience of an international contract. So, there was no harm in trying. At that moment, however, I was in India where another misfortune was awaiting me.

YET ANOTHER MISFORTUNE STALKS

According to the plan, I was in Patna for a week. I was going to return alone to Algeria, three days ahead of Holi. I came to Delhi in the morning to catch the night flight. I got a message in the evening that I should return to Patna immediately as my wife had met with an accident. I reached Patna next morning by a night train. My wife was in a local nursing home. She had gone to the market in a rickshaw. While returning, her rickshaw was hit by another in the crowded street. She fell down along with Shrimant. Her knee was injured; it looked like a fracture. An x-ray was required, but it being Holi, everything was closed. The x-ray report taken the next day revealed a fracture. This would take at least two months to heal. The doctor put her on traction. It meant that she had to be nursed. I had to be with her. There was of course some small mercy! In a crowded street, a lady and a small boy lying on road, could have had it worse!

After about a month, Mr Rane called me. He requested me to come down to Delhi for a day. He wanted to discuss the Committee's Report on Associates' claims. Although it was difficult, I went by the morning flight. The MD complimented me on the high quality of the report. Most of the recommendations were acceptable with minor adjustments. He wanted some clarifications on a recommendation. He sent a telex message to Algeria on the excellent report of the committee. I felt happy for the members of the committee. The MD asked me when I could go back to Algeria. I told him, 'Sir, I have suffered too much and I have doubts about my usefulness'. He said that I need not worry about that because they had found out how useful I was. Well, once again, they had pinned on the services of a person who was on a long leave. There are usually many takers for a foreign project. After a couple of months, when my wife started moving a bit, I once again left for Algeria.

BACK TO ALGERIA

There was a lot of high praise on the report of the Committee on Associates' claims in Ain Temouchent. Even Mr Ramakrishna conceded that he was of course sceptical of the report in the beginning. But it was an excellent job with good technical and contractual reasoning to support the committee's recommendations. Naturally our stock had gone up.

The next logical step was to prefer claims on clients. I wanted to make a test case. So, I prepared the first case with great care, particularly the words appropriate to phrase the claim. This case was about a concreting item which was not a part of the original scope of the contract. The statement I made was this: 'We received your instruction for concreting in the fabrication yard. This work was of course technically essential. We carried out the work because of its urgency. But we find that the work is beyond the scope of the contract. We incurred an expenditure of "x" on this work according to the enclosed statement. Since no contract item provides for it, we request you to reimburse our expenses in carrying out the work.'

I sat down with the French translator to carefully select the words in French to convey the exact meaning of the text in the original English draft. The letter, as soon as it was delivered, caused big commotion in the SNTF office. Mr Slaimia came running down waving the letter. Mr Ramakrishna disappeared from the rear exit when he saw him. Mr Slaimia shouted at me, asking how I had dared to lodge a claim. I asked him to calm down and take a seat. He would not and was plainly furious. He said that I should have known that no claim was admissible in this country.

I took the letter from him and looked at it disinterestedly. I said, 'Oh, claim! You said. That is bad. But Mr Slaimia I cannot find the word "claim" in the letter. Can you show me because my French is really poor?' He took the letter back and read it once again. But he could not find any word that meant claim. He said that it was clearly to that effect. I said, 'Come on, Mr Slaimia. That is not a claim. We have carried out this work, you know that. In fact, we do not find this work in the scope of the contract. Can you kindly point out under which scheduled item of the contract, this work is covered? We will charge the amount spent by us accordingly. We have submitted that the expenditure was incurred by the company on your instruction and on your behalf on an essential item. This expenditure can be reimbursed by you, if you wish. If you do not wish to do that, you can forget about this. Because of our good relations, we considered it appropriate to bring this to your notice. There is no need to be agitated, Mr Slaimia.'

Immediately, he was quiet and pensive. He slowly said, 'Mr Jaruhar, as I now think deeply on it, I am obliged to you. We would not have known about it otherwise. We are actually in debt now because you have spent the money for our work and on our behalf. You know that in Islam, it is the duty of a son to repay even his father's debt. A debt has to be paid by the son if his father cannot repay it in his lifetime. We must find a way of reimbursing you. It is my responsibility, Mr Jaruhar, and I thank you very much.' The man was thundering when he came, but was apologetic and left like a lamb. Thus, the jinx was broken because he said that if I had anything else like that, I should let him know.

Mr Ramakrishna came back later. He was apprehensive. He asked others about what had actually happened when Mr Slaimia came into the office. He told the others that he had to leave the office to avoid a scene. He had told everyone else that I must have received an earful. I told him about what had happened in detail. I told him that Mr Slaimia had after all agreed in principle with our submission. Mr Ramakrishna was dumbstruck and looked incredulously at me—not believing in what I was telling him.

I had believed that any person in the modern-day would sincerely wish to pay back what one owed. The only problem was that it was an issue related to religious belief. We were able to overcome the emotional issue by not making a demand. It was a gentle submission to the person, noting that he owed the amount to us. It was certainly a great credit to Mr Slaimia. Like a good and progressive friend, he seized upon the real import of our submission. It had turned out to be a 'win-win' situation by the grace of God. This issue had made all the others sceptical about my approach. The director (works) ran away through the rear door to avoid a confrontation!

I BECOME THE TEAM LEADER—DIRECTOR (WORKS)

Mr Slaimia agreed to settle the dues of the IRCON after the line was formally commissioned. Well that was quite reasonable. According to the contract, the line had to be commissioned and handed over to the SNTF in two stages. In the first stage known as temporary handing over, the SNTF would operate the line and IRCON would have to maintain it for a year. After one year, the defects, if any, had to be rectified and then permanently handed over to the SNTF. Thus, on 4 May 1988—the date of completion—a temporary handing over was to put into effect. The SNTF had in course of time issued FNC (*Fiche' de non-conformity*'—list of deficiencies). According to the procedure, they had to be replied to after rectification and accepted by the SNTF. They were particular about the documentation. Mr Slaimia did not agree to temporary handing over the line on this account. The date of completion had ended and gone by. Mr Slaimia was unhappy with Mr Ramakrishna and had told me that the line would not be taken over as long as he was there. There was a provision of penalty in the contract, if it were to go beyond the date of temporary handing over. The Associates requested Mr Rane, the MD, to replace Mr Ramakrishna. Mr Rane wanted me to take over. I insisted that he should seek Mr Slaimia's consent also. I told Mr Slaimia separately, 'I will not take over as the DW if you insist on slamming the penalty for delayed handing over. That would bring me a bad name.' He told me that all problems would be resolved if I became the DW. He also said this to Mr Rane. Mr Ramakrishna thus left Algeria and I finally took command over the project.

There were problems galore. Director Finance Mr Barua had told us that he would be satisfied with a profit of even one dollar. The temporary hand-over was of utmost importance to stop the clicking of the penalty clock. The accrued penalty had to be waived off thereafter. The financial closure of the project, including settlement of Associates' accounts, was the next step. After a year's maintenance, the line had to be finally handed over.

All machinery and plants were brought to Algeria under temporary import without the payment of custom duty. That meant that all the imported machinery had to be re-exported out of the country; this undertaking was covered by bank guarantee (BG) of over 10 million dinars. If the IRCON failed to ship out, the BG could be encashed. Besides there were other issues whose implications were not clear. That is the one reason why I always hold that financial closure of a project is as important as the physical completion. Without this, the entire profitability of an enterprise can be in serious jeopardy.

CONTRACTUAL AND FINANCIAL ISSUES

I related to Mr Rane the full account of all the pending issues that had the potential to sink the company. He could not believe how the senior project heads had compromised the interests of a commercial enterprise. Mr Ramakrishna would often say that he had come here only to physically complete the work and that the financial aspect was not his concern. In all fairness, the higher-ups in the corporate office could also not be absolved of the responsibility because they had failed to appreciate the seriousness of contractual glitches.

I now had full authority to haul the company out of this mess. With a prayer to God, I moved to address them. In the beginning, many were sceptical of my powers. They tried to intercede with Mr Rane directly by taking advantage of their proximity with him. But thanks to Mr Rane, he never encouraged such attempts. As a result, my position was consolidated and I could act with confidence. Thankfully, results were favourable and I came out as the undisputed leader.

Temporary handing over without penalty

All the old FNC which were not complied with were collected and reconciled with the SNTF. Associates' engineers were asked to liaise with the SNTF engineers and all the reported deficiencies were checked again. All corrective actions were taken, as necessary. Many of them were already complied with, but were not reported. A report with the full disclosure of the deficiencies cited in the FNC was prepared after reconciliation with the SNTF. They were asked to inspect the line again. Because of an improved rapport with Slaimia, there was no problem and the temporary hand-over of the line was completed in an impressive ceremony. All the accrued penalty of over a month was also fully waived. Mr Rane was extremely happy and profusely commended and congratulated me and my team. This happened within three weeks of my taking over as the DW. It was a feather in our cap. Without this, there would have been nothing to write back home.

Claim and export of plants

The Associates' accounts had to be settled before all the engineers concerned were repatriated. This was however linked with proposals the IRCON had submitted to the SNTF for reimbursement. I requested Mr Slaimia to expedite their disposal. On my suggestion, he appointed a committee to discuss all the bills with our engineers. Fortunately, it went off smoothly. In a month's time, all the outstanding issues were settled. The IRCON was finally paid over ten million US dollars (contract value was ninety-five million US dollars), as reimbursement. This was a landmark achievement and beyond anybody's wildest imagination. This completely changed the balance sheet of the IRCON as well as those of the Associates. There were savings for the SNTF also. They were thus equally happy with the settlement.

The shipment of equipment was a serious and knotty issue. There were several BGs taken to cover the import duty to be paid in the case that the equipment imported for the project were not shipped out. Under one BG, 6 or 7 equipment were covered. Unless each one of them was shipped out that particular BG could not be released. Some machines had become junk. Though it was foolish to export them to India but failure to do that was costlier. Obviously, it was a policy mistake.

We went about it in a methodical manner. We fixed a shipping agency and a custom clearing agent to take care of multiple documentations. All the doubts of custom officers were cleared by a thorough interaction. Thus, when the ship called on port, the equipment did not have to wait long for custom clearance. The shipment was smooth. Our success in actual export of these equipment raised our credibility with the banks and custom authorities. It served us in good stead while dealing with other outstanding issues with Algerian authorities. All the bank guarantees were finally released. It was another sigh of relief because many in the corporate office had grave doubts about the issue. When it was done the prophets of doom did not know where to look!

SOCIAL SECURITY BREACH—PENALTY

But they did not have to wait for too long. Social security laws in Algeria are enforced strictly. The government has undertaken the responsibility to cover all persons against any misfortune be it a calamity or simple healthcare issues including unemployment. The social security department CASORAN looked after such affairs. All the employees had to be registered with this department. Every employer had to deposit a prescribed sum for this purpose.

Serious breach of social security

The IRCON had defaulted payment of insurance fee for almost a year. This related to the period when the contract was suspended during 1984-85. This was not taken seriously in the beginning by CASORAN. Notices issued by them were replied to in a routine manner. They served their final notice just when I took over as the DW. Unfortunately, it was also replied to without much thought.

The department issued a penalty order of four million dinars—mercifully no prosecution against the company's head was launched. It was a big shock. Legal experts and social law consultants advised us to appeal on the grounds that the outstanding fee had already been paid. In our earlier representations, the same grounds were cited but it was not obviously accepted by them. The Appellate Authority promptly rejected the appeal. Our last chance was to go to the National Appellate Board. This board sat once in a quarter. We were told that the Board seldom reversed the order of Appellate Authority. We had about three months to appeal and decided what our appeal should be after proper study and wider consultation.

I wanted to meet the CASORAN chief who was also a member of the National Appellate Board. He was passing by Ain Temouchent. I invited him for a cup of coffee which he accepted. I talked about the project and particularly about many difficulties and challenges faced during execution. I also highlighted how we earned savings for the SNTF by introducing good engineering practices. It was emphasized how the company was more particular about professional integrity while effecting cost cuts rather than its own turnover. He was impressed.

While discussing the penalty issue, he underlined how a serious view was taken against any default in payment. In CASORAN, there was an impression that foreign companies often overlooked employees' welfare and hence, serious view was taken of a defaulting. I politely pointed out, 'I don't know about other companies but for us it was a solemn mission under South-South Cooperation to complete the work in time with utmost professional integrity. Tell me where was the reason for us to volunteer and suggest cutting down unwarranted costs in the project and thus suffering a loss in turnover for the company? When Algeria went through financial constraints in 1984-85, the company poured eight million US dollars to keep the work going. No other foreign enterprise would have done so. They would have packed off and filed claims in the International Court of Arbitrators. The IRCON failed to pay its dues during this period when it carried on with the work with its own money without waiting for payment from the SNTF. This was the reason for delay. There was no intentional default on employees' welfare.' He was impressed with my submission as they had not known about the background. He advised me to appeal to the National Appellate Board in this context.

It was thus clear from the meeting that the Appellate Board suspected that all foreign enterprises deliberately defaulted on payment and that welfare of their employees was not their priority. They were governed by commercial interests. We decided that our appeal should convince them that we were different in this respect. We wanted to convey that the default was unintentional and was forced by a situation where the Algerian client was unable to pay to the IRCON. To highlight this point we wanted to say how the company had carried out the work without receiving any money from the clients, who were suffering from the financial crunch. It was totally unheard of in any international contract. The ultimate proof of the best intention and bona fides of the company lay in the fact that it had injected eight million US dollars of its own money into the project! No foreign company would have done that.

Mr Slaimia strongly supported our case. The SNTF endorsed that the company had demonstrated a high degree of professionalism in their work and were not governed purely by commercial interests. Because of our support, the SNTF indeed affected considerable savings at the expense of the company's turnover. They arranged for eight million US dollars to tide over the financial constraints Algeria faced during 1984-85. It was unprecedented and demonstrated their friendly disposition. They looked after their employees' welfare.

We similarly briefed other Appellate Board members. It created a positive image for the company. Thus, the National Appellate Board had a fair understanding of us. The Board eventually upheld our appeal. They just cautioned us while waiving off the entire penalty of four million dinars (0.67 million USD)! There was a great sigh of relief. Mr Rane could not believe this. I thanked Slaimia for his support. The case had seemed hopeless. No foreign company was ever let off without a punishment. This could have killed the company. Thank God! Nothing succeeds like success!

MINISTER'S AWARD AS APPRECIATION

When I had taken over as DW in July 1988, many issues had cast their pall of gloom. Without their satisfactory resolution, there was no hope of the company coming good. The top management had serious concerns about them. They were elated when the issues were resolved within a year. I was nominated for railway minister's award for the maximum foreign exchange earnings and excellent financial closure. Madhavrao Scindia handed over the medal and the award during the IRCON's Annual Day in Delhi on 28 May 1989. When I climbed to the dais to receive the award, he looked at me curiously. He asked me if he had seen me earlier. Mr Balachandran told him that I had also been the deputy CE at Tezpur. He was very happy to know that I was earning laurels elsewhere too.

Mr Rane began to tell others that they should learn how to prepare claim documents and file cases from me. He was not very impressed when I first joined the IRCON. But gradually he became my greatest supporter. Even after leaving the IRCON, we would meet quite often and talk of the good old days. May his soul rest in peace. The IRCON would never forget him for taking it to the great height it is today.

CONCLUDING MY TENURE WITH THE MESSAGE OF COOPERATION

The only remaining issue was the final hand-over of the project to the SNTF. Another small work was a concrete sleeper plant set up by the IRCON in Benisaf.

The concrete sleeper factory in Benisaf—a model of cooperation

This factory was designed to produce five hundred twin block concrete sleepers per day. The plant naturally had a large number of teething problems. We quickly resolved them to stabilize production. I insisted that the operation should be passed on to local Algerians after training them well. Once, the Algerian transport minister visited the plant. The production was around 540 sleepers. I told the minister that this plant continuously produced upward of five hundred sleepers under the management and control of Algerian workers and technicians. We completed the transfer with the plant, technology, training and assimilation of the knowledge. He could not believe it. He appreciated our attitude, lacking in other foreign agencies.

Track parameters were recorded by oscillograph car at hundred kmph before finally handing it over. The recording was superlative. The line was handed over to the SNTF in a brief and impressive ceremony.

I bid goodbye to Mr Slaimia

After a month or so, I finally left for London in September 1989, a final repatriation. That was end of my Algerian experience. I carried with me the profound love and affection of people. Mr Slaimia accompanied me to London. It was a very nice gesture. While parting he said that Algeria would never forget me and would be grateful to me. He still remains a very close friend. He continues to give me a bear hug whenever he comes to India. He even invited me to come to Algeria to do some work together once again. I cannot conclude the Algerian experience without saying a few words about Mr Slaimia. He was a person with a lot of energy and enthusiasm. He led the project with passion and emotion. I am also convinced that a project has to be owned and nurtured with unfettered emotion and one should not be shy of demonstrating it. Look at Mr Balachandran and Mr Slaimia and you will be easily convinced that they actually were in love with the project. I am myself a victim of this symptom and I do not mind it at all!

The Algerian experience was an excellent opportunity indeed. It was painful and trying but the compensation was enormous. This was my last official foreign trip. But I did not know that then. But it was most rewarding one. Thank you, Algeria!

8

BACK TO THE INDIAN RAILWAYS

STRUGGLE FOR POSTING

The Algerian experience was undoubtedly an exciting one. But I belonged to the Indian Railways. Mr Rane, while talking on the subject, had told me that I should seriously think on the subject of returning to the Indian Railways. He felt, 'Unless you have a good chance of becoming general manager and upwards, it is no good to return. You see, here you can be the managing director of IRCON one day if you opt for the IRCON.'

The IRCON is a contracting agency which drafted the IR officers for senior positions on a deputation basis. But the company wanted these officers to have the attitude of a contractor. After a service of over fifteen years, these officers normally acquired the warped mindset of government servants. Thus, they would normally conduct themselves like clients. This Algerian fiasco could clearly be traced back to this attitudinal problem. I had talked about this perspective which many find difficult to change. This had been a problem for me and more seriously for the organization. Mr Rane, however, was quite clear that I did not suffer from any such warp. I think it was an exception and it must be attributed to our deep involvement with the Brahmaputra Bridge. A contractor was treated as a subordinate and his interests were looked after. This in turn also forced similar change in the attitude of the contractor. I had, however, chosen to be a railway engineer. It was therefore my lot now. I had to render my services to the Indian Railways. With deep respect to Mr Rane, I returned to the Indian Railways from Algeria.

I had met Mr Prasad, ME, during the IRCON's annual day in May 1989 when I was in Delhi to receive an award from MR. He had told me, 'Please tell me when you come back. We will find a suitable posting, no problem.' He had become the chairman Railway Board in August 1989. I congratulated him by telex and mentioned that I would be back in September 1989. He assured me that the ME would look after my posting.

I was promoted to the senior administrative grade (SAG that is, CE) in

Algeria. I reported to E. Sreedharan, ME, on 29 September 1989. I had expected to be posted in a good railway. I however learnt that after a foreign posting, it was mandatory to undergo a cool-off period of service in a less popular railway like the Northeast Frontier Railway, the Eastern Railway, the South Eastern Railway or the North Eastern Railway. Even a posting in the RDSO Lucknow was considered unpopular. Mr Sreedharan wanted to post me to the RDSO. I was taken aback because I had established myself as a good construction engineer. I wondered what I would do in the RDSO. I had all along worked in the so-called unpopular Eastern region including almost eight years in NF Railway. It was unfair to categorize me with the others who had never seen the east during their career. But that did not cut any ice. The ME wanted good, practical engineers for the RDSO. I wanted a month's leave before I joined. He had of course no objection to that.

Mr Prasad welcomed me with a lot of warmth when I saw him. He had become a grandfather. He himself served me sweets on a plate. I was touched by his affection. After pleasantries, he asked me about my posting. I briefed him about the development. He smiled and said, 'So, you did not come to me first. You went to the ME because he is the boss.' I said, 'Sir, my approach to your room is only through the ME. I could not do otherwise.' He laughed and spoke to the ME on intercom: 'Sreedharan, I understand Jaruhar has met you. He did a wonderful job at Tezpur. As general manager, I had asked you to visit Tezpur but you could not. I understand that he is being posted to the RDSO. It would be a total waste. He should go to a good railway.' I was not aware of his response but eventually my posting order as director (research), the RDSO was issued. In spite of the strong recommendations from Mr Prasad, the RDSO was to be my destination. My leave had been sanctioned. I went to Patna to be with my family.

RDSO—RESEARCH IS MY NEXT CALL

I joined as director (research) on 3 November 1989 after a month. My re-induction to the Indian Railways came with some unpleasant experiences. Shravani was down with jaundice. As soon as she recovered, I left for Lucknow. She was due for her tenth standard Indian Certificate Secondary Board Examination. We had to therefore settle down quickly.

Well, there was hardly any priority or guideline for research work. I called for a briefing on the task at hand while meeting with my joint directors. After all, many projects for research and study were taken up. They had been running for over five years. We were not a classical research organization. I emphasized that we could not afford endless research. I told them that our emphasis had to be on trials or studies of a product before they were used in the railways. This was a major shift in the paradigm and it surprised many. Some even questioned my authority to change the priority. But nevertheless, projects were reviewed to shortlist them on the basis of their usefulness. The focus was on usefulness, practicability and simplicity of the result. I never bothered about the views of purists in the matter. As usual, I seemed to be getting away with a different approach. It was fine because I was convinced of what I was doing.

I SUFFER ANOTHER MISHAP

The Babri Masjid issue had become contentious at that time. The General Election was around the corner. The opposition party had united under the banner of the United Front led by V.P. Singh. The party came to power in November 1989. The scene was quite exciting. I remember, on a huge screen erected in Hazratganj, election results were displayed. Each result was followed by the loud burst of crackers. V.P. Singh was elected as the PM.

On 28 November 1989 I left for Calcutta by the *Punjab Mail*. I had to inspect track fittings on trial near Dhanbad after a meeting in Calcutta. I planned to go to Patna from there. A bungalow had already been allotted to me in the RDSO and my family had to move to Lucknow. My baggage had also arrived in Delhi from Algeria. My other household affects in Patna were moved by road.

We were the only two passengers in the first AC compartment. The train passed Sitarampur Junction station at about 4 a.m. There are four tracks beyond that to Howrah. Suddenly there was a big jerk. I found that I had fallen and was lying on the floor. I was not able to get up. There were shouts all around me. I knew there had been an accident. My co-passenger woke to see me lying on the floor. He asked why I was sleeping on the floor. After which, he turned over and went off to sleep again!

Three trains collide—a bizarre accident

I got up with great difficulty. I called the coach attendant who informed that the accident was serious and there were many casualties. I took the torch from him and came out in the dark. I asked Mr B.D. Kumar, my joint director travelling in the adjoining second AC coach, to join me. He had been hit in the forehead but was alright. In my coach an elderly gentleman had been hit as his luggage fell on him. He was in pain but the injury was not serious. I was horrified to see that three trains had collided in this accident!

A down cattle special goods train on down slow line had derailed first infringing on the down main line. The *Punjab Mail*, running at fast speed on the down main line, had hit the derailed cattle special wagons infringing on the down main line. After hitting the goods train, three coaches of our train capsized fouling the Up main line. A Up goods train coming at fast speed from the opposite direction, also derailed after being hit by the derailed coaches of the mail train. It was still dark as I moved along with the help of a torch. There was noise from all round me. The scene was unnerving indeed. The guard of the Up Goods train was asked to protect the line. Phone lines were damaged disrupting communication. The goods train engine was dispatched to the next station to inform about the accident. The GT road ran parallel and as the dawn broke, bus/truck drivers and villages came to our rescue. The injured passengers were taken to hospitals.

The accident relief train arrived after some time with divisional officers of Asansol. Mr Mitra, the DRM, knew me. As the senior-most railway officer at the site of accident, I briefed him about the action taken. He kept looking very intently at me while I spoke, he said, 'Jaruhar, you need immediate attention. I find blood coming out of your chest. Wait here in this coach while I ask some doctor to have a look at you.' I had not noticed my injury so far! I had some pain but I had attributed it to the injury sustained on falling from my berth. After examination, the doctor found my ribs were fractured. I requested the DRM to send me to Calcutta for further examination by an orthopaedic surgeon. He arranged for my travel to Howrah where someone took me to an orthopaedic hospital. Dr Ghosh, a renowned orthopaedic surgeon, confirmed that there was a fracture of three ribs. He said that it would take about three months to recover.

I walked out of the hospital with my rib cage strapped down with bandages. It was painful to even cough. I carried on with the normal work, but my movements were restricted. In Dhanbad, when my elder brother unaware of my condition came towards me for a bear hug I retreated but he would have none of that until I cried out in pain. On my return to Patna, Shrimant dashed for me. Well, that too, an uncalled-for tragedy!

Every railwayman is trained to attend to an accident

An accident involving three trains was unheard of and hence unique. Something surely had kept me driving even after I had been hurt. I recalled the lesson that I learnt in the Staff College, Vadodara, as a probationer, about the duty of railwaymen during an accident! The responsibility of a senior officer is very high in the case of an accident. Any dereliction of duty in case of an accident is unpardonable. The deep sense of duty and attachment is engrained in the body and soul of all railwaymen.

I was the first Railways' officer to reach the train accident site close to Tezpur where two passenger trains had a head-on collision. I organized a rescue operation with the help of the district administration. I never thought that I was in a construction organization. We set up a kitchen at the site for those engaged in restoration work. GM (open line) Mr Raghvan was pleasantly surprised and spoke about it to Mr Balachandran.

As an ME, I had to deal with a disciplinary case against a SAG officer, related to a *Rajdhani Express* accident near Gaya in October 2001. More than a hundred people had died in the accident. This officer had also travelled by the same train. Luckily, his coach was unaffected and nothing happened to him. But he just left the site and went home. By the time disciplinary proceedings were completed, he had retired. His pensionary benefits were withheld because of this case. He had appealed against the penalty. In his defence, he had submitted that he had been too dazed after the accident. He was unable to think of anything because of the trauma. Others had put him in a car and sent him home.

An incident like this would undoubtedly cause extreme trauma to a person. The ability to face such tragic events varied from person to person. The problem in his case was his credibility. Had he actually suffered such an extreme trauma? Could he not, despite the traumatic experience, attend to the accident? In spite of my rib cage being fractured, I performed my duties. Another person in that situation might not be able to do so. But in my view, this event adjudged the officer's ability to stand up to a difficult situation. In the annual confidential report (ACR) of an officer, there is a column which calls for the assessment of the reporting officer regarding the capacity of the reported officer to face an emergency situation. One could be accordingly graded because this is considered an important attribute, especially in case of an officer for senior and important assignments like DRM, GM, PHOD, etc. Unless, it was a case of gross dereliction, punishment of a person who has retired, did not seem necessary. I am not sure if others would agree with me. The case was disposed of with a reprimand. His pensionary benefits were restored to him.

WE MOVED OUT OF THE RDSO

Having moved our bag and baggage to Lucknow, we settled down quickly. Shreya and Shrimant had to go to school and their admission was arranged with some difficulty. For the first time, there was enough time to help the children in their studies. We were set for a long innings at the RDSO. A stay of 4 to 5 years was usual.

I am summoned by the ME for Gandak Bridge

George Fernandes was the railway minister in the new government. He decided to start the construction of a rail bridge over the Gandak River near Chitauni. The work was sanctioned long ago but was frozen because of financial constraints as well as technical problems.

This bridge would restore the old connection between Chitauni and Bagaha which was washed away in 1923. George Fernandes visited the site on 7 January 1990 to lay a new foundation stone. This time, the decision was to construct a rail-cum-road bridge. He was in Lucknow on 8 January 1990, where he discussed about a person who could execute the work. V.K. Agarwal, the DRM Lucknow, may have mentioned me, for he called me up to warn me about what could be my future assignment.

After a week, Mr Sreedharan called me from Guwahati. He told me that I was being posted as CE of the project. Mr Rangnath had possibly told him that only I could do the difficult work. I was asked to meet him in Delhi. I was quite upset. When I met him he straightaway asked me to go to Gorakhpur. I told him, 'Sir, I came to the RDSO only a month and half ago. I have arranged for admission of my children in Lucknow at considerable expense. I am not interested in this transfer.' He told me that the Gorakhpur posting was non-negotiable.

I was immediately relieved and asked to join at Gorakhpur. My family had left for Patna. I reached Patna on the morning of 20 January 1990. My sojourn in the RDSO was hardly sixty days. The shortest tenure record of forty days was held by Mr Balachandran. I was the silver medallist. I was left feeling very unpleasant. I had never been forced like this earlier. I felt that I was being penalized for being good. Some senior mechanical engineer friends like Massihuzamman and Anirudh Mittal were rather surprised. 'Why was an acclaimed engineer like me not being looked after and groomed,' they asked. Well, it was a good thought but, in the end, one has to bear one's own cross!

9
THE GREAT RIVER GANDAK BECKONS

I left Lucknow—unsung and unwept—with a few of my belongings. Nobody had noticed my departure from the RDSO. My PA was very good and he took care of my household effects. After a day in Patna, I left for Gorakhpur from Hajipur side. I reached in the evening. Executive Engineer Sirtaj Prasad—an elderly gentleman—received me at the station. I was taken to the rest house. From there, I went and saw the GM, Gauri Shankar, a dynamic personality, whom I knew very well from my Brahmaputra days. He was happy to see me but he asked me to see CE (survey & construction, S&C). That was perhaps to ensure that I do not come to him directly. A gentle reminder, of course!

Unwanted chief engineer construction

There was not a word of welcome from CE (S&C) J.C. Gupta when I reported to him. He was having a telephonic conversation with a deputy CE for over half an hour. After that interminable phone conversation, he just asked his PA that a joining report should be taken from me. I was told subsequently that the ME had called for a meeting in the Board's office a day later. We were to leave for Delhi.

I had no time to see the site. I had a sketchy idea of the project from the records. Anyway, I accompanied all of them for the meeting. What an entourage! Led by the GM, the party consisted of CE (S&C), two CEs (C), including me, one deputy CE (planning & design), two chief draftsmen and other junior officials. I had never ever seen such a large contingent for a technical meeting. I as GM or ME would never allow officers to be accompanied by their subordinates. I believed that when an officer went for a meeting, he had to be prepared for it. He could, of course, take his subordinate for help. But he should wait in the anteroom and could be called only if necessary. Anyway, this was an important meeting and not many knew the subject, and so presence of others was perhaps understandable. Even I was only one day into the project.

BASIC PRINCIPLE OF RIVER TRAINING

My antenna raised on basic river training

Mr Sreedharan, ME, said that the work had to start immediately. The CE (S&C) told him that the tender for part construction of the approach bank was under finalization. My antenna was immediately raised. I told the ME that constructing a part of the bank inside a river was not possible and should never be done. Both the guide bundh and the two adjoining approach banks had to be done in one go. There was a loud protest. Mr Gupta said that his proposal was supported by model studies. He looked at me jeeringly and commented on my remarks, which were made without even seeing the site! I said, 'It is a basic principle of river training, and I need not visit a site for this. Model study may comment on hydraulic behaviour of a partly built structure. But it cannot say how the subsequently constructed portion of the bank can be joined with it. It is easy to visualize that the flood will scour the front head of the bank, leaving deep scour holes. It will be impossible to join this with the subsequently constructed work.' This was just common sense and everyone in the room could visualize this. It had, thus, a profound impact. Mr Gupta was furious. He told the ME, 'Sir, he wants to overrule everything. No big contractor will ever come to work in the area.' I told him, 'I am confident that parties like Jai Prakash, HCC will participate, if I asked them. Otherwise, I will request the ME to intervene in the matter.' That was it.

Both the GM and the ME supported me. But the office of the CE (construction) was upset and antagonized. I had planned to go to the site directly after returning to Gorakhpur. Two deputy CEs were recently posted for the project. They were asked to meet me at the station. I worked on broad planning in the train. It was not difficult because I knew the subject like the back of my hand.

VISIT TO THE GREAT GANDAK SITE

I must give some background of the project, to enable readers to appreciate the nuances and complexities associated with it.

The Great Gandak and the project site

The Great Gandak, the major Himalayan tributary of the Ganga, is known as Narayani or Saligrami in Nepal. The origin of the river is in the central mountain basin of Nepal, known as Sapt Gandaki or the country of seven Gandaks. The seven tributaries that form the main stream of the river Great Gandak originate from this land. This basin is bounded by Dhaulagiri 8,209 metres (26,926 feet) high in the west and by Manna and Rasuagrahi in the east. The river assumes its name, the Great Gandak, after the confluence of the Kali Gandaki and Trishuli Ganga. Kali Gandaki has its source beyond the Himalayan range in Tibet. Trishuli Ganga rises north of Kathmandu beyond the Ladakali range.

The Great Gandak flows in the plains of India through a deep gorge near Tribeni (Valmikinagar). A barrage was constructed here in 1966 under Indo-Nepal cooperation. Part of the barrage is in Nepal and the rest is in Bihar. The river flows for a few kilometres westward beyond Tribeni, then southwards between Uttar Pradesh and Bihar. It flows through West Champaran and Saran districts of Bihar and finally joins the Ganga near Patna. Out of its total length of 580 km from the source to the outfall, it flows 45 km in UP, 274 km in Bihar and the rest in Nepal.

The Gandak Bridge that the British built

The Champaran district of Bihar has a large forest cover, whose rich agricultural and forest produce attracted British attention. Motihari is the district headquarters of Champaran. It has a prominent mention in the Indian history of freedom struggle. The British had exploited the agricultural and forest produce of the area. Mahatma Gandhi, after returning from his successful non-violence (satyagraha) experiment in South Africa, launched the famous non-violence struggle from Motihari against the atrocities committed by British landlords, who owned indigo plantations. His experiment was successful, and it became the main theme of the struggle for Indian Independence.

The British built a meter gauge railway line in 1912 that connects Motihari to Gorakhpur. The line, which had a meter gauge bridge on Gandak between Chitauni in Uttar Pradesh and Bagaha in Bihar, was meant to transport the agricultural and forest produce of the area. Gandak then hugged the left bank on Bagaha side. But in 1924, the river shifted to its right, on the Uttar Pradesh side. The bridge was eventually outflanked. The right guide bund, constructed in parts, gave way and the piers also collapsed. Since then, the communication lines between Bihar and Uttar Pradesh through Bagaha and Chitauni had remained disrupted.

Back then, station master of Chitauni was an Englishman. The bridge was washed away around 11:30 p.m. He had recorded a note in the station diary around 9.30 p.m. about how the river was attacking the bridge with full force. He had noted, 'The bridge is in imminent danger and all trains must be stopped.' This is the courage and commitment of a railwayman, the hallmark of all true railwaymen.

The demand for a new bridge

There was constant public demand to restore the link. This could not be done due to techno-economic considerations. Mr Fenton, a renowned hydraulic engineer, had said way back in 1949 that it was not possible to divert the river to flow through its original position under the bridge. The bridge thus could not be restored. There was no serious attempt thereafter to restore communication. Beyond the barrage, the river has a steep bed slope varying from rocky to boulder stage. About twenty-three kilometre upstream of the proposed bridge the river comes into an alluvial (or on plains) stage. The river generates high flow velocity due to the steep bed slope. After entering the alluvial stage, the river is braided (gets divided into more than one channel) and flows into several streams in a wide khadir (a khadir is total expanse or width over which a river with braided channels may flow. In actual practice the width could be much larger but the river can flow in any part depending upon hydrological conditions. For example, here the total width or Khadir was nearly nine km but the actual channel width of the river was about two km). The river near the proposed bridge location was nearly nine-km wide. The river oscillated between the left and right banks, and the process had been the cause of severe floods.

A major flood in 1971 caused extensive damage to the Nautar Chitauni area. K.L. Rao was then the Union irrigation minister. He was an eminent engineer. He inspected the flood damages. As an outcome of this, the Gandak High Level Committee (GHLC) was constituted. The committee submitted its report in May 1972. The committee recommended setting up of a number of control points in its report, to channelise the river into a central stream. They were long-term measures. The first control point (a control point is a set of structures through which the river is bound to flow) was recommended along cross section 47, about seven km downstream of Birbhar spur (a spur is a bank-like construction on a river bank to deflect the flow of the river away from the bank. It is thus a flood protection measure). This control point would consist of two guide bundhs with two connecting approach embankments to Uttar Pradesh and Bihar. Taking advantage of the control point, the Railways was persuaded to construct a bridge across the guide bundhs to restore the broken rail link between Bagaha and Chitauni. The committee felt that the project would have thus two objectives fulfilled—flood control and restoration of rail link. The project would be financially viable as the governments of Uttar Pradesh and Bihar as well as the Central Water Commission (CWC) could share the cost of the project. On this broad premise, the work was sanctioned by the Railways and the foundation stone was laid in 1977 by Prime Minister Indira Gandhi.

THE GREAT RIVER GANDAK BECKONS

But there were other technical problems which were not resolved. Except for constructing an eight-km link line from Bagaha to Valmikinagar on the Bihar side, no other work was undertaken. VCA Padmanabhan also visited the site. He found the river training work very difficult if not impossible. The work was practically shelved by the Railways. The Planning Commission appointed Mr Balachandran in 1987 as a one-man committee. According to his report, the bridge was desirable at the location, but it had too many technical snags to undertake the project. The Planning Commission in 1987 recommended shelving of the project.

CHITAUNI BAGAHA RAIL LINK PROJECT REVIVED

George Fernandes was elected as a member of Parliament from Muzaffarpur, which is close to Bagaha. In the course of the election campaign, he had promised to take up this project, if elected. That is how he had come to Chitauni in January 1990. Both the state governments agreed to share the additional cost for the road bridge in equal proportion. The work was taken up under 'urgency certificate'.

Two deputy CEs met me at Gorakhpur station as I arrived from Delhi. Ram Gopal was posted at Khadda and R. G. Singh at Bagaha. They had just been promoted but had no organization of any sort with them. We immediately moved to the site about ninety km away from Gorakhpur. They had no experience in major construction work let alone river training works. I of course did not consider this as a handicap but rather as advantageous. Broad design parameters had to be fixed. Detailed hydrological survey and field survey was also required.

An awesome site—we take a plunge

The site was awe-inspiring. More than eight km wide, the other end of the river bank was not visible. We walked across the bed by trying to keep ourselves as close to the alignment..

Imagine, nothing had been done to fix up the alignment so far. There were no hydraulic data on water level, water current and discharge in various channels. This was the basic distinction between a construction and a flood control engineer. The construction engineer was more concerned about the particulars of dry weather discharge in contrast to the flood control engineer who was concerned about flood discharge. Dry weather discharge gave valuable guidance about the construction technique to be adopted. As we walked along the bed, I explained all this to my deputy chief engineers. Walking on sand is very difficult and strenuous. So, we had to take short breaks. With the help of boats, we crossed two main channels. We could reach the other side of the river by 3 p.m.

Bagaha end was in the Madanpur reserve forest which boasted of tigers. More than tigers, the place was infamous for dacoits who kidnapped people for ransom. This threat was more potent than tigers. I never saw a tiger in the five years I spent on the project. I, of course, saw groups of dacoits with whom we had ample interactions.

The winter sun was setting for the day. Everyone was anxious to get out of the forest as quickly as possible. There is a famous temple of Goddess Narayani in the forest. Even dacoits regularly worshipped Her. So, we thought we were quite safe. We prayed to Mother to seek Her blessings. The Gandak, in the old days, hugged the bank near the temple. After the prayer, we left by jeep for Valmikinagar Barrage guest house. After crossing the forest, everyone was relieved. I was not aware of the lurking danger but my other colleagues knew better and were naturally more apprehensive.

Even though it was quite dark, the sight of Valmikinagar was magnificent. It was a moonlit night. The Great Gandak flowing in a deep gorge was a sheer delight. The guesthouse of the Bihar Irrigation Department was on one side and the western bank was in Nepal. Those days it was very famous for imported goods.

We were tired but while the dinner was being prepared, we finalized the initial programme for the project. Next day after breakfast, we returned to Gorakhpur via the western canal travelling through Nepal and a part in Uttar Pradesh. The journey was very educative and we had a fairly good idea of the entire project.

THE PROJECT MOVED FORWARD

The immediate necessity was to shift my personal effects from Lucknow and to get all the three children admitted to suitable schools. I was given a suite in the officers' rest house. It had a garage so my household effects were dumped there. Luckily, both Shrimant and Shreya got admitted to Carmel Convent School. Shravani, after her Indian School Certificate examination, where she performed impressively, was admitted to Kendriya Vidyalaya in Class 11. I also got a regular house by June 1990 which enabled us to settle down quickly.

We face hostilities bravely

The office was beset with problems and handicaps. It was clear after a while that I was not welcome in the organization. J.C. Gupta once candidly admitted that the Railway Board had insulted them by not trusting them and posting a rank outsider like me. He was rude and arrogant; an abrasive person. He minced no words in showing his mistrust and disdain for me.

It was clear that unless I had at least one trustworthy person to look after design and tender, I would soon be crippled. So, I requested the ME to post J.P. Das, who has an AEN at that time. He had worked with me in Tezpur and was technically sound. He was on deputation to the IRCON in Nepal. He was immediately pulled out and posted under me. He protested against the transfer. But when he found that he was being posted under me, he had no reservations. The ME was aware of the power politics in Gorakhpur. He therefore suggested that I could be made independent of CE (S&C). I knew it would not work. I told him that it was my job to work in the organization and still deliver. I could not survive as an independent entity. He informed me that a CAO was being posted soon. I would not have to suffer the hassle every day thereafter. Ramesh Chandra joined as the first CAO. He was a nice person. He was a batchmate of Mr Gupta but totally different in disposition. It made things much better.

The second biggest problem was a plethora of reports and studies carried out by different agencies over the last fifteen years. Many reports contradicted each other. Many believed that a hydraulic structure could be designed by model studies alone. Such studies were only indicative of the hydraulic behaviour of the structure. The designer has to take into account factors like bed layout, lean period discharge, time available for construction and a possible methodology. These factors would actually govern the design. From theoretical considerations, a bridge of 1,500 metres would have been adequate in the Brahmaputra. But it was not possible to construct such a bridge. On the basis of these essential factors, a three-km long bridge had to be constructed.

Pritam Singh chairs the technical advisory group

It would not have been administratively possible for me to ride over old recommendations all by myself. On my suggestion, a technical advisory group (TAG) was formed by the ME to finalize all design parameters for the bridge. The project cost would be shared by Uttar Pradesh, Bihar, the CWC and the Railways. It was therefore prudent to draw experts from all of them in the TAG, so that the technical features and adequacy could be open to examination by the co-sharers of the project.

The composition of the TAG was important. We decided to induct persons who had practical experience besides exposure in design. It was difficult, but we could form a good TAG. I personally requested Pritam Singh, the former chairman of the CWC, to chair the group. He was also the chairman of the TAG for the Brahmaputra Bridge. He knew me very well and was respected by all. He agreed to my request. He deserves all the credit for a very good job, despite his age.

Immediately after the first site visit, a gauge was set up for recording daily water levels. It provided crucial data for many important technical decisions. We decided to set up a base line on either side to fix the bridge alignment. This work was entrusted to the Survey of India.

Nobody in the North Eastern Railway (NER) had heard of astronomical survey to fix alignment and to set up base line. Jokes were shared about me when someone wanted to know the progress of the work. Mr Gupta would say, 'Arrey! The bridge expert is measuring waves of the river (referring to setting up of water gauge to take water levels) at present. He is also looking at stars and counting them (reference to astronomical survey). Only when he has finished counting the waves and the stars can he perhaps start any construction activity.' I once confronted him and asked how he would fix pier locations over a stretch of more than eight km without geodetic survey. How could he fix the low water level for fixing the foundation level—bottom of well cap or the bottom of stone apron? He had no answer because he did not know.

A DISASTER STALLED—WIN POWERFUL SUPPORT

Without my knowledge, the CE (S&C) accepted the tender for the construction of one km of approach bank. I was not consulted about this although it was discussed in the ME's room in our first meeting. I came to know about it after the tender had been accepted. I immediately met the ME in Delhi. I explained once again how the bridge could not be constructed at that location after this work was done. The river would attack the mole head forming deep scour holes. Joining old and new work would become impossible. It would meet the same fate as the old Chitauni Bridge had. The logic was irrefutable. The ME asked Mr Gupta on the phone, 'Why did you finalize the tender? It was decided not to take up the work during an earlier meeting. Why was Jaruhar not consulted?' The ME asked him to withdraw the letter of acceptance forthwith. Fortunately, the letter had not been issued (it was under vetting by Finance) and hence it was cancelled. But as a result, I earned everyone's wrath.

We win support amongst people due to our clean image

My well-wishers had already warned me about mafia activities in Gorakhpur. This tender for about ₹3 crore was being awarded to a company owned by a renowned legislator, Ganesh Shankar Pandey. Whatever his reputation, he was extremely pleasant to me.

As a legislator, he had also been campaigning for the construction of the bridge. I explained to him that it would never be possible to construct the bridge if the work was executed. I gave the simple example of Birbhur Spur. It had been done in an exactly similar manner. He quickly understood. I informed him that there would be enough tenders which he could bid for. Construction of the bridge would give him political mileage. He admitted that he was actually misinformed. He had also come to know of my clean image. He told me, 'It is also my duty to ensure construction of the bridge. It is my duty to support a person enjoying sound technical expertise and a clean reputation. Most of the engineers here are after earning money only. I know how to deal with them.' From that day, I earned a good friend and a well-wisher who was truly strong.

Some goons manhandled the CE (S&C) at his residence, when he had gone for lunch. It was not difficult to guess the reason and the people behind the assault. Many had anticipated a similar fate for me, but I received a respectful treatment instead. J.C. Gupta, having great experience of the area, had boasted of his networking with the mafia. He had projected himself as the only one to get such a massive work done. He was instead humiliated and assaulted. With God's blessings, sincerity, hard work and honesty were rewarded. I got recognition that I sorely needed, to establish myself.

The shadow of mafia influence was indeed real. One could not bid for a railway contract without taking approval from the group. Hari Shankar Tiwari and Ganesh Pandey, both MLAs, had a lot of clout. In such prevailing circumstances, the fact that we could operate without any real interference from them, is sheer good luck. There used to be an annual sports event organized by them in which all senior officers, including those in the District Administration, Judiciary were invited. All those who were invited had to go including the GM. I was also invited and I was wondering what I should do because it was a private affair. My colleagues told me that there was no option but to mark your attendance because it was a measure to demonstrate their hold on the beaurocracy and on all those who mattered. But I got a telephone call from Pandey ji that it was not necessary for me to go. That was great, and it was thus also a demonstration of the fact that I was in a different class.

BOULDER TRANSPORT BY RAIL ON PUBLIC TARIFF

Large quantities of boulders were required for protection work on the left and right banks. At least 80 per cent of the total requirement had to be collected in advance before the actual work could start. We inspected and surveyed all quarries in terms of their yield and their lead from the two banks. Out of five lakh cubic metres (CUM) of boulders, two lakh CUM were required for the Bagaha end and three lakh CUM at the Chitauni end.

For the Bagaha end, boulders had to come from Jamalpur quarries with a lead of over three hundred km. We examined both rail and road options for the transport. Rail transport turned out to be the cheapest option. But this required BG/MG transhipment. Garhara was the natural transhipment yard but its capacity was not adequate. It was also not advisable to depend upon a single point. Kaparpura near Kanti, a station away from Muzaffarpur, was therefore selected as another point for transhipment. Kanti has a big thermal power station served by the BG line. The metre gauge haul from Kaparpura to Bagaha/Valmikinagar Road station was smaller. This would improve the turnaround of metre gauge stocks—an important consideration.

Likewise, for Chitauni, the Mirzapur quarries on the Northern Railway trunk route of the Allahabad division were the main source. Mirzapur, Manduadih and Varanasi city stations were selected as multiple loading points on the MG route. We also located Gorakhpur Cantt on BG for meter gauge transhipment.

We enlist support of the traffic department

I was warned that the rail route would never materialize and therefore road transport was the only dependable option. I knew that this was a risky business but I had a very good ally in Mr Kedia, the CFTM (chief freight traffic manager). I accepted the offer of the CFTM to carry boulder on commercial tariff instead of the RMC (railway material consignment) applicable for transport of departmental material. The RMC rates were peanuts in comparison to commercial tariff. Kedia was immediately enthusiastic. My argument was that it was not strictly Railways' work. It was being funded by other government agencies as well. The GM jumped at the idea of four million tonne of additional revenue earning traffic accruing to the Railways. It was a big boost for the Railways and, as a result, the entire traffic department removed all obstacles in the way to ensure a smooth and free flowing operation. A more difficult job was, however, to finalize the boulder contracts.

BOULDER CONTRACTS HAD A PROBLEM—
WE OVERCOME THE NEXUS

Tenders were originally called for a supply of two lakh CUM boulders from Jamalpur. Tender files were put in front of me one evening, but they were gone the next day. The tender superintendent informed me that the files were called back by Mr Gupta. It came to the CAO's notice and eventually all files were back on my table. This further fuelled the hostility against us. Mr Gupta was sceptical of my ability to finalize complex tenders. No doubt, tenders were big and difficult, but I was confident of overcoming difficulties.

There were twelve offers. Considering their past performance and financial capability, no single party could supply two lakh CUM. The offered rates varied from ₹86 to 125 per CUM. I requested the Tender Committee members to visit Jamalpur quarry. It was unusual, but I insisted on it, so that the committee had a first-hand idea of the work. It would also explain the reasons for the wide variation in offered rates. The tender committee had a very good picture of the large quarry and could appreciate the reasons for the wide variation in rates. Every supplier has his own depot spread over a two km area of the quarry. Lead of different depots varied widely hence the wide variation in the rates. The committee also witnessed a live gunfight towards the end of inspection, confirming prevailing criminal activities in the area. The tender proceedings turned out to be a classical one where varying rates were justified. This was a topic of intense debate but the arguments were irrefutable and based on spot assessment. The case was investigated by many including the CBI. Finally, the decision was found to be pragmatic and transparent.

The supply for Chitauni had a complex problem. Our deputy CE, H.K. Singh, an extremely painstaking and methodical officer, carried out an intensive investigation on the Mirzapur quarry. Detailed data were very useful. The initially offered rates were very high. Even after one round of negotiation, the rate was around ₹300 per CUM as against our estimate of ₹150. All the tenderers were called for an informal discussion. We confronted them with our rate analysis. They soon discovered that our knowledge of the quarry was better than theirs. They therefore accepted our analysis with minor modifications like royalty payment, quarry road repair charges, octroi tax and some other contingent expenditure. All that added up to ₹165 per CUM. ₹2. 50 was offered to account for wastages, etc. The overall cost thus worked out to ₹167.50 per CUM way down from ₹300 per CUM. A great achievement! My senior colleague Mohan Lal, another veteran of the NER, had emphatically told me that ₹300 was very reasonable and we could not get a better deal. We had succeeded to the utter dismay of my colleagues and the prophets of doom. We were not only able to finalize tenders with considerable savings but we also proved them wrong once again. I was soon known as an astute babu who could calculate and reel off figures to silence opponents. My motto was this: either you convince me or you get convinced!

Lessons in tender negotiation

This is a lesson in negotiation. One should have all the detailed information and data before entering into a negotiation. An informal discussion beforehand is often useful. Negotiation with inadequate preparation is like flying a kite without the knowledge of it. In this case, the bidders gave up once they knew that we had all details.

I always treated the contractors as my subordinates, entitled to receive as much of consideration as was due with respect. This is a million dollars adage, known to pay rich dividends. We had a smooth passage through infamous, intense mafia activities in tenders. There was practically no interference; rather, we got a lot of respect. Our words carried weight, which surprised the old-timers. There is no doubt that moral values do exert a lot of influence on others.

PRAGMATIC DESIGN OF GUIDE BUNDH AND BRIDGE

The design of the bridge and protective works was another important issue. As I said, this project was being contemplated for a long time. The designs for the protective work were already prepared. According to this design, heavy concrete blocks and very thick boulder aprons were provided. The depth of foundation was much more—almost equal to the Brahmaputra Bridge, which carried a design discharge four times that of the Gandak.

On closer examination, we found that the results and data from the model studies were incorrectly interpreted. The design thus had to be revamped. Bridge spans were chosen based on theoretical application of Lacey's formula without considering feasibility of construction. According to the design, the guide bundh was located in a running channel. It would not be possible to build it in a running channel. Purely from the feasibility of construction, two more spans had to be added so that the guide bunds were located away from the running water. Concrete blocks were totally unsuitable on alluvium (sandy deposits—a major characterstic of Indo-Gangetic plain) deposits and was expensive. These changes had to be examined and approved by the TAG.

The TAG meeting was accordingly convened. The TAG was in total agreement with me. The design principles that were proposed were similar to Tezpur. Pritam Singh endorsed them as suitable to be adopted as a revised design. After site inspection, UPIRI, Roorkee was requested to test the revised span arrangement by adding two more spans. Model studies confirmed the suitability and feasibility of our proposal. But this was based on the present-day configuration of live and active channels, which could change after the floods just before the commencement of construction. The final span arrangement would therefore have to be determined by checking the configuration of the channels after the flood. Accordingly, we decided to hold the TAG meeting in October 1993, just after the flood and before actual commencement of work.

The design was accordingly finalized and it brought down the cost by over 30 per cent. It conformed to good engineering practices and was comparable to similar structures elsewhere. It gave us a lot of satisfaction. As usual, it gave rise to raised eyebrows and a hue and cry. How had, the earlier design, finalized after considerable deliberation by several technical committees, given up? But endorsement by the TAG was solid, well-deliberated and backed by experiences of past successful, similar structures. More importantly, its members had impeccable reputation. Detractors failed to get any takers. My decision to have a committee of renowned experts was thus vindicated.

There was a huge saving of more than ₹37 crore in an estimate of ₹166 crore. I never mentioned this fact anywhere, but my boss, CAO, Ramesh Chandra, took notice of this fact. He added this in my achievement in the annual confidential report for the year. He told me that I should have mentioned it myself. I thanked him. 'Sir, I was more worried about tackling criticism of our action to modify the old design. I did not wish to highlight it as an achievement lest it should serve to accentuate the criticism.'

FINANCING—A VERY CRUCIAL ISSUE

The financing of the project was the most crucial issue. Broadly, the project cost had three basic components—control point structures (guide bundh and two approach banks), rail bridge and road bridge.

According to the initial agreement, the cost of control point structures had to be shared equally among the governments of Uttar Pradesh, Bihar and the Ministry of Water Resources. The Railways had to bear the cost of the rail bridge. Uttar Pradesh and Bihar had to share the additional cost of the road bridge, in equal proportions.

Based on these broad principles, a draft MoU was prepared for acceptance by all the parties. It also laid down the schedule for the release of funds by them. All other stakeholders had suffered from a resource crunch and thus, although broadly agreeing, they found it difficult to release the funds. They approached the Planning Commission for fund allocation for this work under the State Plan. The Rail Budget was separate, so the Railways had no problem in providing the funds as per its share. The work thus continued with funds available from the Railways.

Funding was crucial

We vigorously pursued the funds from all participants of the project without success. The Railway Board decided in 1992 that it would not be prudent to spend the Railways' money alone, particularly in the absence of any commitment from other partners. We were asked not to enter into any fresh financial commitment in the project.

Narasimha Rao led a new government at the Centre. Y.P. Anand had joined as a new ME. He was earlier a CE in the North Eastern Railway and had then taken considerable interest in this project. He prided himself for walking across the alignment once. This feat was equalled by me. We sought his advice for our future course of action. He asked me to continue with the work. He said that the FC had issued those orders without considering its political implications. All the politicians interested in the project were told that work would stop unless the state governments paid their share of funds. This would have led to an adverse public reaction. Both state governments were thus prevailed upon to reconfirm their commitment. All of them had bowed down to intense lobbying, which not only reconfirmed their commitment, but also released ₹5 crore as part of their share. Accordingly, the restriction was formally withdrawn by the Board.

Y.P. ANAND—A GREAT MOVING FORCE

Mr Anand was a dynamic force in the project. He was totally convinced of the success of the project and echoed the people's aspirations. He asked us to continue till the Railways' share was available. He was sure that as soon as field work commenced other parties would be forced to give their share. He said, 'Underplay the cost as a strategy and tell a lie if necessary!'

Underplaying the cost was not possible. It would have been unethical and unprofessional. I suggested that we propose a change in the ratio of cost sharing for the approach bank. My logic behind the suggestion was that the Railways was, in any case, to construct the railway line. For constructing a road bridge, as decided subsequently, the cross section of the approach bank of railway line had to be suitably increased to accommodate the road. Hence, this additional work to provide a road bridge would incur an incremental cost, which state governments had to pay. This logic could be acceptable. Thus, the share of the two state governments would reduce with the corresponding rise in the Railways' share. He liked the suggestion. He praised and complimented me. Executive Director (works) K.P. Singh was with me. Mr Anand told K.P. Singh, 'The chap is brilliant.'

I redrafted the MoU accordingly. But I did not send the revised draft to the other participants. Mr Anand became the chairman of the Railway Board in due course. He was also member engineering of the Board. The FA&CAO in his monthly progress letter to the FC mentioned how the Railways' share had gone up. The FC brought this to the notice of Mr Anand with a request to check this aspect.

Mr Anand was upset. He called me and reprimanded me. I was taken aback and told him, 'Sir, please recall we had discussed this suggestion and you had actually appreciated my logic. You had complimented me.' But he ignored that and said, 'You have failed to look after the Railways' interest and should be sacked!' My God that was a limit crossed! K.P. Singh was a witness but he said nothing in my defence. Mr Anand was a simple person given to living and following the Gandhian way of life. I told him, 'I am sorry, if you do not believe me, you can sack me'. An embarrassed K.P. Singh intervened and took me away. He reminded me of an earlier incident where he had advised me to not counter Mr Anand back because it infuriated him.

On that occasion, Mr Anand had called me late in the evening in Gorakhpur. I was down with fever and alone in the house. He asked me why fieldwork could not start from November 1991. I explained that the guide bundh work could not start without boulders. The tender for the main work was also not finalized. He said that it could be done straight away. He said that he could not afford a CE whose only job was collecting boulders. That ticked me off. I had not come to do this project on my own but had been forced to. I replied, 'Sir, you can always do that. Since you consider me a bridge expert, I will not advise you to start the work without having at least 80 per cent of boulders at the site. This work is not a normal railway work but is being funded by three other participants. If boulders do not come, there is a chance of a catastrophe. Other participants will blame the Railways. Nobody will be able to defend the Railways' case. Please remember this.'

My response stunned him. He sent Mr Kumar, advisor (works), and K.P. Singh to Gorakhpur for a review. They were in absolute agreement with my assessment. Mr Kumar said, 'You do not know Mr Anand well. He would have got your point later on. But when contradicted, he is furious.' The team was amazed to see our arrangements for boulder transport. Their report convinced the ME completely. He would thereafter cite my arguments to justify why the work could not be taken up during 1991-92 seasons. I was amused. He subsequently praised me on my planning.

The issue related to the revised MoU was quickly settled. He was happy and claimed credit for correcting the MoU. Well, I did not mind as his support was most crucial. The project, without any doubt, could go ahead only because of his support. These pinpricks were like a few grey spots in a person's make up. He appreciated me and I remember him with reverence. At least, it was much better than my interactions with Mr Sreedharan. I was asked to send a bar chart for the project. According to my estimate, the project would take five years to complete. The bar chart was accordingly submitted.

I had told the GM, Mr Gauri Shankar, who had also agreed with me. The bar chart approved by the Board was, however, totally different—showing completion time as three years. I had neither opened nor had I seen the chart. I had not expected it to be different from what I had submitted. Mr Shankar pointed this out. I saw the Board's chart then. It showed even a well foundation during flood! I told Mr Salelkar, EDW, that it was impractical. 'Do not worry. Work according to your chart. The ME has prepared this just to show MR,' he said.

I told him that if a plan was approved by the Board, it had to be followed. Otherwise, even if the work was completed as per a practical schedule it would be seen as one and a half year behind the approved schedule based on impractical assumptions. I returned the approved plan back to the Board, insisting upon them to approve my plan and I continued to work accordingly. There was no murmur from the Board thereafter. After retirement, Mr Sreedharan became MD, Konkan Railway Corporation Limited (KRCL). George Fernandes became more interested in the Konkan Railway. His interest in the Gandak Project had gradually waned. Under the circumstances, the project moved only because of Y.P. Anand. Locally, the GM, Mr Bhatnagar, who succeeded Gauri Shankar, did not favour the project. Left to himself, he would have wound up the work.

MAIN TENDERS ARE FINALIZED

We had all the details available from the Tezpur Bridge tender documents, which were prepared by me. So, the documents were finalized without any delay. I spoke to all the leading contractors whom I knew personally inviting them to participate in the tendering process. They responded and four top contractors were prequalified. My detractors were sceptical about it. Although it looked presumptuous to claim before the ME that they would come only because of me, it proved to be true, which in turn boosted my reputation. Surely, God had answered my wishes.

The first ever prebid conference to evolve consensus

Tender documents were well-drawn and tested. The contractors were quite happy with them. Nevertheless, I invited them to Gorakhpur for a pre-bid discussion. We told them about the possible pitfalls. After that, they were conducted through the site by two deputy CEs. After the site visit, pre-bid conference was held for suggestions and clarification. The pre-bid conference was unheard of in those days and a lot of eyebrows were raised at it. The FA&CAO was also present to listen to the views of the bidders. Initial briefing was advantageous because it forced them to look at those aspects in particular. They could not afford to overlook them. Important points during the pre-bid conference were:

- The position of two abutments was not fixed. It would depend upon the actual configuration of the main channel. That meant that the length of the right or left approach bank could vary.
- Contractors would need a temporary bridge across the first channel to transport machinery to the guide bundh location.
- Boulders were to be issued by the Railways on the basis of stack measurements. After completing the actual pitching work, the quantity issued in stack and that which was used in the actual work was to be reconciled. Mechanism for this was explained.
- The area was prone to disturbance due to poor law and order, as well as mafia activities. They should work towards building plans of adequate contingency for this. Although measures to provide police security would be taken, the Railways' administration could not take any responsibility for this.

Although the entire work was divided into three separate tenders, it was essentially integrated—the impact of one affected the other two also. All work had to be done in a sequence, and therefore, everyone was asked to consider the job in its entirety and evaluate the risk factor judiciously, before bidding. It was well appreciated by all and encouraged them. Pre-bid conference was a new exercise. This concept enabled everyone to be aware of the likely pitfalls and constraints and their views, which would need to be considered by the clients. I am glad that it has now found wide acceptance.

With suitable clarifications and modifications after pre-bid conference, tenders for following three packages were called:

1. 1.5-km long elliptical right guide bundh and 3-km long right approach bank;
2. 1.5-km long elliptical left guide bundh and 5.14-km long left approach bank; and
3. Foundations and substructures of the main bridge (14 spans of 61 metre with 12-metre diameter circular well and 42 metres below the low water level).

Tenders were opened in January 1992. It was our intention to send recommendations to the tender committee latest by the first week of March so that tenders could be finalized by May/June 1992. That would provide us with three months to mobilize for the work. Work could thus start in October 1992 after the flood. I requested the tender committee members to finalize the recommendations within a week to avoid any kind of pressure. We worked overtime and sent recommendations of the tender committee through the GM in about ten days' time.

Eyebrows were raised during the tender committee proceedings

Many eyebrows were raised in the Board while examining the tender and its proceedings. There were several rounds of discussions which elicited various kinds of information. But it was clear: there was no adequate appreciation for the work of training of the Gandak River, or for the construction of the bridge, which had many special features. We could not convince them that there was no point in comparing this to an ordinary work. I was sure that if the officers from the Board would visit the site, they would be in a better position to appreciate the enormity of the work. I invited them to the site and I showed them how awesome the river looked. They were unable to see the other bank. Then they walked on the bed and travelled by boat. They saw the dense forest about which so much has been written and spoken. By the time we reached the other end it was dark. Executive Director Finance Mrs Banerjee, a nice lady, was plainly scared upon seeing the dense forest. The satellite picture of the river as it left Nepal totally convinced them of the enormity of the job. Subsequently, there was no problem. The Tender Committee proceedings were processed with speed and urgency. The documents contained elaborate analyses based on sound engineering practice and could be compared with what had been adopted for the Tezpur Bridge on the Brahmaputra. All technical parameters had the endorsement of the TAG comprising the best talents available in the country. With some minor modifications, tenders were finally accepted in June 1992. The recommendation for the road bridge was however not accepted because two state governments did not provide funds. It fitted our projected timeframe entirely.

ISSUES AFFECTING THE START OF THE WORK

Issues like funding, forestry clearance, land acquisition and security were vital before construction work could begin.

Funding by other participants was uncertain

The estimated project cost was ₹166 crore. Bihar's share was ₹26 crore while Uttar Pradesh had to provide ₹29 crore. Ministries of Water Resources and Railways' shares were ₹22 crore and ₹89 crore respectively. Despite our intense chase, the other three participants had paid only a nominal sum. The picture was disappointing. The Planning Commission was requested to take up the issue and a meeting was held to discuss it. All the three stakeholders had suffered from serious budgetary constraints. They did not have any provision for this work in their state plan. They wanted exclusive funds from the Central government. The Planning Commission agreed to assist them. Some funds thereafter were released by the state governments.

I was usually an unwelcome person in the state's secretariat. The state's principal secretary of water resources looked acutely embarrassed whenever I called upon them.

Lalu Prasad Yadav, the CM, called for a meeting on 26 March 1992 in Patna, to review railway projects in Bihar. He was critical of the pace of the other railway projects in Bihar but was defensive the moment I requested him to release funds for the project. Lalu ji asked the principal secretary, 'Dubey ji, why has the fund not been released? I have committed to the railway minister.' Mr Dubey told him that the file had been put up for his approval. Lalu ji was upset. He told him that he should have brought the file himself. The current financial year had only three more days so I requested him to expedite the release.

I told V.S. Dubey after the meeting that the fund release should now be easy. He smiled and said, 'Arrey! Jaruhar sahib, you are seeing this drama for the first time. For us it is not new. Anyway, your deputy can wait and see me tomorrow.' My deputy waited till 31 March, but there were no orders on file to release the fund. The file was returned on 1 April with the remark that due to constraints, funds cannot be released to the Railways. Mr Dubey informed me with a wry smile, 'Look I told you.'

The principal secretary of Uttar Pradesh continued to be apologetic. The Ministry of Water Resources said that they would release the funds only after the state governments had given their share. It was a humiliating experience but we persisted doggedly. We also mounted a lot of political pressure. I was once told by a peon in Lucknow that the secretary had left from the back door when I arrived at his office, saying that he had suddenly been called by the minister. But luckily, things somehow progressed. As the physical work started, all the participants began to feel a lot of pressure. In fact, someone told me that they were apprehensive that the Railways might abandon the work. They were surprised by our dogged persistence.

FORESTRY CLEARANCE FOR BAGAHA SIDE FOREST

On the Bagaha side, the alignment passed through the Madanpur reserve forest. A report on the environmental impact had to be prepared for forestry clearance, a complex process. Bihar's forest officers had serious reservations. They insisted on the identification of alternative land for afforestation before the case was processed. We also wanted permission for temporary stacking of boulders in the forest area. The district administration was however very co-operative under a dynamic DM, Krishnaiah. He swiftly processed all these. After the clearance from the forest department, the case had to go to the standing committee on environment for the recommendation of the transfer of forest land. Principal Secretary Forest Mr Subramanian was an enterprising man. He rode over the forest officers' objections and forwarded the case to the Union environment ministry with recommendations to transfer the land. Mr Dubey, principal secretary water resources, was a great force. Mr Subramanian held him in high esteem. He told Mr Subramanian, 'This project will change Bihar. Mr Jaruhar is a renowned engineer whose perseverance and sincerity is infectious. If we cannot help him with money, we can at least make his work as easy as possible.' Mr Subramanian while recommending the case to Delhi, told me that these forest officers were poor-sighted and could not see beyond the forest. He said, 'As long as I am here, I will ensure that you do not suffer. We will make it that much simpler. That will be our contribution.' Hats off! I told others that Mr Dubey and Mr Subramanian did not belong to Bihar but they were very keen that the state should benefit from the project. They often went out of their way. But in contrast, the officers from Bihar brought in all kinds of issues to bog down the project!

We got adequate support from the Central Environment Board. The local MP of Bagaha had spoken to the IG Forests in Delhi, an IPS officer from Bihar. He backed us with many valuable suggestions. We argued that the River Gandak attacked the forest every year and caused great damage to fauna and flora of the area. After the construction of the bridge, the wide river would be controlled to flow into a central channel. This would help in reclaiming about five km of forest land downstream which was swamped by the river. R.G. Singh, our able deputy CE argued the case superbly. It was due to his silent but persistent approach that the forestry clearance was obtained in time, from the Union environment ministry.

The State Forest Department had to issue the final order. The Railways had to deposit ₹4 crore as compensation. Again, the team of Mr Subramanian and Mr Dubey came to our rescue. I told Mr Dubey that the Bihar government was committed to pay over ₹15 crore. I suggested that Mr Subramanian and he agree to offset this sum against the state's share of the project. In a meeting between the two principal secretaries, Mr Subramanian accepted this arrangement on written assurance of Mr Dubey, which was put on the file. The entire issue was thus settled. Again, the two gentlemen went out of their way to resolve an issue. The forest officers' cried wolf, but Mr Subramanian silenced them with a curt remark: 'It was the decision of the government.' How the funds would be adjusted was his prerogative.

Most of the trees to be cut were teak, which unscrupulous elements wanted to exploit. I did not want my officers to be harassed by disgruntled elements in the forest department. I explained it to Mr Subramanian and requested that the DM should provide police protection during the felling of trees. Trees should be removed under the direct supervision of the police and forest officer. He did one step better. He inspected the area himself and requested the DM, Krishnaiah, to organize felling and accounting for the trees. This took the wind out of their sails. The felling was done smoothly and without any mishap. So, we were ready to take up the construction in the forest area in time.

LAND ACQUISITION IN THE BED OF RIVER GANDAK

Land acquisition proceeded smoothly and most of it was acquired in time. The central channel however shifted by a hundred metres towards Bagaha after the 1992 flood. The right abutment and guide bundh also had to be shifted accordingly. This called for acquisition of additional land immediately. A normal land acquisition process would have taken a long time. Hence, private negotiations were resorted to. Deputy CE H.K. Singh effectively managed it by rehabilitating two families.

This also called for additional acquisition on Bagaha side. R.G. Singh managed this with the assistance of district administration. Thus land acquisition, involving two states, may have bogged down the project easily. But the two dedicated deputy CEs with their team developed effective rapport with district administration at all levels, to speed up the process. I must give the team all the credit.

Great credit must be given to Mr Krishnaiah, IAS, the young DM who provided all the support and who had to be seen to be believed. I particularly salute him and may his soul rest in peace. He was brutally murdered while travelling on an official visit—in his official staff car!

THE SITE SECURITY—THE BIGGEST CHALLENGE

Security was a serious issue. The mafia in Gorakhpur had influence and interfered in all aspects of contracts. The construction of two guide bundhs and two approach banks involved over thirty lakh CUM of earthwork and five lakh CUM of boulders in one season of 160 days. The local mafia elements had a lot of clout in the area and had to be reckoned with.

It was a costly project involving heavy transactions of money. This interested dacoits who had the mafia's tacit support. They indulged in kidnapping for ransom. The threat of kidnapping of the project officials was thus potent. Such an incident would surely drive away contractors. This was the last thing I wished for in the course of the project!

The site was strategically located. On one side of river was Uttar Pradesh and Bihar on the other; Nepal was in the north. Bihar's side had thick forest cover and the Himalayan range was just twenty km away. Dacoits easily crossed over from one side to another, escaping the security. It was thus a serious issue.

We addressed the problem in a systematic manner. We enlisted the support of DC of Gorakhpur Mr Tolia and DC of Muzaffarpur Mr Biswas. I had a warm relationship with both of them. Both were well-informed. Mr Biswas had researched on the tribes known as Tharu, who had settled on Himalayan foothills on the Bihar side. The women of the tribe were mostly royal princesses from Rajasthan who after being persecuted by Mughals, had left Rajasthan with their male servants. In due course of time, they settled down in these forests and eventually married their servants. But they still commanded power over them. The women would eat first and after eating would touch the thali with their feet. The men would only eat after that. This was a matriarchal society.

Lalu ji quickly addresses the security concern

On my request, a sort of flag meeting was held at the site to draw the security drill. Proper co-ordination was the key. They decided to set up one more police check post on the Bagaha side. On the request of the Bihar side commissioner, I also raised the subject of security with the chief minister of Bihar, Lalu ji. The conversation was very interesting. Gopalgunj was Lalu ji's constituency where he had a great deal of clout. This is an adjoining district of West Champaran. Most of the operation was involved near Bettiah. This significant conversation between us was held in Patna in March 1992.

Myself: Sir, you will be glad to know that all arrangements have been made to start work on Bagaha-Chitauni Bridge this October (1992).

CM: This is very good news. We have been waiting for it for a long time.

Myself: Sir, we have organized everything, but there is a problem. Dacoits rule the area and I am afraid that even if a single person is kidnapped, no one would work. Everyone will run away.

CM: Dacoits! What are you talking about? Please tell them everyone would be shot dead.

Myself: Sir, the problem is very real. I have talked at all levels in the district administration. The senior superintendent of police and the DIG range say that they would do their best. But I thought it fit to bring it to your personal notice that without proper security protection, it will not be possible to do the work.

CM: What are you talking? I do not know since when these dacoits are operating. Please connect me to the director general of police (DGP). I must set it right.

His secretary tried to connect to the DGP, but he did not succeed as the DGP was out. There were no cell phones in those days. Then he asked for the IGP to be connected. When he came on the line, the CM spoke to him.

CM: 'Arrey! Listen. I have the Railways' chief engineer with me. He is in charge of Gandak Bridge. He says there are lots of dacoits in the Madanpur forest area. How come, I did not know about them? Anyway, you should shoot all of them. Hang a few by the tree so that people know that they are dead. Ok.'

Then he turned towards me and told me, 'Now, Chief Engineer Sahib, you become absolutely free from any worry on account of dacoits. Your people can work peacefully.'

So, he solved the problem in a phone call! My purpose was served in any case as I was determined to bring it to the personal notice of the CM. I knew that the government machinery had limitations. We had to find our own solution. But the official machinery had to be fully briefed, and they could not feign ignorance.

'MINI CHAMBAL'—A NOVEL APPROACH

It was my firm conviction that local stakeholders must be involved in the project. In this case, apart from others, the groups of dacoits also had a stake. The construction of the bridge was surely going to affect their lives. The economic deprivation of the area was the basic reason for this. Undoubtedly, dacoits also wished to have a piece of the cake of economic activity in the area. There was nothing wrong in their wish to share the wealth. But to snatch the piece of cake by force was not an acceptable modality. It is abhorred by any civilized society. We could not undertake to socially reform them. It was beyond our scope or domain. We, however, believed that the wealth should be shared. The group might be appropriately involved in this process in a right and civilized manner. It would at least give them a chance to correct their image. It was a gamble or a philosophy that we contemplated in strict confidence. We decided that we could perhaps try it.

A new philosophy and approach

We had a large number of detractors. They did not wish for us to succeed. So, we always maintained a low profile. Main contractors were taken into confidence. They were asked to offload smaller, non-critical work to such local parties. The idea was to trust them and give them a chance to perform. Once they had earned money in honest way, they would surely shun criminal activities. We were against payment of any 'hafta' or protection money. This was the basic presumption. Everyone wanted to earn their money in an honourable manner. The local subcontractor of guide bundh (Mr Salluddin) was a willing partner. He was the most interested party to ensure uninterrupted work.

This was the working hypothesis and strategy in our minds. We went ahead under the capable leadership of our deputy CE, R. G. Singh. I must give him full credit for bringing all the dreaded parties to a conference of a kind. He was able to convince them that this was the best way to earn honourable money and give up their criminal way of earning a livelihood. It turned out to be an attractive package.

The result was extremely encouraging. The contractors worked in peace without fear. It surprised our detractors. I travelled by jeep late at nights or during early hours through the jungle, not once but many times during the peak construction period. I also spent a night in the newly built rest house at Valmikinagar station, located inside the forest. Fortunately, I never came across a tiger or a dacoit, for which the Madanpur reserve forest was well known. I often walked on the alignment at night without any disturbance whatsoever. An area where none dared to set foot after sunset now provided a peaceful working atmosphere. In my view, we must salute the basic strength of human values, which can rise above everything else when addressed properly. In my humble ways, I also pay my deep respects to all those, who had worked behind the scene to bring about this remarkable transformation. I will talk about it later because now I must return to the actual construction of the bridge, which was a challenge because of its technical aspects as well as adverse external influence.

THE WORKING SEASON BEGINS IN OCTOBER 1992

Despite all odds, we were ready to take a plunge into the river just after the flood of 1992. Normally by the end of October, the barrage gates are closed and the eastern and western canals running through Bihar and Uttar Pradesh are opened. This brings down the river discharge considerably. It helps in the diversion of river channels and mobilization for construction work. The canals however were closed that year. Consequently, there was a high river discharge. Due to adequate rainfall in the command area that year, there was no demand for irrigation water. The irrigation department took this opportunity to close the canals and undertook their annual repair. Canals were planned to be opened by mid-January 1993. This had completely upset our plan. We could not wait until then because the time available after that would be inadequate to complete the work.

The river had three broad channels. Channel 1 was the closest to the right bank. Channel 2 was the main channel, located in the middle and roughly four km away from the right bank. Channel 3 was a small one near the left side. Apart from this, Rahua nala also crossed the alignment approximately two km from the left bank. Channel 3 and Rahua nala had a considerably smaller flow. But this channel could not be closed till harvesting was over in February or March. But it was possible to construct a temporary bridge across them to transport heavy earth-moving equipment to the left side.

The real problem was in Channel 1(it was in three parts, two of which were small, but the third one was quite big) which was one hundred metres from the right bank. It carried a considerable discharge of over 180-250 cumecs. Unless something was done, heavy machinery could not be taken to the central area to take up right guide bundh. Channel 2 had shifted eastward after the flood. A temporary pile bridge across Channel 1 was planned to transport the equipment to the main island. A temporary timber bridge would take a month. We did not take any chances and transported heavy equipment on a barge.

TAG VISITS THE SITE—REVIEW OF THE WORK STRATEGY

The TAG meeting was convened on 16 October 1992 at the site. The group saw the actual site conditions. The methodology proposed for construction was also explained. The left guide bundh was critically located. Its mole head was under water. It was impossible to construct the guide bundh under those conditions.

Two additional spans at the design stage were proposed exactly for such exigencies. The members saw huge discharge flowing through Channel 1, and thus they had serious doubts about closing of the channel. The real problem was about Channel 2, which was flowing with a high current over the area where the mole head of the left guide bundh would have come. The TAG took note of the problem, which ordinarily would need two additional spans. Pritam Singh was very humble after the inspection. He acknowledged that I was in an unenviable position. He said, 'I know Mr Jaruhar from the Brahmaputra. I have full trust in his ability. We must entrust this to his command and back up his decisions. I know that adding two or three more spans will be good, but I am confident that Mr Jaruhar will do without any additional spans. I shall personally be very happy, if he does so.'

The meeting of the TAG was over. I told my team that we were now on our own. I called for suggestions. Mr Venketraman, the president of the company (Continental Construction Limited) and an ex-CE of the Railways (a batchmate of Y.P. Anand, ME), suggested constructing a bundh right up to Birbhur spur. I told him that we were encountering problems in constructing a four-km bundh. How were we to construct a nine-km bundh (Birbhur spur was nine km away)? After that, there was no word from anyone. All of them agreed that they did not have any experience. Since I was the best person around, I was asked to take the lead.

RIVER TRAINING STRATEGY IS DEVISED

I told Mr Venketraman, 'Very well then. All of you should have faith in me and follow me because the methods I propose are rather inexpensive. But it calls for a war-like action. There may be a chance of a failure, but I am reasonably sure that with the blessings of Narayani, we will overcome all difficulties.'

This generated a lot of goodwill. My own team had a rock-like confidence in me. I would walk on islands along the channel looking for the best location to try the diversion. It was evident that unless the flow in Channel 1 was reduced considerably by suitable diversion upstream from the present level of 180-250 cumec, it would not be possible to close the channel at the point where the approach bank crossed it. That meant that its flow had to be diverted into the main Channel 2 upstream: also, the latter had to be straightened so that the channel shifted rightward to leave the ground free from any flow, where the left guide bundh would come. Unless that was done, it would not be possible to construct the left guide bundh and the right approach embankments. My deputy CE and contractor's engineers walked behind me in a disciplined manner. At some spot, I would stop to gauge the river.

In a project like this, it is essential to define the problem and study all possible options to achieve the objectives. For success in river training, it is essential to lay the entire operation on board so that it may be discussed with the operating lieutenants. It is also vital that everyone involved understood the significance and importance of each stage of the operation. Above all, the schedule and timeframe stipulated for each activity had to be clearly understood. The sequence and the problem were defined as under:

- The flow from Channel 1 having three parts would be diverted to Channel 2, the main channel upstream, at the most suitable point identified by us. It would reduce the flow considerably and was thereafter to be closed on the right approach embankment.
- Channel 2, the main channel on the downstream of the bridge was eroding the bank where the tail of the right guide bundh would have come. It had to be diverted away from there, to provide space to lay the boulder apron to protect the tail of right guide bundh.
- Channel 2 on the upstream had formed a loop sweeping almost seven hundred metres of the area where the mole head and shank of the left guide bundh would be located. Unless the flow was straightened away from this location, this portion of the guide bundh being as it was in flowing water, could not be constructed.
- Diversion and closure of Rahua nala on the left approach bank after harvesting in April.
- Closure of Channel 3 on the left approach embankment after harvesting in April.

The sequence and time frame were important. The actual design and execution have been dealt with in a separate technical paper. Without going into the detail it can be said that the channels were trained in the sequence planned.

The river training work called for a lot of courage. Channel 1 was first closed and its flow was diverted into Channel 2 before the latter was straightened. The flow in the Channel 2, which was in a loop, had to be diverted into an old channel of the river, now lying dormant. It was necessary so that the area, where the left guide bundh would have come, would become free from flowing water. It was done by closing the Channel 2 just downstream of the mouth of the activated old channel. When only about twenty metres of the portion remained to be closed, the flow in the channel became very violent. It was early January. The sky had been cast with smog for the last 2 or 3 days. There was no sun, and it was biting cold. I told R.G. Singh that this was the moment for the project. We either lived or died. The fellow took it literally. He jumped into a new excavator, and drove into the gap to block the flow. The subcontractor (Mr Salaluddin) followed him in another excavator, literally blocking the flow. The roar suddenly stopped and water started rising in the channel. I was worried but I knew that the rising water was a good sign. High afflux would drive the flow through the old channel. It happened exactly like that. The Channel No. 2 was thus straightened, making the area available for the construction of molehead and shank of the left guide bundh.

There had been a similar situation in the Brahmaputra. Those who have not seen a scene like this, would not believe it or have no idea of how it looked. It was awe-inspiring, and one was reminded of God at the sight of the fury of the river. Very recently, Mr Balachandran had described the scene while watching the final closure of the South Channel of the Brahmaputra in his book *Agony and Ecstasy*. I quote from his book:

> An army of earth moving machinery like bull dozers, tractors, dumpers, excavators, graders, etc. was mobilized. There were also stacks of big size boulders at site. We located some machines in the char (Island), ferrying them by boats. To close the South channel, we (the work was executed departmentally, that is, no contractor was employed) started dumping boulders from the char as well as the South bank continuously for about eighteen hours—I was standing at the site for the whole period, with my heart literally in my mouth. With the South channel width gradually reducing, the velocity was increasing rapidly, threatening to outflank the south bank, till suddenly the river swung to the north, cutting the char and merging with the North Channel! It was a do-or-die situation and I was mentally resigned to getting the boot, if the river had breached the South bank and flooded the villages—in any case, there was no worse posting was there for me on the IR! The relief was so intense that my eyes got blurred due to tears of joy—I thanked my mentor Mr Padmanabhan for teaching me to take risks, if I had to succeed. This was the first river training ever attempted on the Brahmaputra—our river of sorrows, for the flood havocs that occur year after year. On hindsight, it was perhaps God's will that I should have the privilege of taming this river and create a history of sorts!

He also recalled in an email to me, 'I recollect us standing together on the South Bank through the night and me telling U that nothing worse could happen to me, whereas U could get into difficulties, if our attempt to close the south Channel failed!'

This mail was sent to me by Mr Balachandran recently, it captured his imagination of a scene when he was the ME and I stood by his side at the Brahmaputra. The scene was now being repeated in more or less a similar way at Gandak. I salute the courage of the deputy chief engineer. He later told me that he had so much faith in me. When I had uttered those words, he thought the moment of reckoning had arrived. If we could plunge in, history could be made. Goddess Narayani, which the river epitomized, had beckoned like that. There was no way but to respond to that. But for brave acts as these, we could not have succeeded. It was probably our day, and Narayani chose to bless us. It was certainly God's will that people like us with great handicaps, made an attempt to convince the river to abandon its path. It never occurred to me what would have happened to me, if we had failed, but if something had happened to my brave men, I would not have found any place to hide myself. Thank God!

RIVER NARAYANI FINALLY YIELDS AND ALLOWS WORK

It was the day people thought we could now complete the work. The news spread fast. Someone must also have told A.S. Bhatnagar (GM) that the work was progressing at a feverish pitch. He was until now, very sceptical of our ability and was perhaps shocked when he heard about what was going on. I was at the site when I was asked to speak to him. He said that he had heard about the fast pace of the work; and so, I invited him to visit the site.

Mr Bhatnagar visits the site

He arrived the very next day. He was totally overwhelmed by the sight of a huge fleet of plants and machinery. We had also started well foundation works at six locations. It was essential to complete at least two well foundations on either side before two guide bunds were completed and the adjoining gaps could be closed. The GM walked across the alignment. He was a stickler for quality. I told him that he could select any location from which the earthwork could be tested to ascertain its quality. The deputy CE took a sample from the location selected by him. The test result was excellent. He was overwhelmed. He had never in his life seen a work of this magnitude with such superb managerial and quality control. He confessed that he had never thought that Indian engineers were capable of executing such work. After that, he ate a good lunch of puri and bhaji that we used to serve in the camp on the river bed. He found the experience unforgettable.

He arranged for coverage by the press. We got a good coverage in the print media and suddenly everyone appeared to be talking about the work. We started getting scores of visitors, much to the disappointment of our detractors. Some of them were amazed by the scale and magnitude of the operation.

Safety precautions for the flash flood

In work of this nature, it is always better to be safe than be sorry. The first safety rule is to be prepared for a flash flood, which is very common in all Himalayan rivers. April is the most dangerous month because rains are common on the upper reaches. Melting of snow is also a common feature. The month of April has no demand for irrigation water. Canals are therefore closed for annual maintenance. Although we had a good liaison with the irrigation department and the barrage authorities, I played safe. We were prepared for a discharge of 20 to 30 per cent of design discharge. We insisted on part pitching of the approach embankment, placing one row of apron in front of the approach embankment. A 15-metre wide apron was laid in front of the embankment where Channel No.1 flowed before its closure. The guide bunds were completed. No borrowing of earth was allowed from the downstream side as a matter of rule to prevent formation of hydraulic gradient through the bank. I had once been very angry when it was not observed.

A flash flood actually occurred on 1 April 1993. The barrage gates were opened without any warning. There was a heavy discharge down the river. I was informed about it in the afternoon. The superintending engineer of the Uttar Pradesh irrigation department informed me that the whole area had been submerged. He asked me what I was going to do. 'Sleep', I said. He was shocked. I said that if everything was breached as reported by him there was no point in my going during the night.

I however did go during the night. As expected, there was huge ponding in front of the right approach bank. It was natural because the flow initially followed through its old course. The water started flowing along the right guide bundh from the pond. With taut nerves, we continuously took the gauge level and measured the current of water.

The gauge level became steady after a while and then started falling. It was a good sign because the riverbed was getting scoured to take additional discharge. It induced flow along the bank. The hydraulic flow pattern followed beautifully. The pond level fell steadily. The guide bund functioned very well. After the forty-eight hour watch, we were quite relaxed. The news that everything was breached had spread. People came to witness the catastrophe. They were disappointed. The river channel had actually straightened. The initial precautions had actually saved us. Work was resumed and completed by May 1993, as planned.

My deputy CEs were happy. Their quiet composure in our company actually sent out a very encouraging signal. We thanked Goddess Narayani for keeping her promise. We also decided to construct a temple on the tail of the left guide bund in her honour and requested her to flow through the bridge without ever altering her course! A different story of which comes a little later.

The economic benefits of the construction flows to the locals

Miscellaneous work like grass turf pitching of slopes needed a lot of labour. It was not easily available. We requested our 'friends' to bring the Tharu tribe from the hill. They were paid ₹80 per head per day. They were picked up earlier in the day and then dropped in the evening. Very hard working by nature, they learnt the work very quickly. It was a new experience for them. They had not seen a currency note till then. They dealt with barter system for purchasing of clothes, spices and salt. They would barter these for their agricultural produce. More often than not, they used to get a raw deal from local tradesmen. They were surprised to receive their first fifty-rupee note. It could buy many things. They had never imagined that. Naturally, they were very excited. On average, a family would earn more than ₹3,000 a month. It was a fortune for them. It was actually a new social awakening. I was personally very happy because the project also meant something for the locals in economic terms. I mention this tribe because of their historical relevance. But besides them, so many were recipients of benefits of the economic activity taking place in the area. Such people were always encouraged. They also wished us well.

Main river training work completed in the first season

The main working season came to a close by the end of May 1993. We had completed both guide bunds, and both approach embankments up to formation levels as well as six well foundations, including both abutments. The newly constructed banks had to be protected from rain cuts. We had experimented with geo-jute grids, putting them just below the slope of the two banks. Elaborate drainage arrangements were made. The result was excellent. We were criticized for using the river bed material in construction of the guide bund and approach embankments. Being sandy material, they were prone to rain cuts. But this was the standard specification. With properly designed protection work, drainage and turf, there was practically no problem. People had to be alert during the first season. Stone pitching was provided as precaution over a layer of filter on the upstream side of the embankment up to the highest pond level. I recall that a member of the TAG was critical of this, but in high floods, when the pond upstream is full, there is severe wave action, particularly when it is windy. The normal turfing is generally not adequate against such wave action. The stone pitching over a layer of filter is very effective. I could demonstrate this when the TAG visited post construction.

GUIDE BUNDH COMPLETED—A TRAINED RIVER BRINGS ENORMOUS BENEFITS

The efficient functioning of both guide bunds was very satisfying indeed. The straightened river was flowing parallel to the guide bunds in a classic, textbook manner. Almost four km of stretch on the right bank, which used to be perpetually under water, was now dry. The river had left the right bank and had shifted between the two guide bunds. There was a deposit of a carpet of thick very fertile silt layer because of ponding. The land that had been engulfed by the river since 1924 was reclaimed. It had also turned into a very fertile land. Old farmers came to claim the land. After a brief pooja, they began cultivation. One old man came to see us. He wanted to meet the CE who had completed the work. They showed directed him to me. He said, 'Sahib, I was a lad of sixteen years when Narayani took away our land. I had never expected to see the land returned to me in my life time in such a beautiful shape. People say that you have made it possible. Many engineers in the past said that it was not possible.' Saying this, he fell down at my feet. It happened so suddenly that I was totally embarrassed because he was as old as my father. But all of us were touched by his emotion. The common people treated us with a kind of reverence that I had not seen earlier.

The Uttar Pradesh irrigation department dumped boulders worth ₹5 crore every year on the right bank. The protection and repair of the right protection bank was no longer required. This would cause a huge perpetual saving. This may not have, of course, pleased many because this work was a perpetual source of earning!

I called another meeting of the TAG at the site to inspect the finished work. Luckily for us, there was a huge flood before the rainy season finally withdrew. They could see guide bunds functioning beautifully. We also got pictures from the satellite through the National Remote Sensing Agency. These clearly showed the straightened portion of the river after construction of the guide bunds and approach embankments. The comparison of the latest satellite picture with the earlier picture was very revealing. It clearly established that because of the creation of control point, the river was now straight for 8 to 10 km on the upstream and downstream side against a stretch of five km as originally visualized, at the design stage. More than fifty square kilometres of land was reclaimed, which in terms of social benefits compensated much beyond the cost of construction.

It was only the Bihar Forest Department that was unhappy because of some upstream forest land being swamped. But it was entirely a short-sighted view. The overall impact of the benefits to the forest could be assessed by the following:

- The entire forest in the affected area was in the river bed. This had become available due to shifting of the river sixty years ago, towards UP. According to the hydraulic cycle, the flow could once again revert to the Bihar side. So, the forest was in perpetual danger of inundation.
- The river regime was now well established and defined. It had reclaimed a huge stretch much larger than the affected portion which was now available for plantation.
- The damaging effect of Rahua nala was now contained. The whole area was now available for the plantation of different species. Incidentally, it had also provided much needed water holes for the wild animals.
- The entire Madanpur forest was now protected and a huge sum which the government was planning to spend, to protect it from flood, was no longer necessary.

The TAG was very happy. They thanked and complimented us profusely. I was able to fulfil the expectations of my peers like Pritam Singh who was overwhelmed. I cannot but say that the ratification and acceptance of the work by the TAG humbled me and made my teammates, justifiably proud.

BRIDGE SUBSTRUCTURE COMPLETED IN THE SECOND SEASON

All remaining foundation work was completed during 1993-94, including the piers. The contract for steel superstructure was also fixed. The work on the first span was also completed.

Funding had remained as elusive. But our stature rose rapidly. The superintending engineer from Uttar Pradesh narrated his meeting with the principal secretary. During the progress review, he told the secretary that the guide bundh had been successfully completed by the Railways. According to him, the secretary literally jumped up from his chair in utter disbelief. He said that they were now morally bound to release funds. A lot of pressure was also now being exerted on the state governments for funding. With the retirement of Mr Anand in January 1994, we lost solid support from the Board. But thanks to him, the most critical part of project was over.

Some highlights of interest

Some highlights were given to the media. The earthwork involved equalled to that required to construct a double lane road between Delhi and Gorakhpur.

This comparison captured the imagination of the people. The total earthwork involved was close to thirty-seven lakh CUM executed in about 150 days. But even if compared to work like the Brahmaputra Bridge in Tezpur, the achievement is quite revealing as the following table would show:

S. N.	Description	Gandak Bridge (Actual Execution 1992-94)	Brahmaputra Bridge at Tezpur (Actual Execution 1981-86)
A	*Guide bund and approach banks*		
1	Total earthwork in one working season	36.42 lakh CUM (150 days, 92-93)	18.25 lakh CUM (135 days, 84-85)
2	Total boulder work in one season	4.80 lakh CUM	6.90 lakh CUM
3	Maximum earthwork in a day	32,100 CUM	16,800 CUM
4	Maximum quantity of boulder in a day	5,260 CUM	9,350 CUM
5	Maximum work value in a day (contractor's payment)	₹35.44 Lakh (1992-93)	₹11.60 Lakh (1984-85)
B	*Bridge*		
1	Total concreting involved (without superstructure)	63,000 CUM	1,70,000 CUM
2	Total sinking involved	637.50 metre	1320 metre
3	Maximum concreting in a working season	36,000 CUM (57% of total quantity, 1992-93)	71,000 CUM (41.50% of total quantity, 1982-83)
4	Maximum sinking in one working season	336 metre (53% of total quantity, 1992-93)	703 metre (53% of total quantity, 1982-83)
5	Maximum concreting done in a day	1079 CUM (1992-93)	960 CUM (1982-83)
6	Maximum aggregate sinking in a day	8 metre	19 metre
7	Average rate of sinking on one well	2.10 metre/day	1.30 metre/day
8	Maximum cement consumed in one season	11,500 metric ton	23,800 metric ton

Source: Collated by the author from various sources.

The comparison is not easy. In terms of gross logistics and overall challenges, the Gandak Bridge would fare well with the Brahmaputra Bridge.

This will perhaps encourage my compatriots who worked valiantly for this project. I had the greatest satisfaction of having been involved in both the difficult projects. It was again satisfying to complete a ₹166-crore work with a saving of ₹37 crore. The participants of the projects should be happy too.

For completing the work within the time frame and with no cost overrun, the project team deserved a great deal of credit. We had assembled a team of total novices in the beginning of 1990. We were given no chance at all. On top of it, Mr Padmanabhan had reportedly advised people not to take up this project. According to him, one would run the risk of losing one's provident fund deposit! The eminent engineer Fenton had said that it was impossible to train the river to its original regime.

However, God and destiny had willed it otherwise. It was a matter of regret that no recognition was given for an excellent execution of the project. It only made it clear to me that fame and infamy was willed by God. If neither of it was given to us, it must be some part of His grand scheme of Karma! No?

Challenges had always excited me. So, there being none, I felt quite uncomfortable. I wanted to do something different. Managing a division was an interesting and challenging assignment. However, a post like the DRM was proving to be full of pulls and pushes. It was distasteful but could not be helped. Well, I will pick up the episode concerning my posting as the DRM a bit later.

WE PRAY AT THE TEMPLE OF GODDESS NARAYANI—'FRIENDS' ALSO PRAY WITH US

We had all resolved to set up a temple for Goddess Narayani on the tail of the left guide bund. It was our tribute to the river. She had allowed us to carry out the construction as planned. In the process, she had agreed graciously to change her braided course for a straighter approach. We prayed to her to stick to her changed regime without abandoning her course as she had done more than sixty years ago.

The old temple of the goddess was in the Madanpur forest by side of the bank. This was a very famous temple. Even dacoits of mini Chambal offered their prayers there. An annual mela at this location was very famous.

The temple was built accordingly, and I was asked to perform the pooja. I was the DRM of Firozpur at that time. But we came down to Gorakhpur. My wife and Shrimant, who was about ten years old, accompanied me to the site.

WE PRAY UNDER THE BOOM OF AK-47 FIRE

We crossed the bridge on a trolley. The experience was exotic. The sight of heavy cultivation of sugarcane and wheat was simply superb. Who would have really thought that it would become a reality? There were a number of people standing by the side of the railway line to greet us. My eyes were full of tears at witnessing this sight. The old picture of the river, spreading over a stretch of eight km with only wild grass and forest came back to remind me how things were eventually transformed.

But the best sight awaited us across the bridge. On both sides of the railway line, about 15 or 20 persons in spotless white kurtas and pajamas were standing with AK-47 rifles raised to salute me. It took no time for me to recognize them. They touched my feet. I had wished to go first to the old temple in the Madanpur forest. They took me in a cavalcade of jeeps to the temple. After offering prayers there, we returned to the new temple on the bridge. The priest performed the pooja.

Shrimant, was in awe at seeing so many rifles. He whispered in my ears, 'Papa, can I fire the rifle?' Our friends overheard and said to Shrimant, 'Why not?' They took him in their laps and put his fingers on the triggers. There was a volley of deafening sound as shots rent the air. The boy was simply petrified. He ran across to me, wailing. It took some time to calm him down. My wife did not see any of this and I did not say anything to my wife then. It was only after returning to Gorakhpur, I told her the whole story. My wife was simply scared and asked me how I had the courage to do all this. I got roundly scolded for exposing Shrimant to such people.

THE DIFFERENCE WE MADE—OUR REWARD

It was an experience that I will never forget. These friends told me that before getting work, abduction was their only livelihood. After days of scouting, they would succeed in kidnapping a victim. The police would normally be after them for the first few days. During this period, they would run with the victim from one place to another in the forest. It used to be an awful period. Then ransom notice was followed by prolonged negotiations. Sometimes they had to be content with only ₹5,000 or so.

But after being engaged in the project, they earned more than a lakh of rupees per week. They now visited the local bank in their jeep, with the cheque in their hands and their chest filled with pride. They had never before had that feeling of having honourable money. There was a greater joy in doing work. 'Sir, we all owe our new life to you. We will never forget what you have done for us.' I was really happy because they had joined the mainstream life.

When as ME, I was inspecting the work site near Gopalgunj—the constituency of Lalu Prasad ji— a person came and touched my feet. I had seen him before. I was told that he was a contractor from Bagaha and wanted to meet me. Yes, he was, of course, my old transformed friend. I was happy to learn that he was a good medium-sized contractor. I congratulated him. He was grateful for my help and kindness.

My eyes were full of tears. I thanked God for His mercy. Without it, nothing could happened. It was after all not a flash in the pan. The Great Gandak was really great, and whenever I recalled how things had developed, I felt that the Almighty had been extraordinarily kind to us. Not to forget my good teammates, R.G. Singh and H. K. Singh, the indomitable deputy CEs who had executed it at the risk of their own lives!

10

MANAGING THE DIVISION— FIROZPUR

BOTTLENECKS IN THE POSTING

In the Railways' service, managing a division as the DRM is considered to be an important landmark in one's career. It opens up the channel to promotion to open line general manager and further advancement to the Railway Board. In my case, it turned out to be a nightmare of sorts. Shortlisting of officers for posting as DRM is a long-established system in the Indian Railways. The DRM is a general category post for which officers of different services are eligible to be shortlisted. Some norms are laid down for selection for the post. But Y. P. Anand as the CRB had expressed that those who had had a sufficiently longer tenure in the open line turned out to be better DRMs. He also said that this should be a deciding criterion for selection of the DRM. Quite unnecessary actually! Such views coming from a CRB were quite confusing and also created doubts in the minds of those who were being considered. It turned out to be his personal opinion but enough to set many a tongue wagging!

Mr Anand thought that an open line officer was better versed with nuances of running railways. Till 1992-93 I had served the majority of my years in construction. Thus, my critics felt that in face of what the CRB opined, I may not be included in the DRM's panel. There was abundant sympathy, particularly because I was otherwise well placed in my career. I was not in the construction department due to my own choice. The administration had posted me as a construction engineer for prestigious projects. It would thus be unfortunate if I lost out for no fault of mine. A special course for the prospective DRM was being conducted at Railway Staff College, Vadodara. My name did not appear in the list. Someone told my wife that I had eventually missed the bus!

I went to Delhi in January 1994 to find out whether I appeared in the panel of DRM. Raj Kumar, ME, promised to find out. Then I met Anirudh Mithal, EDCC (executive director co-ordination) to the CRB. We were in Kanchrapara and we had hit off well. I told him what was being talked about. He had a hearty laugh and said that he would check and tell me. He confirmed after some time that I was very much there in the panel and that I need not worry about it. Oh! That was a big relief. All the talk of open line work was a loose one then.

Mr Mithal had also discussed with the CRB, Mr A.N. Shukla, and subsequently told me that the CRB had agreed to post me as DRM of the Jhansi division. I wanted to be nearer Delhi to look after my eldest daughter Shravani, who was in Lady Sri Ram College for Women in Delhi. But it did not happen that way. Mr Shukla retired in March 1994 and things changed thereafter. The member traffic (Mr Bhatnagar) presumably did not favour my posting at Jhansi. So, I lost. The ME was helpless. He told me that I might get Alipurduar in the NF Railway. I was surprised because I had already served the NF Railway for about eight years. Someone who had never worked in that area should have been chosen. I was looking for a more demanding assignment. So I met Mr Masihuzaman, (Mr Masih in short), secretary Railway Board, who also held the post of GM, Northern Railway. He was also an ex-Eastern Railway man. He promised to do his best.

Then one day, he asked me to go to the Firozpur division. Now I was alarmed because Punjab suffered from a severe bout of terrorism. My wife thought Alipurduar would be better. I met Mr Mithal [he was promoted as additional general manager (AGM) Northern Railway] and Mr Masih. Both of them advised me to go to Firozpur. It had many challenges and I could be counted if I succeeded. I agreed to their suggestion. But I had to wait for two more months for the orders to materialize.

POSTED AT FIROZPUR AFTER A LONG WAIT

I was in office on Saturday, when Mr Sandhu, DRM, Firozpur congratulated me over the phone on being posted as the DRM. He wanted to know about my joining programme, and so on. Luckily the order had already come by fax from the Board. It was issued on Friday. (By sheer coincidence, all important orders were issued from the Board on Friday evening, the last working day of the week.) I had planned to go to Pokhra in Nepal on a holiday with my family, on a trip we had planned earlier.

I spoke to Mr Masih to thank him. I told him that I planned to join after visiting Pokhra. He said, 'Nothing doing. You do not know how difficult it was for me to have you posted at Firozpur. I had to get it changed by Minister of Railways (MR) Mr Jaffer Sharief, who has now gone to Dubai. He will be back in 4 or 5 days' time. There is bound to be a great deal of noise and pressure on the

MR when he returns from Dubai. So, you must join immediately. There are large numbers of hill stations in your division. You can visit them if you like'. That's it. Our GM, Mr Viz, was out of Gorakhpur and was expected on Wednesday. Mr Masih told him to release me quickly. I was released immediately.

So on 26 May 1994, I left for Delhi forgoing the much planned Pokhra trip. I reached on the morning of 27 May. I was met by some senior officers from Firozpur. I met Mr Masih in Baroda House. He immediately made me join at Delhi itself. He also called me for the Punctuality Meeting in his room, where I could meet all the senior principal head of the department (PHOD) officers. It was with such an eventful introduction to the senior officers that my journey as DRM began. Mr Masih asked me to go to Firozpur in the evening. So, I left Delhi Main by the *Jammu Mail* to Ludhiana from where a special train took me to Firozpur early in the morning.

I LEARN OF PUNJAB

The transplantation of paddy was the most interesting scene from the train. The fields were full of irrigated water with neatly planted paddy. An amazing sight, because in our parts, paddy is sown only in the rainy season and never in the full white heat of summer. Because of the water and the very high day temperature, the humidity level was rightly very high. After all, I was in Punjab, very close to Pakistani border. Punjab had led the green revolution in the country and harvesting of three crops in a year was very common in the area.

Punjab means the 'land of five rivers'—Ravi, Jhelum, Chenab, Sutlej and Beas. After the Partition, Ravi, Sutlej and Beas were the main rivers in Indian Punjab. In the pre-Partition period, Punjab was the land of heroes and warriors led by Guru Govind Singh. It had produced many martyrs. They had fought many invading kings, as the Indian history recounts. Punjab has been the main producer of foodgrains in the country. Valour, farming, courage and an adventurous lifestyle were the hallmark of the people of Punjab. It was evident everywhere and was somewhat infectious.

HEARTY WELCOME OF A SORT

I was welcomed heartily. A big farewell was given to my predecessor, Mr Sandhu. Seeing the strength of the audience, it was clear that he was a very popular DRM—a real sardar and true *'Punjab ka puttar'*.

As I learnt more subsequently, I found him to be a large-hearted person. He enjoyed life even while serving as a DRM in a very difficult period with militancy in Punjab at its peak. A Parliamentary Committee on Rajbhasha was visiting Palampur the next day to meet the divisional officers. I left for Pathankot in the evening from where I reached Palampur next day by road. It is a beautiful hill station in Kangra Valley overlooking the Shivalik range of hills of the Himalayas. The mountain narrow gauge line from Pathankot to Jogindernagar was a very interesting engineering construction and travelling on it was a beautiful experience.

Superfast train derails to accord a hearty welcome!

Interacting with the committee was not much of a problem. The committee was going to Amritsar the next day. We reached Pathankot in the afternoon on the way to Amritsar. Just after lunch, I was informed of the derailment of the Jammu-Rajkot Superfast Express short of Jalandhar. It was a huge shock. I requested Chief Rajbhasha Officer Nagrath to manage the meeting. I left Pathankot by road. After a two-hour drive, we arrived at the site of accident. Some local Railway officers and civil authorities had already arrived from Jalandhar. They had moved the stranded passengers. The first sight of seven derailed coaches was unnerving. But fortunately, no passenger had been injured. Only one bearer in the pantry car had a minor burn injury as hot water had fallen on his toes. It was simply miraculous.

Jalandhar-Pathankot is a single line section. The section had to be restored after removing derailed coaches. The GM arrived at the site around 10 p.m. with the headquarter officers. They said, 'First things first! You have been given a resounding welcome by the division. You are bound to have a very successful tenure as the DRM in the division'. What a welcome indeed!

There were plenty of suggestions from the headquarters' team. I was absolutely new. After patiently listening to them, I told the GM, 'Sir, I thank you for your generous suggestions. I will take them into account. But my most important task is to restore the traffic. It is already 10 p.m. Please allow me to work. I request you to take away your officers and let me have a free hand'. He smiled appreciatively at me. He told his officers to return to Delhi and told them to allow the DRM a free hand. They were taken aback. I asked the branch officers to take their own decisions and if they wished, they could consult me.

This ensured that work went smoothly without any interventions. We restored the traffic by 6 a.m.—an achievement. I earned their respect in plenty. That was, of course, important and welcome. But the accident was certainly not. Who would want a welcome like that?

STRATEGIC LOCATION OF THE DIVISION

Firozpur is an old division of the Indian Railways. The line from Bhatinda was part of the North West Frontier Railway going through Pakistan to Peshawar. This section in former times was known as SPR (South Punjab Railway). Many still fondly called it SPR. The Partition truncated the section—the Pakistani Border being only nine km away. River Sutlej divided the two countries. The old line went to Lahore from there. My career had started from Kanchrapara in West Bengal, very close to East Pakistan. I had seen the 1971 Indo-Pakistan war which led to the creation of Bangladesh. The pendulum in my career had swung the full circle. I was now in the western frontier of India, closest to Pakistan. A coincidence!

People had vivid memories of earlier wars with Pakistan. Two Pakistani shells had fallen in the Railways' area during the 1971 war, one near the DRM's bungalow and other near the loco shed. Large craters in the ground bore testimony to the event. Firozpur was the terminal division of the Indian Railways. All trains had to compulsorily terminate in the division. From these considerations, the division played a very strategic role not only for the security of the country but also from Indian Railways' point of view.

Militancy had taken a heavy toll

Punjab was the worst victim of terrorism and militancy. It had suffered for a long fifteen years. The youth had fallen an easy prey to the allure, campaign or threat by the extremists who had affiliation across the border. Sane people and parents had lost complete control over the misguided youth. Gradually, life had become unsafe. Nobody moved out after dusk. Industries had suffered a great deal. Punjab, once a front runner in the Indian economy, now faced a huge setback.

Trains as usual were the easy target. Thoroughfare was badly affected. From the security point of view, no trains ran after dark. All trains moved in a block piloted by the security forces. Blasts on the railway lines were common. While going to a site of an accident in a special train, officers were once attacked by terrorists, using AK-47 fire. The presence of mind of the driver saved them. These incidents led to a collapse of morale. The result was neglect of maintenance of assets including railway tracks. Supervision and inspections become ineffective or at best perfunctory. Jalandhar-Pathankot, a hundred-km section, had thirty-four speed restrictions due to weak tracks which crippled train movement. It was also prone to accidents.

I had gone to Amritsar on my first visit with my family while returning from Pathankot. We wished to pray at the holy shrine. For security reasons, the police had advised me to cross the Sutlej-Beas area before dark. We could see armed police posted every hundred metres on both sides of the road. We were given armed security patrol to accompany us. A barrage had been built across Sutlej, just after the confluence of Beas with Sutlej. The terrain is undulating and full of grass—an ideal hideout for terrorists coming from Pakistan as the border is not far away. Plainly, everyone was looking worried and they were keen to see our car clear the area before dark. In June, the sun sets around 8 p.m. in western Punjab. Besides, the deserted road allowed the car to travel very fast, and so we reached Firozpur without any problem.

STOCKTAKING IN THE WAKE OF TERRORISM

In short, the first glimpse of the division brought up some critically urgent issues. Managerial inputs were required for the reconstruction of the division. But I had to settle down quickly before taking up the arduous task. The DRM's house known as 'Rail House', is a huge, old building dating back to 1867. The GM was initially hesitant when I asked for his permission to go to Gorakhpur to bring my family, but he eventually agreed. I was back in Firozpur with my bag and baggage in three days. We were finally home on 27 June—Shreya's birthday.

Apart from loss of morale, the long spell of militancy had eroded staff discipline. People were known to drink even in office. The popular saying was: 'Do not take anyone seriously in Punjab after dark'. Taking advantage of the lack of command in the organization, the trade unions had exploited the situation and taken over control of all staff interests. It was, of course, natural for such an organization to fill in the gap created by lack of authority.

In many ways, the conditions were identical to what I had faced in Kanchrapara as a young AEN. The political climate was similar with uncertainty and poor law and order conditions. Unions called the shots because of mistrust in the administrative machinery. It called for some changes in the setup. A few changes were initiated after conferring with Mr Masih. We discussed the general position of the division every morning on phone. He would invite me for lunch whenever I was in Delhi.

RECONSTRUCTION STRATEGY FOR THE DIVISION

I worked out a detailed plan for the reconstruction of the division in a time-bound manner. This was prepared after discussion with my branch officers.

Enlarge our area of influence

The planning was based on our own resources with practically no help from the headquarters. I had insisted on this. People normally demand all sorts of assistance for making a change. This is the easiest way out. This does not bring any personal commitment. More often than not, the solution and the problem are conveniently passed on to the boss. My ADRM, an experienced civil engineer, said that complete track renewal of the Jalandhar-Pathankot section was required to lift all speed restrictions. The situation was bad. Once, a senior DEN's push trolley had derailed! The track renewal would cost ₹5 crore. The territorial chief engineer, Mr US Pandey, pushed the estimate to ₹6 crore. This work would have to be included in Railways' annual works programme and needed to be sanctioned by the Parliament. That would take more than a year.

There was no time for that. Tie bars of CST 9 sleepers were rusted because of long neglect, and they were unable to hold the gauge. The engineering team was led by a dynamic young Sr DEN (coordination), Surinder Pal. He checked up with each PWI. They had enough permanent way material in their stores. Every fourth sleeper was replaced by a new sleeper. This enabled the gauge to be held on the track—an important safety requirement. The distance between inner faces of two rails is known as gauge. Thus casual renewal was done on actual need basis. This created an excellent synergy, and all the team members took this as an opportunity. I gave them an example of how the first high-speed train was introduced on the IR with CST 9 sleeper track on 90 R rails. This was the power of expanding one's area of influence. In other words, it highlights what one could do with one's available resources. The key is to use one's resource fully and also to clearly define the functional goal. In this case, it was to ensure safety and to remove umpteen speed restrictions.

We build bridges

In my first interaction with the union, I talked about my reputation and expertise in building important bridges. I now sought to build bridges between the staff and the administration. There was a retort from the divisional secretary of the union. He thought that such a bridge was normally built by the union. 'What sort of a bridge does the DRM want to build? This should be left to the union,' he said. But the fact is that the administration must be reachable and provide accessibility to the staff to reach it. If it failed, a chasm would be created. If others built a bridge, the chasm would never be filled—it would only grow. The mainstream staff did not identify themselves with the organizational goals. Thus, the divide grew wider with time. Both had become like two banks of a river. This reminded me of a popular saying by Mark Twain—'East is east and West is west and never the twain shall meet.' For even a small thing, an employee would come in company of a union leader. It was a sure sign of breakage in the communication. It was neither in the overall interest of the union nor the administration.

Subtle and effective action had to be initiated on this front in order to break the ice. The branch officers were asked to address staff grievances as part of their regular inspection. This experiment was a proven one. It started showing good results. The division had to be rebuilt after the traumatic ruin wrought by the long spell of militancy. And obviously, the first rebuilding block had to be the railwaymen.

The staff's welfare was of utmost importance. We had a dynamic senior divisional personnel officer (Sr DPO), Jaswant Rai. The Sr DPO is the real image of the DRM. Long use of ad hoc procedures had led to unprincipled decisions. We slowly but firmly moved away from the old regime. It was welcomed by a large number of staff. But a few, belonging to an influential coterie, detested it vehemently. It was my good luck that the Sr DPO was of impeccable integrity. I always held him in high esteem and supported him strongly. As a result, some good elements in the union like the divisional secretary of the Northern Railwaymen's Union (NRMU), Mr Gautam, came forward to support us. This led to us enlarging our area of influence. This was vital to carry out structural improvements in the working of the division.

ACCIDENTS ARE ARRESTED—THEY DECLINE

The large number of accidents in the division were a matter of serious concern and therefore of utmost urgency. More than thirty accidents were reported in a month—an accident almost every day. The issue was systematically analysed by studying past cases. Tank wagon siding in Pathankot was a point, where frequent derailments took place. The siding had a short reverse curve taking off from the main line—its geometry not being good. The track parameters of the siding were improved to be as good as top-class main line, besides improving its geometry. Accidents on this siding were thus, eliminated altogether. In the monthly POM, it was hard to defend those accidents. Suddenly, after the fourth month, the number of accidents came down to half, and in the next month, it became zero. Chief Safety Officer Sudarshan Seth asked, 'How did you bring down the accidents to zero? Any medicine used?' There was of course no magic wand but we had focused on the maintenance of the track and paid thorough attention to the rolling stock. Planned and systematic efforts as a team had led to excellent results. Reversing the trend and bringing back the number of accidents to zero from the level of one per day spoke volumes on the commitment and zeal of the team. Speed restrictions were gradually removed. In the Ludhiana-Pathankot section, time loss came down to sixteen minutes from forty-nine minutes provided in the working timetable. Whenever a new restriction was imposed, it was mandatory to give a timetable to lift it. This was reviewed in the daily operating meeting. Traffic block was considered as an investment with certain assured quantifiable returns in train operation. The Sr DOM was informed about the returns that were expected.

This created a new work culture. The Sr DOM was quite keen to grant traffic blocks because he knew what advantage he would gain in return. The main thrust was train operation which was linked to revenue earning. Thus, for routine activity like rake examination, the Sr DME (C&W) would interact with the Sr DOM to plan the order of rake examination. The idea was that the rake should be available for loading according to the daily traffic forecast position of loading. Every activity had a link with the business plan of the division.

The running of trains was the paramount objective of all the departments. Thus, the target or objective of each department had to support the central goal or objective of the division. It was an important lesson but in course of time, it was often lost sight of. There is a mistaken impression that one should see the department's own goal first. The organizational goal could come later. Quite often when organizational objectives are achieved, departmental objectives are automatically achieved. If they are not, then they were not worth achieving in the first place. This was how we were able to create a record of laying of the tracks for the track relaying train (TRT) in a single day. This was due to the strong synergy that had developed between the branch officers concerned. When a common goal is identified and accepted by all in an organization, it leads to the release of remarkable synergy-like atomic fusion which only grows.

Rotational transfer for increasing transparency

There is a general policy of rotational transfer of staff particularly of those occupying sensitive seats in the division. This had not been enforced in the division. No rotational transfer had taken place during the last fifteen years. It is a normal function that is necessary to ensure transparency in working, particularly in the area where the division has to interact with the public. Rotational transfer deters the formation of a nexus at the cutting-edge level in such cases.

No branch officer, however, was willing to invoke the rotational transfer. In our internal discussions, they felt that the division had once again started delivering and a rotational transfer might upset the apple cart. 'Let sleeping dogs lie' was their logic and there was nothing wrong with it. There were of course no two opinions about the correctness of the measure. I believed that if it was correct then we ought to go ahead with it. There was resistance among the employees for the transfer. The resistance was due to the disturbance it caused in the schooling session of their wards. In some cases, it was on medical grounds—family members required specialized treatment at a particular place. In some cases, their spouse was employed in other state government departments. They could not move unless the spouse was also transferred to another department. In such cases, a suitable position had to be found where the spouse could also be posted. This caused some problems but given adequate notice, it was possible to make adjustments. So, the crux of the problem was to give timely notice to the employee so that they could organize for such matters.

A list of such persons staying at a station or post for over five years was prepared. They were informed during the month of December that they would be transferred in March, at the end of the school session. They were asked to make one choice out of three choices of stations where they could be posted. Unions were also consulted. We had agreed to consider requests from employees to defer such transfers on genuine grounds. I had also agreed that the unions could also recommend up to five such cases. The transfer could be deferred for a year only. Grounds like school session, sickness or spouse working in other departments, could only be considered for deferring such a transfer. It went off smoothly. More than 85 per cent of the rotational transfers were successfully carried out. This also broke a prevalent myth which claimed that unions would not allow such transfers. Withholding transfers for a year in deserving cases ensured commitment of the staff and both sides felt as if they had won.

INTRODUCTION OF THE DMU

Transfers in the Railways are routinely done and all concerned have accepted this as a part of their service requirements. As in the case of any change, there is bound to be resistance from the affected persons but if they are taken into confidence and the entire process is transparent and well-managed, it has a favourable response. A large cross-section of the railwaymen had fairly appreciated such issues. Some hawks in the union were however not amused. They felt that the union had lost its hold on the administration. They felt that there was a need to assert their authority to retain the supremacy of the union in affairs of the division.

In the Indian Railways, steam tractions, particularly on broad gauge were wound up long ago. But in the Firozpur division, many branch lines had steam traction. On 6 December 1995, the last steam engine on the IR was withdrawn from this division.

After the closure of the steam shed in the Firozpur division, diesel multiple units (DMU) were to be introduced for the first time in India, on all branch lines. They were faster and more efficient. The Firozpur division was selected for the DMU trial. We believed that only a single driver could run the DMU and no assistant driver was necessary. In the Eastern Railway, for the main line electric multiple units (MEMU), an assistant driver was also provided. The NRMU wanted an assistant driver on the same basis. The decision of the Eastern Railway to provide an assistant driver was arbitrary and illogical and could not be technically justified. The union's demand was unacceptable. We tried to convince them, but the hawks within the union were adamant. We did not want to force this issue but continued with our efforts to persuade them. The situation was tough because it had precedence, however unprincipled it may be. We had learnt from the mistake and it was not necessary to commit a mistake again. It needed patience to resolve the issue. This caused some frustration in headquarters' office. Some were inclined to agree with the union. During the meeting with the GM, I pointedly asked, 'It appears the headquarters does not mind having an assistant driver. I should know because I don't want to fight a losing battle. If we give in to an unprincipled demand, we will slip back to days of militancy. But if I have your support, I have the will to fight.' There was a pin-drop silence. The general manager agreed with my views. He asked the team to stand by me—a moral victory.

The dialogue with the union was tough. They tried to stop willing people from working. I told them that the police would be called if they intimidated the willing staff. I explained that the assistant driver had no role whatsoever. Even in suburban railways of the Western and Central Railway, EMUs (electrical multiple units), a similar train, did not require any assistant driver. I requested them to allow the trial run. Their headquarters leaders of the union agreed with our logic and they prevailed upon the locals to allow the trial run. I offered to send in a team consisting of union's representatives and officers to study the system elsewhere. Ultimately this was also not necessary. Uttariya Railway Mazdoor Union (URMU) did not want to visit. I told the NMRU that such a visit would only highlight their ignorance and reflect badly on them.

The issue thus resolved, the DMU had a successful trial run. In an impressive public function at Jalandhar, the DMU was flagged off by the CRB Mr Ashok Bhatnagar. I was grateful for the support from Mr Masih. Besides, the support from the late Mr Bajpayee the then vice president of the NRMU and Shiva Gopal Mishra, the present president and Mr Gautama, divisional secretary, were invaluable. Their far-sightedness as union leaders made them place organizational interest above the union and it was truly commendable.

Mr Bhatnagar, CRB, was happy and had dinner with all officers in Amritsar. He was my strong critic but he praised me for doing a wonderful job in introducing the DMU. He said, 'But for your perseverance and good leadership, the IR would have incurred huge operating expenses. So, I have decided to reward you. Please tell me what you would like to have.' I was surprised because I never expected a reward from Mr Bhatnagar. I said, 'Sir, I am honoured by your appreciation. That is all I wanted'. Others said that Mr Bhatnagar did not give awards easily. Since he wished to do that, he must be genuinely pleased. I said, 'Sir, I am grateful. A token amount of ₹5 or ₹10,000 will do.' 'Oh! You do not know what you have done. Another DRM in the Eastern Railway agreed to allow an assistant driver in an identical situation. Even I thought that in view of this precedence, it would be difficult to convince the union. But you persisted with your conviction. I sanction an award of ₹25,000.' First, ₹25,000 was quite a sum in those days. Second, it had come from Mr Bhatnagar, who was known to be very selective and discreet. I thanked him and accepted this with great humility and as a token of appreciation for all of my team.

I was really happy. We had embarked upon reconstruction of this division after the damage it had suffered from a long spell of militancy in Punjab. The division had a turnaround, which had been made possible through a lot of effort and the sacrifices of so many. The reward was recognition of the good work. It was not as a compensation or mark of sympathy for our sufferings. This reward had brought us back and made us capable of reckoning with others. We accepted it with our heads held high.

I told my team that we would not talk of the scars we carried or seek any sympathy for them. But we would demonstrate our resolve to march forward. We would talk of new milestones we had set up for ourselves. We would make a great effort. We would display much more grit and determination and fight for qualities for which Punjab was known for and respected in the country. I must say with all honesty that they responded as true Punjabis. Hats off to them!

PAKISTANI RANGERS SALUTE AT THE BORDER

On the bank of Sutlej, on the Indian side of the border near Hussainiwala, is the sacred place where famous martyrs—Bhagat Singh, Sukhdev and Rajguru were hastily cremated by the British after they were hanged in Lahore Central Jail. They were hanged at 7.33 p.m. on 23 March 1931, a day in advance of the schedule. It was most unusual and was done in fear of riots. Sahidi Mela takes place here every year on this day. The division runs a special train for the mela to enable people to offer homage to the martyrs of Punjab. It is a very emotional scene even today. The rail bridge over the Sutlej River, which was disabled during the 1965 war, stands as a testimony to the rail connection that existed between the two countries. It connected the Lahore-Karachi rail line.

The border post is manned by the Border Security Force and Pakistani rangers. The lowering of the flags of both the countries at sunset is marked by a parade and salute. The colourful spectacle is witnessed by visitors from both countries. As the DRM, I was once the chief guest of the ceremony. Pakistani rangers welcomed me with a guard of honour. After an inspection of their unit, I presented a basket of fruits, sweets and a bottle of rum. Crossing the border had evoked an eerie feeling. I was possibly the only civilian other than a head of state to receive a guard of honour by Pakistani rangers. There is no difference between the people of the two countries. Only a line divides them—a line drawn by someone who did not even belong to either of the countries. A similar ceremony is held at Wagah near Amritsar, which is a road connection between the two countries. The ceremony at Wagah is more popular, but the one near Hussainwala though smaller is more beautiful!

INDO-PAK RAIL TRAFFIC

India and Pakistan have a running rail link between Amritsar and Lahore. Atari is the last railway station on the Indian side and is the only international station to have arrangements like immigration and customs to deal with passengers. The *Samjhauta Express* is a through train from Lahore to Delhi. There are some trains that run between Lahore and Amritsar. There is also a considerable parcel and freight traffic. Outward parcel traffic includes books, print materials, different types of spices, onion, ginger, etc. The outward freight includes fertilizer, gypsum, etc. Inward parcel includes dry fruits, dates, etc.; while inward freight includes rock salt and occasionally, cement.

We had to interact over the phone with the DS of Lahore of Pakistani Railway for interchange of problems. There was a provision for a flag meeting between the two. The next meeting was scheduled in India. There were several issues between the two railway systems for which such a meeting to ensure coordination was required. But even though, the meeting was long overdue and keenly needed, no meeting took place during my tenure.

A Pakistani loco was required to haul the train from Atari to Lahore. The Pakistani loco was very irregular at the first place. Even if the Pakistani loco came, it was often unable to pull the load. On such an occasion, a Indian loco had to push the load from behind to enable the train to just cross the border. Pakistan had four-wheeler stocks which had become obsolete in the IR. I will mention two episodes connected with Pakistani traffic. They will highlight the responsibility of the division in handling Indo-Pak rail traffic, with international ramifications.

Chaos about onion traffic

Pakistan imported onions and potatoes from international markets. Due to some break in the supply line up in November 1996, there was a serious shortage of onions and potatoes for their domestic consumption. This caused sudden shoot up of their export from India. Everyone in India who wanted to export onions threw his hat in the ring. There was a great pressure on the local parcel office to handle the huge export offerings. The situation got out of hand and the senior divisional commercial manager brought this full blown-out chaos to my notice.

It took me some time to understand the business. Normally 2 or 3 parcel wagons were attached to the local train between Lahore and Amritsar running twice a week. Apart from onions, some other perishables like paan were also sent. Traffic was booked on first-come-first-serve basis. But the traffic offerings at hand were far beyond the rail capacity. Thus, the pressure to clear the traffic mounted.

A transparent procedure had to be set up to clear the traffic. There was no procedure that gave a fair chance to a small supplier who also wished to avail this business opportunity. All traders were called for a meeting. It was decided that no trader could book more than three packages of a stipulated size. They would have to submit their offer in a tender box. This would be sealed by 12 p.m., to be opened before all by the area officer at Amritsar. A list would be prepared on that basis. Parcels of those approved in the list would be accepted for loading. This reduced pressure and ensured that even the small operator could do business.

Parcels had accumulated in the office. All unauthorized parcels (those not in the approved list) were removed with the help of the police. The procedure though not exactly according to the rules, suited the situation. But it was quite transparent, equitable and was formulated by a consensus. Even the court refused to intervene in the process. The headquarters' commercial officers were nowhere to be seen to offer their help. According to them, it was the job of the local parcel clerk. Preposterous! The chief operations manager (COM) was however very helpful. He was satisfied with the spirit behind the procedure, we had introduced. He also allowed the attachment of four extra wagons. Once I took over the command directly, all the pressure was transferred on to me.

I had acted in the best possible way and it was my job to hold the baby. I could not have then, and I have never after, abdicated responsibility that comes attached with the job. I have never left my subordinates unprotected. The result was a gleaming success. My own officers recognized that I possessed grit.

As a management principle, here was an important lesson. A leader cannot walk away from any crisis. He must stand up to a situation and should be willing to take decisions. A common-sense solution that leads to the maximum good for all and which protected the interest of the weaker elements of the stakeholders of the community is bound to be good and would uphold under any public scrutiny.

I recall an episode related to us while we were on probation. An assistant commercial superintendent (ACS) in the Western Railway (WR) was deputed at Bombay Central Station to deal with any passenger problem. A very well-dressed person entered the office of the station superintendent one evening. He introduced himself as the Nawab of Jamnagar. He had to go to Ahmadabad by the evening train. He did not have cash to buy the ticket but was prepared to give a cheque. His entire conduct was very imposing. The ACS allowed him to get a ticket by cheque and recorded the reason for doing so. As per the rules, a cheque was not permissible for sale of rail ticket. Unfortunately, the cheque bounced. The officer was hauled up for an obvious breach.

The GM observed that the officer was deputed to look after the problems of passengers on the spot. In this case, the officer was convinced of the antecedent of the passenger. He had to take a decision, which he did. It was an entirely different matter that a particular decision had ultimately been proven wrong. Some decisions go wrong sometimes. It would be wrong to punish a person who had shown an initiative for the good of the organization. He was exonerated by the GM.

It used to thrill us in those days. We marvelled at the wisdom and vision of the GM. I always believed that if one went by one's conviction, things would seldom go wrong. Even if they did, one should stick to it. The best batsman in the world at times gets out even after applying the best cricketing technique. I believed that those enjoying a clean and good public reputation always had an advantage. The course of action taken by us in this case clearly demonstrated why something was good, regardless of whether it followed the rules or the procedure. This is the best aspect of value engineering. And, a good lesson in management.

LOGICAL INTERCHANGE AT ATARI

Soon after joining as the DRM, another decision in respect of the Indo-Pak rail traffic was taken. Several issues connected with the Indo-Pak rail traffic at Atari were discussed in a meeting held in Chandigarh. The customs

Brahmaputra Bridge under construction

Left to right: Myself, P.S. Hari Rao, Seetharaman, Debes Mukherjee and K. Balachandran

The completed Brahmaputra Bridge, September 1986

With former Chief of Army Staff General A.S. Vaidya at the Brahmaputra Bridge site

Myself and Vipin Sharma (extreme left), deputy CE, being introduced to former prime Minister Rajiv Gandhi during the commissioning of the Brahmaputra Bridge, 16 April 1987

At URWICK Management Centre with Course Director Robert George. I am in the centre

On a visit to Heidelberg, Germany, July 1984

Launching of a girder in Algeria

Former Railway Minister Madhavrao Scindia presenting an award to me for outstanding performance in the Algerian project, 1985

Handing over the completed Algeria rail project to director of Algerian Railways, July 1987

The most critical operation to close the main channel of the Gandak River, December 1992

The closure and diversion of a river channel on the Gandak

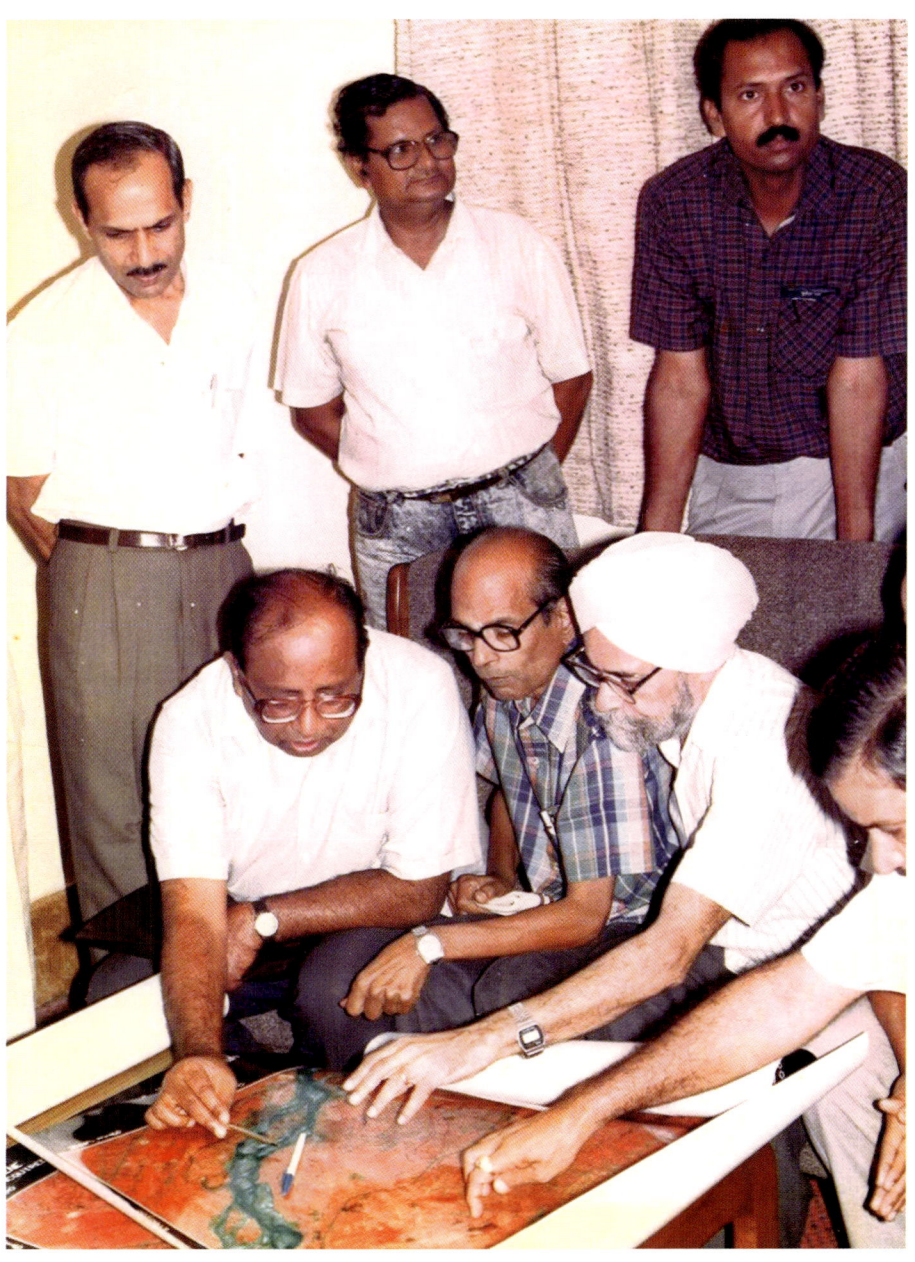

Myself showing the map of the straightened Gandak after construction to Punnuswamy and Pritam Singh, chairman, TAG

Receiving an award on behalf of the Firozpur division for the most improved performance from V.K. Agarwal, April 1995

With former Railway Minister C.K. Jaffer Sharief to flag off the Shatabdi Express from Amritsar, 1995

At the inauguration of the newly-created North Central Railway zone in Allahabad, former Human Resource Development Minister Murli Manohar Joshi and former Railway Minister Nitish Kumar, April 2003

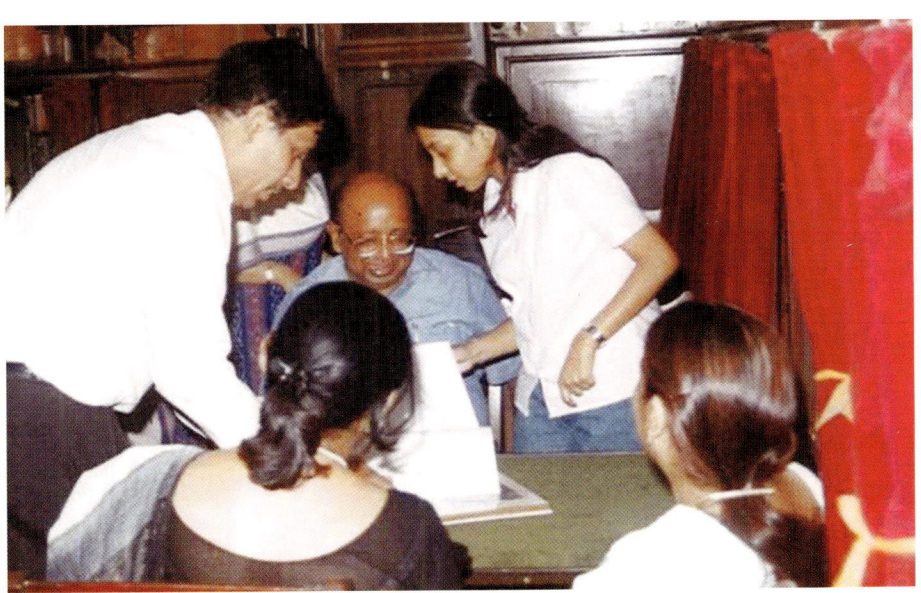

Inside the special coach of King George V, April 2003

Minister of State Bandaru Dattatreya (second from left); Minister of Railways Nitish Kumar; myself; Union Urban Development Minister Jagmohan; I.I.M.S Rana, chairman Railway Board; Sandeep Silas

Left to right: Myself; Mr Nitish Kumar; Anubha Jaruhar, president, NRWWO; Vinoo Mathur, secretary Railway Board

Welcoming former Prime Minister Atal Bihari Vajpayee in Faizabad, January 2004

Welcoming former President Dr A.P.J. Abdul Kalam at the Safdarjung Station, January 2004

Explaining the features of the Kashmir rail project to former Prime Minister Manmohan Singh in Udhampur, April 2005

At the Bhilai Steel plant to inspect the newly set up facility for developing world class rail technology, January 2006

Inspecting the innovative right-angle crossing constructed at Manmad workshop of the Central Railway in my capacity of Member Engineering, July 2006

On my retirement as Member Engineering from the Railway Board. Left to right: Jena, MS; Shivdasan, FC; Ghoshdastidar, MT; myself, ME; J.P. Batra, chairman; Ramesh Chandra, ML; A.K. Rao, MM; Mathew John, secretary; Chaudhary, PPS to CRB; 31 January 2007

During my days as secretary Railway Board, 2002–03

With my wife Anubha as newly-weds, March 1972

Left to right: My eldest daughter, Shravani; son, Shrimant; myself; my wife, Anubha; daughter, Shreya

*A recent family photo from a vacation in Greece.
Left to right: Manav (son-in-law), Shreya with her daughter Mishika,
myself, Anubha, Shravani and Shrimant*

department and the immigration was managed by the Punjab Police and the Ministry of External Affairs; general law and order in the Railway premises was managed by the government railway police; general intelligence by the Intelligence Bureau; border security by the Border Security Force. I was, of course, from the Railways.

The handling and placement of the Amritsar-bound Pakistani train at Amritsar posed several serious security issues. After customs and immigration check at Atari, the Pakistani train entered Amritsar for passengers to disembark. The present arrangement was considered inconvenient and suffered from certain security risk. The train could not be thoroughly checked at Atari. A Pakistani criminal could easily hide unlawful goods in the underframe of a train. It was not possible to check or prevent such a thing. It could be easily removed upon the arrival of the train at Amritsar, which is a big and crowded place. It was also not possible to watch the train at Amritsar.

A more rational arrangement was to terminate the rake at Atari. After complete security, immigration and custom check at Atari, passengers could board the Indian rake for Amritsar. The Pakistani rake could be kept under better watch at an isolated location at Atari. This arrangement was better, even from the perspective of the Railways. It saved costly space in Amritsar Yard. I had thus no hesitation in agreeing to it. The changeover took place with immediate effect. I was complimented for the decision, which was long overdue. Even the officers from the headquarters were happy and appreciated the good initiative.

Pak pilgrims held up

The arrangement ran smoothly for almost a year. In January 1995, after the outbreak of plague in Surat, Pakistan closed its border and refused entry to Pakistani Sikh pilgrims, who were returning from Nanded—the famous Sikh shrine in Maharashtra. Pakistan insisted that the five hundred odd pilgrims, including women and children, had to be quarantined. It was a classical diplomatic case which had to be dealt with by the Ministry of External Affairs (MEA). The plight of these pilgrims was pathetic in such an acute winter. The district administration had to take the charge. Jaffer Sharief—the minister of the Railways— asked me to look after them properly. But I did not have to take any action. The villagers had formed help-groups by setting up a langer (free community kitchen). Arrangements for hot water, milk, and so on were made. Women helped in looking after the children. The pilgrims were thus looked after in the best possible manner, with perfect Punjabi hospitality. The situation continued like that for five days.

I was in Delhi for a meeting and was due to return in the evening. Deputy Chief Operating Manager Mani Anand frantically wanted to talk to me around 5 p.m. as I returned to the inspection carriage. She told me that the MR had discussed with the CRB how the Pakistani passengers stranded at Atari were being handled. Mr Bhatnagar reassured the MR that there was nothing to worry about as the passengers were in Amritsar, which had all the facilities. Mr Bhatnagar was formerly COM of the Northern Railway and had signed the Indo-Pak Rail treaty. He was aware of the interchange rules. Thus, he was shocked when the MR told him that the passengers were in Atari, not Amritsar. He was annoyed and asked the Northern Railway to explain how the interchange point had been changed. The COM, in order to ward of the pressure, found it convenient to name the DRM who had done this without consulting the headquarters.

They were of course correct. I did not formally consult the headquarters before the change. I was also not aware of the existence of the provision in the holy accord between the two countries. Obviously, I did not have the authority to change it. But I had informed all including the GM. Nobody had pointed out that I had overstepped my authority. Instead I was complimented on the bold initiative. The action was correct. Just imagine the situation after the border had been closed! With the interchange at Amritsar, all passengers would have been in a crowded city like Amritsar causing a serious security threat. All the authorities like Punjab Police, Customs, Border Security Force and Intelligence Bureau were in much better command to control the situation at Atari by sealing off the area. It did not affect our Railway's operation either. Amritsar would have had serious repercussion with one line blocked for a week.

Thus, the logic of change in the interchange station was fully tested and vindicated but for the blessed provision in the accord. They wanted to shoot me down for daring to act beyond the statute. It had no real significance except for the technicality or the propriety it possessed.

I could not speak to the CRB as he was out. I talked to Govind Ballabh, the COM. He told me that as the CRB was in a foul mood, he could not explain it to him. I told him that the decision, if incorrect, could be reversed. But he smilingly said, 'Jaruhar ji, please do not get upset. What you have done is the correct thing, which you can also see. You should sleep over it and we will see about it.' I asked the director general of the railway police also. He said that the new system was working so well that there was no need to change it. I said that it was against the accord. In my view, the ground reality was cardinal and it could not be overlooked simply because it was not part of the rule in the book. We therefore decided to do nothing. The system continues even today without any change in the sacrosanct accord. Indian and Pakistani Railways have run rather well with these changes.

A good decision is 'swayam sidhha'

God was certainly kind. I continued to do my job without losing my head. Everyone was quite happy about the arrangement. I was ME when the *Thar Express* was to be introduced on 19 February 2006 across Munabo in Rajasthan border to Khokhrapur in Pakistan. There was a meter gauge line linking Karachi to Hyderabad. This link was disrupted after the 1965 war. I asked L.R. Thaper, additional member traffic transportation, who was deputed to oversee the interchange arrangements, if sufficient thought was given to deciding the modality of the interchange between the two railway systems, particularly after the experience of Atari. Thaper was the chief freight traffic manager in the Northern Railway when the Atari incident had taken place. We had a good laugh.

It was a memorable episode. A good decision will always appear logical. It should serve a maximum number of people. It is a decision that is often natural and easy to take. Such a decision is also easy to defend. In our culture, it is called 'Swayam Sidhha', which means 'it is its own proof'. This decision proved its merit, by the events.

TOUGH MEASURES—APPLICATION OF 14(2)

A number of initiatives were taken for the division to win back its original glory. Divisional performance in every sphere had improved. Loading and revenue earning were the highest in the Northern Railway. Safety performance was excellent now. The division very deservedly was judged as having shown an outstanding recovery, during 1994-95. It claimed the runners-up Divisional Shield in the Railway Week function the following year.

Some pockets in industrial relationship however still caused concern. We had a healthy relationship with the NRMU. But the URMU (affiliated to the National Federation of Indian Railway) often brought petty personal problems. These were not congenial to the general health of the organization. It was the narrow outlook of the local leadership. Although I enjoyed the personal regard of both the local and the apex level leadership, some problems often cropped up at the field level. This upset the general industrial peace.

My officers complained that the group created problems during routine inspection. It was possible to resolve any issue in a constructive manner, so I was prepared to look into them. But a status quo had to be maintained during the time the issue was under consideration. There could not be an instantaneous resolution of a problem and therefore there was no point in pressurizing lower functionaries. Acts of indiscipline on this account was unacceptable. Most of the time, we were inclined to have a favourable response to issues referred to us but it was made clear that the answer could also be a 'No', which had to be accepted.

Ludhiana was a difficult pocket. The union office bearers were unable to rein in the hawks in their rank and file. So, we often gave them time to resolve their internal differences. A good administrator should promote the growth of the union. In my view both needed each other in the democratic set-up we worked in.

The Divisional Rail Users Consultative Committee (DRUCC) is a forum to interact with rail users in the division. The DRM is its chairman. The DRUCC meeting had not been held in the division for over fifteen years, since the advent of militancy. The division served the states of Haryana, J&K and Himachal Pradesh besides Punjab. The committee was reconstituted with a lot of effort. Its first meeting was being held in Ludhiana. I arrived from Ferozepur for the meeting. A deputation of local branch of the URMU wanted an urgent meeting with me. I told them that I could meet them after the DRUCC meet. They were however insistent. Clearly there was a design to embarrass me. It was imprudent to use force. I therefore gave them just fifteen minutes after which I went for the meeting.

Discipline had to be maintained

The divisional secretary met me subsequently and he apologized for the indiscreet action of the local branch which had caused inconvenience to me. It was a lie because I knew that it was his handiwork. The divisional secretary had brought a case regarding the operating branch for my consideration. I told him that I had to discuss this with the SRDOM before responding to his plea. As a point, I did not discuss an issue with the branch officer in the presence of union office bearers. It was a policy to help both sides. But my promise to revert to the divisional secretary was disregarded by the local branch of the union, which gheraoed the SR DOM on the same issue, when he went to Ludhiana on inspection. He was kept confined in the yard. I was annoyed. I got the officer released. I told the divisional secretary that their conduct had violated the acceptable norm practiced in such cases. He again noted that it was regrettable saying that the local branch had acted in his absence. The excuse was unacceptable. The time had come for stringent measures to restore a disciplined conduct.

We thought of various alternatives. We were convinced that the normal application of discipline rules, was not possible. Witnesses were unlikely to depose in such situation. A tough measure like the application of Rule 14(2) of the Discipline & Appeal Rules (DAR) would send a strong signal down the line. It was an extraordinary measure, it dispensed with the normal disciplinary procedure. According to the rules, the disciplinary authority had to satisfy himself that normal departmental inquiry was not possible. For this, there had to be a reasonable doubt based on evidence of intimidation, criminal offence and violence. The process took some time. Meanwhile, their people caused more acts of indiscipline. Evidence of such activities was proof of reasonable apprehension in the mind of the disciplinary officer that the atmosphere was vitiated causing fears in the mind of witnesses to come forward to depose in the case. It was reasonable to assume that no departmental inquiry under the Discipline & Appeal Rules was possible under such circumstances. The assistant divisional secretary, who had taken a leading role in instigating people to harass and confine the railway officer, was taken up under Rule 14(2). He was given a chargesheet and removed from service under this rule.

Tough measures have a salutary effect

In Punjab, losing a job is taken very seriously. There was a strong shock-wave-like reaction. But it was clear that one could not cross the limit. The divisional secretary came down running and said that it was not fair. He was under intense pressure. He had been set free but another person who had acted at his behest had lost his job. He pleaded that action be taken against him. I politely said that since he had been out of Ludhiana, no action could be taken against him.

This stopped acts of anarchy and discipline returned immediately. I received threats including one against my family. But we were firm. In the headquarters, the union requested the GM to intervene. The Officers Association passed a resolution condemning the physical humiliation of the officer, and supporting my action.

The GM refused to intervene in the matter initially. But obviously there was a lot of pressure on him. Whenever I went to Delhi, the top union leaders would meet me and ask me to forgive the person. They told me that the local leaders were ready to apologize. I said that the apology could not be sought at Delhi and it had to be sought from the victim. The case ran for more than three months, which was sufficient to drive the basic point home. Officers who had been charged including the union divisional secretary apologized with an undertaking of good conduct. The action was withdrawn. It brought back the good working atmosphere in the division. As long as I remained in command, we had a harmonious industrial relationship in the division. It revived a good working culture once.

NRWWO HELPS THE RAILWAYMEN—WELFARE MEASURES

The long stint of militancy had deprived the division of its normal extra-curricular activities. We wanted to revive them and fully involve the railwaymen and their families. The Northern Railway Women's Welfare Organisation of the Division (NRWWO) ran welfare activities for the families of railwaymen. This was headed by the wife of the DRM. We encouraged ladies to undertake voluntary activities. They ran primary schools, handicraft centres, provided help to the seriously-ill, looked after the physically challenged children, ran computer centres for railway children and gave scholarships to needy children, etc. Thus, they complemented the efforts of the railway administration.

Anubha worked very hard in this direction. The employees were very happy with the welfare schemes of the NRWWO. Their mission was to identify genuine persons who needed help. They ensured that the help reached the farthest corner of the division. I was amazed at the missionary zeal of the ladies and the sincerity of the purpose shown by its president, Anubha, my dear wife. They evolved novel means like a rail mela to collect funds for welfare activities. It became a runaway success in the town.

The first Rail Mela was organized in February 1995 and was a memorable one. It was cold and raining. The ladies were disappointed with the weather playing spoilsport. But it improved dramatically in the afternoon. It attracted a large number of people. The second one was equally successful, the next year. My wife had the satisfaction of handing over a comfortable balance, even after carrying out a large number of welfare activities. The generous help from NRWWO for the staff and the families was a breath of fresh air that helped drive away years of bottled negativity. It restored normalcy to life in the Railways, which senior members of the staff later fondly recollected. As the DRM, this was a big gain for me. I thanked my wife and her devoted associates for uplifting the morale of the division. Watching them work closely, I appreciated their sincerity and dedication in return for nothing.

INTER-DIVISIONAL CULTURAL MEET

About the same time, the headquarters office asked us to host an annual inter-divisional cultural meet in Firozpur. Because of the short notice, officers were unsure. They thought that the artists from other divisions might not endure the cold December month. The temperature outside during this time goes down to sub-zero. Often there would be a thin layer of frost in my lawn in the morning. Apart from the physical discomfort, the fear of militants still loomed large. But eventually we accepted the challenge. It was sure to uplift our morale besides sending a firm signal to all around that the division had bounced back. That was certainly very important.

The meet was successfully organized. All the participants were looked after very well. Our divisional mechanical engineer (power) generously stationed a steam locomotive near the dormitory to provide enough hot water from its boiler for their wash, etc. The coal-fired heaters kept the rooms warm, and thus their stay was quite comfortable. They were also treated with the best of the famous Punjabi hospitality. The meet was colourful and well-organized. Quite interestingly, the divisional team went on to win the championship. That was the icing on the cake indeed!

COLOURFUL INAUGURAL CEREMONY FOR THE NEW TRAINS

The division had emerged from the trauma of militancy. Any good work made headlines. A number of new trains were introduced from Jammu or Amritsar. These trains became quite popular. All these services were introduced after a colourful inaugural ceremony. We became experts in organizing such functions. Out of more than a dozen of such functions, I will recount two for different reasons.

Amritsar Shatabdi Express—a runaway success

The *Shatabdi Express* from Amritsar was to be flagged off by Jaffer Sharief, the MR. I was told that he wanted to meet the family of one Mr Shah in Amritsar. His office could not provide the contact details, so Mr Shah could not be contacted. The MR spoke to me again to enquire about the family. I told him that we could not contact them for want of a contact address. He immediately gave me the telephone number. It was quite evident that it was important for the minister. The area officer was dispatched to meet the family. They were told that the minister would visit them after the function. An invitation card for the function was also given to them.

The MR came to Amritsar by IRCON's private aircraft. Immediately after landing at about 8 a.m., he asked me whether Shah's family could be located. I told him that we could go there after the function. He said, 'You do not understand. Once I go to the venue, people will never let me leave. I may not get any time to visit the family later. I have to return to Delhi by 11 a.m. to attend the Parliament. So, we will go now'.

Now that called for a complete change in the programme. For security reasons, the minister had to be properly escorted. The police had to be informed in advance. I requested him to freshen up in the Circuit House. Such last-minute change in the VIP's itinerary was normally refused in Punjab. But because of our good rapport with the senior superintendent of police, we could take the minister to the house of Mr Shah.

The minister was very pleased to meet Mr Shah and his family. He told me later that once when he had to go to London for medical attention, when he was not in power, Mr Shah had looked after him. He was thus deeply indebted to him. Mr Shah was apparently in some business in Bombay. The minister had promised to visit his family at Amritsar. He told them that he had consented to be the chief guest of the function only because of the opportunity to visit Amritsar. He was obviously in no hurry. I had to remind him very politely that people were waiting for the function and we were already late by almost an hour.

He got up reluctantly, taking the family along. He asked me to seat them in the front row. The minister was very gracious to mention that he was late for the function because he had to meet Mr Shah's family. The gesture touched me. If only more people remembered acts of kindness with gratitude!

Sachkhand Express

I had gone to Jammu to visit some people injured in a level crossing accident. After a visit to the hospital, I returned to the railway station around 4 p.m. when the general manager phoned to say, 'Jaruhar, MR Mr Kalmadi will inaugurate *Sachkhand Express* connecting Amritsar to Nanded.'

This train had been demanded for long as it connected the famous holy Sikh shrine at Nanded. I requested Mr Agarwal for a detailed programme. With a laugh he said, 'You have to do it tomorrow at 8 a.m. The minister will come by IRCON's plane. He has to return to Delhi by 9.30 a.m.' I said nothing. Frankly, its gravity did not strike me at all. The GM asked me if it was fine. I said, 'I beg your pardon, Sir. You mean tomorrow morning at 8? Where is the new rake? You know I am at Jammu and it is 4 p.m. already.' He said, 'Yes, it is at 8 a.m. and the new rake should reach Amritsar some time during the night. Anything else, you want?' I laughed very loudly and said, 'I need good luck in plenty.' He also laughed and hung up.

Imagine, we had hardly twelve hours left. I asked the ADRM to move to Amritsar immediately. The security clearance and security arrangements were to be made by the District Police. We were quite methodical in this respect. So, it progressed very fast. I reached directly from Jammu by about 9 p.m. The team was already in place from Firozpur. Even the invitation cards that had been printed locally were distributed to all the important dignitaries by 10 p.m. The district administration was very cooperative. We worked the whole night.

The rake arrived at 2 in the night. It was washed and brought duly decked with flowers around 7 in the morning. This was the time when I left for the airport to receive Mr Suresh Kalmadi, the minister.

The fresh morning air did me a world of good and by the time I arrived at the airport, I was feeling much better. Mr Agarwal came out first from the aircraft and smiled at me. I told him that everything was almost ready. MR was apologetic for not giving any notice. The function was excellent. On his way back, the minister told me, 'I am surprised how you organized it at such short notice.' The GM said that they deserved an award. The minister sanctioned an award of ₹50,000. We were overwhelmed.

CHALLENGES AND SKILLS—USEFUL LESSONS FOR THE DRM

Managing a division came with a lot of challenges. People adopted different means and followed different approaches. The division is the cutting edge of Railways' operation. All policies are implemented here. Quite frequently anything done in a division would become the benchmark. It is however pertinent to understand the central idea for the proper functioning of the division.

The division had to ensure that all trains ran safely and with utmost utilization of its capacity. The satisfaction of rail users was also a central objective. This must be central to the psyche of the entire rail staff. The DRM must find out ways and means to ensure that. Broadly speaking, the DRM must manage the technical and financial aspects including the management of external and internal influences.

They are also applicable to major projects. I will describe them to the extent that they might concern the DRM.

DRM's role in the management of technical and financial functions

Officers and other staff members are quite competent in the technical and financial management functions of the division. The DRM is normally not expected to, and, in my belief, should not involve himself in the intricacies of technical or financial management except to coordinate with various groups. The real role of the DRM should be to ensure that all departments eventually achieve the organizational goal.

An example in ensuring this aspect is a case in point. February and March, the last two months of a financial year, usually engaged each department in the division to attain their own annual target. While pursuing this, the mechanical (C&W) department had to send wagons to Jagadhari Workshop for intermediate overhaul (IOH). The workshop was chasing every division for sending such wagons which needed IOH.

The Food Corporation of India (FCI) wanted to load foodgrains from the depot during this period. We were keen to take up additional revenue loading. Thus, wagons were required for the next three months. I asked the Sr DME if he could defer booking these wagons for the IOH after March. He wanted dispensation from the CME. I easily got it from the GM. Thus, in a conflict in technical management, the DRM had to intervene. Beyond that, officers must be allowed to work with full freedom.

Management of internal and external influences

But the real challenge is in managing the internal and external influences. Intra-departmental conflicts in the division have to be managed by the DRM. A long-term view in industrial relationship has an important bearing on the functioning of all departments. External influences have to be dealt with, solely by the DRM. It is also important that branch officers are briefed so that they appreciate the intricacies of these interactions. It helps the branch officers in two ways. First, it enables them to understand and appreciate these forces and it also guides them on how to conduct themselves in order to safeguard the overall interest of the division. Second, the young officers need to be exposed to the experience for their own development as future leaders.

Political functionaries—important external influence

Once, an MP from Phagwara, Mrs Santosh Chaudhary, wanted me to meet her to discuss some problems in her constituency. She requested me to tell people from her constituency what she had done for them. I told them how effective she had been in pursuing their problems. I also told them that in some cases, there was delay because of technical constraints. She asked me to stop the demolition of unauthorized structures near the station. I asked my officers to hold it up for a day. It was carried out after she was gone. It was discreet, but had a profound effect.

Public leaders have to keep the people of their constituency in good humour. There was a branch line going from Phagwara to Roha on the banks of the Beas River. Traffic was suspended on this section during militancy. She pleaded to open the line to traffic. The Railways and the Punjab Police were not keen on opening the line. I reassured her that the service would be resumed after the introduction of the DMU. Meanwhile, our engineers removed one of the sidings from Roha station. There was an undergoing drive to generate revenue by collecting scraps which included dismantling unused lines. It was an initiative from the minister and the Sr DEN removed this under this drive.

She was upset with me. She told me that instead of resuming the train services as promised, the railway line had been dismantled. I was not aware of that. I told her that I would revert after checking up. The Sr DEN told me that the track was indeed dismantled. I was annoyed and asked him, 'You knew we had to resume train services in the section. Why did you dismantle the line?' He told me that the traffic department had cleared it as surplus. 'But only the extra siding has been removed and it will not affect the train service', he said. I explained the full background to the MP and reassured her that my promise would stay in place. I also told her that if she insisted, the dismantled line could be put back.

At noon, Jaffer Sharief was to present the rail budget in the Parliament. I was in front of the TV, waiting to hear the speech. Just then, I got a call from the minister. He wanted to speak to me. I thought that it must be his personal assistant. Surely the minister must be too preoccupied with the budget to bother calling a DRM. I was therefore surprised when the MR himself came on the line. He said, 'Arrey, DRM sahib, Santosh Chaudhary ji (the MP) is saying that you have dismantled the track. You promised to resume the train services. She is upset and will not allow me to present the budget unless her problem is sorted out.' I said, 'Sir, I have already spoken to her. I have told her that the line dismantled was redundant and will not affect train service. Dismantling was done to generate additional scrap, according to your directives. I have also told her that the line could be put back if she insisted.' He was very happy. I could hear him talking to the MP. He was asking her why she did not tell him that the DRM had already spoken to her.

An alert DRM can save an organization from embarrassment

Thus an alert DRM can save the organization from a lot of embarrassment. Interacting with representatives is an important duty. Failure to do this can send wrong signals. It is not possible to accede to all of their requests. But if properly explained, the position is usually appreciated.

Another incident would illustrate this aspect. The DMU service was to be introduced in Phagwara-Roha section. All the arrangements were made including the public function. Just a day ahead, the DEN told me that the CRS sanction for the DMU was not available for the section.

The DMU was a new stock. After the trial, the CRS gave an omnibus sanction to run the DMU in the Firozpur division. Since this particular section was then closed, it had not been included in the list. It was a Sunday and the office of the CRS was closed. But he promised to accord approval on Monday. Though initially upset, the MP appreciated the predicament. I suggested, 'Madam, you can travel in the DMU with me and thus the train will be inaugurated. You may tell the public that the commercial service will start a day later.'

This clicked and she arrived at the venue in style. She announced the resuming of train services in the section. The function was a great success. She paid a glorious tribute to me in her speech. She explained to the public that the DRM had arranged for the inauguration but tickets could only be sold from the next day when the commercial service would formally commence. Thus, by good application, it was possible to create a win-win situation for all. The role of the DRM in such a situation is very crucial.

RTSA—SURVIVAL TESTS AS THE DRM

The DRM has also to deal with some unpleasant situations. An honest and straightforward approach always helped. I cannot forget one such incident regarding appointment of the RTSA (rail travel service agent).

The Sr DCM told me that he had invited applications for the appointment of the RTSA for Ludhiana, Jammu, Jalandhar city, Amritsar and Pathankot stations. I did not then know about the RTSA. I was disgusted to find out that they were nothing but authorized touts who collected requests for train reservation on payment of a fee of ₹16 or so per ticket. The Railway Board had introduced this scheme some time back. There were already 4 or 5 agents at these stations. We did not want any more of them. According to the guidelines issued by the Board, the agent required office premises, telephone, etc. Hundreds of applicants could meet the minimum qualifying criteria. It was impossible to select 4 or 5 out of them. This would have been a sure case that led to an indefensible vigilance complaint.

I earn ire of the MR

I asked the Sr DCM if he correctly understood the procedure for the selection of a suitable RTSA from several applicants all of whom met the minimum qualifying criteria. Being a traffic officer, he did not really appreciate the nuances of tendering process. He was hence extremely worried when I explained them. He already had received one or two complaints from a local MP. Some others had also spoken against it. I asked him to get more representations on the subject. He was able to get representation from three more MPs including one from L.K. Advani. In view of a large representation against the procedure, I recorded that this needed examination, pending which the selection was cancelled.

That brought immediate relief. But a few went to the minister against the cancellation. I told the GM that the selection procedure is difficult and is likely to give rise to avoidable complaints. Mr Agarwal was the chief vigilance officer of the Railways before his appointment as GM. But he refused to interfere saying that such appointments in Delhi were being regularly done. So, I sent a note detailing our reservations and addressing the lacunae in the procedure. We requested the headquarters to address them and advise us suitably in the matter. Mr Khalique, OSD (officer on special duty), to minister phoned me once to find why the RTSA selection was cancelled. I explained it in detail but he was not convinced. He asked me to approve one case for Ludhiana which was pending clarification from the headquarters. I said that I could not do it on my own unless ordered by the minister's office. He said that there would be no problem about that.

After a couple of days, a gentleman came to me with a letter from the OSD. He said that the minister's office had issued orders as I desired. The letter said that the MR had seen the application for appointment of the RTSA at Ludhiana. Mr X might be considered for appointment as the RTSA. I told him, 'I am sorry but I cannot act on the letter. It says that this might be considered for appointment. If I have to appoint you, it has to be done by following due procedure which cannot be dispensed with.' He was exasperated. He said that he had spent lot of money already. I politely explained the reason why I could not act on the letter. Although, he seemed to appreciate my compulsion he still had to report to Khalique, who must have been upset. He had not expected a DRM to return his letter without taking any action.

Quite late one night when I had gone to bed, Khalique called me. He was quite pleasant and enquired about my welfare. Then he gently asked why no action was taken on MR's orders. I explained as best I could. Then he said, 'Please speak to the MR'. I knew that the MR would not be pleasant. I immediately guessed that Mr X must have reported against me and would certainly be present while MR talked to me. It was my moment of survival. If I could hold on such a situation it might not happen again. All these thoughts passed through my mind while I waited for the MR to come on the line. He presently came on the line and the conversation went thus:

MR (almost shouting): 'Arrey, what type of a DRM we have? I have 58 DRMs and do you think I have time to check if our instructions are being complied with or not? The OSD already issued an order and you have refused to obey. I have to issue orders to post you to NF Railway immediately.'

Myself: 'Sir, it was not an order. It only said that I should consider appointing Mr X as the RTSA. There were more than 1,000 applications for this. Sir, I was in NF Railway for eight years.'

MR: 'So, what is the difference? Such orders are always issued like that.'

Myself: 'But Sir, there are already many complaints from MPs in this case. One of the complainants is Mr Advani. There are six other MPs also complaining about this.'

The mention of Mr Advani immediately brought down the heat. The MR paused and asked:

MR: 'But why MPs are complaining?'

Myself: 'They are saying that the selection procedure is faulty and it would lead to favouritism. Under these circumstances, if I appoint Mr X as per the letter from OSD, it will be difficult to defend the action—either from my side or from your side.'

MR: 'What have you done so far?'

Myself: 'Sir I have cancelled the tender notice and I have written to the headquarters for clarifications. I understand that it has been referred to the Board for clarification. This could be issued quickly if you kindly order it, Sir.'

MR: 'Yes, I will see. Ok.'

That was it. My wife thought I was speaking to someone. But when I told her that the MR was on the line, she was upset. How could I have spoken to the railway minister like that?

In fact, I too, had not completely realized it. The reputation of the minister in this respect was terrible. I survived due to sheer luck. God had been kind to me once again! I must, however, underline that being truthful and sincere is the best defence. I felt sorry for Mr X. But he did not take my advice. The selection procedure for the RTSA was full of loopholes. It could not ensure fair play and left a lot to subjectivity. That was dangerous.

Mr X would not wait. He approached Mr Suresh Kalmadi when he became the MR. Fresh applications for the RTSA were called. I could not stop it. The headquarters advised us to appoint the RTSA for more stations in the division.

It was sometime in March 1996. The General Election was due in April/May. The Sr DCM was asked to give a notice period of two months instead of forty-five days. The results of the General Election would be due by the first week of May 1996. We proposed to decide the case around that time. My tenure was to be completed in May 1996. The election results were against the ruling party. I asked the Sr DCM for a fresh review of the RTSA, pending which the selection notice was cancelled. He winked at me and both of us were greatly relieved.

I do not know about Mr X. But when I was heading the vigilance department as chief vigilance officer of the ministry, I started a campaign against the policy of appointing the RTSA. There was a parliamentary question on it. During briefing, I explained as secretary Railway Board, about its flaws to Nitish Kumar, the MR. The system was done away with. Good riddance! That was after almost five years!

THE DIVISION IS REWARDED BY CHAIRMAN RAILWAY BOARD

Towards the end of my term, the CRB Ashok Bhatnagar visited Jammu and also Mata Vaishno Devi. He inspected the section from Jammu to Ludhiana on his return. He had heard of the measures taken by us to improve the section. He found the services to be very good. He told all, 'Look at the DRM. He has used his internal resources to upgrade the section. He has improved the safety performance of the division. It is now our duty to lend him material support by giving him out of turn sanction so that he is able to complete overdue renewal programme.' He was lavish in his praise while announcing an award of ₹50,000 to the division. Coming from Mr Bhatnagar, it was a great feat indeed.

INTER-DIVISIONAL RIVALRY BY THE DRM CAN BE COMICAL

In divisional working, there are times one was compared with one's fellow DRM. I did not believe in the game, but others played it frequently. You might call it a type of brinkmanship but one should be aware of this. I cannot but mention this in passing while talking about S.K. Agarwal, DRM, Ambala.

Manali—is it in Firozpur division?

I was in Delhi for the POM. I was told that the member engineering would visit Manali. Mr Bhatnagar was visiting Jammu on the same day. According to the protocol, I had to accompany the chairman. I spoke to Raj Kumar, ME, on the phone about his trip to Manali.

He was apparently annoyed. He asked me how I was concerned. He was surprised when I told him that Manali was in the Firozpur division. He said, 'What are you talking about? Agarwal (DRM Ambala) had been requesting me for a long time for a Manali visit as it was in his division. If I knew that Manali was in Firozpur, I would have certainly told you. (It was quite surprising because Mr Raj Kumar had been the GM, Northern Railway till recently before becoming ME.) But in any case, Agarwal should have informed you'. He told me that the programme was already worked out by DRM Ambala so nothing else was required. I asked Agarwal why he did not tell me. It would have caused a breach of protocol if I had not spoken to the ME. He told me unabashedly that it did not matter if he looked after him or if I did that. 'As it is, you are busy with the CRB at Jammu so it would be alright if I pitch in on your behalf. No? We must rise to such occasions, you know,' he said nonchalantly. But I sent my senior DEN to Chandigarh to accompany the ME and to ensure the presence of the division during his visit to Manali. It was good in many ways. The ME did inspect our installations in Manali but he availed the facilities and hospitality provided by Ambala division.

Soon after this, a train was to be flagged off from Fazilka, a border railway station of Firozpur. Because of its importance, Jaffer Sharief was the chief guest. He had also planned to go to Manali. But our insider information was that the MR might not go to Manali but his family would. When I told the GM, he smiled and said, 'Why Manali also is in Ambala as claimed by Agarwal? He should take care of the trip while you concentrate on the Fazilka function.' He winked at me and told the DRM Ambala accordingly.

Mr Agarwal was furious for being unnecessarily dragged to carry this difficult task. 'There are sixteen-odd members in the minister's family. They are very demanding and whole operation will be very expensive,' he said. Sympathizing, I said that being still busy with the Fazilka function, I could not do much. But I promised to send someone with as much of help as possible. 'After all, Agarwal, Manali is as much in your division, as you had told the ME not very long ago. And in any case, we must pitch in for each other. No?' I said.

He would have murdered me if he could. But in all fairness, he had started this game. According to divine law, retribution comes often in the most enigmatic way.

BEAUTIFUL HILL STATIONS—PRIDE OF THE DIVISION

The Firozpur division has many famous hill stations. They include Palampur, Kangra, Dalhousie, Dharmshala and Kulu, Manali, etc., in Himachal Pradesh and Srinagar, Pahalgam, Gulmarg, Amarnath, etc., in Jammu and Kashmir (J&K). Hill stations in Himachal Pradesh brought in many tourists whereas Kashmir had very few because of serious security concerns. The Railways had very good guest houses in Palampur and Manali.

Beautiful Kangra Valley—and its train

The Kangra Valley hill train to Palampur and up to Jogindernagar is a treat to watch. The narrow gauge line though popular is quite difficult to maintain. This line was built by British engineers primarily for the construction of Ranjit Sagar Dam on the River Beas.

Jogindernagar about 2,300 feet high has a power plant. A winch operated trolley takes you to the top. It was meant for the transportation of material. Pulling the trolley on 1 in 6 grades by the winch is awe-inspiring. After travelling up and down once, I decided that it was too dangerous to do it again. The view overlooking the Shivalik range from the top of the hill was absolutely breathtaking! The Palampur rest house is an absolute beauty. This house was purchased from a British landlord. The view from the verandah is beyond description. A perennial stream flows through the guest house. The water is cold and comes from the mountains. It is a small heaven there.

The Kangra Valley train runs through an excellent landscape. Main difference between the Kalka Shimla line and the Kangra Valley line was in its approach towards construction. Whereas Kalka Shimla line crossed many hills through tunnels, the Kangra line chugged along the ridge. Tunnels are therefore few in number. Both lines have their own elegance and beauty and have attracted tourists from everywhere. I tried to bring this line on to a regular tourist map by combining the through service with roads and Himachal tourism. I was not successful because I lacked patronage. I looked forward to some entrepreneur who would seize the potential of the area to convert the entire operation into a viable proposition.

Near Palampur is also the home of the famous painter the late Dr Saheb Verma. His paintings are vibrant. They presented pictures of folks of Punjab and Himachal Pradesh. His all-time great paintings, in my view, are those of 'Sohani Mahiwal' and 'Ranjit Singh'. His small home is a known place for people to visit. I was often welcomed with great deal of warmth whenever I found the time to go there. I had made a lot of effort to improve the services of the hill train. This included improving the maintenance of diesel locomotives and their reliability and also better track maintenance, which consequently improved the general speed and led to a reduction of the running time between Pathankot and Palampur.

JAMMU AND KASHMIR—A BEAUTIFUL STATE

The tenure of DRM Firozpur without some description of J&K would not be complete. Kashmir can best be described as closest to heaven: as Emperor Jahangir said, 'If there is a heaven on the earth it is here, it is here!'

But the political disturbances in the state by militants with generous support from across the border brought untold misery and violence. Fortunately, railway line went up to Jammu. J&K has three broad regions—Kashmir known as valley,

Ladakh and Jammu. The cultural background also varies between the three regions. The valley portion is divine and its natural beauty defies description. This is dominated by Muslims while Jammu has a large Hindu population. The valley has been under the grip of militancy for a long time. But without any railway line, it had no impact on the working of the railway unlike in Punjab. The only installations the Railway had were beautiful holiday homes and rest houses located in Srinagar, Gulmarg, etc., and of course one out agency at Srinagar. These guest houses were very popular during the good old days. In the wake of militancy, the holiday home in Gulmarg was taken over by militants and was subsequently burnt down. The rest house in Srinagar was also burnt down by them. It was then taken over by the CRPF. The out agency was closed down after the licensee ran away with railway money.

I could not go to Srinagar to start services of the out agency once again. The security arrangements were too demanding. I did not relish the thought of moving under a protective ring of armed security men. The government was however very keen to reopen the out agency in Srinagar. By that time, the passenger reservation system (PRS) was also in force. We had a tie-up with the post office in Srinagar to open the PRS in their office. This was operated by the staff of the post office. This became very popular in time to come.

Jammu remained a very active railway hub, serving many areas of J&K. Apart from the famous holy shrine at Vaishno Devi, which attracted a large number of pilgrims from all parts of the country, Jammu station catered for people going to the valley by road. Furthermore, huge Army and paramilitary personnel deployed in different parts of J&K used Jammu as a rail head. All major supplies for the valley like foodgrains, coal, POL, fertilizer, cement and construction materials were carried by rail to Jammu and then onwards by road. This included both civil and military supplies. Operationally, Ludhiana-Jalandhar-Pathankot-Jammu line was very vital for the sustenance of J&K.

As long as Punjab was on the extremists' agenda, their pressure on Jammu was insignificant. The Pathankot-Jammu single line section crossed many important rivers. The area between Sambha and Jammu was very close to Pakistani border—at some places just three km away. According to the civil and military authorities, after Punjab, militant activities started to pick up in and around Jammu. The top civilian authority at Jammu mentioned how young armed people were forced across the border for disruptive activities. Many times, unexploded bombs were found in bushes near Jammu Railway station.

During the later part of my tenure in Firozpur in 1995-96, such activities became frequent and Jammu station became a soft target for the terrorists. Two attempts were made to blow the railway line near Sambha station. Once,

Shalimar Express had just passed when the railway line was blown up by bombs. In the second case, the explosion took place ahead of an express train. In both cases the escape was miraculous. According to the police, the extremists crossed the border under cover of darkness. It was difficult to distinguish them from any Indian villager returning from his field. As a result, continuous patrolling of the track by combined patrol of the Railway Protection Special Force (RPSF) and state police was introduced. A pilot engine was run ahead of a group of trains leaving Jammu in the evening, to take care of any untoward incident.

When I returned to the Northern Railway as its GM in 2003 it had already blown up to serious proportions. J&K had the misfortune to witness so many senseless acts of violence. The people of the state who had lived peacefully, earning their livelihood from a flourishing tourism industry were driven to abject poverty. It is a tale all right-minded people deserve to know. Parents saw their young children being driven to terrorism as they were misled that it was meant for gaining absolute freedom. It soon became an illusion. Only the perpetrators of crime flourished. I will talk more about it when I revisit J&K during my tenure as GM, Northern Railway.

DUMPED, I BID FAREWELL TO FIROZPUR

Normally the DRM's tenure was for two years. Accordingly, I was completing my tenure in May 1996. Many rated my performance as very good. They wished for an extension in my tenure, which would be justified and welcome.

In the morning of 16 May 1996, the GM informed me that Raj Kumar was ordered to take over from me. He was at that time DRM Lucknow (NE Railway). I was taken aback. I had expected to complete my two years tenure on 27 May at least. Although it did not matter but there was no tearing hurry to replace me. Mr Agarwal agreed to sort out the problem, after I spoke to him. He asked Raj Kumar to join after 27 May. Many were of course eyeing this post. Mr Kalmadi before relinquishing his office had ordered the change. So, Raj Kumar landed on 26 May 1996 and I handed over the charge of the division on 27 May 1996. I received a touching farewell interestingly from the trade unions. Two years had been very eventful and when I left Firozpur, it was with a great deal of satisfaction.

11

RETURN TO WILDERNESS

My choice of the title 'Return to Wilderness' is rather bizarre. Nevertheless, I have chosen it and correctly so. You may have to wait a bit to appreciate its appropriateness.

After being relieved from the post of DRM, I had to return to my department, but no orders for my further posting had been issued. My children were in crucial years, academically. Shravani was completing political science from Lady Shri Ram College of Women. Shreya had just completed her tenth board examination. For her, the next two years were crucial. Shrimant was in Class VIII. Thus, I wished to be in Delhi for at least the next two years. For my career also, a stint in the Board was essential. I had spoken to ME Mr Raj Kumar on these lines in April. He had assured me, 'Do not worry. We will take care. Tell me when the DRM orders are issued.'

After the DRM orders were issued, I requested him to post me as CE (SAG) in the Northern Railway. For some strange reason, he was curt and told me, 'Do not talk to me directly. Speak to the secretary Railway Board.' I felt hurt because he had asked me to speak to him after the DRM orders were issued. As per extant conventions, outgoing DRMs are always shown greater consideration in subsequent postings. Well, I could do nothing about it.

V.K. Agarwal, GM, was also upset when I told him about it. He had also spoken to the ME earlier. He spoke to him on the RAX, 'Sir, Jaruhar is coming out of DRM, Firozpur. I had mentioned to you that he wanted to be in Delhi. I am prepared to accept him in Northern. He has done a wonderful job as DRM in a very difficult situation, and for most part of his career he has been in difficult areas. It will be good if his request is accepted. Please issue orders accordingly.' The ME agreed and the orders for posting me to the Northern Railway, were issued. The principal CE had agreed to accommodate me in Baroda House as CE (track machines).

I SEEK MY MOORINGS AS CHIEF ENGINEER

The residential accommodation in Delhi was the most serious problem. I was lucky to get a transit flat at the State Entry Road. It served my immediate purpose. I got a room in the construction office to put our kit that had been transported from Firozpur. After graduation, Shravani had gone for a management programme in Jaipur. Shreya and Shrimant found it difficult to get admitted to a school. Being in the middle of the session, all schools had closed their admission programmes. But thanks to Veer Raghvan the noted educationist and one of the directors of Bharatiya Vidya Bhavan, both were admitted in school. I was thus ready for the next show at Baroda House as CE (track machines).

I had no real experience with track machines so far. The entire fleet of track machines of the Northern Railway was centrally controlled at the headquarters level. Besides, the Northern Railway had a workshop in Allahabad for maintenance, repair and periodic overhauling of the entire fleet of track machines of the Indian Railways. The performance of track machines was monitored by the Board as it is highly capital intensive.

The Track Machine Organization (TMO) did not have healthy working conditions for its men. This was a matter of perpetual complaint. Unfortunately, traffic blocks for track machines were not regularly available on high density routes where machine maintenance would be most advantageous. Because of indifferent availability of blocks, there was a tendency to deploy machines on unimportant routes. This was against the organizational goal. The maintenance of machines also had some problems. Procurement of critical spare parts suffered long procedural delays. Reliability of machine depended upon genuine spare parts manufactured by original equipment manufacturers (OEMs).

In short, the TMO needed immediate attention in order to turn it in to an effective and efficient unit in track maintenance. Many maladies afflicting the unit were identified.

Territorial chief engineer for the Allahabad division

Apart from a functional duty related to track machines, the CE (track machines) was also the territorial CE of the Allahabad division. The division occupied an extremely important position in the Indian Railways. Important commodities like coal, iron and steel moved in this division. All eyes were set on this division to perform without any hold up. As the territorial CE, I was responsible for ensuring a proper coordination of all the maintenance activities in the division.

ONE COULD BE LOST IN THE WILDERNESS!

A DRM has full wherewithal within the proper chain of command. A territorial CE has to fend for himself. The change was sudden and very pronounced one. Even for attending to an accident, he has to pick up his own kit and figure out how to reach the site by himself. On arrival at the site, he has to find his own bearings. This state of affairs is akin to being in the wilderness. One could easily be lost.

No authority is vested under a territorial CE. Unless blessed with a commanding personality and conduct, he would easily be cold-shouldered by divisional officers. The PHOD normally interacted directly with the divisional officers without involving him. As such, it was desirable, but any decision could become lopsided if the territorial CE was not in the picture. The PHOD has no qualms and is quite comfortable in dealing with him as the DRM but not when he is a territorial CE.

I recall in the former days; the DRM's tenure was longer—not just two years. A DRM usually served more than one division. He would eventually become PHOD. The tenure of two years is inadequate. In the first year, he learns the ropes. When he starts delivering, the bell rings for him. There is lot of merit in the argument for a longer tenure. A posting as DRM was considered as a status symbol and kind of social embellishment. The body of the Officers' Association therefore requested that the chance be given to as many officers as possible. It was considered as a welfare goal and accordingly, the government decided to have two-year fixed tenure for the DRM. How far this policy has served organizational interests was a crucial question that remained unanswered. Remember, Ayn Rand in *Atlas Shrugged* has dealt with a similar theme—that seeking personal satisfaction at the expense of organizational goal could be disastrous indeed.

Instead of moaning, I had to quickly adapt to the changed circumstances. With slips inevitable at the start, the best way out of the wilderness was to make myself useful. I decided to grow my areas of influence. I had useful contacts as the DRM. I used them to my full advantage. The work culture, set-up and ambience created a feeling of being in a jungle, but there was no need to succumb to it. The feeling had to be banished.

Track machines issues, challenges and approach to a solution

Three factors basically affected the productivity of track machines—availability of traffic blocks, reliability including downtime of machines and depleted morale of workmen.

The Track Machine Organization has handicaps

Improvement in quality of workmanship called for technological input and the use of the best engineering practices. The DENs were asked to associate themselves with track machine operators. The DENs knew about track defects better. So, they were in a better position to give technical inputs to the operators, who in turn, then could come up with the best suited results. This had encouraging results. Besides, close interaction also helped in improving the working conditions at the work sites. This was the plus point.

The traffic block had been a long-standing issue between the traffic and engineering officers. Despite a series of joint circulars signed by none less than member engineering and member traffic, the four-hour stipulated traffic block for track machines had never materialized. Even when Shanti Narayan was the GM of the Northern Railway as well as the MT, the availability of traffic blocks did not improve. For good train operations, proper track maintenance is an absolute requirement. This needed appreciation. The traffic block was an inescapable requirement and not some kind of favour.

The machine required minimum time to move from its base. Besides the time taken to travel, time was required for setting it up before it could commence working. Likewise, the machine needed time for winding up before it returned to the base yard. The preparatory time differed from machine to machine. Thus, a block of less than two hours for a tie tamping machine was useless. For a ballast cleaning machine, a block of less than three hours was unproductive and hence unacceptable. This was a basic need to maintain good health of the track. It was not a luxury and if ignored, it could lead to the breakdown of infrastructure and could put the organization at peril.

The concept of traffic block as an investment

It will be unfair to believe that traffic officers needed to be convinced that traffic blocks were unavoidable. But they had also seen that trains ran without maintenance and unless there was an absolute emergency, traffic blocks could be deferred. It was a dangerous outlook. According to them, the train services did not improve even after a traffic block and machines broke down frequently in the mid-section causing huge hold up. The reliability of track machines was questioned. But fortunately, the COM, Govind Ballabh, was an exceptional traffic officer. He often said that traffic officers suffered from a mental block. After all, heavens did not fall if there was a hold-up because of an accident! With his support, traffic blocks were given with more regularity. Actually, my performance in the Firozpur division in this respect came very handy. I was determined that the quality of the track after machine maintenance was superior and more durable. The performance was measured in terms of running time saved either due to the removal of existing restrictions or due to a reduction in duration of the restrictions time to make the train movement faster. The grant of traffic block was an investment. It was therefore our duty as engineers to ensure a commensurate return on the investment in measurable terms. Improving speed and removal of standing restrictions to have a direct impact on through put could be safely considered as a yardstick of measurement.

Addressing the quality and the downtime of machines

The second aspect of the machine operation was its reliability and the optimum availability of the machine by cutting down its breakdown time. It was also important to set up a procedure for speedy evacuation of the machine in case of a breakdown. Extensive discussions with all concerned led to interesting results or issues. Briefly described they were:

Poor maintenance practices: They were not enough annual maintenance contracts (AMC) with OEMs.

Inadequate stock of spare parts: Procurement process by the stores department was long and more often than not, the parts procured did not match the quality of the OEM.

Maintenance work not properly monitored: It needed training and improvement of skill of artisans.

Poor communication: Mobile phones were not available in those days. In case of any failure, the site staff had to wait to be called on railway phones. These were either not readily available or there was a very low priority in getting telephone connection.

With good support from controller of stores and the finance officers concerned, a system to have a running rate contact was approved for the supply of genuine spare parts and introduced. This system was already in practice for diesel and electric engines. Besides, the unit exchange practice was also introduced. The entire defective unit was replaced and sent to the manufacturer's workshop for quality repair with high reliability.

These measures immediately improved downtime and reliability made a quantum jump. It was essential to have a properly analysed schedule listing out commonly used spare parts for each machine based on experience of the TMO plus recommendations of the OEM. Fortunately, the engineers concerned were thorough and a committed lot like Hitesh Khanna, Bali and Achal Jain, etc. This helped in finalizing the list for purchase and monitoring.

Communication was not a very serious issue. Thanks to the Bharat Sanchar Nigam Limited (BSNL) network, public phones were available very widely and getting an STD connection was cheap and easy. We allowed them to use DOT phones freely with payments made through cash imprest. Of course, the person could also contact his family. It was an essential step in improving our working conditions.

Improving working conditions—refurbished camp coaches

The working conditions had many aspects. Some of the employees had to go out of their homes with machines. Normally a roster of fifteen days was set for them. In between two outstation spells of duties there was a spell of a fifteen-day stay at the headquarters. This had to be strictly controlled. Most of the complaints were regarding the poor living conditions. With the active involvement of divisional engineers, the position vastly improved.

The camp coaches provided to them were horrible. The rolling stock programme of the Board did not give adequate priority for camp coaches in the face of a greater demand for passenger coaches. I had the experience of refurbishing an inspection carriage, carried out by the railway workshop, by suitably modifying a damaged general service coach. Such coaches had to be hunted out. Every railway workshop could produce a few coaches like this. We were ready with two camp coaches, custom-built and furnished for the workmen, in six months' time. It was unbelievable and this boosted the morale of the workmen a great deal.

There was nothing magical or novel in taking these measures. Most of them were already known and some initiatives had been taken already. But being a DRM, I had some advantage. I could push them faster. I was fortunate because in a total time of nine months (June 1996 to March 1997) that I spent as CE (TMC), I could give shape to some, with the active support of my team.

MEANINGFUL AS TERRITORIAL CHIEF ENGINEER

New ideas have to be owned

As a territorial CE, I tried to be useful for the division. The latest track recording of Ghaziabad-Tundla section—both the Up and Down line had shown a deterioration in the aspect of its running. There were enormous inputs in maintenance of track and therefore this slide in track parameters was not understandable. This required a thorough investigation and analysis of results. The response of the division in this respect was typically evasive.

Like any other person, DENs also suffered from personal egos, which would not permit the acceptance of new ideas easily especially those coming from the territorial chief engineer. But he had to assist in solving these problems. Unless the personal ego was addressed, the new idea could not succeed. *It is important to ensure that a new idea is owned—who authored or whose idea it is, is not important.* I simply asked the field engineers to analyse how peaks in track recording chart (denoting defects in track parameters) were distributed on the overall section. The answer was obvious. About 80 per cent of bad peaks were in station yards—precisely between two outermost points. The curves in the midsection accounted for most of other remaining peaks. Thus, attention obviously had to be focused on station yards. There could not be any dispute about that. So, station yards in disrepute were isolated. This idea was owned by them.

Outstanding results—owned by all with credit to the territorial chief

Recently on a programme basis, old turnouts were replaced by fan-shaped ones. But the analysis of track recording showed that the running instead of improving had become worse. Why? A loaded question which did not have any defence. It was obvious that the geometry of the layout was defective. A fan-shaped turnout has a superior curvature that allows for smooth movement of a vehicle. Why should there be a jerk? That meant that the overall dimension was not as per the drawing. That is, it was possible that the overall length of the turnout was either a few millimetres too long or short. It is possible because that aspect is normally not checked with a standard template. For inserting the turnout during traffic block, PWI would normally cut the rail in advance according to dimensions *as per the drawing*. If the dimension of the assembly did not exactly match the drawing, he would force the turnout within the available gap. This would cause a distinct kink.

No PWI would accept that he did not check the overall length of the assembly before inserting it. This had to be verified. Now the idea was owned by them. I had only helped them along. On my advice, an accurate survey of the yard by using level and theodolite between fifty metres ahead of the outermost point on one end to fifty metres on the other end was carried out. In less than three weeks' time, the survey was completed. Bad locations were identified and rectified within a month. The next recording showed a quantum improvement, with spectacular results beyond belief. They accepted me as their undisputed leader—not only merely as just another territorial CE who came for dinner and some drinks!

SPATE OF DERAILMENTS IN THE GMC (KANPUR)—OBJECTIVE ASSESSMENT

GMC (Kanpur)—a vital yard had a spate of derailments. On a single day, there were six derailments. The engineering department was indicted for bad maintenance. The DRM was also convinced of this.

The sequence of events and site measurements recorded were analysed. All track parameters were within the acceptable limits. Possible causes of derailment could be track defects, incorrect layout, bad train running (over-speeding), signalling defects and bad rolling stocks. It was being said that the layout of the yard was difficult. But this aspect could not be held responsible because traffic had run without any problem so far. The layout was difficult because of a constraint of space. But this was common in many other places. This called for a need for cautious running. It was not a case of bad track parameters. It was wrong to hold engineering department responsible.

Since I loudly disputed the findings, the case was put up to the GM for acceptance of an accident enquiry report. The GM called me and the chief safety officer (CSO) for a discussion. I marshalled my arguments in a logical manner. The GM was convinced. The engineering department was acquitted of the charge, in the report. My senior DEN, Satish Agnihotri, had been unhappy because the young man had worked hard but there was no one to listen to or support his argument. Very pleased with the outcome, even today, he never fails to mention my effort in this regard.

TIME TO GO TO THE BOARD

There was a talk of my migrating to the Railway Board. In my view, it was necessary to serve in the Board to acquire the much needed experience. One morning, Kanwarjit Singh (who I also called KJ), advisor vigilance, called me to say that my orders as executive director vigilance (E) in the Board had been issued.

It was 22 March 1997. I was to leave for Patna on that day. I had recently lost my father-in-law. My wife was already in Patna. But I was asked to join immediately in the Board on the same day before I left for Patna.

12

ENTER THE RAILWAY BOARD

FIRST POSTING IN THE BOARD IN VIGILANCE

'Entre, Railway Board, sil vous plait (Please enter the Railway Board, if you please).'

It did not happen any way like that. It had its own measure of yes or no. Kanwarjit Singh had once asked me if I would accept a posting as executive director in the Vigilance Directorate. Vigilance posting is an ex-cadre appointment and the officer's willingness is essential. More importantly, many were not comfortable with Vigilance. To me, it was a challenge. The proposal for my posting was accordingly initiated to obtain approval of the MR. I think that someone had advised the minister's cell against my posting and hence the proposal was dumped. Whatever the truth, the minister's approval was not forthcoming.

Months passed without any tangible development. I told Mr Ravindra, the new ME, about it. He was surprised and asked me why I had not mentioned it earlier. He requested the minister to approve my posting. The original note could not be located in the office. A fresh note was dictated and the minister's approval was taken personally. Orders were issued in the evening.

Kanwarjit Singh asked me to join straight away. He was apprehensive that the lobby in the minister's cell might persuade the MR to change the order. I had to go to Patna on that day. But I joined as executive director vigilance (E) in the forenoon before proceeding to Patna in the evening.

I served the Board in two spells. I was entering the Board after twenty-nine years of service—about eight years ahead of superannuation. I had a great deal of experience. Government service was extended to sixty years after the Fifth Pay Commission awards. I occupied many important positions during my ten years of remaining service. Except for a little spell, less than two years as GM, the rest was spent in the Board.

RAILWAY BOARD OPENS UP A NEW VISTA

Railway Board, an apex organization of the Indian Railways, has two levels of functioning. The Ministry of Railways deals with policy formulation and implementation. The Board comprised various directorates. The top tier of the Board is the secretariat of the ministry comprising the chairman and members including the secretary. The Board functions are set down by the Railway Board Act of 1905.

I was convinced that those aspiring to be members of the Railway Board (preferably the GM also) should have tenure in the Board. It opens a new vista and provides vital experience without which many have been seen to fumble in the initial stages. An appointment in the Board came at the right time for me, after a spell as the DRM. I had acquired a stature, which augured well for my stint in the Board.

The vigilance organization—a novel experience

I had little idea of the vigilance department. As it was an ex-cadre assignment, I had no past knowledge or experience. Kanwarjit Singh was my predecessor before being promoted as advisor vigilance. This was a precedence that was for a long time. EDV (E) was senior appointment No.2 in the directorate. The advisor vigilance was the chief vigilance officer of the Ministry of Railways.

KJ would time and again in the initial stage, lay great emphasis upon upright conduct as a vigilance officer—and ask us to be a clean person with regard to integrity. I was amused because one could not become clean or acquire integrity overnight. I decided to conduct myself as usual. People had accepted me without ever questioning my integrity. It was not necessary for me to demonstrate it afresh.

In this respect, I recall how a colleague CE (construction) of mine in Gorakhpur would come to the office in a tattered shirt. He wanted everyone to note his frugal lifestyle which he believed would demonstrate his integrity. At the drop of a hat, he would mention that he possessed only two shirts. Likewise, he would announce that his bank balance that day was the same as it was before he had joined the Railways. In short, he took pride in telling people that he lived a simple life, that his meagre income could only afford so much. But he had an infamous reputation, so people simply laughed at his self-proclaimed honesty. My deputy CE was once with me for some meeting when someone wanted to meet him urgently. He went out to meet him and returned after some time to resume our discussion. He told me later about how a contractor was humiliated in the office by that CE. That contractor confessed to my deputy CE that the CE had demanded ₹1,000 for approving extension in the contract period. When the contractor denied having so much money, the CE forcibly put his hand in the contractor's pocket, to take out the money. In the scuffle, the contractor's shirt was torn but all the CE could get was only ₹100. That infuriated him further. He had wanted at least ₹500 more. With this kind of reputation any claims of honesty is absurd and would only fetch laughter and scorn.

Structure of the vigilance

The Railway Board Vigilance supervised vigilance activities over the entire Railway system. Policy directives were issued by the Central Vigilance Commission (CVC), which did not have the requisite constitutional strength earlier. In course of time, it became a constitutional authority with adequate power. The CVC consisted of the central vigilance commissioner (CVC) and two vigilance commissioners.

The vigilance organization had three-fold functions—preventive, punitive and complaint investigation. In all three functions, action emanated normally from the Zonal Railways. In some cases, where the Railway Board or GM was involved, action was initiated by Board Vigilance. On the basis of the investigation, misconduct was brought to light and action proposed to be put into effect against the railway servant. In case of a gazetted officer, the advice of the CVC is to be obtained for the course of action proposed. Thus, the Vigilance Organization was better known as witch-hunters. Many in the Railways were afraid of the mere mention of its name.

I once called R.K. Singh, then ED (track) to ask if I could drop into his room for tea. He welcomed me but he was visibly alarmed. He asked if all was well. The CVC, too, once told me how many were uncomfortable in his presence. A depressing thought indeed! My good old friend Arun Biswas had told me that he had declined the vigilance posting earlier. He said that he was afraid of the hostility he would draw from his old friends!

INITIATIVES FOR POSITIVE PERCEPTION OF THE VIGILANCE

My two directors put forward their annual performance report. They had cited number of vigilance cases they had registered or disposed of as a measure of their performance. I was shocked initially but that was apparently the practice even in CVC. I knew it was fundamentally wrong somewhere.

Long overdue change in paradigm

In my perception, the vigilance department was a part of Indian Railways and its mission and objective was to transport public goods and passengers efficiently and effectively. The vigilance department had to promote and supplement the corporate mission objective. The organization had a workforce where some were good and some bad. If catching people and punishing them becomes the measure of performance of the vigilance department, then soon all would be run down, leaving very few to carry on with the corporate goal. Railwaymen are public servants with public accountability. They have to be open to public scrutiny. The vigilance organization could not be merely fault-finders. It had to assist railwaymen in discharging their duty in tune with the corporate mission objective. The vigilance organization had the information and wherewithal in this respect. The department had to focus on positives rather than counting how many were booked by it. We perceived that the change in the paradigm was long overdue.

Examination of past cases confirmed that the majority of officers acted in good faith. They acted with common prudence while taking financial decisions but failed to leave behind evidence of such application for subsequent scrutiny. This was basic to the canons of financial propriety. This tenet was taught to us as probationers in the Railway Staff College, Baroda. It unfortunately became only a quotation. Very few took steps to ensure and demonstrate how this principle was applied.

Thus, a large percentage of officers suffered from ignorance and needed education. Tender and contracts and selection processes were the two main areas where mistakes were common. With help of case studies, a training module was designed to help officers to take decisions in a logical and simple manner.

In our assessment, 85 per cent of the railwaymen are basically good, but ignorant. Good, effective and practical training could easily help this group. Another 10 per cent are knowledgeable but had crossed the line for lack of supervision or fear of any action. They could also be addressed. The course module talked of the consequences of not following the correct action.

Lastly, the last 5 per cent constituted real diehards. Carrying out harsh punitive measures was the best action against them. They had to be effectively weeded out. There was no doubt that they were a powerful lot. They wielded great influence and were close to the centre of power. They often occupied important positions.

WE INITIATE CHANGES

Introducing a change like this was not easy. Many in the Vigilance Directorate believed that offering such training was not their job, and it could even become counter-productive. They felt that training could make rogues smarter! I believed that our role was to deter corrupt activities and promote good conduct.

We could not adopt a negative attitude and measure our success by the number of vigilance cases instituted. Fortunately, my two very competent directors—Anurag Sharma and B.D. Garg—supported me fully. They became active allies in my initiative. KJ, first cautious but later became very supportive.

Practical training modules were helpful

Many educative programme capsules for tender and contracts as well as for departmental selections were prepared. The JA and selection grade officers and above were our target area. We also specially targeted DRMs and PHOD officers. It was an instant success for the DRMs many of whom had no experience of tenders. The DRM is a senior officer but a lonely one, unable to seek guidance on the subject. Traffic officers, mechanical engineers were such examples. For departmental selection, officers of all disciplines suffered from a lack of experience and exposure. I told the DRMs that they were free to seek my advice if required. That was encouraging and I received calls from them quite frequently. The training programme eventually became a regular course in the Railway Staff College. Evidently officers were keen on the knowledge and as it came from experienced persons it was welcome.

The CVC was briefed about the programme. Tender and contracts were dealt with very exhaustively. The responsibilities of individual members of the Tender Committee were explained in detail. Likewise, the tender accepting authority also had a checklist for guidance. There was of course nothing new in them. But these points were collected to enable the Tender Committee members to deliberate on the offers in a more objective and transparent manner. The CVC circulated them among other departments for their guidance.

I believed that I held public money in solemn trust. So at each stage of financial implication, I asked myself if I could defend or justify my decisions or actions. This often led to an intense internal debate. If the action proposed did not satisfy my conscious auditing, it could not be justified. The module was framed with this basic underlying philosophy.

The image of the vigilance organization was transformed. We were perceived as a proactive group and not merely fault-finders and fixers. Along with these steps, we also initiated actions to train our own workforce in proper vigilance management.

VIGILANCE ACTIVITY TO SUPPORT CORPORATE MISSION

The top management was unhappy with a large section of staff being involved in vigilance cases. They were unavailable for full and active duty. The analysis showed many pending Discipline and Appeals Rules (DAR) cases—some for over five years. It was bad for the staff morale as well.

Besides, many officers were on the 'Agreed List'. This list is the product of an annual exercise between the CBI and the Railways' vigilance organization. It contained names of officers whose integrity was suspect, but against whom we could not find any established case. General managers were directed not to post such officers in 'sensitive' posts. The administration had problems with accommodating such officers because of a limited number of non-sensitive posts.

A two-pronged strategy was developed for the purpose. All the DAR cases were closely monitored by posting them on the data bank of Board Vigilance. The first list prepared sometime in November 1997 had more than nine hundred pending DAR cases. The size of the problem was staggering.

A massive training programme was launched for dealing with DAR cases both for deputy chief personnel officers (G) and deputy CAO (G) who monitored them in the Railways. Retired officers of good reputation were inducted as inquiry officers. Exclusive training in conduct of the DAR inquiry was given to them. Quarterly review of the DAR cases was conducted. Bad cases of delay were brought to the notice of GMs. The results of an intense monitoring and system improvement were very rewarding. The list showed only five hundred pending cases—down from nine hundred cases in a span of six months. This steadily improved and even the CVC took note of our efforts. We were soon a role model for them.

There was no point in placing a large number of suspects in the 'Agreed' list. It caused unnecessary administrative problems. I took up the issue with the joint director CBI (coordination). He appreciated my point of view. We made sure that not more than seven officers from the Railways were put on the list. That meant there was a maximum of two persons from a department in a zonal railway. This became vastly manageable.

PROVISION OF SINGLE DIRECTIVE

Prime Minister I.K. Gujral in his speech to the nation on Independence Day in 1998 announced that corruption in public life would be removed. This raised a lot of hue and cry and all anti-corruption departments were readied. The CBI complained that administrative ministries were reluctant to accord sanctions for prosecution against officers under the Prevention of Corruption Act, 1989. This permission was necessary in accordance with the famous provision known as 'Single Directive', to protect officers of joint secretary and above. This was based on the view that the decision making process at higher levels was quite complex.

If prosecution was launched without a proper consideration of the situation, it would deter senior public servants from acting in public interest. This provision in the Act was considered discriminatory and controversial. The Supreme Court accepted the plea of provision being discriminatory in a PIL filed before it, and struck it down

But the administrative machinery including political parties soon realized that it was dangerous to do away with this provision. I had supported the view to retain the protection clause in the Act to protect well-meaning officers from avoidable prosecution. In my view, complexities of tender and contract cases of a department were often not duly appreciated by others. It was therefore necessary for the administrative ministry to apply its mind before deciding to proceed in the court of law. I had a substantial discussion with the CBI officers, but most of them were adamant to do away with this provision. In this context, I will relate a very interesting case.

Provision of single directive helped well-meaning officers

The case was for the sanction of a prosecution against four senior officers of the Western Railway. All of them were members of the tender committee—the FA&CAO, the AGM and the CE (construction) in charge of a gauge conversion project near Jaipur. The GM—the accepted authority—was also named as culprit but was let off because he agreed to be a prosecution's witness. Except the FA&CAO, all others had retired.

The DIG of the CBI called me one afternoon and requested me to issue a sanction to prosecute the officers. To be honest, I did not know the procedure and the nuances of the Prevention of Corruption Act. In practice, such sanction was being issued in a routine manner. But KJ told me that all the officers had a good reputation and therefore the case looked fishy. The sanction could be denied on good and sound reasons only. I decided to meet joint director CBI immediately in Mumbai. I fixed up an appointment with him for the next day. I read up on the act and case studies on the flight to Mumbai and by the time I landed in Mumbai, I was fairly well-informed about the essence of the legal provisions contained in the Prevention of Corruption Act.

The case related to award of a ballast supply contract for the gauge conversion project on single tender basis. According to the report, a contract for supply of ballast was awarded by the officers on high rates by entering into a criminal conspiracy. The CAO had briefed me about the case in Mumbai before I met with the CBI. In Jaipur area, a large number of construction activities were undertaken by many government departments. With a large number of contracts in operation, hands of all established ballast suppliers in the area were full. They were therefore unable to meet fresh demands. Thus, a limited tender calling for supply of ballast from existing competent suppliers had shown poor response. The gauge conversion work was nearing completion. It could not be opened to the traffic unless the track was ballasted. The existing meter gauge line was already blocked. There was a hue and cry by the public to commission the broad gauge line, without any undue delay. It became an issue where for want of a nail—the war was lost. Under such compelling circumstances, the CE in charge of the construction had decided to bring in a new agency to break the impasse created by existing suppliers.

He scouted out a suitable new quarry and a suitable operator for the work. He found an alternative source which had to be developed. It was the only option. They accordingly awarded the work to the party on a single tender basis. The rates fixed were however quite reasonable and lower than those quoted by established suppliers in the failed limited tender. These rates were however higher than some existing supply rates fixed long ago and which had eventually failed. Old rates were no longer viable because of high demand. This background information was relevant, but the CBI did not bring this out in their report. I met the joint director CBI. I explained how in light of this context, the conduct of the officers looked reasonable and just. I clarified that the provisions of single directive were relavant in light of such cases. I explained that the department only could provide the necessary input to judge the action of officers. Such relevant information was only available with them. Only the Railways could consider and explain the urgency about opening of a closed line for public transport. But without such consideration, even he and I could be handed a chargesheet. He agreed with me when I presented the facts. The case was sent to the CVC for advice with full facts. The case had caused a commotion in the CBI headquarters and the joint director had invited me for a presentation on the case to the CBI headquarters. Finally, the CVC, in light of our comments, accepted our recommendation and advised closure of the case without any action.

This case gave me useful insight into the Prevention of Corruption Act. I educated officers to be careful in their conduct. It also helped in proper dealing with such cases to protect genuine officers. The vigilance department was seen as being helpful and not a witch-hunter—a positive and encouraging feedback. The credit for this must go to KJ who prompted me to apply our minds afresh on the subject. The CBI also appreciated our view and their respect for us grew, which was encouraging indeed.

HARD-CORE ELEMENTS ARE RATTLED

There were also some offenders who typically constituted 5 per cent of the workforce. They were hard core elements with a large following, who challenged our credibility. But I had an energetic and daredevil director (vigilance)—Anurag Sharma, a bundle of energy with a 'never say die' spirit. Large value contracts like the supply of concrete, wooden sleepers and track fittings were dealt with by the Railway Board. There were many complaints in these contracts. But these persons dealing with such contracts had the reputation of being good achievers. They claimed to have caused the Railways to make a good amount of savings. But the manner of fixing contract quantity and its distribution was arbitrary, lacking in transparency. Around this time, one could see a horde of suppliers, flocking the corridors of the Board. It was an obnoxious scene that brought a bad name to the Railways! These cases were taken up and it caused a furore because they pulled out quite a few skeletons from the cupboard. KJ's support was invaluable. He could take on anyone and that emboldened us. The people in the MR's cell were particularly unhappy.

There was an intense political pressure to close the case. In the heat, Kanwarjit Singh was shifted. Some MP went gunning for him at the behest of a powerful lobby. A question was raised in the Parliament about his conduct in a trivial case. I had to defend that case. In her written reply to the starred Parliament question, Railway Minister Mamata Banerjee answered that the advisor vigilance was being transferred and the case against him was being referred to the CBI for inquiry.

We were stunned by the reply and so was CRB Ashok Kumar, who told me that this was done by the minister. KJ, who was an above-board officer and nobody could even think of any blemish in his integrity. I knew him from our short stint in the NF Railway, when he was posted there for a short while after returning from a foreign posting. I always thanked him for the support and courage and it has continued even now when both of us have retired from the same post—ME. This case was totally out of context relating to his tenure as CE, Northern Railway and was regarding the supply of HT wire which was a Board contract. We in the Board were convinced that he had no role in the case and it was being taken totally out of context in order to retaliate against the high and mighty in the Board. KJ is not a person to ever act with any vendetta; in fact, he was at pains to grill us to be careful while taking up any case. For him, the principle of British jurisprudence was supreme, 'Let thousands of scoundrels go but never punish one innocent.' We had learnt this from him.

The case was sent to the CBI for inquiry. I could not stop the injustice. All I could do was sympathise with KJ. Corrupt, power-wielding men were hitting him below the belt. Eventually, after inquiry, the CBI advised the Board that there was no substance in the complaint and gave a clean chit to KJ. It was a moral victory for me because I had promised Mrs Kanwarjit that no harm would come to him and he would eventually be a Board member. She had told me that how badly this had affected them. When I had informed her at Pune where KJ was posted, she had begun to cry.

I AM ADVISOR VIGILANCE BY DEFAULT

Thus, by default I became advisor vigilance. I was busy with my daughter's wedding. It was solemnized on 16 January 2001. Orders were issued by the Board on 18 January. I finally took over on 21 January 2001 in my existing grade. I was eventually promoted to higher administrative grade (HAG) on 8 April 2001.

There was change in the ministry also. With the arrival of Nitish Kumar, our morale was restored after having suffered from a severe battering. Many in the Board felt that the investigation of a Board case tarnished the Railways' image and hence Vigilance should avoid taking up such cases. I could not buy that argument simply because many down the line pointed their fingers at the Board. If nothing was done at this level, the credibility of Railways as an organization was sure to suffer a dent.

A PHOD in S&T engineering was involved in a selection case for Group B officers. He carried out the selection every six months. According to the complaint, only those who had paid his wife would pass. He was a high flier. I once casually asked him how the success rate in Group B selection was so low in the Railways. He replied very brusquely that he insisted on quality. He said that unless the candidate met his exacting standards, he would not accept them. Very lofty indeed!

We carefully looked at the cases. The selection was to fill a quota of assistant S&T engineers in Group B from internal departmental candidates in Group C who had an engineering degree through a limited departmental test. Thus, a candidate who failed in the first test was unlikely to pass with flying colours in the next test held after six months. The Group C staff with an engineering degree in the Railways were limited in number. There is no other source to fill the quota. The head of the department, we thought, should have tried to select the best among the available candidates. It was a moot point—the Group B officer was required to discharge a particular functional duty and not all were called to be top grade designers. Then, what was the crying need to set such a high bar which was totally futile to fill the post required for less demanding services? This led to a possible conclusion that it was an excuse to hold an examination every six months. A workable hypothesis!

An examination of the answer books of the candidates brought out the modus operandi of the operation. The person finally selected was awarded full marks for an incorrect answer. The officer clarified that marks were given for following the correct procedure. Then why were others not awarded? He was awarded full marks for personality traits in a viva voce test whereas in the previous test he was only given 60 per cent. Well, one knows that personality traits do not improve dramatically in the course of six months.

The officer was rattled and came to me in an agitated manner. As advisor vigilance, I met all the officers facing vigilance cases. I always listened to them with an open mind. The opportunity was also taken to convince the person of his misconduct, if there was irrefutable evidence. He told me that he was being questioned for his effort to select the most suitable candidate and for being uncompromising in this respect. I told him that it was a laudable attempt but the points brought out in the course of the investigation militated against his mission. The argument was so forceful that he had no answer. But he requested to be let off because he was due to become GM and could also become a Board member. Despite several pressures exerted by the Board and even in the CVC, his conduct could not be condoned. His case went as an appeal to the UPSC, but the Commission upheld the charge.

INTERESTING LEGAL CLARIFICATION IN THE DAR CASES

DAR based on the principle of preponderance of probability

The principle of preponderance of probability was the most important precept adopted in departmental proceedings. But in the case of judicial proceedings, the governing principle was that the charge had to be established beyond all reasonable doubt. This difference is important and many people are confused on this account.

The Supreme Court in many rulings on this basis has clarified that in departmental proceedings, the relationship between the disciplinary officer and the employee was that of a master and servant, where the master was not obliged to hold a judicial court to judge conduct of his servant. The evidence required to prove his culpability was not exacting in departmental proceedings. In judicial proceedings, the proof has to be beyond all reasonable doubt. This distinction was often confused while dealing with departmental cases.

Natural justice satisfied if set rules are followed

Likewise, the principle of 'natural justice' was often cited in judicial proceedings, which was different in the case of departmental cases. The apex court has ruled that if departmental rules, which were already laid out, were followed, then it would be presumed that the principle of natural justice had been followed.

In one case, according to the Railway Servants DAR, a charged officer (CO) was awarded a minor penalty by the disciplinary authority (DA). He was issued a major penalty chargesheet but after considering his representation the DA awarded a minor penalty. He appealed against the penalty order on the plea that a no show-cause notice was issued before awarding a minor penalty, which was a breach of 'natural justice'. The DA rules clearly provided that after considering the representation of the CO on a major penalty chargesheet, the DA had three options. If he was satisfied with his representation, he can drop the charges and exonerate the CO. Otherwise he would have to remit the case to departmental inquiry. Thirdly, if he is satisfied that the seriousness of the misconduct did not warrant a major penalty, he could award a suitable minor penalty without any further reference to the charged officer. The appeal was referred to the UPSC (in cases of all Class I officers where the president is DA, advice of the UPSC is mandatory) for their advice. They agreed with the CO and advised to uphold his appeal. The UPSC advised that the principle of natural justice was not observed before awarding minor penalty notwithstanding the provision in the DAR. Ultimately, citing the Supreme Court ruling, the case was sent to the DoPT who agreed with us. Consequently, the UPSC also withdrew its advice thus upholding the action taken by us.

The apex court in its judgment had relied upon the fact that the servant should know the rules and conduct himself accordingly. These rules could be different from the rules issued by another department on the same subject. As long as the rules were followed, the person could not complain.

In one case, the officer represented that he did not receive the chargesheet because the address was wrong. He should have been advised through the newspaper. According to the DAR, we were not obliged to do so although some departments had this rule. The court also said that it was the duty of a public servant to keep the office posted with his correct address.

These were often dilatory tactics adopted by some charged officers, who were assisted by defence counsels with a legal background. This often confused the disciplinary authority or inquiry officer as they were without proper understanding or training in law. So, we trained them with good case histories and judicial pronouncements on such matters. They were firmly told that this was not a court and the case had to be dealt with in accordance with the DAR. This paid us rich dividends. The credibility of the vigilance department rose because of our professional knowledge of these DA rules.

THE VIGILANCE DEPARTMENT CONTRIBUTED TO EARNINGS

I always felt that the vigilance organization like any other department of the Indian Railways should have a role in supplementing the activity of the organization. We discussed this aspect amongst ourselves. This change could bring about a positive direction to the efforts of the department.

Auction of scrap had a lot of complaints

Complaints regarding the auction of surplus and scrap stores engaged our serious attention. According to the complaint, the auction was usually cornered by some mafia who manipulated the process. Our minister was very critical and wanted concrete action. During a meeting called by him, the additional member (stores) vehemently defended the existing system. I rebutted his claim by citing cases where irregularities had been found. On the other hand, he had no evidence to sustain his claim. I said, 'Efficacy of a system is judged by quality system checks. You have no test result to support your statement.' He was quite upset but I stuck to my guns. Vigilance tests had outlined the presence of all types of irregularities. The minister was furious. He told him that Vigilance had at least carried out some checks and they had ultimately confirmed the complaints received by him. The stores department had no evidence to offer. So where was the basis of assurance given by the additional member (AM) stores?

Two days later, our team on source information intercepted a truck after it left Tughlakabad Store Depot with scraps that had not been weighed. Delivery documentations were incomplete and it carried three tons extra. Clearly, everyone had connived in the misconduct. This convinced the minister. On my recommendation, a task force was set up to streamline the procedure with clear-cut individual accountability. The entire process became more transparent. It also helped buyers of the scrap to receive the delivery of material with ease and thus was more user-friendly.

Vigilance reported earning to the organization

Vigilance checks led to the plugging of loss in revenue. We decided to quantify the earnings attributable to vigilance checks under three categories—tender and contracts, stores and released material, and traffic under charge. A monthly report on the earnings/savings accrued was submitted to the Board and the CVC.

The first report showed an earnings of ₹4 crore. It made waves, and the minister sent a note of appreciation. The Indian Railways spent around ₹26 lakh on the vigilance department. It had earned much more. It was thus fully self-reliant, and this positively contributed to the revenue of the Indian Railways. The CVC was very pleased and reported to the government accordingly. He also asked other departments to follow the Railways' module. This was a positive act, winning glory for the department and a rightful place in the organization for me.

COMPLAINTS ABOUT PASSENGER RESERVATION

There were complaints about train reservation particularly during the summer and festive seasons like Durga Pooja and Diwali. The system was monitored. Under a new procedure, extra coaches or even a new train were ordered to clear the rush. Coordination between the Railways' officials was the key in this respect. We ensured that a good coordination was in place between chief passenger transport manager (CPTM) and chief commercial manager (CCM). During summer, the operating department was asked to increase the number of coaches as many trains had a standard composition of sixteen coaches only.

A lady called me when she could not secure train reservation for her son to Bangalore (Bengaluru now) on a particular date. The Karnataka government conducted the entrance examination for its engineering colleges on a particular date. Students from all parts of India, including Bihar, travelled in large numbers. I requested the Board to run as many trains as possible to clear the rush. With six extra trains from all over, all waitlisted passengers were cleared. The lady called to thank me. Her son had confirmed reservation for Bangalore.

Actions like this removed public complaints, and illegal touts' activities disappeared. It brought a good name to the organization. Some operating officers were quite proactive, and I must place on record the initiative of Vivek Sahai as DRM Bombay in clearing an extraordinary rush for the eastern part of the country.

In the entire endeavour, touts and agents who fleeced ordinary passengers found no scope for their nefarious activities. The key was to eliminate the gap between the demand and the supply rather than spending time and energy in catching the touts. This was a good lesson and gradually the approach was accepted.

Judicial intervention in the DAR

In any court, the most important matter for any legal scrutiny is as follows:

- Whether the chargesheet is served according to the rules.
- Whether the disciplinary officer has applied his mind to the representation of the charged officer and has remitted the case to inquiry after passing the suitable speaking order. A line like, 'I have carefully gone through the representation of the charged officer who has denied the charges. Under the circumstances, it is essential to inquire into the case to ascertain the facts. I accordingly remit the case to inquiry would make the case legally sound'.
- Whether the departmental inquiry is conducted as per the rules. This is essential for natural justice. The inquiry officer must dispose of the objections of the charged officer through suitable speaking orders.
- After the receipt of the inquiry report, it must be ascertained whether it was given to the charged officer for his representation.
- Whether the DA passed the detailed speaking order after considering, point by point submission of the charged officer. There should be reasoned analysis of the proved charges. He should thereafter impose penalty as per rules.

If these principles are followed, the court would not normally interfere with the decision. It would not even question the quantum of punishment awarded.

In one case, the minister as the DA had imposed a minor penalty of withholding of increment in the time scale in consultation with the UPSC. The officer was a tender accepting authority in a composite case. The executive engineer—the convenor of the tender committee—was awarded the penalty of 'censure' by a different DA.

The tender accepting authority represented in the court that his role was minor in comparison to that of the convenor of the tender committee. He pleaded that his penalty could not have been more severe. The court agreed with this view and ordered the DA, that is, the MR, to revise the penalty.

The MR was not happy. I advised the joint secretary (E) that the minister need not revise the order. The action was justified. It was a composite case with two more charged officers with different DAs. Each DA had applied his mind independently. The rules did not allow the DA to consult each other in such cases. It was not possible to arrive at a common quantum of punishment. It depended on the DA's appreciation of the case. According to the apex court, the DA could not be questioned about the quantum of punishment if it had correctly applied its mind. The case was accordingly upheld by the court.

Terrorist attack on the Parliament

Although this incident was probably the most heinous crime against Indian democracy and has nothing to do with Vigilance, I describe it because it happened when I was advisor vigilance. The minister Nitish Kumar had called for a final briefing on the Parliament question in the Parliament Office at 10 a.m. on 13 December 2001. The briefing was over by 10.50 or so. The minister told me that he wanted to discuss something with Dasharathi, member mechanical (MM), and me. He said that the question hour was from 11 a.m., but it was likely that the house would be adjourned because the Opposition was boycotting George Fernandes, defence minister, on the Kargil issue. He said that if the house was adjourned he would discuss it with us in his Parliament Office, else in the Rail Bhawan. So, both of us waited for him in his room. After a while, we were informed that both houses had been adjourned as expected. Other officers left for the Rail Bhawan after that. After about half an hour, Nitish ji sent a message that he was busy in the Central Hall and that we should return to the Rail Bhawan, where the discussion would be held.

When the MM and I started walking back to the Rail Bhawan, we saw a battery of newsmen and TV photographers waiting for other ministers to come out. The Rail Bhawan is just across the Parliament, at a five-minute walk. As soon as we crossed the road, I saw people running here and there inside the Parliament. There was smoke and sounds of firing. My first thought was that demonstrators were being dispersed by the police—a very unlikely occurrence, of course. As soon as I came to my office on the fifth floor, my secretary Janaki ran out and informed me that the Parliament had been attacked by terrorists. I could see firing from my room, going on from all sides and at that very moment a man was struck down and blown away immediately. He was a suicide bomber with explosives strapped to his body. It was followed by complete silence. The scene was shocking. We had never thought that the temple of democracy could ever be violated. There were five terrorists in a white Ambassador car with home ministry and Parliament labels. All of them were killed. Six policemen and one gardener also lost their lives. The TV cameras were there and some daring photographers filmed the incident live.

I had told my wife in the morning that I would send her the car after I returned from the Parliament. When she heard the news on TV she was alarmed. I called her to calm her down. My son was in school and wanted to come to my office immediately. I told him that he should not move until someone came to fetch him. There was an atmosphere of fear and deathly silence. But fortunately, people acted responsibly. I need not describe how the politicians conducted themselves. MPs locked themselves inside the house and were reportedly paralysed with fear as they did not know where the terrorists would come from. As for me, the scene is etched in my memory and I wonder how the perpetrators of crime against democracy could be so daring. It was much later that I realized what a close shave I really had. I had emerged from the same gate from where the terrorists attacked barely five minutes later!

SOME AWKWARD OR EMBARRASSING MOMENTS

There were many awkward situations while working in Vigilance but the one I found most disturbing was about my own batchmate. He was at that time posted as executive director (standards) in the RDSO. Some products like rubber liners and plates were manufactured by some approved RDSO vendors. According to the CBI, samples were not tested properly by the inspection team. Rejected samples were not destroyed as per the rules. According to the report, the rejected samples were subsequently re-supplied in connivance of the RDSO team. The CBI wanted to register a case against the team, which included my batchmate. Normally such permissions were routine. According to the CBI report, he did not apply himself correctly and had even allowed tampering of the test results. My mate was my senior, and both of us had a very good chance to become board members. One of us might even eventually become the chairman.

The permission to the CBI to register the case would have certainly ruined his chances to become a member. He would certainly assume that I had deliberately removed a strong competitor from the race. Nobody would forgive me. My director on examination felt that it would be difficult to defend the case. I argued that this was a routine inspection by a RDSO team, and linking the executive director (standards), who is a senior person, is unnecessary as there was no direct evidence of actual interference. I recommended that this kind of permission not be given to register the case. I consulted the advisor vigilance also. The board agreed with me and it was eventually denied.

The SP of the CBI discussed the case with me. After a great deal of arguments, he said, 'Sir, I reluctantly agree with you because you are well-respected, but I can tell you that you are making a mistake about your batchmate.' After a long time, I told my batchmate about what had happened. I don't think he appreciated it. The story is long but eventually he used all his guile to prevent me from becoming a board member. He did not succeed, but the damage was done. But the good and redeeming part of it was that he did mention this episode during his farewell address upon his retirement.

He said, 'If Jaruhar had wanted he could have very easily allowed the CBI to ruin my career, but he did not!'

WHY CORRUPTION WOULD CONTINUE

The larger question, continuously haunting us was why after joining as a Class I officer, many went astray. During our time, seniors very proudly said that a Class I officer was a class in itself and could always be trusted with regard to his integrity!

Unfortunately, nobody is prepared to hazard a guess about the integrity of such officers today. It is also true of elite services like the IAS. Initially everyone is innocent like a child, but as he grows in his career, the demands made of him outgrow his income. This has always been like that, but most of the officers never crossed the line of respectable conduct or the 'Laksman rekha', despite the worst temptation. Offerings as some kind of consideration for the services are categorized as follows:

(i) Nazrana: A small gift given at the time of a festival or occasion to show one's gratitude.
(ii) Sukrana: A gift as a mark of thanks for a job done—mostly voluntarily without a favour.
(iii) Mehnatana: It was a fee for a job, demanded in advance.
(iv) Jabrana: A forcible demand made before the job was done.

The first two categories were prevalent earlier as common courtesy and they fell on the right side of the Laksman rekha. Being quite common, perhaps, no serious consideration was made of this type.

The most priceless quality of contentment is no longer regarded as a human virtue. So, people have indulged in the other two types. It has caused serious damage to society. Is it a social malady? We may pass judgment on the conduct of such persons, but there is also 'karma', which will take care of it in its own time. Whether it happens now or later is hardly important. Only our Lord knows. Is it not so?

13

SECRETARY RAILWAY BOARD

MY SELECTION AS SECRETARY RAILWAY BOARD

I was buying vegetables in Sarojini Nagar Market, New Delhi, on a Saturday in February 2002 when R.K. Singh, secretary Railway Board told me that the MR had selected me to succeed him as the next secretary of the Railway Board. There was a chain of vacancies coming up after the retirement of R.N. Malhotra, CRB, on 31 March 2002. The ME, Mr Rana, was to succeed him as the CRB. Kanwarjit Singh, GM, Northern Railway, was to take over as the next ME. R.K. Singh was being posted as GM, Northern Railway. In the din of the market, his voice was not clear but he asked me to see the MR.

I told my wife of the development. I was in the Railway Board by 12:30 p.m. Nitish ji welcomed me and said, 'I am glad to select you for the post. I am sure that you will also do very well as secretary as you did as advisor vigilance. The posting may take effect in about a month.' I thanked him for his confidence in me. I also wanted time to arrange my replacement, which required the CVC's consent. I proposed Shiv Kumar, EDVE, to be posted as advisor vigilance. This was according to established precedence. The minister approved my proposal and the CVC also cleared the appointment in due course.

R.K. Singh took over as GM, Northern on 31 March 2002 as scheduled. But there was no corresponding order for me. He continued looking after as secretary Railway Board as an additional charge. R.C.P. Singh, IAS, the minister's PS, told me that the MR was keen to notify the first phase of reorganization of the Railways. Two new zonal railways viz. the East Central Railway and the North Western Railway with their headquarters in Hajipur and Jaipur respectively were to be created under this phase. This was a crucial decision and the MR wanted R.K. Singh to pilot it.

The notification to create two new zones was issued on 14 June 2002. My orders were issued on 18 June with the approval of the minister. I took over the charge from R.K. Singh in the evening. Formal approval of the ACC for my appointment as the secretary Railway Board was also issued in due course.

I was in the panel of the GM, and the ACC approved my appointment in the GM's grade.

HISTORICAL BACKGROUND AND STRUCTURE OF THE RAILWAY BOARD

The Railway Board was set up under the Railway Board Act, 1904. Hitherto in the early 1900s, the Railways was a mixture of various types, administered by a railway branch under the PWD. Thomas Robertson—the railway commissioner—recommended the abolition of railway branch under the PWD and its replacement by a separate Railway Board with more powers.

The Railway Board Act, 1904

Under the Railway Board Act, 1904 the new Railway Board was set up in 1905. In course of time, more autonomy and powers were given to the Board. Initially it had three members, but gradually the Board grew to consist of seven members. The Board has a secretary who acts in all statutory matters under the Railway Act and the Railway Board Act. He is known to hold the statuette in the true sense. He participates in all the Board's meetings and is a part of the Board. A very distinctive feature of the secretary is: 'he is the Secretary to the Board and not the Secretary of the Board'.

I had a dream

I had a dream of being the secretary Railway Board, and I was! I was aware of my humble background. It was indeed a handicap. All my predecessors were giants of personality. But after having worked as advisor vigilance, I was quite confident of possessing the necessary sheen to do justice to the post. In my life, I had never asked anyone for a particular assignment except once. As the EDVE, I requested V.K. Agarwal, the CRB, to consider me for this post. That was a definite indiscretion. He just gave me an enigmatic smile and quite rightly said nothing about it.

There are two unique and one-off posts in the Railways, in terms of importance—one is the post of secretary Railway Board and another advisor vigilance, Railway Board. I was grateful to God for being selected for both assignments. It was particularly significant because I was clearly the underdog. Many were disappointed by my appointment. Very few were confident of my capability. One of them was definitely Nitish Kumar, the railway minister and Kanwarjit Singh, my earlier boss and now the ME.

INITIAL PERIOD OF TRIAL

I was keen and determined to prove my detractors wrong. I did not have to wait for long for an opportunity to demonstrate my capabilities. It seemed that many crucial tasks were just waiting for me.

There was a hue and cry as soon as the notification for new zones was issued. Hajipur and Jaipur zones were to become operational with effect from 1 October 2002. The minister was in Patna the day I had taken over. Strong protest rose from West Bengal because Hajipur Zone was to be carved off from the Eastern and the North Eastern Railways. Someone had also spoken to the prime minister and the president. The PM spoke to Nitish Kumar in Lucknow about the political rumblings in the new zones. There were protests from many quarters. Many retired railwaymen of eminence also strongly protested against the decision.

The MR was apparently upset. When the PM spoke to him regarding the protest on the decision, the MR got an impression that it was necessary to brief the PM before acting further on the notification. He asked me to hold back all action on it accordingly.

Official as well as domestic emergency

I was asked to handle large public protests. Unfortunately, my wife was admitted to a hospital suddenly. Tests had shown the presence of gall stones. Shravani was already sick with the same ailment. Her surgery was already planned on 2 July 2002. I was with my wife in the Central Hospital. The hospital cabin had virtually become a control room for secretary Railway Board. The famous surgeon, Dr Kripalani, was to perform surgery on my daughter. He had no time for the next three weeks if the surgery planned for 2 July was deferred. The MR had to meet the PM on 2 July and the president on 4 July. Our doctors advised me to go ahead with the scheduled surgery. They assured me that it could be managed in my absence. I had no choice.

Shravani was taken inside the operation theatre at 8.30 in the morning. The operation was over around 9.30. She was brought out around 10.30 from the operation theatre and taken to the recovery room. Sedated, she still held my hand and would not let me go. The post-surgery stage was difficult for her because of severe nausea.

R.C.P. Singh called me after the operation. He asked me to return to Rail Bhawan as others could now look after her. The minister wanted me for an urgent discussion. I told my wife that everything had gone well. I had to go to the minister immediately. She smiled understandingly. I returned to the hospital only after 3 p.m. Shravani was in a pitiable state but she calmed down on seeing me and by 5 p.m. she was much better. This was one of the most difficult days in my life. It was only because of God that I sailed through. It seemed to me also as a kind of baptism for becoming secretary Railway Board.

In the course of management training, I was asked how to handle a situation like this. The crisis was caused by a domestic emergency which required my presence. At the same time, the boss insisted that I handle a sensitive case. I had said that I must pause for a moment to evaluate the two conflicting demands. If both could be handled by staggering the sequence, there was no problem. Otherwise, family came first. A difficult answer! Obviously, the family and boss both had to appreciate it maturely as called for under transactional analysis (described in the book, *I am OK, You're OK*). I am of course not talking about national issues which certainly called for a different yardstick.

I would fail if I could not be by my family's side in their hour of need. I had promised to stand by them. All along I had believed in this axiom. I told my younger friends about this in no uncertain terms. That was how my boss and my family both supported me in my respective duties.

REORGANIZATION OF THE INDIAN RAILWAYS—A MOMENTOUS AND HISTORIC EVENT

The reorganization of the Indian Railways was undoubtedly the most vexing question that secretary Railway Board was concerned with. I must describe it as this threatened to destroy the entire fabric of the Indian Railways.

Pre-Independence reorganization of the Railways

The Railways in India before Independence was a big mixed bag. In early 1890, there were around nine categories of railways in India in terms of ownership and control. They were:

(i) government-owned lines operated by private companies;
(ii) government-owned lines operated by the government;
(iii) private-owned lines operated by private companies with guarantees from the government;
(iv) short local lines owned and operated by the district board;
(v) lines owned and operated by private companies with government assistance but no guarantees;
(vi) lines owned and operated by princely states;
(vii) lines owned by princely states but operated by private companies;
(viii) lines owned by princely states but operated by the government; and

(ix) lines in foreign territories like Portuguese (Goa) and French (Pondicherry).

With growing public use, there were many complaints against private railways. During the First World War in 1914-18, many inadequacies of the system also came to light. The British appointed the Acworth Committee in 1921 to go into the functioning of the railway system in India. The committee brought in sweeping changes. As a result, all privately owned railways came under government control. Bengal Nagpur railway was the last privately-owned railway to come under government control in 1944.

Post-Independence reorganization of the Railways

After Independence, all railways came under government control. The Railway Board took up the consolidation and reorganization of railway system in India. With integration of all princely states during 1949-50, princely railway lines were also taken over. Between 1951 and 1958, eight zones were created. South the Central Railway with its headquarters in Secunderabad was the ninth zone created in 1966.

The historic reorganization of 1996-97

Thus, there were nine zones operating till 1996-97. It was felt that growing public use called for making the system more operationally and managerially effective. Some exercises were undertaken to reorganize the system further. The Railway Reform Commission in 1984 had recommended the creation of four new zones.

However, no further step was taken in this regard until Ram Vilas Paswan, the MR, took up the subject. After considerable deliberation, the Union Cabinet approved setting up of six new zones in 1996 by readjusting the jurisdictions of the existing nine zones. They were:

S. N.	Names of New Zones	Proposed Headquarters	Adjustment with Existing Zones
1	East Central Railway (ECR)	Hajipur	Eastern and North Eastern Railways
2	North Western Railway (NWR)	Jaipur	Northern and Western Railways
3	North Central Railway (NCR)	Allahabad	Northern and Central Railways
4	South Western Railway (SWR)	Bangalore	Central, Southern & South-Central Railways
5	East Coast Railway (ECoR)	Bhubaneswar	South Eastern Railway
6	West Central Railway (WCR)	Jabalpur	Central and Western Railways

Source: Compiled by the author based on the record and public notification in *Gazette of India.*

The headquarters of the SWR was subsequently changed to Hubli by the next government led by Atal Bihari Vajpayee. One more zone was also created with its headquarters in Bilaspur in 2001. The reorganization was expected to improve operational performance besides encouraging the development of backward areas as some zones were being set up in such areas.

Re-organization decision on the back-burner

The decision was taken also in response to demands in political circles, but implementation of the decision was not seriously pursued. The Railway Board posted an officer on special duty with a skeleton staff for setting up new zones. Many in the Railways felt that the decision was politically motivated.

The Indian Railways was passing through serious economic constraint. Such massive reorganization was therefore not considered desirable. This was also the time when the Rakesh Mohan Committee report recommended total restructuring of the Indian Railways as the present format was ill-equipped to deliver results. The Cabinet decision was almost wiped out from the minds of the top-echelons of the ministry. The Railway Board had earlier created posts of the OSD for the new zones in the rank of GMs but subsequently, in order to economize, the posts were downgraded to the HAG levels.

The new government pushes the proposal amidst resistance

Mamata Banerjee was the railway minister in the Atal Bihari Vajpayee government which came to power in 2000. Nitish Kumar succeeded her after she quit the coalition in 2001. He actively pursued the proposal despite great resistance within the organization. The Railway Board in a resolution in January 2002 dismissed the proposal as being unsound and not in the Railways' interest. Nitish Kumar however questioned the propriety of the Board's resolution. He told R.N. Malhotra, CRB, that the Board could not undo the Cabinet's decision. The minister thus ignored the Board's resolution and went ahead with the Cabinet's decision. The Board accordingly notified the operation of two new zones in the first phase in June 2002—one in Hajipur and another in Jaipur. This is when I took over as secretary Railway Board.

NOTIFICATION FOR NEW ZONES UNLEASHES PROTESTS

The notification unleashed severe protests from all round—the most vociferous one was from West Bengal. The Eastern Railway after its bifurcation had to part with three important divisions of Dhanbad, Danapur and Mughalsarai. Dhanbad served as a rich coal belt and also had other minerals. Mughalsarai and Danapur served as major links to and from West Bengal. The apprehension was that the truncated Eastern Railway would lose its place of pride and attention as commercial focus would shift to Bihar.

Creation of the NWR was welcome. Both the Northern and the Western Railways favoured the partition of their two meter gauge divisions—Jodhpur and Bikaner of the NR and Jaipur and Ajmer of the WR. The then chief minister of Rajasthan, Ashok Ghelot, welcomed the decentralization of the Railways' operational management and applauded the emphasis on efficiency that the creation of the new zone aimed to achieve.

An all-party delegation of MPs from West Bengal led by Subhash Chakravarty, the West Bengal transport minister, called on Nitish Kumar on 9 July 2002 to protest against the proposed bifurcation of the Eastern Railway. Lalu Prasad initially had supported the creation of the ECR but he was lukewarm later in his approach. He thought that this would help Nitish Kumar politically. Thus, when political parties from West Bengal levelled a charge of creating the new zone on basis of state boundaries, ruling political parties from Bihar initially chose to be silent. But stung by criticism in political circles, the Bihar government eventually sent its own delegation, urging the minister to stand firm on the decision because of the potential immense economic benefits to Bihar.

MAIN ISSUES AGAINST THE CREATION OF NEW ZONES

The strongest allegation against the proposal was its arbitrariness. It would eventually lead to balkanization of the country. Besides, it was also alleged to be politically motivated, intended to harm the interest of West Bengal. There was also grave concern about the staff posted in the headquarters office of the Eastern Railway, Calcutta. They were mostly Bengali and it was feared that they would be dislocated after the creation of ECR. Regarding the train's operation also, it was stated that this would lead to delays in train services because of an increased number of interchanges. (An interchange is typically required at the boundary of each zonal railway to facilitate change of crew, etc.) Given the present economic constraints, the IR could not afford such a costly proposal. They called for a review of the proposal by an expert committee.

Even two recognized unions—the NFIR and the AIRF—went against the decision. The Federation of Railway Officers' Association (FROA) passed a resolution rejecting the move. Only the Indian Railway RPF Association and the Indian Railway Promotee Officers Federation (IRPOF) supported the move. This was a piquant situation. The Railway Board was asked to re-examine the allegations. The Board did not see any justification to bring in another committee of experts. The Railway Board possessed the necessary expertise on the subject. Moreover, in the past, the subject had already been examined by experts like Mr Gujral and a committee of additional members. In 1984, the Railway Reform Commission had actually recommended the creation of four new zones.

Examination by the Railway Board

The subject was taken up by the Board in its meeting. Members were however sharply divided on the issue. The Board had passed a resolution in 2002 against the proposed reorganization and put it up to the minister for his orders. Some members wanted to know how that resolution was disposed of. The minister had not passed any order.

I urged the Board to consider the implication of its resolution of January 2002. The Board had prepared a Cabinet note on the subject, which was placed before the Cabinet for consideration. The Union Cabinet decided to create seven new zones based on the ministry's proposal, contained in the Cabinet note. The Board could not reject the Cabinet's decision subsequently. Review of a Cabinet decision was possible only if some facts in the Cabinet note had changed in light of new development. In that case also, it was for the minister to call for the revision by the Cabinet. If he chose otherwise, the decision would have to be implemented.

Fortunately, many members saw my point. They agreed to consider the special note put before them with the agenda. The representation contained several issues on which the Board had to comment on after due deliberation. Some were factually incorrect. Apprehensions in the representations had to be discounted while elaborating advantages likely to accrue after reorganization. The Board's deliberation was pointed and focused on discounting issues which were untrue or irrelevant. For example, it was not necessary to change the crew at each interchange point which could cause delay. The minister keenly awaited the outcome of the Board's deliberation with concern. He was therefore pleased with the way the Board had deliberated on the issues.

I dictated the minutes of the proceedings immediately after Board's meeting. The draft was ready by 8 p.m. After the CRB's approval, the draft was circulated to members. Member mechanical had already left the Rail Bhawan. I sent his PS along with the draft minutes. With difficulty, he was located in a temple. I was sorry for it but it was unavoidable. He came to me in the morning with the approved draft. He looked distinctly displeased and said, 'What you are doing is not correct. The history of the Indian Railways will remember you for its dismemberment. You will not be forgiven.' That was the curse I had to carry!

The MR saw the Board's proceedings and remarked on how I had found the time to finalize the minutes of the meeting and have it duly corrected and approved by all seven Board members. He told me that the proceedings were perhaps too lengthy and could have been shorter. From my experience in vigilance, I knew that the court, in course of judicial scrutiny, would examine if all points or charges raised by the petitioners were duly examined and suitable orders were passed on them. I had taken that precaution. When the case finally came before the court, it was satisfied that the Board had examined them before arriving at the decision with reasons as recorded in the minutes of Board proceedings.

A Cabinet note was prepared to brief the Cabinet. Ordinarily a Cabinet note is never longer than ten pages. Our note ran about twenty-five pages. The additional secretary in the Cabinet Secretariat returned the papers. But I explained that it was necessary for the Cabinet to examine all the points the petitioners had raised against the Cabinet's decision. This was again found very useful later on. The Cabinet approved the note. Thus, the earlier decision was ratified by the Cabinet without any change. It was good in many ways.

MAIN PLANK OF THE ARGUMENTS

As soon as the Cabinet reiterated the earlier decision, there rose a large numbers of protests from many quarters. Chief Minister of West Bengal Buddhadeb Bhattacharjee came down to meet the PM. The MR was not in Delhi so I was asked to go to 6 Race Course (the residence of PM) to be available for any clarification during discussion. But the PM handled it very well and my assistance was not called for at all. The CM opposed the move to create new zones on the grounds that it would impair operational efficiencies, would cause dislocation of personnel and would raise conflicting regional demands on an invaluable national asset.

The main plank of arguments to rebut the allegations was:

- There was no division on the basis of state boundary. The Dhanbad division had part of West Bengal. Mughalsarai also contained part of Uttar Pradesh. Thus, the ECR containing only Bihar was factually incorrect.
- The operation would certainly improve as accessibility to most of the area was better from Hajipur. This was also true for two divisions of Sonepur and Samastipur taken from the North Eastern Railway.
- Only willing persons would be transferred to the headquarters from the Eastern or the North Eastern Railway. In Group C, many were willing to go to Hajipur. The same policy was also applicable to Group B officers.

The chief minister of West Bengal repeatedly emphasized the operational parameters to preserve the Railways' wider role of national integration. He had obviously avoided the protest to bring other issues for discussion between the two states.

OTHER FIVE ZONES NOTIFIED FOR OPERATION

The Board notified on 4 July 2002 the creation of remaining five new zones—North Central Railway, Allahabad; East Coast Railway Bhubaneswar; South Western Railway, Hubli; West Central Railway, Jabalpur; South East Central Railway, Bilaspur were to be operational with effect from 1 April 2003. The Cabinet approval for Bilaspur had stated, 'The Cabinet approved creation of a new zone with its headquarters at Bilaspur'. In the case of all other zones, it had specified the name of the zone while issuing the notification. The MR was out of Delhi, I simply put its name as 'South East Central Railway' and signed the gazette notification. On his return I told the MR. He smiled and said, 'So you have christened the new zone. I compliment you because it is quite apt.' The Board also notified the creation of eight new divisions at Nanded, Agra, Guntur, Raipur, Ranchi, Pune, Rangiya and Ahmedabad with effect from 1 April 2003.

The Railway Board was aware that large scale shifting of personnel from one zonal headquarters to another would cause difficulties and problems. As a result of this, a policy decision was taken that no Group B, C and D personnel would be shifted without their express consent. But surprisingly, both the federations the AIRF and the NFIR joined hands with the Officers' Association to oppose the issue in the court. They filed a public interest litigation in Delhi High Court against the decision of the government to create new zones.

It was 5th of August 2002 when around 6 p.m. I received a copy of the petition forwarded by the court's registrar. The MR was not in the office but was informed in the evening. He checked up with some advocates to ascertain the position of the case for hearing.

Around 7.30 p.m., the MR informed me that the case was coming up before the chief justice of the Delhi High Court the very next day, before 11.30 a.m. That was a smart thing done by the petitioners. They had arranged everything in a very hushed manner. The court might grant a stay on the order, if no one from Railways was present. This would not have been in our interest. But the MR moved very fast. He requested Solicitor General (SG) Harish Salve—a learned and famous counsel—to appear on our behalf. The SG called for a briefing around 9 a.m. of 6 August 2002.

We prepared the brief during the night. I cannot say that it was very good. The briefing was better. The MR came to Mr Salve's residence for the briefing. Mr Salve felt that the judgment of the Karnataka High Court regarding the change of headquarters of South West Railway from Bangalore to Hubli was important. The high court had said that it was an administrative issue, the court could not interfere, if the government had already taken the decision. Even the apex court in 2001 had refused to intervene in the matter.

The matter came up in the court of Chief Justice Sinha around 11.30 a.m. There was a spirited argument by the petitioners' counsel Prashant Bhushan. The SG replied very briefly that the government had taken this decision after due deliberation. It came under the purview of executive governance. The Karnataka High Court and the Supreme Court in a similar situation had decided that it could not interfere with the executive decision regarding the governance of the Railways. The government had decided to create more districts in a state or more states for administrative convenience. In a democracy, a political party leads the government. There is nothing wrong if the party sought public views on a subject. But based on this reason alone, a decision could not be called political. The arguments were incisive. The court rejected the petition at the stage of admission. This round rightly belonged to Nitish Kumar. But for his initiative, the case would have taken a wrong turn. Although Nitish Kumar gave me a lot of credit for this, it was his magnanimity which encouraged all of us.

THE PIL IN THE SUPREME COURT

The victory at Delhi High Court was only a small consolation. The case was certain to come up for appeal in the Supreme Court. We had set up reliable machinery to monitor it so that we were not caught off guard again. Someone gave us a copy of the petitioners' draft also. Shanti Bhushan, a former law minister and a very senior advocate of the Supreme Court, would appear for the petitioners. From the draft, it was easy to prepare a rejoinder in advance. We wanted Mr Salve to appear but Soli Sorabjee, attorney general of India (AG), himself decided to appear on behalf of the Railways.

Attorney General of India Soli Sorabjee takes up the case

Mr Sorabjee had a team of 6 or 7 juniors helping him. He spoke rapidly, and brought our notice to a lot of details. He was not easily satisfied. At times, I had to remind him about the real objective of our defence. I feared that he might mess up the details and figures in the court. Normally, the counsel has to make a strong submission as soon as the case is mentioned in the Supreme Court, otherwise it might just pass it over. The counsels from both sides were celebrities, and hence it was unlikely to be thrown without proper submission by the advocates. A senior counsel has to attend different courts for other cases.

It is the responsibility of his juniors to monitor the progress of cases before the Bench. They have to inform the AG in time to enable him to be present when the case is taken up by the Bench.

Mr Sorabjee was appearing in another court when he was informed that the case would come up in ten minutes. He started but meanwhile some other cases moved faster. Hence when our case was called, Mr Sorabjee was just entering the court. Taking advantage of the situation, the counsel of the appellant moved that the case be admitted for hearing. The judges said that they could see Mr Sorabjee coming. Mr Sorabjee apologized and said, 'Your Honour, I am extremely sorry because I was attending another Bench. I would have come in time but for huge rush in the gallery. I had to make my way through them. Sir, you would recall that I pleaded earlier also that the court should do something to remove the crowd to make the passage clear for movement of older persons like us.' It was very well taken and he said that he had no objection if the case was admitted for hearing. He pleaded for a quick hearing so that this urgent case was disposed of. The court agreed to deal this within a month.

I knew that nobody had liked it. The court had of course not granted any stay but there were going to be changes in February 2003 in the Bench, due to the retirement of the chief justice who headed the Bench. But the AG had his own arguments. He justified his decision by saying that he did not want the impression that he avoided a hearing on the case. Because of his readiness, he said the Bench could be prevailed upon for an early hearing. Despite our disappointment I was inclined to agree with the AG's line of thinking.

The main contention of the respondents

After a month or so, the case came up for hearing. Shanti Bhushan argued vehemently. His argument was based upon the following points:

- The decision was arbitrary and taken on political considerations. He quoted the railway minister in public meetings where he had talked of such action being taken in support of his argument.
- He contended that the government had created new zones for development of the backward areas. The minister had publicly pointed out that development could be speeded up by relocating the headquarters of the new zone in a backward area. According to the counsel, this was not the duty of the Railways.
- This would create serious impediments to flow of traffic because trains would stop at each zonal boundary as locomotive and crew would be changed for every train.

- The formation of seven zones would create public inconvenience and would lead to balkanization of the country. It would be very costly and would unnecessarily drain the public exchequer.
- The railway officers and staff federation were against this and that is why they had joined hands to oppose the move. Even members of the Railway Board were against it. They had submitted a resolution against the formation of new zones. No action was taken by the minister on the resolution so far.

Submission by the AG—eloquent and incisive

The points were answered by the AG. The submission by Soil Sorabjee was so fluent and effective that I was totally swept off my feet. It was simply glorious. These were the qualities which had earned him respect as an eloquent counsel. He never lost the rhythm and his thoughts were so well marshalled that the Bench was rapt in attention. At one point, the appellants produced a copy of the Board's resolution where the entire Board, led by Mr Malhotra had rejected the decision taken by the Cabinet. The document was confidential, so the Bench asked their counsel how it had been obtained as it came under the purview of the Official Secrets Act, 1923. The Bench asked the AG if he would make an objection to the introduction of the confidential document by the petitioners. Soli Sorabjee just smiled and with a wave of his hands, he said, 'Your Honour! If they think it is going to help their cause I have no objection because I have nothing to hide.' Justice Rajendra Babu, heading the Bench along with Justice G.P. Mathur, were both not at all happy. He did not approve of senior counsels flaunting official documents, which a normal person was not privy to. But as the AG himself had no objection he did not press the matter any further.

Soli Sorabjee thereafter produced all the minutes of the meetings of the Board and the Cabinet notes which contained all the objections raised by the petitioners. Since the documents were confidential, he requested the Bench to see them. He argued that all the issues had been fully examined and thereafter the highest decision-making authority in the government had decided on the issue. The Railway Board was itself a group of experts. It had after due examination come to the conclusion that the creation of new zones was administratively essential. The existing Central Railway with its headquarters in Mumbai was unable to superintend the area near Faridabad which was closer to Delhi. On the same plea, Singrauli area was 1,500 km away from Mumbai. The people of this area had claimed that it was not possible for them to travel as far as Mumbai to seek their business. A minister besides being in charge of his ministry, was also a political representative of the area, There was nothing wrong if he had addressed the people in a political meeting informing them of the decision of the government to create new zones.

The crux of the argument was that the government in its wisdom had arrived at a decision which it believed was correct. In view of the large number of documents and consultations before taking the decision, it could not be called an arbitrary decision. Train operations were not obstructed because of interchange points but had improved. To cap the argument, a report on the performance of two new zones, NWR and ECR, was placed before the court. The report showed considerable improvements in freight earnings and tonnage carried by the two zones. Mr Sorabjee concluded that the decision was well deliberated. Even if it were wrong it could not be challenged. But fortunately, the results were better and not worse as the petitioners would have all believe.

LANDMARK JUDGMENT OF THE APEX COURT—A HISTORIC EVENT

It was an extraordinary performance. The Bench was evidently convinced. The petitioners looked dejected. The landmark judgment came on 13 March 2003, completely vindicating our stand. The judgment delivered by Chief Justice Rajendra Babu and Justice Mathur covered a wide perspective and many issues. I wish to quote from it for proper appreciation by the readers.

A landmark judgment of the apex court

The apex court, in this connection, quoted its earlier judgment in *BALCO Employees' Union (Regd.) vs Union of India and others in 2002*, wherein it observed, 'It is evident that it is neither within the domain of the courts nor the scope of judicial review to embark upon an enquiry as to whether a particular policy is wise or whether better public policy can be evolved. Nor are our *Courts* inclined to strike down a policy at the behest of a petitioner merely because it has been urged that a different policy would have been fairer or wiser or more scientific or more logical.'

It further stated, 'In examining a question of this nature where a policy is evolved by the Government judicial review thereof is limited. When a policy according to which or the purpose for which discretion is to be exercised is clearly expressed in the statute, it cannot be said to be an unrestricted discretion. On matters affecting policy and requiring technical expertise, Court would leave the matter for decision of those who are qualified to address the issues. Unless the policy or action is inconsistent with the constitution and the laws or arbitrary or irrational or abuse of power, the Court will not interfere with such matters.'

The Supreme Court further said, 'It has been contended that the objective of developing backward areas or to meet public demand new zones have been formed and such a step will not be consistent with efficiency in administration. These two factors are noticed not in isolation but along with other criteria as increase in traffic load and accessibility. *Therefore, the* contention ignores all the factors taken into consideration and therefore is not tenable. Even otherwise, to meet the demands for backward areas cannot by itself be inconsistent with efficiency. When Railway is a public utility service it has to take care of all areas including backward areas. In doing so, providing service, efficient supervision and keeping the equipment and other material in good and *workable* condition are all important factors. Such services can be appropriately extended if there is an exclusive zone to cater to such areas. If more facilities become available in those zones, naturally efficiency would go up.

'Therefore, the concept of "efficiency" should not be approached in a doctrinaire or pedantic manner. Thus, formation of zones in backward areas for providing proper facilities and services will improve the efficiency and not retard it. Merely setting up a new zone in a backward area, particularly when it fulfills another criterion to which we have already adverted.'

It further added, 'Even if we assume that there is a force in the material placed by the petitioners that by forming new Railway zones efficiency in the railway administration would not enhance, the reasons given by the Government and material placed by them in support of forming new railway zones is no less or even more forceful. Further, when technical questions arise and experts in the field have expressed various views and all those aspects have been taken into consideration by the Government in deciding the matter, could it still be said that this court should reexamine to interfere with the same. The wholesome rule in regard to judicial interference in administrative decisions is that if the Government takes in to consideration all relevant factors, eschew from considering irrelevant factors and reasonably within the parameters of the law, courts would keep off the same. The question before the Court is whether formation of zones is for efficient administration of Railways. On this aspect we have considered the rival contentions including the material placed before the Government of India and the criteria evolved for formation of the zones. The test whether such formation of zones is for the purpose of efficient administration of Railways have been fully considered by the Government before taking decision while such consideration was lacking in Muddappa's case. Hence that decision cannot be of any assistance to appellant. We have applied the principles set out in other decisions relied upon by the appellant to the facts of the case in reaching our conclusions in this matter.' The Supreme Court further observed, 'It is only in 1996 a decision was taken by the Government for a zone at Hajipur.

If formation of a zone at Hajipur as its headquarters fulfils the norms set up by the Government and there is enough statistical data in that regard, it becomes difficult for us to state that the same is malafide. Allegations regarding malafides cannot be vaguely made and it must be specific and clear. In this context, the concerned Minister who is stated to be involved in the formation of new zone at Hajipur is not made a party who can meet the allegations.

'If benefit of a zonal headquarter in a particular place is more suited than any other place in zone it would not affect the ultimate functioning of the railway administration. Thus, all contentions of petitioners stand rejected. These petitions stand dismissed.'

The judgment is hailed by all

Nitish Kumar was very pleased with the way the entire case was conducted. Railway Legal Advisor Mr Malhotra was a pillar of strength. The support given by the secretariat branch was marvellous. Everyone was proud of the secretary's branch in the Railway Board. I must fully compliment the team led by Mehra, joint secretary, Gera, deputy secretary, and others for their exemplary devotion to duty.

The secretary's branch was an excellent organ of the Board. It would never let any secretary down. It would also ensure that no mistake was ever committed while dealing with any case. After all, it was the last post in the hierarchy. Without it, mistakes could have happened, causing acute embarrassment to the ministry. But I have never seen any mistake during my entire tenure. I am justly proud of it.

MAKING NEW ZONES FORMALLY OPERATIONAL

The jurisdiction of new zones had to be defined before the start of their operation. The task was difficult. Factors like crew changing points, gang beats, PWI's jurisdictions and traffic patterns had to be taken into account.

The Board set up a committee for this. It interacted with the zonal railways and divisions. Some existing anomalies in the jurisdictions were also studied. This was a mammoth task. The ECR and the NWR were to become operational on 1 October 2002. Their jurisdictions were finalized first by the committee.

Since reorganization was under the Railway Act, all Gazette notifications were signed by the secretary railway Board. According to some rumours, Nitish Kumar had to plead with N. Chandrababu Naidu, the heavyweight chief minister of Andhra Pradesh and the convenor of the National Democratic Alliance (NDA). This was not true. The MR had spoken to him in my presence. He readily agreed to the Waltair division being made a part of East Coast Railway. He had also agreed to the bifurcation of South Central Railway. He was generally supportive of the reorganization of the Railways. In my view, such gossip was truly mischievous.

NWR and ECR become operational on 1 October 2002

Two new zones were brought into operation on 1 October 2002 as notified, in a simple but impressive ceremony. Jaipur was well-decked for the festive moment and a large crowd had gathered in the temporary office premises. The programme included the reading of a Gazette notification by the secretary Railway Board appointing R.M. Agarwal as the first GM of the NWR in the presence of GMs of the Northern and the Western Railways. The programme was beautifully compered by the legendary Jasdev Singh.

From there, we arrived in Patna by a service flight at 1.40 p.m. The crowd at Hajipur was huge and the enthusiasm of the local people was tremendous. It was very difficult to conduct the proceedings, but I managed to read the Gazette notification, appointing S.C. Gupta as the first GM of the ECR. Nitish Kumar was happy about it. He was clearly the hero at both the functions.

Other five zones also become operational on 1 April 2003

After the Supreme Court verdict, similar preparations for making the other five zones operational with effect from 1 April 2003 were made. Nitish Kumar launched the operation in Allahabad, Jabalpur and Bhubaneswar zones on 1 April 2003. I had gone to Allahabad from Delhi along with the CRB on a chartered flight. The MR arrived by train from Patna. Allahabad zone was made operational, first by appointing I.P.S. Anand as the first GM of the NCR, in a very impressive function. After that, the MR went to Jabalpur to inaugurate the zone. Stanley Babu was appointed the first GM, West Central Railway. The MR reached Bhubaneswar in the evening to inaugurate the East Coast Railway by appointing G.P. Garg as its first GM. At Bhubaneswar, Naveen Patnaik, the CM was himself present at the function which was colourful. Hubli was launched by Bandaru Dattatreya, minister of state for railways. The South East Central Railway although made operational with effect from 1 April was dedicated to the nation by Atal Bihari Vajpayee, the then prime minister of India, in Bilaspur on 5 April 2003.

After the verdict, the leaders of the federations which included the AIRF, the NFRI, Railway Officers, IRPOF and the Railway Protection Force called upon the minister and promised to extend full support to the Railways after its reorganization. Thus, all hostility ceased. The minister was also magnanimous and welcomed their support in all sincerity.

150 YEARS OF RAILWAYS IN INDIA—A MEMORABLE EVENT

The first train in India ran on 16 April 1853 from Bombay to Thane—a modest beginning by the Great Indian Peninsular Railways, a private company. It was decided to celebrate 150 years of the Indian Railways in 2002 in a year-long programme beginning on 16 April 2002. This coincided with the annual Railway Week Celebrations.

Sandeep Silas, director public relations—a moving force

This programme was monitored by the secretary Railway Board. Many events took place all over the country. Most importantly, a two-rupee coin was issued to commemorate the event. A small memento was also designed and it was presented to all the representatives of the international community in India in their respective embassies or high commissions. This gesture was highly appreciated. The GM of the South Eastern Railway had organized a camp in which all the celebrity artists of West Bengal participated. They painted pictures depicting activities connected with the railways. It was a unique experience and led to a large number of masterpieces.

Sandeep Sailas, the director of public relations in the Board, was a moving force behind the celebrations. He is a great adventurer and has penned many books. I honestly confess that apart from administrative support, he needed nothing. His initiative was amazing.

The grand finale was a three-hour long laser show choreographed by the famous Shiamak Davar in Jawaharlal Nehru Stadium on 16 April 2003. This was a thrilling depiction of a colourful story of the Indian Railways. It was an outstanding hit and the crowd, especially the younger ones went into a frenzy.

As a part of the celebrations, we also ran a well-decorated train depicting India's achievement including the struggle for Independence. It was an instant hit with all, particularly among the children, and was a comprehensible lesson in Indian history. The train was flagged off from New Delhi on 15 August 2002. It had great contribution from Sandeep. A vivid tableau of the Indian Railways, which was a stunning piece displayed in the Republic Day Parade on 26 January 2003 as a part of 150th year of the Railways in India, was also his contribution.

NEW DELHI RAJDHANI EXPRESS ACCIDENT

The secretary Railway Board is not directly concerned with accidents in the railways. These are basically the responsibility of zonal railways. In serious accidents, the minister normally visits the site with the Board members. After a telephonic briefing, a report has to be sent to the Cabinet secretary in such cases. He in turn advises the PM including the home minister. In case the PM is out of the country, the report is sent to him by the Cabinet secretary. For any further clarification, the Prime Minister's Office (PMO) would directly contact the secretary Railway Board.

The icon of the Indian Railways

2301 Up *Howrah-Delhi Rajdhani Express* met with an accident at 10.43 p.m. on 9 September 2002 near Gaya (between Gaya and Rafiganj stations of Gaya Mughalsarai section of Eastern Railway). This was my first major case which I dealt with as secretary Railway Board. The train had left Howrah at 5 p.m., and while travelling on the section, derailed just ahead of the masonry arch bridge over the Dhave River. The train was travelling at more than 100 kmph. After derailment, the train moved over the bridge and four of its coaches either fell into the river or were precariously hanging from the bridge.

The *Rajdhani Express* is an icon of the Indian Railways. This was the first fast train introduced at a speed of 130 kmph way back in 1970. It had rightly occupied its place of pride in the Indian Railways. Its involvement in an accident was therefore of very serious concern. I was informed at about 12:40 at night by Satish Agnihotri, the EDCC. Nitish Kumar, who was travelling to Delhi from Patna was informed of the accident at Mughalsarai. He proceeded to the site in an accident relief train from Mughalsarai. The Board members (ME, MM, ML and CRB) wanted to leave for the site immediately. I was requested to arrange a special Air Force plane for the party.

I managed to speak to the joint secretary (Air) on the RAX at his residence. Being late, everyone took some time to respond but he reassured me that he would get back to me in time after fixing up all the details. He, later, informed me that it was not possible to take off during the night.

Our chairman was very vexed and jittery, but I requested him to be patient. Probably someone had advised him to speak to the chief of the Air Force. He called him up but was brusquely asked to contact the defence ministry who dealt with all civil operations. After about forty-five minutes, joint secretary (Air) provided full details of the chartered Air Force flight. The aircraft was ordered to be ready at 6 a.m. from the Air Force Technical Area in Palam. A formal memo with the list of passengers had to be sent to him. That was finalized in consultation with the CRB and sent through the protocol officer to the defence ministry in the South Block. Since the minister was to return on the flight in the evening, formal permission from the PMO was also required. By the time these were complied with, it was 4.30 in the morning. Razdan, the protocol officer called me at 6.05 from the airport as the special plane took off from Palam. I went to bed to catch up on some sleep because I knew it was just the beginning and many things would have to be done including informing the PM who was in Frankfurt on his way to the US.

The media report causes outcry in the country

By next morning there was big furore. When I reached the Rail Bhawan around 9.30 a.m., the mood was of a national calamity and there was deathly silence. I called the emergency control room for the latest update. The toll at that time was around twenty-eight persons dead. The train was carrying more than six hundred passengers. Nobody had imagined that the icon of Indian Railways would be involved in a terrible accident like this. The media was bursting with all kinds of reports. In those days of animation, they merrily produced a likely cause of the accident by showing an animation on TV. This caused a great deal of despair and outcry in the country. I tried to put forward a suitable press release by giving the factual position as known at that time. But in the face of a colourful masaledar report, no one gave a penny to the official version. Mr Sudhir Chandra, member staff and I briefed the Cabinet secretary followed by a formal report. We could only give the number of deaths by counting the bodies recovered by the rescue team. The media did not have that kind of responsibility. It counted everyone travelling in the train as dead. The report was also sent to the PM in Frankfurt. Many queries were received from his office. The PM also spoke to the MR at the site of the accident.

The first report from the site was from the press conference and was addressed by the minister and Board members around 3.30 p.m. The arch bridge had not collapsed as the media had vividly reported through the animation. The Board member explained in the press conference that one piece of the rail had been found cut about sixty feet ahead of the bridge. Thus, there was a gap due to the cutting and removing of the rail piece. But at that speed, high momentum of the train had carried it over the gap to the bridge where coaches had derailed. Some coaches after the derailment also fell into the small river.

It appeared to be an act of sabotage. The minister had told me later that even the local deputy inspector general of police (DIG) of the Government Railway Police (GRP) had admitted it. But the picture changed with the arrival of Lalu ji. He was the president of the Rashtriya Janata Dal (RJD), the ruling party in the state and a former CM. His wife, Rabri Devi, was the chief minister. He vehemently denied the sabotage theory. He evidently wanted to deny any responsibility of the state. He instead blamed the Railways for shoddy upkeep of the bridges which he deemed responsible for the accident. He proved this point by showing cobwebs under the bridge to indicate that there was utter neglect in maintenance by the Railways! The media found the entire description very interesting because not a single person called the utter bluff. The state government launched a vicious campaign against Nitish ji. Clearly, the whole issue had lost its national importance and regrettably turned into a political conflict between the two arch rivals of Bihar. It was a pity because it unwittingly provided cover to the enemies of the country.

A MOMENT OF GLOOM IN THE RAIL BHAWAN

By evening, the entire nation was in alarm. The Board's team, along with the minister, returned to Delhi from the site around 8 p.m. The Board members came to the Rail Bhawan straight from the airport for a press conference to be addressed by the CRB. The conference hall was full. I had never seen such a huge turnout of the media.

The conference—a disastrous outcome

After the initial briefing, the media came straight to the cause of the accident. They pointedly asked how the Board members had reached the conclusion that it was an act of sabotage. Sitting by his side, I immediately nudged the CRB to dodge the question. But Mr Rana brushing me aside, emphatically described it as an open-and-shut sabotage case. He even described the entire modus operandi. The lid was off and nothing could save the situation.

Mr Rana, a simple person when provoked would say what he felt. But it lacked of discretion. The media immediately left the conference hall. They had a juicy story on their hands. There was an immediate splash all over the newspapers about the accident being the handiwork of extremists. The chairman had also talked of the act being carried out by Pakistan's Inter-Services Intelligence (ISI). It was a damning explosion in the media and diplomatic circles. The home minister was upset and asked how such a statement had been made. A report was called from the Bihar government, which stoutly denied the theory of sabotage. The senior superintendent of police also wanted to question Mr Rana on his charge of the ISI's involvement. A police team from Bihar called on the CRB for a statement.

The accident toll rose with the recovery of more bodies from the coaches the next day, while the debate raged on about the 'sabotage'. There was not a solemn moment for the unfortunate victims either dead or injured. The minister had an awful time facing an unrelenting volley of issues thrown up by the media. The total toll was 119 dead and 250 injured. For the Railways, it was a time of gloom. It did not know how to recover from the shadow of this case. It was perhaps the darkest moment for the Railways.

Attempt to discredit the CRS inquiry and vilify him

The entire issue now depended on a statutory accident inquiry by the Commissioner of Railway Safety (CRS), Mahesh Chand, Eastern Circle Kolkata. The inquiry began on 16 September 2002 in Gaya.

Bihar Police filed a report before the commissioner stating that the site sketch prepared by railway officers was 'doctored' to support the sabotage theory. This was an attempt to interfere with the inquiry. There was another report in the media that Mahesh Chand was appointed as CRS by the railway minister in an underhand way. According to the allegation, Mahesh Chand had vigilance cases against him. His appointment had come through by overriding the ongoing vigilance cases against him. The media claimed that it was only logical that a person like him could be favourably biased towards the Railways!

This was a preposterous attempt to vilify the commissioner. I had dealt with his case as advisor vigilance. Mahesh Chand had applied for the post of CRS which is under the Ministry of Civil Aviation. He was selected by the UPSC. Before his appointment, his vigilance clearance was sought in the routine way. The vigilance department of the South Eastern Railway had taken up some cases for investigation where his name had appeared. According to the DoP&T guidelines, which were based on the judgment of the Supreme Court, his selection could not be withheld merely on the ground of vigilance investigation. We had furnished the factual position to the UPSC. Since cases were under investigation and no view was taken on his involvement in those cases till then, his appointment was approved by the government in 2001. When the file was put up to Nitish ji to release the officer from the Railways, the MR had asked for clarification on this aspect. He was released because the rules did not bar such an appointment. It was unthinkable to assume that he was appointed as the CRS in 2001, so that he might help Nitish Kumar during the Rajdhani accident in 2002! This was stretching one's imagination far beyond the realm of credibility.

But those were the days when all kinds of pot shots were being taken at the railway ministry. I felt sorry for our minister who was honestly trying to build up the organization in a transparent manner. He was sensitive to criticism. For quite some time, he did not attend the office in the Rail Bhawan. The PM was supportive and he gradually restored his confidence.

Anyway, the CRS went on with the inquiry. The interim report was submitted to the Railways in October 2002. The report confirmed that the accident was caused by subversive activity. Just before the arrival of the *Rajdhani Express*, fish plates were removed from a closure rail ahead of the bridge. The modus operandi was simple. But because of the political wrangling, real miscreants received such unwarranted protection. They were the real enemies of the nation and regardless of political differences, they should have been hounded.

ACCIDENTS RATTLE RAILWAY MINISTRY

Accidents had rattled the tenure of Nitish Kumar. He was an upright person. In his previous tenure, the Gaisal accident took place on 2 August 1999 involving the collision of two passenger trains—*Avadh Assam Express* and *Brahmaputra Mail*. Taking moral responsibility, he had resigned. In his present tenure, accidents had once again become his bête noire. I dealt with eight serious accidents in my tenure as secretary. But from these emerged, historical initiatives to bring the IR back on the rails.

Nitish ji was scheduled to meet the PM on 3 January 2003. He had planned to brief the PM on the performance of the Railways. The Ghatandur train crash took place on 2 January. It was reported to the minister at about 6 a.m. He went to see the PM and apologetically offered his resignation. The PM did not accept the resignation but told him that only he could improve the Railways. The MR took it as a challenge and encouraged historic initiatives for the Indian Railways. They were as follows:

Special rail safety fund

The Railways was unable to renew its assets like tracks, bridges, rolling stocks and signalling equipment due to its weak financial health. Justice Khanna of Railway Safety and Review Committee (RSRC) had recommended that the government should come up with special initiatives to wipe out arrears in asset renewal particularly because the Ministry of Railways lacked financial resources to wipe out such huge arrears in maintenance.

The government had responded by creating a special non-lapsable corpus of ₹17,000 crore to undertake the renewal of all overdue assets as of 1 October 2001. This was a five-year programme for which a major contribution of ₹12,000 crore came from the central exchequer (free of dividend). The balance amount of ₹5,000 crore was proposed to be raised by levying a special safety surcharge from passenger fare.

This in my view was a visionary approach by the government led by Atal Bihari Vajpayee given shape by the then finance minister Yashwant Sinha. The element of non-lapsable fund was the unique key. Apart from meeting overdue renewal cost, the fund also met the cost of improvement for the replaced assets.

The government placed a Green Book in the Parliament listing all assets to be replaced in the course of its programme. This programme became the background of the Railways' turnaround in later years.

National Rail Vikas Yojana

On 15 August 2002, the prime minister announced important initiatives for the Indian Railways. With the backdrop of the 150th anniversary of the Railways, he paid tribute to the great institution which had contributed immensely to India's economic progress and national integration. He said that putting the Railways on a path of fast-track growth would be a befitting tribute to it. Thus, a major development plan called National Rail Vikas Yojana (NRVY) was launched.

The plan envisaged undertaking the removal of capacity bottlenecks in the critical sections of the railway network at an investment of ₹15,000 crore over the next five years. The projects included were as follows:

- Strengthening of the Golden Quadrilateral and its diagonals to enable the Railways to run more long-distance mail/express and freight trains at a cost of ₹8,000 crore;
- Strengthening of rail connectivity to ports and development of multimodal corridors to hinterland at a cost of ₹3,000 crore;
- Construction of four mega bridges—two over the Ganga River (in Patna and Monger in Bihar), one over the Brahmaputra River and one over the Kosi River—at a cost of ₹3,500 crore;
- For accelerated completion of the last mile and other important projects ₹763 crore were allotted.

This important initiative also included the approval of work to construct Udhampur Baramulla railway line in J&K as a national project with direct central funding. It was again a visionary approach for which credit must go to Atal Bihari Vajpayee and Yashwant Sinha.

This was a massive non-budgetary initiative to undertake capacity building for the Indian Railways to enable it to play its role in economic growth, in the wake of an upsurge in Indian economy. In my opinion, these were precursor to the turnaround of the IR in subsequent years.

This was launched from the prime minister's residence at the Race Course in an impressive ceremony on 26 December 2002. Three major projects were launched through a satellite link. They were: Mega Bridge over the Ganga River at Monger, doubling of 151 km Gooty—Pullampetta on the Mumbai-Chennai route and gauge conversion work of 305 km Gandhidham-Palanpur port connectivity work in Gujarat.

The programme was compered by the inimitable Manisha Dubey in her impeccable voice. The PM was extremely pleased and spoke to her. She was chosen by Sandeep Silas who had promoted her in many Railway functions. We organized a special citation and reward for her through the railway minister. Today when I hear her commentary on the Republic Day ceremony at Rajpath, I feel justifiably proud of her.

Administrative reforms and the action plan on safety

The minister presented a white paper in the Parliament on the status of the Railways in 2002. Apart from all the other issues, Chapter IX of the white paper dealt with the measures taken to improve safety. A corporate safety plan was also submitted in the Parliament in August 2003.

The minister also initiated action to improve the quality of rails produced by SAIL's plant in Bhilai. According to the RSRC, rails used by the IR had a high hydrogen content of 4-6 per cent instead of the normal 2 to 3 per cent. Higher hydrogen content reportedly made the rails prone to premature fracture. For ensuring this, a hydrogen degassing plant had to be installed. This was a costly investment of over ₹300 crore. A MoU was signed with SAIL and the Ministry of Railways. Accordingly, SAIL took all measures to improve rail quality and the Railways agreed to purchase rails from Bhilai and not to import rail as long as SAIL met its demand.

Under administrative measures, empowerment of GMs and safety organization were carried out. There was a general complaint against many officers who managed to stay in and around the metro cities and avoided going to less popular posts.

Ten-year rule for transfer

The minister announced that those officers staying for more than ten years at a particular place would be shifted. As secretary, a list of all such officers was prepared. Since they were generally of SAG and above, action had to be taken through the Board.

This came to be known as the infamous ten-year rule. Many high and mighty were involved. They had developed a strong clout. I told the minister that it would be an unpleasant and a thankless job. It was important for the MR to set precedence by not interfering in the process. He promised to stand by me. The first victim was his own EDPG, Mukundan. He had been with the MR for a long time. He asked him to go out of Delhi. This sent a strong message to all around. Once the minister was firm, the process moved forward.

I earned a great deal of displeasure and hostility in the process. But I continued the campaign. Members of the Board were generally cooperative. They however requested me to prevail upon the minister to slow down the process because of antagonism among the officers. I would not like to go into it as I sincerely believed in its necessity. Officers like us had spent more than twenty years in unpopular places. Only a handful of officers who had never moved outside Delhi in their life time, resented it. They had enjoyed the social advantages of a metro city. Their children had received the best of education. Officers in NF Railway were unable to get out of Maligaon.

The MR called me from his residence at about 9.30 one morning. He told me that he had cleared the file sent to him for posting of HAG officers. He said that a proposal of sending an officer to the South Eastern Railway, Kolkata, had also been approved by him. He said, 'But Jaruhar Sahib, I have received a call from someone regarding his transfer. I cannot say no to him. Please try to adjust him in Delhi.' I told him that he was a candidate under the ten-year rule. If not sent out even on promotion, he would never be out of Delhi. He became silent. He said that the person was very close to him. He had respected him too much to say no to him. 'It is a *dharm sankat* (moral dilemma), and you have to bail me out of it,' he said.

I understood and made the necessary changes. I kept the paper ready for his approval. The MR came to the office around 11 a.m. I went to him with the modified order for his approval. As soon as I entered his room, he laughed at me. He told me that I had actually bailed him out by making a very clear and unambiguous statement: 'If I changed the order, I would have no moral authority to enforce these orders.'

The MR said, 'I therefore told him that my problem was very serious. I am bound by my moral conviction. My secretary Railway Board has clarified about the implication of the change. You will have to forgive me for not acceding to your request.' Oh, what greatness! That was known as moral conviction.

The minister had shown this trait a number of times. He was always ready to listen to reason. The DRM Danapur and Sonepur being the local DRM near Patna had exerted a lot of pressure on the minister for a special approval to retain their quarters at Delhi. Since the minister often went to Patna, they narrated how their families suffered due to the two parallel establishments that they were bound to maintain. The MR told me to do it as he had promised them. Once he spoke to me from Patna to take immediate action and put up papers for his approval on his return to Delhi.

I prepared a note to the effect that the two DRMs be permitted to retain their quarters in Delhi. I put up the note before him for approval. His OSD, Chanchal Kumar, and EDPG, Mukundan, were present. They urged the MR to sign the note. But I politely restrained him by saying, 'Sir, you can sign the note. But you have promised to do justice to all. They are not doing any personal favour to you as the DRM. By seeking a special dispensation, they have made an unjust demand. There are many officers like them who also need this favour. Unfortunately, they cannot approach the railway minister. How shall we defend our action? According to the culture of the Indian Railways, the DRM is the head of the family, and his wife has an important role. The DRM is expected to take charge along with his wife. We cannot think of a DRM working out of a suitcase from a rest house and trying to run to Delhi at every opportunity. Sir, I am sorry, but I thought that I must tell you this. This was the reason for my reservations in carrying out your instructions.'

He listened to me intently and smiled. He said, 'Thank you, Jaruhar Sahib, for reminding me about the rule and duties of a DRM and his family. It would have been very unfair and unjust.'

He tore the note and there was complete silence. I thought that he was angry, but then he said, 'I value your judgment and advice. None of my officers pointed out the serious ramification of my action, if it had been taken'.

Inspection carriages stay

The minister was told by some that the inspection carriages (ICs) popularly known as saloons were being misused and that there was no need for them. One officer from his secretariat elaborately described how officers, along with their families, regularly abused the facility. The MR was convinced and had already decided that these carriages should be converted into holiday tourist coaches.

It was understandable in the light of his strong socialist background. He would not tolerate an article of luxury like an inspection carriage. I was silent. The MR then asked me if I had a view on this. I said, 'Sir, you should appreciate the essential use of the IC. If you use the IC for inspection, you will appreciate it better. All officers, particularly in the divisions, have to visit many places including some inconvenient ones. The officers are ready for their work at the arrival of the train. Otherwise, they have to hunt for a room in a rest house to get ready. It is a convenience which facilitates work. They are able to do the night inspection conveniently'.

After that the minister took me and R.K. Singh, GM Northern Railway, for an inspection of the Ambala division. When I showed him what he could inspect from the rear window of a carriage he was very impressed. The idea of banning the IC was killed.

I must thank Nitish ji for his great sense of commitment and the trust he displayed in me. It was a decision which was taken virtually, but he had listened to me, and the great institution of the IR was allowed to be retained ultimately for the good of the organization.

The minister bails me out

An incident highlighting his ability to give praise where it was due occurred during an air journey from Bilaspur. After attending the inaugural ceremony of dedicating the new zone of the SECR by the prime minister on 5 April 2003, we were returning to Delhi by a chartered flight. The MT, the CRB and some other senior officers were also in the party and we all travelled together.

After the evening ceremony, our flight had to take off before darkness set in. The minister was surrounded by many including some from his own party. To save time, we came straight to the airport and asked the pilot to be ready. We were already seated in the aircraft. As soon as the MR boarded the plane, it started taxiing. We were barely able to take off before darkness actually set in. The MR was sitting in the rear. It was a small aircraft with a capacity to seat ten persons. The MR said, 'Arrey, Jaruhar Sahib, where were you? I had told the Governor Mr Sahay that you had also come, and he wanted to meet you.' I told him that I was anxious about the take-off. I had come earlier to make preparations for the take-off.

Then he asked me how the governor and Yashwant Sinha (Union minister of finance) were related. I said that he was distantly related, but if I remembered correctly, both were posted together in Dumka district in Bihar. Mr Sinha was the deputy commissioner and Mr Sahay was the superintendent of police.

Then he told the CRB, 'Do you know Rana Sahib that Jaruhar Sahib is son-in-law of Mr Sinha?' The CRB said that he had never told us and we did not know about it. Nitish ji said, 'Arrey! Neither has he told me. And why should he tell? He did not want any advantage out of the relationship. I came to know about it by chance when I was talking to Mr Sinha. I had mentioned to him that I would ask the secretary Railway Board to send him some documents. Then the FM smiled and told me that Rajiv was his son-in-law. I was taken aback. I asked the FM why he had not told me about the relationship. 'Jaruhar ji is an excellent officer and he did not need any support. But Rana Sahib, look at the character of our *secretary*.'

I was very embarrassed and did not know where to look.

MINISTER INTRODUCES SAMVAD

Many measures or initiatives had been taken to improve the performance of the Railways—particularly the safety performance. The trade union representatives urged the minister to have a direct dialogue with the staff at the grassroots level.

They were likely to tell the minister what really afflicted the Railways.

The idea was superb and appealed to the minister immensely. The railwaymen involved in the operation were in a better position to explain why the accidents were occurring—particularly those attributable to human failures. This would also give them an opportunity to know what was being done at the corporate level. This was a concept and it was coined as 'Samvad'—a dialogue between the top level of management and the field-level operating personnel of the Indian Railways to develop stronger synergy.

Samvad releases vast synergy

The first samvad was planned in Delhi in May 2003. The task was entrusted to the secretary Railway Board. It was held in the auditorium of the Rail Museum. All five federations—the AIRF, the NFIR, Officers Association, the IRPOF and the RPF sponsored the meet. From the Railways, a team of gang men, carriage and wagon loco drivers, station masters and safety inspectors were called. General managers and chief safety officers (CSOs) from zonal railways were also invited. The full Board was also present.

There was no clear-cut structure of the dialogue and hence initially it started in the usual way—like a PNM meeting. During tea time, I told the minister that the actual purpose was not being achieved as it was only leading to open criticism. I then persuaded the general secretary of the NFIR, Mr Raghaviah, to initiate positive dialogue by bringing in constructive suggestions. He was requested to point out the structural deficiency in the IR system which hindered observance of safety rules. U.S. Jha, general secretary, AIRPFA, also turned the dialogue in that direction in his usual flamboyant style. After that, positive suggestions started flowing. These suggestions were examined by the Board in the evening. The minister in his response the next day gave positive assurances for a truly constructive action plan.

Samvad brought all the railwaymen to a common platform. This was the most important gain, and it resulted in a huge synergy. For the first time, the mood changed from one of depression or melancholy to cheerfulness and brightness. This had not happened for long. Many adverse incidents had spread negative energy in the organization. The brightness and cheer brought the whole team together once again. It was decided to hold samvad at other locations also. The minister travelled across the country with encouraging results. Such samvads were also held in divisions and zonal railways. When I became GM, Northern Railway, samvad was organized by the NRMU in Lucknow. Loco drivers voluntarily admitted to problems of alcoholism, which affected their safety performance. It was tackled, and the NGO helped them to overcome the malady. This sent a positive signal and was greatly appreciated by all.

Samvad in my view was an excellent attempt at creating a fabric of goodwill and harmony which the organization had lost over the years. Nobody had thought of its success in the beginning but the concept had gradually swept everybody off their feet. The feeling of bonhomie and looking towards a 'win-win' situation should have been continued, but in course of time, because of the change in political leadership in the country, this faded into oblivion.

Important initiatives brought by samvad

(i) Defreezing of recruitment in safety category

As part of samvad, the decision like defreezing the ban on recruitment of gangmen to fill vacant safety posts was taken. The MR announced that recruitments in the safety category would begin forthwith.

(ii) Improvement in running rooms and staff quarters

Running rooms (A running room is a place where drivers change duties. It has the facility for catering and rest for them. Every driver has to sign in here, when he reports for duty and sign off when he goes off the duty.) did not have adequate facilities. Likewise, there was difficulty in the deployment of running staff. This in turn affected the performance of the running staff (the drivers and guards are called the running staff). A committee was formed to formulate a new policy on the deployment of the running staff. An attempt was made to rationalize deployment of the crew. This in turn brought down the requirements of the running staff. The improvement of running rooms was taken up as a mission area. New quarters for gangmen were also sanctioned. The condition of the level crossing gates was improved. These measures put together improved the working conditions of the safety staff.

(iii) Voluntary retirement scheme for gangmen and loco drivers

The introduction of voluntary retirement scheme for gangmen and loco drivers was a landmark decision. Under this scheme, gangmen and loco drivers older than fifty years could seek voluntary retirement. In turn, the Railways agreed to employ their ward in their place. Employees like drivers or gangmen, as they advanced in age, either lost the sharpness of their reflexes or their physical strength did not permit them to do arduous duties. The scheme would enable such persons to seek honourable premature retirement. A very widely welcome step but unfortunately its implementation was tardy due to legal lacunae.

Thus, the problem of rail safety was tackled for the first time at various levels. The credit must be given to Railway Minister Nitish ji. For him the entire task was dear to his heart. It was good for the organization and it should be ever grateful to him.

IMPORTANT POSTING IN THE RAILWAY BOARD

The secretary was in charge of the establishment of the Rail Bhawan and all the railway officers and thus dealt with important postings. Because of his confidence in me, the minister asked me to deal with all such cases.

Mr Murali, FC, was scheduled to retire in November 2002. The minister was keen that his replacement should have a reasonably long tenure, of not less than two years. He was also desired to have a progressive outlook. Of the two previous FCs, one had a tenure of three months and the other, six months. He was clear that such utterly short tenures did not serve the organization well. From the list of eligible candidates, the names of two persons had emerged. One was already in the rank of secretary in Telecommunication Commission while the other's track record was not good. Another choice was Ms Vijaya Lakshmi—a much better option who had a residual service of three years.

I informally consulted Ashok Saikia, joint secretary in the PMO. He knew the first person quite well and thought that his lack of vision might not make him a good FC. He told me, 'This gentleman is already a secretary. Why move him to another department in the same rank?' But I told him that the Cabinet secretary was favourably disposed towards him. Saikia told me, 'Then send the file after 31 October 2002.' I initially did not appreciate the significance of the date but subsequently realized that the Cabinet secretary was retiring on 31 October 2002 and the new Cabinet secretary Kamal Pandey was taking over.

The minister approved the name of Vijaya Lakshmi as the FC, and she was recommended for appointment as the next FC. She was the first lady FC in the Indian Railways. The approval of the ACC was received in time.

I must thank Saikia for the smooth piloting of the case through the ACC. May his soul rest in peace. He died recently after suffering a great deal from the change of government in 2004.

Departmental Promotion Committee

The secretary Railway Board is part of all the Departmental Promotion Committee (DPC) proceedings. He in consultation with the CRB fixes the meeting of the DPC. Particularly important ones were for GM, HAG officers and additional members of the Railway Board. The role of the secretary is to prepare a list of all eligible officers, preparing dossiers, vacancy positions, annual confidential reports (ACRs) and documents like government resolutions that regulated the appointment. Except in the case of the AM, the secretary DOP is the third member of the DPC of all these posts. The main task for the secretary is to brief the members of the DPC. After deliberations, the proceedings are drawn by the secretary.

In my opinion, the DPC is sacrosanct. All members concerned are expected to do their homework before attending the meeting. But quite often, I had to intervene to ensure that the proceedings were in accordance with the government resolution. It caused some embarrassment at times. For empanelment of the S&T officers into the HAG, Chairman Rana wanted to make an exception with an officer but the secretary DOP did not agree. The chairman finally had to relent. The proceedings were drawn and everyone signed it. The file was sent to the MR for approval. The CRB, however, recorded that although he had signed the proceedings, he was misled by the secretary. He, therefore, wanted a review of the DPC.

I did not know about it. The minister smiled and asked me, 'Why did you mislead the chairman?' This was a serious charge. The chairman was called in by the MR. I requested him to tell me how I had misled him. The CRB said, 'This officer should have been in the panel. But you insisted that the DPC should view his entire record instead of just five years as in other cases. That is how his name could not be included in the panel.' I explained, 'Sir, the officer had only twenty-one points. He had one "Warning/Counselling" issued to him. According to the government resolution, such cases fall into the "grey area" category. According to the government resolution, the DPC should examine the entire career records of such officers and not just the five-year records. That is what secretary, DOP also said.' He had obviously not read the government resolution which he later admitted. His face fell when I showed him the resolution. The MR was very distressed.

It was obviously an unwelcome showdown and it had its repercussions. Officer on special duty, Rajasekaran, agitatedly placed all the ACRs of Board members, including mine before me. The ACRs of Board members contained unwarranted remarks by the chairman Railway Board. My ACR was marked 'Average' and not fit for promotion as 'general manager'. I was shocked but could do nothing about it. I had faced such biased and arbitrary remarks earlier also. One railway minister had recorded that I was not fit for 'open line general manager'. But in the final empanelment, this was ignored because I had held an outstanding record all along. This was treated as aberration. This is because they were annoyed by my refusal to drop a case when I was ED vigilance.

So, I asked the OSD to take the file to the minister as per rule. It was up to him to deal with the remark. I was called again by an unhappy MR. He was annoyed with the indiscreet comments of the CRB. I showed him many meaningless comments by the CRB. He had recorded the FC as not fit for CRB post. According to the government resolution, the FC could not become CRB. So, the remark was not only meaningless but also showed the chairman in poor light. The MR was the accepting authority. He had to record his acceptance.

A boss, of course, has the prerogative to assess someone in his own way. Some degree of subjectivity in such matters is also unavoidable. But the assessment of very senior persons has to be done with care. A person having risen in the hierarchy to become member or secretary after 25 or 30 years of service could not become an 'average' performer overnight. In absence of such care, the credibility of the person writing the report becomes questionable. I did not know what finally transpired but the CRB told me on the phone that he had graded me 'outstanding'. I thanked him politely. I did not ask the MR nor did he tell me anything about it.

A COMICAL EPISODE REGARDING THE POSTING OF THE GM

In time to come, I was duly empanelled as an open line general manager. Ashok Saikia called me on a Saturday afternoon to congratulate me, after the PM had approved the panel. A vacancy of GM was to come up after the retirement of the CRB, Mr Rana on 30 June 2003. I was the next person in the chain to fill the vacancy of the GM. The only question was who would succeed Mr Rana.

For posting as GM, a person should have two major qualifications. First, the residual service left for working as GM must be two years, counting from the date of the vacancy. Second, he or she should be fit to work as an open line general manager. At no point in time, could there be more than seven open line GMs from one particular cadre or service.

An officer of the electrical department was going to miss the bus. After 30 June 2003, he did not have requisite two years' of residual service. He requested that I decline the posting as the GM against the vacancy arising on 30 June so that he could be posted as the GM. I told him that the refusal of posting could go against me. I might not be considered for the post in the new panel which would come into force from 1 July. He told me that the CRB had told him that if I refused the promotion, he would manage everything and would ensure that my progression in career was not impaired in any way. I could not say anything. Firstly, he was a good friend and secondly, being the secretary Railway Board, I knew the rule rather well. I could not imagine how the CRB made such suggestions, and what could he possibly do because he was himself going to retire on 30 June 2003.

I was silent in sheer embarrassment and he took it out to be my consent and reported it to the CRB. I was called by the minister who was furious. He asked, 'What is this that I am hearing? The CRB says that you have agreed to forgo posting as the GM in favour of Mr Grover. I have called Mr Rana to understand what kind of a comic is being staged by the secretary and chairman Railway Board.' I gave him the background of my conversation with the officer.

Mr Rana walked in to the room and patted me saying, 'Well done. We will look after your interest.' The minister had already taken the matter into his hands. He was scathing in his remarks. 'I am shocked how one can think of such a proposal. Do you want to make a joke of this ministry by suggesting a factitious proposal like this? That too where posting of a GM is concerned? Jaruhar ji is at least trying to be humble but how can the CRB and I even imagine entertaining such a crap? I do not want to listen anything further on this, lest I become a laughing stock.'

Yes, utter crap it was and it showed all of us in a very poor light. That was the end of it.

THE POSTING OF THE CRB—A LANDMARK MOVE

The question of posting of the CRB on 30 June 2003 was uppermost in our mind. The minister was keen that the next CRB should have adequate residual service. He should have initiative and drive. The present position was dismal and not very encouraging. Of the likely candidates to fill the position, the options were as follows:

 (i) Sudhir Chandra, member staff, the seniormost member but would retire in two months' time.
 (ii) Mr Dasarathi, member mechanical, was the next senior member with a residual service of three months only.
 (iii) Kanwarjit Singh, member engineering, was the next senior member with a residual service of five months only.

Government Resolution of 1987

According to the resolution of the government of 16 February 1987:

 (i) Officers to be considered for posts of members of the Railway Board (including financial commissioner) (*a*) should normally have balance tenure of service of two years or more from the date of occurrence of the vacancy; and (*b*) should normally have worked for a period of one year in the grade preceding that of member railway board/financial commissioner.

Note: In the context of the above, the preceding grade for member, the Railway Board (other than the FC) would be that of GM (open line) on the Railways.

(ii) The officers to be considered for the post of CRB should normally have a minimum tenure of two years as member Railway Board and/or CRB including at least one year as CRB.

In simpler terms, the CRB will be appointed from members of the Railway Board with two years tenure as member at the time of joining the Railway Board with a balance tenure of one year to work as the CRB. Failing this, the CRB can be appointed from open line GM (having worked for one year) and having balance tenure of two years to serve as the CRB.

In the past, in absence of persons having dual qualifying criteria (of one year as residual service and two years on appointment as member), senior board members having less than a year also were appointed as chairman. There was an example of a chairman with a tenure of eight months only.

In the present circumstances, two other members—electrical and traffic—were both junior to some other GMs like S.M. Singla (GM, S.C. Railway), S.P.S. Jain (GM, Central Railway) and R.K. Singh (GM, Northern Railway). The minister felt that there was no point in appointing senior Board members as chairman with tenure varying from 2 to 5 months. The choice had to therefore go outside the Board. This was a step which had never been taken except if my memory serves right, in the case of Mr Gujral. He was appointed as chairman from GM, Western Railway, when the entire Board was sacked by Mrs Indira Gandhi in 1980. He had only seven months to retire. That was a war-like situation and it would not be appropriate to compare the two situations.

R.K. Singh in contention for the CRB

Much gossip ran rife by May 2003. A lady officer in S.P. Marg Colony, in course of a morning walk, ran towards me to enquire if R.K. Singh was being considered for appointment as the chairman. I had no knowledge of it.

R.K. Singh asked me one Saturday if I could come to Baroda House for a chat. He broached the subject of the appointment. I explained the position and suggested that S.M. Singla could be the next CRB.

He smiled. He said that the provisions contained in the government resolution would have to be fully exhausted before following the rule of seniority. In other words, if no person met the criteria contained in the resolution, the Board could follow the seniority rule. Both Mr Singla and S.P.S. Jain did not have two years as residual service to serve as the CRB although they had completed one year as GM (open line). He said that he had fulfilled both the qualifying criteria. Thus, he should be appointed as the CRB. The cat was out of the bag! The MR discussed this aspect with us and he observed there was no valid reason to bypass R.K. Singh. He asked the CRB to process the case.

I am asked to pilot the proposal

After a couple of days, the minister called me up from his residence one afternoon. He had asked Mr Rana, the CRB, to meet the Cabinet secretary to discuss R. K. Singh's proposal before it was sent formally. He said, 'Mr Rana has confused the matter. The Cabinet secretary says that the proposal is not acceptable. I have told him that Mr Jaruhar, *secretary* Railway Board will meet him to clarify and explain the proposal. Jaruhar Sahib, I was expecting this! I know that it was appropriate that the *chairman* Railway Board should meet the Cabinet *secretary* first. But Mr Rana has failed. We have to take the Cabinet *secretary* into confidence on the proposal before it is sent formally. You should go and convince him.' I said that I would first discuss the proposal with Mr Mukherjee, joint secretary, who dealt with and processed the case. The Cabinet secretary in any case would ask him before making up his mind. The MR turned towards his PS, R.C.P Singh, and said, 'Ramchandra Babu, look at the difference in approach. He has already started making the right moves.'

I knew Mukherjee well and had a good rapport with him. So, there was no problem when I met him. He was patient but plainly looked sceptical about the proposal. He said that working with the Ministry of Railways was difficult. It was in the habit of mooting all kinds of proposals. He said, 'Look, there is a precedence of the CRB or member with tenure of three months also. It will be difficult to defend such a proposal. There is bound to be a hostile reaction including some one going to the Court.'

His argument had force. I said, 'But look at the other side, about the person who fulfils all qualifying criteria. The government decides to ignore his claim without assigning any reason. How are we going to explain ourselves or defend our action in the court? Let us not forget that the Government Resolution of 1987 was framed at the instance of a directive of the apex court. It aimed at tenure-linked norms for appointment of Board members for good governance. If we select a senior person with inadequate service disregarding the objective underlined in the government resolution, we are only serving a person's personal aspiration with no regard for good governance. Mr Mukherjee, let us decide what we want—complaint from a person who was senior but not eligible or good governance? For a moment don't think of injustice as an issue. We will end up with three CRBs with varying tenure of 2 to 5 months. That is your logic. Any thought for governance?'

Formal proposal of R.K. Singh sent to the ACC

He was totally floored by the argument but insisted that the Railways should confirm that it would henceforth follow the government resolution in letter and spirit. I signed the note of assurance with great promptitude. The discussion had gone on for two hours. After complete satisfaction, the Cabinet secretary was briefed. He listened carefully and was satisfied. He told me that the minister may send the proposal accordingly. I came back to the Rail Bhawan to brief the minister. But he personally spoke to him, 'Pandey ji, Jaruhar Sahib has discussed with you and you are satisfied. The proposal will go today.'

It was a Friday. I had planned to go to Kota that evening. I wanted to visit Ranthambore forest to see tigers after the inspection. It was already 4 p.m. The programme had to be cancelled and I told the MR accordingly. He was embarrassed but he suggested that I still try. I drafted the proposal with the help of Rajasekaran. The chairman had already gone home so I sent the file to him at 8 p.m. for his approval. After which, I took the file to the MR. Unfortunately, he was busy with a party meeting. George Fernandes, the defence minister and two other MPs were with him. I waited till 8.30 p.m. After an SOS, he immediately called me in. He took about ten minutes to read and sign the file. I signed the formal proposal. The papers and the file were handed over to the OSD with instructions to deliver it to the Cabinet secretary the next morning. I came home and ate some dinner and was off to the station—just in time to catch the train. It was a great feat!

THE POSTING PROPOSAL OF THE CRB SUFFERS A SETBACK

When I returned from Kota on Monday, I was told that the proposal had been received by the Cabinet secretariat and it was being processed. It was the first week of June and I thought that things were in order. There was nothing to worry.

The proposal has a setback

However, there was intense lobbying from others. Everyone appeared to have thrown their hat in the ring. The Cabinet secretary had apparently wilted under intense pressure and had taken the safest way out. He claimed that the proposal of the Ministry of Railways would cause heartburn. He took the line that in the past, persons with lesser tenure had been appointed as the CRB in order to honour seniority. He showed incidents with precedence where the government had decided to post persons with even three months of residual service as the secretary to the Government of India. Taking this plea, he recommended the appointment of Mr Dasarathi as the CRB. He had three months of service left. He sent the file to the home minister who in turn, agreeing with the Cabinet secretary sent it to the PM for approval.

Although done very secretly, the MR learnt of it when the file reached the PM. There was a serious rail accident on 23 June 2003. The MR was busy till 26 June due to this. He spoke to the PM about the proposal. A meeting was called by the PM of all the ACC members (home minister & MR) where the Cabinet secretary and the principal secretary to the PM, Mr Brajesh Mishra, were also present. After the discussions, the PM said that the 1987 resolution could not be ignored. The Railways was going through a crisis at present. It was necessary that a person of longer tenure took charge of the affairs. Thus, the proposal was taken away by the Cabinet secretary on 28 June 2003. He processed the case exactly as proposed by the MR. The file reached the PM on the 29th evening. The PS to the PM took the file to the PM in the morning of 30 June 2003. Around 9.30 a.m. the PM signed it, and soon after that I was informed about it. When informed while he was at his residence, the MR was very happy and asked me to get the order immediately. I told him not to worry. With reasons, I did not want the file to reach before 5 p.m. He understood and appreciated my sense of caution.

After that I told R.K. Singh about it around 11.30 a.m. I requested that he keep in touch with me. I asked Mr Rajshekhran to go to the DOP & T around 4.30 p.m. The letter came to me by 5.15 p.m. I then got the approval of the MR by hand, and issued the letter, appointing R.K. Singh, GM, Northern Railway as chairman Railway Board. I had asked Satish Agnihotri, EDCC, to escort Mr Singh to the Rail Bhawan. I received him in the Rail Bhawan. By 6.15 p.m. he was installed as the next CRB.

Aftermath of the appointment of R.K. Singh

By all means, it was a historic moment and not without reason, it led to criticisms and very hostile reactions. The most stringent criticism was against the minister, Nitish Kumar, for playing the 'caste card'. R.K. Singh and he apparently belonged to the same caste. One day he asked R.C.P. Singh in my presence if R.K. Singh also was of the same caste. He confirmed it. Nitish ji was hurt. I honestly believed that it was an unfair charge. As I knew him, he would have never gone such a distance on the basis of caste. The resolution was completely explicit in its content. It would have been unfair to deny the job to R.K. Singh.

The most virulent claim rose from Mr Parthasarthy, the person who had missed out to Ms Vijaya Lakshmi in the run-up to the FC. He represented that he could not become the CRB because of the casteism that had been perpetrated by Nitish Kumar. It was completely baseless. The 1987 Resolution of the government did not envisage that the FC could become the CRB. The Cabinet secretary took it up with him because it was unbecoming of a serving officer to level such a charge. A minor penalty chargesheet was served and he was duly 'censured'. He went to court against the order but the case was eventually dismissed.

Serious resentment—MM walks out in protest

Mr Dasarathi openly protested against the appointment. He refused to work as member mechanical (MM) with R.K. Singh. He immediately sought voluntary retirement. He was held in high esteem by the minister. It shook him up a great deal. But he was perhaps, batting for GM, Southern Railway (SR) who had one year left in July 2003. If Mr Dasarathi's retirement was accepted, he would become MM. Mr Dasarathi was requested to continue till the monsoon session of the Parliament. The minister also explained that he should not take him amiss. R.K. Singh was appointed as chairman in larger interest of the organization. R.K. Singh also went to placate him, but Mr Dasarathi was unrelenting.

The minister did not accept his resignation. Thus, he had to continue as the MM. Other Board members like B.S. Sudhir Chandra did not react because he was in any case retiring in a month's time. KJ, ME, was a bit hurt. He was promised that he would be the next CRB even if it was for five months. But he was quite a sport about it. S.C. Gupta, ML, and K.K. Agarwal, MT, had no stakes.

There was resentment against me for piloting the case. Some thought that I had manipulated the situation to secure the post of GM, Northern Railway. It was also alleged that I had set the precedence for my posting as the next CRB. The case was processed in accordance with provisions in the Government Resolution of 1987. I had no role in the resolution. Despite our pleading, the Cabinet secretary eventually had taken a different line. But for MR's intervention, the story would have been different. I was next in line to be posted as GM. I was posted as GM, Northern, since a vacancy arose there. Thus, I could not have been involved in any manipulation. If the government resolution was to be followed, I had of course the chance to become the next CRB.

Unprincipled placatory approach

Two senior GMs, S.M. Singla of the SCR and S.P.S. Jain of the CR, had serious complaints. Proposal was to be made for the posting of member staff in August. The MR asked me if Mr Singla would be willing. He had no reservations when I asked him. Thus, decks were cleared for his appointment. S.P.S. Jain also agreed to take on the position as the ME when KJ was to retire in November 2003. Dust appeared to have settled. R.K. Singh had an excellent reputation of being suave, so the ruffled feathers were calmed, rapidly.

R.K Singh had to make adjustments and compromises. The cadre of mechanical engineers had the greatest grudge against him, which received special consideration. After my posting as GM, Northern Railway, he requested Nitish ji to post R.D. Bhandari (an IRSME officer posted as CME in Southern Railway) as secretary Railway Board. Otherwise, V.K. Kaul, an IRSE officer was shortlisted to be posted as secretary. He would have had a longer tenure. Mr Bhandari was soon posted as GM, SER (in about four months' time) and it did not serve anybody's cause.

After I left as secretary, the importance of the office of secretary Railway Board was systematically decimated. It was certainly because of the unprincipled posting as well as an attempt to disregard its authority.

I cannot absolve myself of the blame. Being the secretary, I could have and should have considered this and explained it to the MR. But at that time, the greater priority was to provide support and comfort to R.K. Singh, who had walked over many seniors to become the chairman. The MR was also very keen on this. I had therefore no other way than to keep the counsel to myself. A poor excuse indeed!

MINISTER RESIGNED—SHADOW OF POLITICAL INTERACTION

R.K. Singh had joined as chairman on 30 June 2003, and in the course of another twenty-five days, I had become GM, Northern Railway. But these were crucial days. Because of some intraparty wrangling; Nitish ji had resigned as the MR.

This had more to do with intraparty politics. He was openly criticized by his own party's MP. He had stopped coming to the office. All kinds of persuasive tactics had failed. R.K. Singh gave an impression of not being interested. I then called Mr Jha, the general secretary of the All India RPF Association (AIRPF). He was close to the MR and held me in high respect. I requested a formal meeting with all the five federation heads—the AIRF, the NFIR, the IRPOF, Officers Association and the AIRPF. I suggested that they issue a joint appeal to Nitish ji to withdraw his resignation. This would demonstrate their unity, strength and respect for the minister. They agreed and jointly went to the MR residence to request that he withdraw his resignation.

I also went to Nitish ji and made an emotional appeal, stating that that the Railways was in a crucial stage. I requested him to forget the political push and pull and to rise above it. I do not know why I did this. But he smiled and said nothing. He met the delegation and listened to them. He was moved by their appeal. He told them that he would decide his future course of action in a day's time. Soon after, he came back and told us that he would return to the

Rail Bhawan. I organized a befitting welcome for him. The crowd to welcome him was amazing. I requested R.K. Singh to escort him to the Rail Bhawan but he chose to be in the Rail Bhawan.

I, of course, acted on my impulse, driven by pure emotion. I was not aware of any transgression of norms of the established protocol. There was no question of being as aligned with any political side. That was simply ridiculous. Nitish ji was still the minister. Where was the breach in protocol if I visited him and sought his advice? I think some wanted to be cautious so that they were not seen as too close to Nitish ji.

It would be unfair on my part to pass any judgment on anyone's conduct, but it looked odd to me at that time. History is very cruel. It replays the action at some point for witnesses to make an evaluation of one's conduct. I have only underlined this. The person in question chose to conduct himself differently, when a change in ministry looked imminent. It only established that people wore a different face in public affairs! I have purposefully chosen to be obscure and not explicit in recounting the incident. I believe that judging the conduct of a person is the prerogative of history, which is, after all the custodian of all events!

Fifth Pay Commission Awards—more Board members

The Pay Commission had recommended:

- The post of member staff and additional member staff should be encadred into the IRPS (Indian Railway Personnel Service).
- Two new posts of members of the Board should be created—one for stores and another for the S&T department.

The recommendations were not accepted by the government because the IRPS was a young service. The MS had to be a senior person. The concept of comparable seniority was brought in. The senior-most person in the IRPS was junior to the GM. He could not exercise effective control. Thus, the post of MS was not considered to be in cadre of the IRPS. Moreover, the MS also had to come from a serving GM (open line). No IRPS officer was senior enough in such a case. The present arrangement of drawing the MS from the list of serving GMs (open line) with the requisite qualifying criteria had to continue.

But in the case of additional member staff (AMS), the concept of comparable seniority was again factored in. This led to resentment. The matter went to court. The court wanted a definition of comparable seniority. An attempt was also being made to sabotage the case. I did not like this and I took the matter into my own hands. It had to be explained to the court that the governance was the prerogative of the executives. It had decided that a difference of normally

2 to 3 years in this case was considered comparable seniority. The petition on this basis was rejected. But in time to come, the first IRPS officer became AM staff in 2 to 3 years' time.

Regarding two more members to the Board, there was intense debate and lobbying at different levels. There was a genuine concern for the Board to be a compact body. It could not be reduced to representing each cadre in the Railways. The government did not accept the recommendations of the Pay Commission, but agreed to create two posts of director generals (DGs), one each for the S&T and the stores departments. Om Prakash, GM, North Eastern Railway—a senior stores officer—was close to Nitish ji. He prevailed upon him to move his case for appointment as DG store. The post had not been created by the Cabinet formally. After its creation, a government resolution to regulate appointment of the DG would have been required. This would take time. Om Prakash did not have even a year of residual service and his retirement was due in May 2004. But after I left as secretary, the case was referred to the Ministry of Finance. And look at the power of lobbying! The Ministry of Finance approved the creation of two posts of members instead of the DG. This was nowhere called for. The Cabinet secretary threw the case out as unwarranted.

I bid goodbye as secretary Railway Board

On 25 July 2003, my orders posting me as GM, Northern Railway was received around 6 p.m. The OSD brought the order of the ACC. The formal order of the Board was also issued in consultation with the MR. Around 7 p.m., I went to the residence of the minister to seek his blessings before I joined as GM, Northern Railway. He was all smiles and accepted the sweets which I offered. Meanwhile, the CRB also joined us. The MR said, 'Jaruhar Sahib, I am very happy. You have made me proud. I wish you the very best and I look forward to your return to the Rail Bhawan soon.' I did not understand and I replied, 'Sir, as secretary Railway Board, I was free to walk in to your room. But now as GM, I have to seek an appointment to meet you.' He laughed and said, 'Arrey no! Till such time as a new *secretary* takes over, which will not be less than a month, you must double up as *secretary* Railway Board, much in the same way as your predecessor R.K. Singh had done. You must work hard and follow the path he has travelled.' This was said with a wink and I understood what he meant!

14

MANAGING ZONAL RAILWAY: NORTHERN RAILWAY

I TAKE OVER AS GENERAL MANAGER WITH HUMILITY

I reported to Baroda House—headquarters of the Northern Railway at around 7.30 p.m. I was escorted by Vinay Kumar Singh, secretary to the GM. It was with a feeling of awe and with the weight of grave responsibility that I entered the portals of Baroda House and gradually climbed up to my room.

The most beautiful building designed by Lutyens—Sir Edwin Landseer Lutyens—the famous English architect—would fill anyone with awe, but the thought that I was chosen to preside over the affairs of the Northern Railway from this architectural masterpiece for the next couple of years was simply momentous. Its dome signified the formal cover the Northern Railway received from its GM who occupied the powerful room. I was designated to hold this fort now, I did not expect any senior officer to meet or greet me at that hour. But I was surprised to meet many due to an enormously capable and efficient secretary. The news of my posting had spread fast. I was receiving calls on my cell phone continuously from all over, congratulating me on the appointment. I had managed to call my wife. I told her that I was on the way to Baroda House after having met the MR. She, as usual, just heard it and smiled. V.K. Singh had kept the charge papers ready which I signed. I was thus installed as GM, Northern Railway around 7.40 p.m. on 25 July 2003.

Many PHOD officers came to felicitate me. Mr Awasthi, the chief security commissioner (CSC), RPF, invited me for the passing out parade of RPF officers in Lucknow, held on 27 July. The CRB was the chief guest. I was undecided about it, but Satish Agnihotri requested that I go there. I left for home around 9 p.m., only to find a host of TV channels waiting for me. I quickly finished with them and only then could I be with my family.

The post of GM is a statutory appointment under the Railway Act, 1989. The GM had all the powers to superintend the running of the railways. Having been secretary, I had a clear picture of the importance of the post and its various implications.

CONCEPT OF FUNCTIONAL DIVISION OF RESPONSIBILITY

Next day was a Saturday and a holiday but I called all the PHOD officers for a meeting in my room. After exchanging pleasantries, I was specific in my emphasis on our prime responsibility as public transporter. It was clearly a way to transport public goods and passengers in the most effective, safe and economic way. Thus, it was to be our main mission and focus of all of our activities. It was an important statement which had to be appreciated by all present.

Concept of functional responsibility group

Train running has basically three essential features namely train operation, commercial activity and safety of operation. These three services form the core group. It could be called the central operating team. The three departments involved in the group were operating, commercial and safety. Their departmental heads must seek business, provide services to the public and conduct it safely.

But for running a train, other departments had to provide services like rail tracks and bridges, coaches, wagons, locomotives besides electric traction and electrical services, and S&T. The four departments responsible for providing these services were engineering, mechanical, electrical and S&T. These could be called the service provider group. They had to provide services to the core operation group responsible for the rail business. Without their support, the operation group could not function.

For the entire operation, these two groups needed support from seven departments namely finance, personnel, stores, medical, security, public relations and general management (SDGM). The quality of the service or realization of the mission objective would entirely depend upon the quality of support provided by the support group. Besides, the construction department under the chief administrative officer (CAO) formed a support group entrusted with the task of creating infrastructure and capacity augmentation under the plan head.

Functional division enforced synergy

The organizational structure based on a functional approach facilitated the assignment of priorities in that order. For example, the departmental targets must complement the corporate targets. It was easy for everyone to direct their attention accordingly. For example, it was necessary to carry traffic through Mughalsarai-Varanasi-Lucknow-Moradabad section as the main trunk route of the Allahabad division was saturated. The Moradabad and the Lucknow divisions had somewhat suffered in terms of inputs in the past. Both divisions had piled up arrears of maintenance. All departments were therefore asked to coordinate their activities in such a manner that construction works related to signalling and civil engineering were bunched together under the same traffic blocks. Thus, the central underlying idea was that after the work was completed, the train would run at an unrestricted speed in that section. It created an enormous synergy among all the departments. The departmental resources were thus focused to achieve an optimum traffic output.

My role as general manager

All were thus conditioned to think in terms of the corporate mission goal. They were asked to prepare their plan and make presentations accordingly. This meeting was rather informal but it soon became about the sharing of mission objectives and path-finding exercises.

As GM, I believed that it was my duty to set goals. I made it clear that I was really a GM without any particular expertise. Thus, I would not generally respond to any call for bridge or civil engineering but instead I would help them realize their task. It was necessary to imbibe the spirit in the true sense of the word. I do not know what the others thought of me after the meeting. But I was pretty sure that I had begun the way I should have. I knew that I would be on trial for some time. My associates would keenly observe me for any flaw or chink in the armour. I had one immediate feedback: 'No general manager had spoken to them like this and I was a different kettle of fish!' Well, it was welcome and I wanted to be like that.

FIRST VISIT TO LUCKNOW

Next morning, I attended the RPF programme in Lucknow. It was a crisp programme. The RPF officers had not expected or visualized that a regular GM would be posted ahead of this ceremony. CSC Mr Awasthi was keen to invite me for this programme as soon as he learnt of my appointment. I attended it mainly because R.K. Singh was coming to Lucknow for the first time, after becoming CRB. He belonged to Uttar Pradesh and had received his education in and around Lucknow. He had been DRM, Lucknow, Northern Railway. He was also ADRM (additional divisional manager) of the Lucknow division of the North Eastern Railway when I was CE (construction) in that railway.

The body of trade apprentices appeals

After the programme, many people called on me. The body of young trade apprentices was the most important among them. They had been agitating for a long time for regular appointments in the Railways. They had also met Nitish Kumar when I was secretary Railway Board. Under the Apprenticeship Act, the Railways was obliged to provide them with training, but were not bound to appoint them after the apprenticeship was over. Any recruitment in the government had to be opened to all through regular selection by the RRB, etc. So, notwithstanding the fact that they were trained and readily available hands, they could not be appointed directly without going through the open selection process. I decided to do something about it—not because they were agitating but because they were useful hands, and the Railway was acutely short on safety category staff. One possible option, that I saw was to appoint them as substitutes, but it required in-depth consideration.

Planned recruitment of apprentices

The first step was to work out the total number of vacancies in technical categories for train operation. There were vacancies in departments like mechanical (in carriage & wagon, diesel loco), electrical (general services, traction, electric loco), engineering (track machines), and S&T. Intake of skilled technical staff had been banned for ages under the overall policy to contain the total manpower in the Railways. All departments had an acute shortage of skilled staff in the safety category. This subject was taken up in Samvad and the MR had lifted the ban in the safety and operational category. Such recruitments were done through the RRB, but its delivery schedule was pretty long. The Railways needed them urgently for their emergency operational needs. The RRB was unable to match the urgent demand in recruitment. The only option was to engage skilled persons like trade apprentices as substitutes. But this option though available earlier was banned by the Railway Board.

A committee of personnel officer, and mechanical engineers was formed to screen the list of trade apprentices. The Railway Board was informed about how the large vacancies in safety category had become a serious threat to safety in train operation. The Railway Board was urged to lift the embargo regarding the appointment of substitutes.

A GM was competent to appoint substitutes as temporary staff for immediate and emergent requirements. This is normally for a period not exceeding 180 days. The grounds of engagement were serious because trained skilled persons were required for safety duty like train examination, track and signalling maintenance works—all related to the safety of train running. A condition was imposed that their services would be terminated after persons recruited through the RRB, who had gone through the prescribed training, were made available. All the conditions for appointment of substitutes were thus complied with. Indents were placed on the RRB for recruitment, but it would take a long time to materialize. The appointment of substitutes was a temporary recruitment, meant exactly for situations like this. All trade apprentices, who were trained and qualified persons duly screened by a special committee, were thus recruited as substitutes. The panel of eligible and qualified apprentices was completely exhausted.

Decades-old problem solved legally—a 'win-win' situation for all

Nobody could believe nor think that the decade long issue would be settled in a smooth and regular manner. According to the rules, substitutes were eligible for regular recruitment if they worked continuously for more than 180 days. The RRB was not expected to complete the selection in a matter of 180 days. Even if they did, they could be easily accommodated because the vacancies were many in number. Trade apprentices were extremely happy. They expressed their gratitude in a large welcome ceremony when I visited Lucknow in the course of an inspection.

NORTHERN RAILWAY—SENSITIVE STAKEHOLDERS

The Northern Railway, after the reorganization of Indian Railways in 2002, had five divisions—Delhi, Ambala, Lucknow, Moradabad and Firozpur. It covered the entire northern India from Jammu in the north to Varanasi in the east. The railway was strategically positioned to have an important border with Pakistan. The strategic defence build-up also required support from the Railways. It served important states like Uttar Pradesh, Haryana, Punjab, J&K, Himachal Pradesh, Uttarakhand and Delhi. More importantly, it served the capital of India—the city of Delhi.

Sensitive stakeholders are very vocal

Apart from the large number of people travelling to and out of Delhi, Northern Railway also served over six hundred members of the Parliament. It therefore served important and sensitive stakeholders. They had high expectations from the Railways. As they were a very vocal lot, they had to be carefully dealt with.

Media personnel—both print and TV—were also important. They were always looking for some story. They had an instant and wide coverage all over the country. Thus, they had to be handled with extreme caution and sensitivity.

All these made the job of the GM very demanding.

The MR and two ministers of state were also in Delhi. They had to be served with extreme care. The MR had to deal with issues brought up by MPs also. Besides, GM, Northern Railway had also to take suitable care of the high offices of the PMO and other Union ministers. It was precisely for these reasons that V.K. Agarwal as GM, Northern Railway had told someone that the GM, Northern Railway was more important than a member Railway Board.

GM had to be alert and innovative

I would not like to draw a direct comparison but there was no argument over the fact that the GM, Northern Railway had to be greatly ingenious and innovative to combat the external influences of severest intensity besides superintending a big zonal railway like Northern.

Just to drive my point home, I wish to describe a small incident. At about 9.15 in the morning when I was leaving for office, someone called me from Delhi Main about the derailment of a commuter train while entering Delhi Main. Before I could get the official version of the account, the media had begun to take up the case to instantly flash it on the TV channel. The Parliament was in session. Now, who had given the feed to the TV channel? Obviously, it was someone from the station—a railwayman. Thus, the media had received the information first before the official version had been conveyed to the GM. TV channels would put up as 'Breaking News' to attract maximum coverage. We knew this modus operandi and accordingly, we had set up our own network.

I immediately called up the CPRO. Sandhu got in touch with the correspondent of the channel with the official version. The truth was that a commuter had thrown a very big bundle from the running train on an adjoining line. It had got stuck in the wheel causing the accident. The police were able to apprehend the culprit and quick action was taken to restore traffic. Thus, the damaging effect of this specific 'breaking news' was vastly diluted. A balanced coverage took the sting out of it.

INTERNAL INFLUENCE—ITS IMPACT ON INDUSTRIAL RELATION

Apart from tackling external influences with the type of sensitivity involved in the Northern Railway, it was also equally important to manage the internal influences. This included trade unions—NRMU (an affiliate of the All India Railwaymen's Federation, AIRF), Uttar Railwaymen's Union (URMU—an affiliate of the National Federation of Indian Railwaymen, NFIR), Association of Indian Railway Protection Force (AIRPF). Besides, two officers' unions—

Federation of Railway Officers' Association (FROA) and Indian Railways Promotee Officers' Federation (IRPOF) were also involved. Other units were the OBC Association and SC & ST Association, which although did not have the status of trade unions, but the government had assigned them the status of welfare societies for the welfare of the two caste groups.

The role of trade unions is vital

These organizations held strong influence over the entire workforce. They formed the bulwark of an industrial relationship. Real strength lay in forging a sincere and strong bond with the workforce directly. But it was also desirable to enlist the support of trade unions. The relationship or interaction with their top leaders was different when one was GM. Obviously that was the highest level in the Railways where issues must be settled. There was no scope to pass the buck on to somewhere else.

This aspect has the widest ramification. Most of the trade unions have some link with political parties on ideological plane. It is, however, important that the internal issues of the Railways are not taken up by these political parties. Such a situation will have detrimental effects on the industrial relationship. They have to be suitably contained within the organization. A place like Delhi has greater chance of such eventuality. The GM must be fully aware of it and he had to deal with them in a very decisive and discreet manner.

THRUST AND CHALLENGES IN OPERATION

The functional based operating system can handle the challenges thrust upon the Railways. The involvement of all concerned is well-defined and their role is made explicit. An action plan was drawn by the PHOD officers in their presentations accordingly. It ensured that the role was completely owned by them. This is the most important step in all ventures as a team. Unless the idea was owned, the success was unlikely to be enduring and the failure likely to be more painful and devastating.

The division—the cutting edge

Divisions had to become effective as a cutting-edge apparatus. They had to own the plan and modify it if necessary. Then it had a greater chance of succeeding. As the DRM, we were asked to market goods traffic. We were unable to seize any deal because the person who was to market a traffic demand, had to have the wherewithal to fulfil the commitment made during marketing. The divisions had to understand the overall dynamics of the traffic flow on the Indian Railways network, which was coordinated by the Railway Board. Thus, the BOXN coal rakes loaded from eastern India for Punjab power houses after the release had to go back to eastern parts empty and were then, available for loading to destinations in eastern India. The Northern Railway did not have a consignment to load for those areas in the BOXN wagons. Punjab had mostly foodgrain traffic which could not be loaded in the BOXN rakes. But Assam coal was loaded in covered BCN wagons rakes. Foodgrains could be loaded in these on the return trip to Northeast destinations. The origin destination analysis known as O-D analysis was thus important.

Divisions had to be strengthened to be efficient. They had to perform well for everyone. Favouritism based on departmental affiliation has to be totally discouraged. This is very important for the GM. It is equally important for any PHOD also. It is quite likely that two DRMs differ in their approach but they may be equally good. It is for the GM to exploit their potential to the maximum.

MORNING BRIEFING TO FOCUS ATTENTION

I organized a daily morning briefing in my room for 15-20 minutes with the COM. This was vital. It was a well laid out drill. I was normally in my room by 9.30-9.45 in the morning. After my usual prayer for about 4 or 5 minutes, my secretary, V.K. Singh, walked into my room. He would brief me about the day's appointments. I would pass on some important instructions. This would take not more than 10 to 15 minutes.

Thereafter, I would receive the COM exactly at 10.10 a.m. I was very well prepared. He would brief me about any plans for the day and the problems faced since yesterday. Any problem that required special assistance was discussed. Any important point with any particular division was highlighted. It was very business-like and hardly lasted for more than 15 or 20 minutes. The entire operational detail was therefore known. It was for the GM to follow up with all divisions so that the programme was fully realized. Once the DRM was asked to monitor loading of so many rakes, they put the entire machinery in motion.

It was essential to cut down all detentions and arrange speedy movement because of rolling stock constraints. Important time factors for this were running time, placement time for rake, loading/unloading time, withdrawal time after loading/unloading and time for placement in C&W running lines.

Minimum time taken for these operations would increase the productivity of the operation. It cut down the unit cost as well. Monitoring was therefore important. I started using the data available from FOIS (freight operation information system), which had data on all important terminals in the Railways.

I thank L.R. Thaper, our COM, for initiating me to the use of this wonderful tool, which had not been used effectively until then.

The division is involved in overall planning

On the basis of FOIS information, I asked a DRM to explain the delay in various operations. He was not aware. I told him where to get the information from and then he was asked to enquire into this. It rattled him a bit but he was back with the report in about 4 to 5 hours. He had all the details and was in a position to remark on undue detention in the terminal.

Once the DRM was himself in the picture and the GM, politely but very firmly, breathing down his neck, the system was activated. Simple operations like informing the merchant, giving precedence to cross the yard, examining the yard layout to improve placement and withdrawal, interacting with the control to give position of loading operation so that the power was moved in time were all taken to ensure that the rake moved as fast as possible. In the longer run, even measures to improve terminal facilities like adequate lighting was undertaken to facilitate loading, even after sunset.

The morning briefing and discussion on operating issues sent a very constructive message down the line. Apart from operating and commercial departments, other service departments started looking critically at avoidable delays. Why wasn't the yard layout re-examined to improve the fluidity of operation? A yard like Shakurbasti had serious problems of rake examination. Power had to cross on average 128 times across the yard in a day. This was not only a time-consuming operation but also a hazardous one. An accident involving a side collision with a passenger train had brought out the real problem and highlighted the issue. The yard layout was revised—improving the complete operation. All avoidable delays were thus reduced. All the departments played a constructive role. They had jointly decided to remove the congenital problem existing in the yard since its inception. I only helped them in casting the estimate for this work. I advised them that there was no point in charging for the cost of points and crossings plus the overhead equipment (OHE). These materials were being shifted from some other locations where they had become surplus or redundant. For this, the labour cost involved in their relocation should only be chargeable. This cut down the cost drastically so that it could be sanctioned by the GM's power, under a lump sum grant. This was the role of the facilitator.

POM IS FOCUSED

It was clearly brought out to the entire team that the running of train was the chief mission of the Northern Railway and soon it became the slogan.

Focus of POM—emphasis on chief mission of the Railways

The POM became an effective forum for strategic planning for the future and for reviewing our past performance. After introductory remarks by the GM, COM was asked to take the floor followed by the CCM and the CSO. They were asked to address not more than 3 or 4 issues. After that, the DRMs were asked to participate in the discussion.

Thus, everyone was prepared and the references were specific. The idea was to generate a participative atmosphere where divisional cutting-edge level would be prepared and strengthened for the mission objective. It was supported and assisted by the service provider unit or support group as the case might be. The service provider group would take over next followed by the support group. This clearly set the tone and approach of the discussions and generated enormous synergy amongst all.

DRMs would actively participate

The DRMs were asked to raise their own points. The principal officers at the headquarters were expected to respond to them. A monitoring team, led by the secretary, was also set up to compile all the issues raised by the DRMs in their monthly letters to be placed before the PHOD concerned. A suitable reply was sent to the DRM immediately. All replies and disposals were personally seen by me. If I did not find them satisfactory, I would ask the PHOD to be clear in his response. It was not possible to comply with all the demands of the DRMs but it was important that all possible and reasonable demands were met with and within a reasonable time. This encouraged the DRMs. They were satisfied that their points were given adequate attention. This enhanced their sincerity and our credibility shot up.

It was not a one-way affair. I recall as the DRM; a particular PHOD had brought all the letters received from the Board. She read them out, calling for suitable action from the division. This did not lead to any answers. I always believed that the purpose of the meeting was to receive feedback and for the development of a plan with open discussions. This called for tremendous discipline at all levels. Without preparations, deliberations would eventually lead to a monologue or would be devoid of credibility. The GM had to be very alert and firm to avoid any digression. I would not allow the main theme and focus to be lost. The meeting would generally end by 4 p.m. Before the meeting was over, the next date for the POM was fixed so that everyone knew about it a month in advance. Thus, it was possible for everyone to plan their schedule for the next month.

Special meeting with the DRMs

After the POM, there was invariably an informal meeting with all the DRMs in my room. They were free to bring forward any problems they had with the headquarters, which they did not wish to speak about in the open forum. If something was amiss, I was told. I, on the other hand, would talk about a sensitive issue, which needed the collective attention of the DRMs. This sitting had become popular and everyone looked forward to it.

It is important that the principal apparatus in the realization of the mission goal is kept in good shape. The problems, including its mental or emotional requirements, have to be addressed adequately and effectively. At the same time, it is also essential that the division does not behave irresponsibly and project its problem on to the shoulder of others or more frequently, upwards. The division should bear its own cross. The GM, on the other hand, must ensure that it receives adequate emotional and physical support to carry on without any distress.

Development of a managerial model for the Railways

As model of managerial capability, we were able to achieve the following:

- Define and establish the mission objective: to run the railway for the carriage of public goods and passengers in the most economic, effective and efficient manner as possible.
- Quantify targets and goals: set in the Board's letter and broadly stipulated the carriage of freight and passenger traffic and to earn in terms of traffic receipts for passengers, freight and sundries. To calculate the effective and economic yardstick, an improvement in the operating ratio was projected to measure our achievement.
- Design and define organizational structure: The organizational structure was already available but it was effectively restructured to achieve our principal mission objective. Operating, service provider and support groups were set up as an example.
- Establish cutting-edge apparatus: Divisions are efficient to achieve organizational goals. They were sensitized, strengthened and suitably supported both in terms of their physical and emotional needs. They

were made more responsive. They were asked to carry their cross and not to shift the blame upwards.
- Define internal influences and measures to tackle them: Internal influence arises primarily from interactions with trade union bodies and the Railway Board. They were likely to hinder normal operations and were clearly identified. They were effectively tackled by opening up a direct line of communication with them.

  As far as the Board was concerned, my stint as secretary Railway Board was of immense value in maintaining good relationships with all. Of course, a personal rapport with the minister and his personal staff was valuable in containing adverse impact of the internal influences. The Northern Railway, because of its location, derived natural strategic advantages as far as the Railway Board was concerned.
- Define external influences and identify the measures to mitigate them: External influences are very important and crucial for the Northern Railway because of its strategic location. The roles played by the media are also crucial and can have a damaging effect if not managed discreetly and with tact. Other important Central government offices like Delhi government including LG, home ministry, defence ministry, urban development ministry and the PMO also had a direct impact on the functioning of the Northern Railway besides the roles played by the MP, Parliament House (its catering was run by the Northern Railway) and political parties at large. Measures were taken to mitigate their impact so that it was possible to operate and function effectively.

The management model helps the team to gel

The entire team soon galvanized into a cohesive and totally charged group. It was therefore no wonder to see that revenue earnings went up and the Railways was in a position to cross the annual target by the end of December 2003.

The MR had come to Baroda House for the launch of some programme. I mentioned the performance of the Railways in my welcoming address. He was pleasantly surprised. He joked with R.K. Singh, 'CRB Sahib, the Board should not have fixed a simple target for Jaruhar Sahib. You see he has already achieved the entire year's earning by the end of December 2003—three months in advance.'

These targets were fixed by the Board for 2003-04 when R.K. Singh was GM, Northern Railway. It was about 15 per cent higher than those achieved by the Northern Railway in the previous year (2002-03) under the stewardship of R.K. Singh. There was a big laugh, but as an offshoot of this, the Board stepped up our financial target in the month of January 2004. It was seemingly impossible to achieve. It was done to slight me, but we nevertheless persevered and worked in a very dedicated manner. It was a great satisfaction to see that it was achieved in the end. I do not know if the Board was disappointed again!

EVOLVING STRATEGY FOR FREIGHT BUSINESS

It was also time to look at the loading pattern from the point of view of revenue earning per rake. Punjab and Haryana are two states that have a surplus of foodgrains and if Western Uttar Pradesh is also included, they accounted for almost 80 per cent of the production of foodgrains in India. There is therefore a heavy procurement of foodgrains from this part of the country, both by the Food Corporation of India (FCI) and private entrepreneurs for distribution elsewhere in the country as well as for export. A foodgrain rake to the southern parts of India like Kerala was extremely profitable. Likewise, the export of foodgrains through Kandla Port in Gujarat was also very rewarding because it provided import traffic like fertilizer on its return trip to Punjab.

Productivity of close circuit rakes and concept of revenue per rake

I mounted heavy pressure on the Board to load these commodities which would fetch a handsome return. I had also formed a number of close circuit (CC) rakes so that the train examination was undertaken only on its return trip or after a run of 5,000 km. These measures improved wagon turn-round considerably. I was encouraged to do so in the beginning because of its productivity. The mechanical department did not favour it because they had safety concerns. This inhibition was successfully overcome by us in the Northern Railway. But after some time, the discipline to return the CC rake to its original destination was not maintained by other railways. For some inexplicable reasons, the Board had adopted a lukewarm attitude in this respect. As a result, most of the CC rakes became defunct. Thus, the pains and initiatives undertaken were simply wasted to the distinct disadvantage of the Indian Railways.

Even foodgrain rakes were being discouraged. I learnt that a large pressure had been created by the cement lobby. According to the Board, cement was a far better paying commodity while foodgrain was subsidized traffic—with Class 80 tariff. Thus, the Board believed that the Railways should only carry foodgrain traffic to the extent committed to food ministry under its social obligation. On the face of it, the logic was forceful. But I argued that it was also necessary to earn maximum revenue per rake. In my view, this had to be the guiding principle and philosophy of the IR.

The mandarins in the traffic department of the Board thought that it was not a big issue because rakes loaded with goods with higher tariff would be automatically more profitable. Thus, they believed that foodgrain rakes could not match the earnings from the high tariff loaded goods. I told Nitish ji that the Board was following what the cement lobby perhaps had advocated. But this policy was not in the interest of the IR. As a typical socialist, he was allergic to such lobbying. So, he reacted sharply and called for a meeting in his room. We carried out a simple calculation of how much a rake would earn if it carried foodgrain from the Punjab area to Kerala vis-à-vis a rake of cement loaded from central India factories to north India consumption centres. The foodgrain rake journey time varied from 50-60 hours but had a very long lead of over 2,000 km. In contrast, the cement rake had short lead of about 200 km and each return trip involved terminal detentions, including a train examination.

The calculation showed that the earning from foodgrain rake, notwithstanding class 80 tariff (with a rebate of 20 per cent), applicable to sponsored foodgrain loading was much higher than that of cement rake with class 130/140 tariff. There was stunned silence and utter disbelief around. They only claimed that many factors had not been included in the comparison. According to us, there was no point in counting common factors like wages of the running staff. It had to be paid regardless of the IR carrying any traffic or not. But to counter the point, I promised to present a statement duly verified by traffic accounts branch. I succeeded in blowing up the myth of tariff class to prove what the Railways should carry. The MR appreciated it but he did not have the time to push it to its logical conclusion. This was perhaps due to his preoccupation with the General Election in May 2004. I am glad that this concept was pursued by the subsequent government with startling results! In revenue earnings, volume, which is a product of weight (tonne) and lead in km known as yield (tonne—km) is more important than merely the tariff class or rate. As a good businessman, a transporter always calculates how much he would earn per unit of transport—whether it is a single truck or a railway rake.

THE PERFORMANCE OF THE NORTHERN RAILWAY—OUTSTANDING AND RECORD BREAKING

The overall performance of the Northern Railway was remarkable. Revenue loading of 42.43 million ton was a record and had surpassed the Board's target by 0.23 million ton. The overall revenue earning of ₹2,894 crore was only second to South East Central Railway (₹2,972.81 crore). The Railway's passenger and other coaching earnings were the highest in the Indian Railways. Its operating ratio was around 92 per cent. Even after reorganization, the Railway had performed very well and made us very proud.

The UIC team led by its chief executive, Mr Phillips was in Delhi to attend a seminar. I invited the team to present our performance and the philosophy behind it. The team was overwhelmed and on their return to Paris, Mr Phillips sent a letter of appreciation. He eventually became a very good friend and even spoke to the heads of other national railways about the progressive team of the Northern Railway.

ENCROACHMENT ON RING RAIL

Local issues in Delhi area are always important. The encroachment on railway land created serious safety problem. The ring rail runs inside Delhi and is an important getaway for all traffic coming from either the Rewari side or Ghaziabad. Trains going to Punjab, avoiding New Delhi, passes through the famous triangle after the Yamuna Bridge and goes via Hazrat Nizamuddin to Bhatinda through the ring rail. Thus, this route is important and carries heavy traffic.

Unfortunately, there was a large-scale encroachment in the area. Encroachers had built hutments by the side of tracks, infringing upon safety distance. The encroachment had made the track dirty. Due to open defecation, it was impossible for the maintenance team to work. A derailed wagon could hit the hutments which were dangerously close to the track. People were in danger but they had patronized political parties of all hues. It was impossible to act against them. Lieutenant Governor Mr Kapoor and later Mr Joshi lent their full support to evacuate them and to shift them away from the danger zone.

The Railways had paid ₹5 crore as its contribution to rehabilitate them. The Municipal Corporation of Delhi (MCD), the executive agency, did not take any steps at all. They had to relocate them on priority. I once called on the LG and told him about it. He almost forced the MCD to move; sanitation was a serious problem. I suggested that the Railways might construct a Sulabh Sauchalay and pay maintenance charges, provided they were run by the MCD. He liked the idea but the MCD would not act because of procedural wrangling.

Eviction and rehabilitation were almost impossible. Once, the CM of Delhi requested me not to press for it as the municipal elections were on. Once Nitish ji told me that there were many Biharis in the list and since Eid and Chhath Pooja were around, I should not force it. The next time, I was told that winter had already set in and it would be very cruel to displace them. This was the reason behind the failure of this drive. The only person who was honest in this respect was Mr Jagmohan, the Union minister of urban development. Once I briefed him about the problem, he immediately withdrew his request. He told me that he did not want to win an election on an incorrect promise. It was ironic that he lost the seat of New Delhi in the 2004 General Election. I do not know if there was a lesson in this but it was sad that a fine person like Mr Jagmohan did not win.

TERRORISM IN J&K

The state of J&K has been a problem state and there are often large-scale acts of terrorism with their origins across the border. The most endangered section prone to attack was between Jammu and Pathankot. Out of the total stretch of ninety km, the difficult stretch was up to Kathua, about sixty-five km from Jammu. The Pakistani border was hardly 2 to 3 km away and militants could just walk to this area, practically at will.

Shalimar Express is attacked by militants

The attack on the *Shalimar Express* on 28 October 2003 showed exactly how fragile security could be. In the night of 28 October 2003, I got a frantic call from Control Room that terrorists had attacked the *Shalimar Express* near Jatwal station about fifty km from Jammu. The train was reportedly set on fire. The Control had no information about the extent of casualties. I sensed grave consequences. Such attacks had taken place in the past also when I was DRM, Firozpur. But each time, the train had miraculously escaped. According to the next report, which came a few minutes later, there was no casualty although five coaches with engine had derailed. A great sense of relief because I had alerted the CRB on the basis of the earlier report!

I left for the site by a special train. Three militants had entered J&K. They hijacked a Tata Sumo and travelled over seventy km to the site of the attack, where they waited by the side of the track near a culvert from where they planned to explode the track using a remote-control device. The place was littered with dry fruits. They had changed out of their black clothes and put on police uniforms. They had also fired at the train but the train windows were shut and there was no damage. After the blast, the perpetrators had run away. They were eventually encountered by the Army picket near the Akhnoor Bridge and killed.

Their escape was providential. Lots of measures were taken by the Railways to patrol the section with the help of the RPSF and the state police, but quite honestly, they could not deter the militants.

I WITNESS ATTACK ON JAMMU STATION

Jammu station was quite vulnerable and its yard was really porous to miscreants. Maintaining the law and order was the responsibility of the state. The state police had asked for complete fencing to be done on all sides of Jammu station, which was not feasible.

I cannot forget 2 January 2004—just a day after the New Year's. My wife had invited our relatives. She had asked me to come home a little early. I reached home by 6.45 p.m. After chatting for a while, I got a call on my cell that something was wrong at Jammu station. I could not reach the area officer. I was therefore connected to the station master (SM). He was speaking in a whisper. I asked him why he could not be louder. He said that the station was under attack. He was hiding under the table. As if in confirmation, he put the phone towards the window, and I could hear AK-47 fire, ringing all through intermittently.

The SM was very brave. Continuously changing his position, he kept on reporting what was going on at the station—a running commentary. Two terrorists, armed with modern weapons and hand grenades, had entered Jammu station around 6.30 p.m. from the foot overbridge on the side of the Indian Oil depot in the city. They started firing indiscriminately. The station was normally very busy and crowded at this time of the day. But Lt Triveni Singh of 26 Infantry Division showed commendable courage. Within ten minutes of the attack, commandos had cordoned off the station. The two terrorists shot and threw grenades at Lt Triveni Singh, but he shot one terrorist dead and moved on to the other. Dodging the grenade attack, he killed the other terrorist also. Gravely injured, he died after saluting the GOC.

The whole episode lasted for about forty-five minutes. Three railwaymen—the station master, an RPF personnel and TTE—stayed on duty, without deserting their position. The SM continued to give me all the details.

While all this was happening, there was complete silence in our drawing room. I sensed that our relatives had an idea of this tragedy. Lt Triveni Singh had shown outstanding courage and ultimately accounted for the two terrorists. But the courage shown by the railway staff was also very commendable. I went to meet them and all were suitably rewarded including the Railway Week Awards by the MR.

TERRORISM AFFECTED CONSTRUCTION OF KASHMIR NEW LINE

Apart from open line work between Jammu and Pathankot, the Railways was engaged in the construction of a new railway line from Jammu to Baramulla.

The section between Jammu and Udhampur, the headquarters of the Army's Northern Command, a stretch of fifty-five km was already under the advanced stage of construction. The work in the section beyond Udhampur to Katra, about thirty-km long, was also in progress. Katra was the gateway to the famous shrine of Mata Vaishno Devi located on the top of the hill. The section between Katra to Qazigund a stretch of about 173 km was the most difficult. It involved a terrain beyond the Chenab River with practically no habitation. It was supposed to be the home of militants. The section between Qazigund to Baramulla about 119-km long was in Kashmir Valley. The work on this section was awarded to the IRCON and they had planned to complete this work early.

The entire project was a stupendous challenge of engineering in the world. Because of international ramifications, it was declared as a national project. Militant activity in the area had continued relentlessly. The project also had to bear the burden of hostility. Those who fielded militants did not want construction of a railway line. Any project to improve ground communication was a threat and was opposed.

On the other hand, locals welcomed the initiative. They had come forward to help in the construction of the line. During my interactions with them, they had appreciated that the line would eventually bring in a source of livelihood and improve conveyance. I had taken this up to highlight the initiative of the government. I tried to explain how the quality of life would change if the line was constructed. My first visit to J&K was aborted due to the accident at Shakurbasti. The next time, I flew to Srinagar along with Rakesh Chopra, the CAO.

MY FIRST VISIT TO SRINAGAR—VERY EVENTFUL

I had planned to meet the chief minister, chief secretary and director general of the police during my visit. I was to meet the press to brief them about the construction programme. Luckily, I met Lt General (retired), S.K. Sinha, the governor of J&K in the flight itself. I knew him, so we conversed in the flight.

I met the CM, Mufti Mohammad Sayeed, in the evening at his residence. He welcomed me warmly and showed a keen interest in the project. He promised to help with sorting out the problems in land acquisition and security. He asked me to meet him next day in his office at the Secretariat. I was also scheduled to meet the chief secretary in the morning. Gopal Sharma, DGP, was well-known and we met him over dinner when all security issues were discussed.

I had a hectic schedule in the morning. I was at breakfast around 9 a.m. D.P.S. Sandhu, CPRO, had come a day in advance to meet the media and organize my meeting with them in the evening. I saw Sandhu entering the hall with a grim face. Mr Chopra remarked that Sandhu was not a bearer of good news as he walked towards me. He informed that the *Jan Shatabdi Express* had derailed around 8.30 at Deoband near Ghaziabad. The train was at a high speed and five coaches had derailed. He told the chief track engineer (CTE), who was travelling by that train that there had been some deaths, but unless the coaches were removed it would not be possible to ascertain the extent of damage and casualty.

Just then the news came of a bomb blast at the main market in Srinagar and firing by terrorists. The loud report of the blast could be heard in the hotel. Soon all mobile phones were jammed. The police were at the hotel soon and zeroed in on Sandhu who was busy calling everybody in Delhi for the details of the accident. The security forces who monitored all calls after the bomb blast had noted a series of calls from the hotel. They jammed the number immediately. They swarmed round Sandhu. It was a tragi-comic scene. Sandhu was a sardar and was taken as a key suspect. They were satisfied after lot of explaining. I decided to return to Delhi to attend to the accident. In any case, all the higher-ups in Kashmir were busy dealing with the bomb blast, which had a heavy toll. I called the CM to express my regrets. But he also happened to know of the train accident. I apologized for not being in a position to keep the appointment with him at 1 p.m. But he, too, was also unavailable because of the blast.

CONSTRUCTION OF THE J&K LINE HAD LOGISTICS PROBLEMS

The project had a number of local contractors working at various places. It was a good thing and I was happy to note that they were giving a fairly good account of themselves.

Involvements of the local population—ownership of an idea

I visited the project site between Anantnag and Baramulla during my next visit to Srinagar. Many villagers met me and complained of waterlogging caused by the construction of an embankment. It was destroying their crops. I found the complaint to be genuine. I asked the CAO to provide more minor bridge openings. This mitigated the waterlogging and gained a lot of goodwill. Likewise, near Udhampur, villagers wanted more level crossings. I prevailed upon the CAO to provide them with it. If one looked at it carefully, the construction of a railway line divided an area. Villagers were faced with the problem of crossing a railway line. Sometimes cultivatable land was on one side whereas habitation was on the other. This was a genuine problem of the community. I openly said that we would provide as many of them as were actually needed. This had a salutary effect.

The most difficult area was the section from Katra to Qazigund. This section of the proposed alignment ran on the other side of the Chenab River whereas the National Highway 1A, the only link to the valley at present, ran on the east of the Chenab. The alignment beyond Riyasi was a hostile and sparsely inhabited terrain.

The survey team needed protection

The survey team had to walk along the proposed alignment to make note of the details of the contour and to carry out an investigation of the soil. Based on the survey plan, the cadastral map was prepared for land acquisition. The survey team had to locate an approach for an alignment particularly for bridges and tunnels. All these data were required for detailed design and bill of quantities for tenders. The team had to stay in a highly militant infested terrain and they had to be provided with full security all round.

This was a tricky affair. A close coordination with the state police, Central armed security forces, Army units and the Intelligence Bureau was essential. A team under the chairmanship of the principal secretary to the PM was formed to coordinate between the various agencies. It comprised the GM, Northern Railway; ME, Railway Board; the home secretary; DGP; and chief secretary, Jammu and Kashmir. The process was slow and painstaking. But it started showing results soon. This area had been till then out of bounds for the security forces. No government official had ever set foot in the area. The government also felt that in order to establish its authority, proper communication was absolutely essential. It was necessary to reach the local populace to bring development to the area and to provide them with means towards economic upliftment.

Gradually, the local population started welcoming the survey team. It was taken as a precursor to escape from the abject poverty that people had been subjected to, since eternity. The PPS to the PM, Mr Nair, encouraged me a great deal. He said that this was the best means to get the area rid of militancy. The area had poor telecommunications services. I suggested that he ask the BSNL to set up microwave towers for mobile phone communication services. On his instructions, good telecommunication was soon put in place. It helped all of us, including the security forces. Thus, it was possible to focus and support the project from an administrative angle.

Deployment of Central paramilitary force was problematic

The home ministry had serious reservations regarding the deployment of additional paramilitary forces. They asked the Ministry of Railways to deploy the RPSF for this purpose. I knew the home secretary well. His father-in-law,

R.P. Singh, was once GM, Northern Railway, and had subsequently retired as member traffic. He had fond memories of his father-in-law as the GM, Northern, so I was given a warm welcome whenever I went to the North Block. I told him that the stand of the home ministry was unreasonable in asking the Ministry of Railways to deploy the RPSF. Law and order was a state subject and hence the Railways could not deploy the RPSF. J&K had agreed to provide security but they wanted additional units of paramilitary forces. The RPSF was anyway deployed in the Northeast and were not trained to deal with terrorism.

The home secretary appreciated the point. He prevailed upon his department to lend support to the state government. I recall he would make it a point to see me off from the North Block. This was a great gesture and I felt deeply moved by it.

THE NEW LINE HAD TECHNICAL CHALLENGES—CHENAB BRIDGE CONCEPT EMERGED

The fifty-five-km long section between Udhampur and Jammu was a difficult construction. Many stretches could not be accessed; they had high mountains on one side and a deep valley on the other. The longest tunnel in this section was more than three-km long. The bridge over the Gambhir River was particularly difficult and had very high piers of over seventy metres. The men and material had to be reached on mule and by making temporary cable bridges. A press party from Delhi was taken to acquaint them with the difficulties and problems of the terrain. They were totally stumped and completely overwhelmed by the dedication of the team. They also spoke to the villagers who were very excited about the project. The plan was to open the section by the end of March 2004 but due to some last-moment problem it was delayed. There was a ban because of the General Election and services could be introduced only after the 2004 elections. The section was formally dedicated to the nation in April 2005 by Prime Minister Manmohan Singh. By that time, I had become member engineering but I also held the post of GM, Northern Railway concurrently. While explaining to him the challenges of the project at Udhampur before the function, I found him responding enthusiastically. We had to build an almost 120-km long service road for construction. The state government could not grant land on temporary acquisition. I said that the government could use this road to connect villages because there was no road whatsoever in that area. The PM readily agreed and told CM Ghulam Nabi Azad to accept the Railways' suggestion.

Katra-Qazigund most challenging—Chenab Bridge

The bridge over the Chenab River was the most challenging engineering feat. Its location was across a high and deep gorge where the river flowed in a span of about six hundred metres. The height was over three hundred metres. The type of structure was an important consideration. The bridge across the river had to be of a single span, and had to be able to withstand intense earthquakes besides high wind. I was in Srinagar for an inspection. Rakesh Chopra the CAO broached the subject. Ankush Krishna was director (works), IRCON. He is a brilliant structural engineer. We had a long brainstorming session during dinner in a houseboat on Dal Lake. After evaluating different options including cable stayed and suspension bridge, we zeroed on to a steel arch bridge. This had many advantages but firm ground to take the skew back of arch was a major consideration in its favour.

We examined this aspect further in the morning. Clearly, it would perhaps be the world's longest railway steel arch bridge and certainly the first of its kind in India. It was therefore appropriate to call for a large brainstorming session on this—where all the known experts could deliberate on it. Mr Chopra told me that such a congregation would be difficult and many might ask for a lot of money. I said that only lunch and travel could be provided, and that experts would consider it an honour to be associated with the biggest engineering feat in the country.

My belief was proved correct. All the experts attended the meeting in Baroda House. After a long session of more than three hours, they were unanimously in favour of a steel arch bridge. Many valuable suggestions were given. We formed a task force to enable the concept and design to be evolved. That is how the design of Chenab Bridge came into being. Even today, I recall the intense discussion to evolve the first concept of Chenab Bridge on a houseboat on Dal Lake in Srinagar. It could not have been more befitting.

TERRORISTS STRIKE—A GRUESOME ACT

The situation in J&K had never been easy because of its security concern. The Railways also had to establish its own liaison to project a picture that we were simply engaged in the construction of the line. The security agencies were having a very difficult time. They had actually borne the brunt of the militants' attack.

I was holding a meeting at around 2.30 p.m. in the conference hall in my office when I received an emergency call from Srinagar on 23 June 2004. The caller informed that around 11:30 in the morning that day two armed persons from Gulzarpora in Awantipore area had kidnapped an engineer of the IRCON, Sudhir Kumar, and his brother, on a visit to Kashmir.

It was a Wednesday, and the fellow had been supervising the work. He was about to leave for lunch. I had visited this area only a few days ago. According to the report of our unit, they waited for them for some time in the hope that they would be let off. Very often, contractor's men were let off after 3 or 4 hours. But no such news came till the evening.

The subsequent report revealed that a local contractor's material supplier, Farooq, and the driver of the Tata Sumo hired by the IRCON were later on released by the militants. This was not good news. I spoke to the CM. I expressed my deep concern about the incident. He was very smooth and reassuring on the phone. 'Oh! GM Sahib, please do not worry. Our people have located them. We are negotiating with them. I am confident that it would be alright very soon,' he said. I asked him if I could tell the family who belonged to Muzaffarnagar in Uttar Pradesh that they need not worry. 'Yes, absolutely so. Please reassure them on my behalf that Insha Allah everything will be fine', he said.

Sudhir Kumar had only recently got married. The worst fear came true when slit-throated bodies of the brothers were recovered later in the month. They had been brutally tortured before being killed.

I spoke to the CM once again. According to him, there had been too much publicity and the militants got scared. They had to kill them. What an explanation! This caused extreme anguish and as a result all work was stopped. All persons deployed were withdrawn. Minister Lalu Prasad ji visited the family to offer condolences. The scene was touching, and to see the young widow's pain was heartbreaking. She was appointed in the Railways, and I told the scouts and guides to look after the young lady and do whatever was possible to rehabilitate her.

INVOLVEMENT IN J&K HAD BEEN LONG AND THE EXPERIENCE INVALUABLE

I have tried to describe J&K as I dealt with my duties as an administrator in the capacity of GM, Northern Railway. I had very little technical inputs in this major construction project. I had earlier dealt with J&K when I was divisional rail manager, Firozpur, from 1994 to 1996. After my promotion as member engineering, I dealt with the project from the standpoint of a construction engineer. It was a unique opportunity and I am justifiably proud that I could see J&K from the stage when militancy had started assuming dangerous proportions till I laid down my office duties in January 2007 on retirement.

But I have one more important reason to remember J&K. It was in the course of many sessions as GM that I would cite my experiences of how I had handled many difficult situations in a project. My chief safety officer (CSO), Ajay Shukla, asked me during these interactions to write down my memories. He believed it could inspire many young persons. He even offered to write it for me if I gave him an outline. He is a well-known writer and his plays are quite famous. *Taj Mahal ka Tender* is a famous play which saw many successful runs all over the country. It is written by him. I must admit that the idea to write my memoir came out of this. I therefore consider J&K as instrumental to my embarking upon this difficult exercise.

SPECTRE OF FIRE IN EMPTY COACH HAUNTS US

New Delhi has always been a place where events swiftly followed one another. Very often, many events could be simply bizarre having no connection with the Railways. But they affected us because they happened in the country's capital. We would often wonder what we had done to deserve them. The fire in empty coaches was a weird and unheard-of event which baffled us.

It started on 13 November 2003 when a fire was reported in an empty coach stationed at Sarai Rohila station. This was an innocuous event. At first, it appeared to be due to an electrical short circuit. The investigation however did not corroborate this theory. A few days later, another empty coach of a terminating rake caught fire at the Delhi Main Station. This happened in broad daylight after the empty rake was shunted into the yard for maintenance.

The third incident took place again at the Delhi Main Station just a couple of days later. The newspapers picked up the mysterious incident. Some reported it as an act of an arsonist or a poltergeist. The Delhi Police and our own RPF took up the matter very seriously. Many precautions were taken against this. Measures like locking up all the coaches before the empty rake was withdrawn, were amongst them. A special task force was formed and intelligence was collected from all known sources. The investigation brought out a simple modus operandi. The arsonist would open an empty coach soon after the placement of the rake in the stabling line. After tearing open the cushion of the seat, he would put camphor tablets and set them on fire. The camphor burnt violently leaving no trace at all. The arsonist would disappear from the other side of the coach. The camphor would soon spread the fire, burning the coach furiously.

Three days later on 6 December 2003, two coaches were set on fire within half an hour at New Delhi Station soon after the arrival of the *Rajdhani Express* from Mumbai. I was there to see the first coach. A large number of officers and police were present. While getting off the coach, I heard about another coach on fire about a hundred metres away. Somebody saw a suspect getting off but failed to catch him.

In all, ten coaches had been burnt in ten incidents. This foxed us and kept us worried for the next three months. The last incident took place on 8 January 2004 when I was in Hardwar with all the PHOD officers concerned for the Kumbh Mela, which was to take place on 14 January. A coach of an empty rake of the *Ashram Express* at Delhi Main Station was set on fire. There was acute pressure on us, and Nitish Kumar ji was extremely upset. He was convinced that CSC RPF Mr Awasthi was not doing enough. The needle of suspicion pointed towards drug addicts frequenting the yard, disgruntled employees out to run down the Railways' reputation, some anti-socials and even ghosts. The Railways had announced an award of ₹50,000 earlier which was raised to ₹1,00,000 to anyone for information leading to the arrest of the arsonist. The police also issued a sketch of a likely culprit. The police was clueless. The Railway Board in its wisdom changed the command of the RPF in the Delhi division, presumably as it had failed to apprehend the culprit on the insistence of the minister.

The police and the RPF officers suspected this to be the handiwork of a gang that wanted to give the security forces a bad name. It was in retaliation to some severe action by the forces, to weed out the criminals around Delhi Main Station. Due to the heat of the operation, the culprits had run away from the Delhi area. Whatever was the truth in their claim, the incidents stopped as calmly as they had begun about three months ago in November 2003. I was told much later that the kingpins were ultimately arrested by the police from Mumbai about a year later. But after January 2004, peace returned to this front. The curtain was drawn on the vexing drama of 'Arsonist or poltergeist?'

DR A.P.J. KALAM TRAVELS BY TRAIN

While we were grappling with the mysterious episode of the fire in the train, President of India Dr A.P.J. Abdul Kalam decided to travel by train from Chandigarh to Delhi. As secretary Railway Board, I had organized his first train journey from Biharsharif to Patna after laying the foundation stone of Harnaut Rail Coach Factory. That journey was a short one (about sixty km) but a great deal of preparations had to be made for the trip. Detailed consultations and coordination meetings were held with the President's Secretariat for this trip. This included Mr Shankar, the secretary, and the president's military secretary. Mr Shankar was a nice and warm person and so was the military secretary.

When the president decided to travel by train from Chandigarh on 5 January 2004, I was called by Mr Shankar to make all arrangements. The president had a two-coach special saloon stabled at the New Delhi station. Built in 1956, it consisted of a dining-cum-visiting-room, a lounge and a bedroom. It also had a kitchen and chambers for the president's staff, including his military secretary and Railways' main coordinator. We asked the ADRM, Delhi division, Rudola, to accompany the president. The train was marshalled with a seven-coach-formation, including two presidential cars. The train carried the support staff, security personnel and a power generating car for power supply to the train. The kitchen was manned by the Railways' elite catering team from the Parliament.

The security was unprecedented in such a case. Patrolling was done by the state police besides Railways' own patrol. Every level crossing was manned by police. In extreme winter in the north India, there was every possibility of a rail fracture or a thick fog, making the operation immobile at times. The president boarded the train around 9.30 p.m. from Chandigarh. He was seen off by our DRM, Ambala, Keshav Chandra. A pilot engine with officers on the foot plate ran ahead of the special train clearing the passage for the president's special. The train was also escorted by a bomb disposal squad and had equipment designed to jam radio signals.

The journey of about 240 km to Delhi normally took about four hours. For security reasons, it was decided to bring him to the Safdarjung railway station. It took fifteen minutes more. I cannot describe the tension caused by the journey. We were praying for a safe trip without any untoward incident. While the control kept us informed of the passage of the train from station to station, the ADRM kept us informed on how the president was being treated. He told us that Dr Kalam was excited and very happy with the dinner served to him. Luckily, the weather was excellent although very cold. I received him at the station at about 1.40 a.m. along with the DRM, Delhi division. He was very pleased and thanked me for the excellent arrangements made on the train. He particularly praised the catering staff led by Mani Anand and Mr Rudola. I had to leave for Moradabad by the 2.45 a.m. train. My wife was also to accompany me. I had sent her to the Old Delhi station in advance. I reached the station just in time and hit the bed totally drained after a gruelling exercise.

THE PRIME MINISTER ALSO TRAVELS ON TRAIN

After the president, the prime minister of India, Atal Bihari Vajpayee, also took a train ride from Katra to Faizabad—a stretch of about sixteen km on 7 February 2004. A new bridge was constructed by the North Eastern Railway on the Sarayu River near Ayodhya. The new line was being inaugurated from Katra. This work had an emotional value for the people. The BJP was keen to cash in on the occasion for the political mileage the trip would carry. Mr Kataria, the firebrand MP from Faizabad, was in charge of the PM's programme. After the inauguration of the new line, the PM was scheduled to travel by train to Faizabad. A political rally was planned in Faizabad.

Nitish ji had briefed the PM on the details of the two train journeys undertaken by the president. The PM asked him to arrange a train journey for him as well. After two decades, an Indian prime minister had decided to travel by train. The last PM to travel by train was Mrs Gandhi in early 1980. She had travelled from Chandigarh to Delhi. Before her, Morarji Desai had travelled by train in 1978.

The security concern was enormous. The IG of the Special Protection Guard (SPG) loathed the project. He told me that he would advise the PM against the train journey. But the PM was quite firm. Thus, all arrangements were made by the SPG. The entire route was patrolled and lined with security personnel. A special platform was built in Faizabad to enable the PM to alight from the train. He was to leave by road from an existing level crossing gate. According to the arrangement, one of the carriages of the MR was modified to suit the PM. Security was reinforced. The line passed through a heavily built area. That was why the SPG was very concerned.

I was to receive the PM in Faizabad. The station superintendent was also a part of the reception party. This fellow was a paan addict. He was constantly chewing it. He was told to stop. But I found him faltering. Apparently, he was missing his paan. So, I asked him to start chewing paan. But the last paan would have to be eaten just before the train had left the previous station. It was a very comical scene but the paan evidently calmed his nerves. The PM was the last to get down from the train. He greeted us and thanked us for the excellent arrangements.

The programme for transporting the PM had a high measure of tension. The exercise and drill adopted for the president had however made us confident. Compared to the president, this trip was a relatively simple affair because the journey lasted for only twenty minutes. We were justly proud to take both the PM and the president on a Northern Railway train within a span of about two months.

LOOKING AFTER THE NORTH EASTERN RAILWAY

I also had to look after the additional charge of GM, North Eastern Railway, in two spells. Once, Om Prakash was admitted to a hospital in Delhi with a cardiac problem. I was given the additional charge of the Railway from 23 March 2004 till first week of May 2004. Subsequently, after his retirement in May 2004, I was again given the charge in addition to the NR on 1 June 2004. This continued till 24 July 2004 when J.P. Batra was posted as a regular GM of NE Railway.

I took the job very seriously. It was not limited to simply attending to office work. The Railway Week is celebrated between 10 April and 16 April every year. I asked the secretary to brief me on the programme. He told me that the function would not be held that year in the absence of a regular GM. It shocked me. The Railway Week has its own sanctity. The official function could not be cancelled, and he was plainly embarrassed when I told him so. A schedule for the Railway Week function was thus fixed. After holding the Northern Railway's function at Baroda House in the morning, I went to Gorakhpur to hold a full-fledged function there. The enthusiasm of the railwaymen was very encouraging. Since I was also GM, North Eastern, the secretary had also put up my name on the honour board. When I went to do the duty again after retirement of Om Prakash, my name had been removed. I paid no notice to this petty act. In contrast, when I looked after North Western Railway, Jaipur, my name was duly put up.

I carried out the duties of two more GMs with the same commitment I showed for my duty as GM, Northern Railway. I tried to bring the same kind of ethos and culture which I had introduced in the Northern Railway. I carried out the annual inspection, and held PNM meetings and POM on a regular basis. It took a heavy toll on me but I strived to do justice as far as it was physically possible.

POLITICAL CHANGES FOLLOW THE 2004 GENERAL ELECTION

The General Election was held in April-May 2004. The National Democratic Alliance (NDA) led by Atal Bihari Vajpayee was confident of returning to power. On the basis of a very good performance in a difficult period, the government had projected the famous slogan of 'India Shining'. Against this, the Congress Party raised the question that even though India might be shining, what was there for the 'aam aadmi' or the common man? This had obviously caught the imagination of the populace. Against all the predictions of media and sundry, the result was a stunning defeat for the NDA. When the results were finally released on 13 May 2004, there was total disbelief everywhere. But it once again demonstrated the strength of Indian democracy. The common man had actually won. The result was not an absolute majority for the Congress Party but there was so much of antipathy against the BJP that it was not difficult to form a coalition government led by the Congress under the banner of the United Progressive Alliance (UPA).

A new government under Manmohan Singh took the office on 22 May 2004. R.K. Singh had told me that Ram Vilas Paswan would be the minister of Railways. According to him, he had already been in touch with him. Someone told me on the morning of 22 May 2004 that Lalu Prasad ji had been nominated as the MR. When I told R.K. Singh, he was clearly upset. After the swearing-in ceremony, I went to the residence of Lalu ji to congratulate him. Many in his party knew me, and so Lalu ji met me enthusiastically. The portfolio had not been announced till then. It was done late in the evening. R.K. Singh, P.K. Goel—DRM, Delhi division—and I went early to his house to formally greet him. Clearly, there had been a change of guard with a new era under the leadership of a new minister in a new government. It was now time to make necessary adjustments in our conduct. There was bound to be some hostility in the new regime against us. It was not difficult to visualize that.

FEAR OF 'HEAD HUNTING'

This did not take any time because there were signals that Lalu ji would be out to upset persons like us who were considered close to Nitish ji. There was a strong political rivalry between them in Bihar. Nitish Kumar was also upset. He invited me for lunch at his residence. I was delayed because of a hold-up on Akbar Road due to VIP movement. He called me up to enquire whether I was actually coming. He was perhaps apprehensive that I might not like to come now. I told him the reason and said that I should be with him in a couple of minutes. He laughed and said, 'Arrey! Many of my past favourites are now afraid to come to this house. They are afraid of being marked and fear persecution.' But I continued to meet him. I was certainly marked or reported at 25 Tughlak Road, the official residence of the new minister, Lalu ji. R.K. Singh, according to reports had stopped visiting Nitish ji.

I recall that Nitish ji was to go to Patna by the *Rajdhani Express*. Around 2.30 p.m., I was told that the Board had not reserved his berth. By convention, a coupe in the First-Class AC was allotted to the former minister. I requested R.K. Singh to look into this because even Lalu ji would not have liked this. But I found him indifferent. I got the reservation done in any case. But by that time, Nitish ji had come to know about it. He was clearly and justifiably upset. He cancelled the train trip and went by flight instead. To the best of my knowledge, he has not undertaken a train journey since then!

The head hunting began soon after. The first test came when the MR made a surprise visit to New Delhi station one evening. I had just returned home from office around 8 p.m. I had some visitors for dinner. My staff car had gone back after dropping me. Someone from the MR cell informed me that the minister had just left the Rail Bhawan for a surprise inspection of the New Delhi Railway Station. My guest dropped me at the station in his car. By the time I reached the station, there was complete chaos. The minister was surrounded by the media. Scores of his party men were too eager to show the dirt to the minister. The DRM, who had arrived ahead of me, was being jostled around. I saw no point in joining the crowd but watched the scene from a distance. Someone however pointed to the minister that the GM was also present.

The MR asked me to come along with him. He started showing me so many things. A large crowd jeered me. It was clearly an exercise to play to the gallery. There was a great deal of humiliation for me as well as the DRM. Around 10 p.m., the MR went away. It was a stage-managed show for the media, to demonstrate how he dealt with officers. After a quick briefing, I returned home.

I called on him at his residence the next morning. He was quite courteous. He however asked me and the DRM to meet him in his office at 4 p.m. Very politely, I told him in the office that the station was admittedly not very clean. It had left much to be desired. There were, however, I pointed out some grave problems also. This station handled an average of 3.80 lakh passengers daily. The number only included those who actually travelled by train. Apart from this, on average, an equal number of people come to either see passengers off or to receive them. I did not have the number of unauthorized persons who had made the station their homes. It was impossible to keep the station spotlessly clean for twenty-four hours like an airport. The problem of the other two stations, Delhi Main and Hazrat Nizamuddin, was no different. This fact hit him with great force. I promised to make all efforts but it was unlikely to come to the expectation of MR.

I had spoken slowly but very candidly. Thankfully, the CRB supported me. I was let off along with the DRM, Goel. When I returned to my office, the CRB told me that the MR had called for a written explanation from me and the DRM. I got a confidential letter from the CRB addressed to me as well as the DRM. It was a chargesheet! I did not pass this on to the DRM but I asked him to give me details to reply. Based on the details furnished by him, I replied to the CRB. This was along the same lines as what I had verbally told the MR. I had also categorically stated that there was no need for the DRM to reply separately. My reply had covered the charges against the DRM also. Mr Goel was touched but I said that the position of the DRM must be preserved. I did not hear anything thereafter. I trust the CRB must have given a decent burial to the memo and my response to that. I thanked R.K. Singh profusely for the support.

The next rubbing came very soon thereafter. We had taken up non-interlocking of the Hazrat Nizamuddin station. Many rehearsals and preparations had been done quite methodically. But on the first day itself everything which could go wrong had gone wrong. Due to a rail fracture on a main line, the line was blocked by the PWI. An engine failure took place soon thereafter, blocking the other line. All movements through Hazrat Nizamuddin were thus totally stopped. It was peak hour for the traffic at about 8 p.m. The repair took longer. Thus, there was a complete chaos all around. Someone called up the minister because his train was delayed. The MR called me at 10.30 p.m. obviously in a foul mood. I told him all about the unforeseen failure which had caused the dislocation. To compound the problem, the Hazrat Nizamuddin station was non-interlocked. Hence the movement had to be slow by manual means observing strict safety precautions. He asked me why I was not at the station. I told him that all senior officers including the AGM were already there. It would have only caused more tension if I had also gone. I assured him that the development was under watch. I promised to inform him as soon as the movement was normalized.

Services were resumed at about midnight. I called the MR at his residence at 12.30 to inform him. His APS told me that the MR had already gone to bed and could not be disturbed. I asked him to wake up the minister since he had asked me to tell him when the services were normalized. The assistant did not dare do that. He, however, promised that he would inform the MR in the morning that I had called around 12.30 a.m. That was the end of it.

These upsetting moves notwithstanding, I continued to perform as well as I could. At the same time, I made efforts to strike up a suitable rapport. In this respect, GM, Northern Railway being in Delhi is always an advantage. Other MPs of his party found me reasonably good and gradually warmed up to me. Being a Bihari probably helped my cause for the first time. The hostilities gradually abated. Or so, it seemed.

UNPRECEDENTED FLOOD CREATES HAVOC IN AMBALA

I had gone on an inspection with the PHOD officers to Bhatinda and beyond in the Ambala division on 3 August 2004. I was told in the evening that a cloud burst had taken place in Himachal Pradesh. This had caused unprecedented rainfall, which had inundated the railway line between Ambala-Ludhiana and also Chandigarh-Ambala section. The downpour continued till 4th August. It caused heavy damage to the double line section between Ambala and Ludhiana at seven locations. Ambala Chandi mandir section was also damaged. One minor bridge was completely washed out. I told my officers to be patient till the rains and the flood abated. It has been my experience that any exercise when the flood is on, turns out to be futile and waste of money and energy. We provided help to people stranded due to disruption in train services. There were damages in some railway colonies also. The staff from these areas had to be evacuated.

I held a detailed inspection on the 5th morning. An action plan to repair the damages was drawn. In a press conference in Chandigarh, I spoke of the damages that had taken place and about our action plan. I fixed a target of ten days for restoration. Although it was a tough job, our marshalling of resources was excellent. The embankment was filled with newly borrowed soil and fully compacted by vibratory compactors borrowed from the Army. The track was laid and packed with tie tamping machines. The section was commissioned with a speed of seventy kmph. Our traffic friends were very happy to see such an excellent track on restoration. Often a section after restoration is unconsolidated and is opened with low speed causing heavy detentions. This was the main line to feed Punjab, Haryana and J&K. I had asked a medical team to camp round the clock since in such situations, workers fall sick and there were also cases of snake bite, which needed immediate treatment.

The NRWWO did an excellent job to provide help to the flood-affected staff. My wife, the president of the NRWWO and Mrs Renu, the wife of the DRM Ambala, and the divisional president, worked quietly, but their help was appreciated by all. The chief bridge engineer (CBE) felt that one bridge would require rebuilding since its abutment seemed tilted. I inspected the bridge and it was clear that the tilt was not due to any damage during the flood. Had it been the case, there would have been other symptoms like cracking elsewhere. There was no such evidence and I convinced them that the bridge had no problem. We worked as a team. I was camping there myself most of the time. There was a great deal of appreciation all around. In contrast, the washout in the ECR remained unattended for almost a month. The MR asked me how I could do the work so quickly and smoothly. I attributed it to teamwork and good leadership.

POSTING AS MEMBER RAILWAY BOARD

The time had come for my posting as a member of the Board. The post of member staff was to fall vacant at the end of October 2004 after the retirement of Mr Singla. The post of Board member is filled from the open line GMs who have completed at least one-year service as GM. He requires a residual service of two years to work as Board member. Amongst the GMs, I was the only one to meet both these criteria. On 31 October 2004, I had a residual service of twenty-seven months and had completed one year as GM (open line). I was pretty sure about my posting, so I did not lobby for the post. Arun Biswas, my batchmate, had once mentioned that R.S. Varshney, the GM, ECR was not reconciled to the idea of my superseding him. I had, however, not paid any attention to this. According to the Government Resolution of 1987, he did not meet those two prequalifying criteria.

I am in for a shock

The GM conference was held on 10 September 2004. A dinner was hosted by the CRB, where the MR was also invited. My colleague, GM, Western, Mr Ansari told me that Varshney had prevailed upon the MR to recommend him for the post of MS as he was senior to me. Mr Ansari was the seniormost GM, if the government resolution was not enforced. He told me that he would lobby for his own case if I did not contest the proposal. I had considered the resolution as sacrosanct. This issue had been debated and examined at length in the Cabinet secretariat only recently, while discussing R.K. Singh's case. After the GM conference, I asked the CRB whether the Board had indeed recommended Varshney for the MS. He dodged the question. He started saying that he did not know how Varshney had prevailed upon Lalu ji. He said that the MR had categorically asked him to bypass my case. I asked him that he knew very well that it was not possible in view of the resolution. But he said, 'Jaruhar, you know that the MR does not understand all this. He has asked me to send the proposal of R.S. Varshney because he is senior to Jaruhar. I am helpless. Unfortunately, you also did not try to mend fences with the minister.' He advised me that I should meet the Cabinet secretary and to do whatever was possible. I was shocked and felt that R.K. Singh should have told me earlier about what was cooking.

I was disappointed and said nothing. R.K. Singh had told me earlier to mend fences with MR. He had advised me to go to the MR and renew or pledge my loyalty to him. It implied, in other words, that I should prostrate before him in total submission. He told me that he had already made his peace with him as it was impossible to work without the approval of the MR. I was aware of what he had done to achieve peace and to what extent he had actually stooped. Of course, it was between the two of them. If he could do what he did, it was fine. Because of my conscience and self-respect, my loyalty could not be pledged at any cost the way it was expected of me. I was sure about it. I had to pay a price for that. I was determined not to go to Prem Chand Gupta, a Cabinet minister and a close confidant of Lalu ji to plead my case. This would commit me to play by their rules. A close relative, who had been the finance secretary with Lalu ji in Bihar, had told me that to preserve one's dignity or honour, it was essential not to seek any favours from Lalu ji.

The Cabinet secretary backs me

So, coming away disappointed, I went to the North Western Railway for an inspection. I was also disappointed with R.K. Singh, but I understood and appreciated his helplessness. He had his own limitations and he was guided by his own conscience. He called me while I was travelling to tell me to go to the Cabinet secretary. I told him that I was out on inspections and that I would decide my next course of action when I was back in Delhi. V.K. Singh, my secretary, was a silent observer. He requested me to do something. I also got a call from the Cabinet secretary's office. I was told that the Board's proposal was against the rules. He requested me to represent my case. I thought that making a case for a post at the level of the secretary would be unbecoming. If the minister, in his wisdom, did not consider me fit, I could do very little about it. I decided against appealing and told him that he had the file before him and also the rules. He was, therefore, in the best position to deal with the case.

The Cabinet secretary backed my case. Disagreeing with the railway ministry, he proposed my name for the post and forwarded it to the home minister and then to the prime minister. The case went ahead smoothly. I was informed on Saturday on 16 October 2004 that my case was approved by the PM. The formal orders were issued on 22 October 2004. Durga Pooja holidays were starting and I had planned to go to Jodhpur and Jaisalmer on inspections with my family. Before I left Delhi on 24 October, R.K. Singh congratulated me. He said that my orders had been received from the establishment officer of DOP&T. He had also spoken to the minister in Patna about it. He apparently had no reservations. So, we happily went to Jodhpur. I got many messages of felicitation.

Lalu ji is upset

The minister returned from Patna after the Pooja holidays. He was upset because the proposal was changed without consulting him. He wrote to the PM that I was not suitable for the post and that there were complaints against me of harassing officers, when I had been in Vigilance. Many rumours were doing the rounds. For the first time, I realized how strong and deep-seated the campaign against me was. I decided to go to the MR. I told him that I had not gone to anyone to plead my case except the CRB. I belonged to Bihar and I was not a Punjabi as had been alleged. I had not harassed anyone during my service, particularly when in Vigilance. But my job as a vigilance officer was an unpleasant task. He was apparently surprised and said that as a Bihari I should have come to him earlier. This was a big joke! He showed his helplessness because he had already committed to Mr Varshney. He had requested the ACC to promote Varshney and me together when the post of member engineering would be vacant on 28 February 2005. It meant a wait of four months. There was no logic behind this but apparently, I could do nothing about it.

The joint secretary in the PMO knew me well. I gave him a note on the rules and implications. I got a call from the PMO one morning at my residence to find out why my appointment was being resisted. I had no clue except that they did not want me as the CRB. If I was promoted now as the MS then I would have clear cut twenty-seven months of residual service. According to the rules, I was eligible for an appointment as chairman after R.K. Singh retired in July 2005. I was told that the PM had obviously seen my case and was satisfied and impressed with my track record. A great deal of pressure was however applied to stall my promotion. It was a subject of talk in the corridors of bureaucracy. The government relented by holding my orders in abeyance. Nobody had ever heard about such an order. People talked of the compulsions of coalition politics. Surprise! This is how an insignificant person like me could upset the coalition!

I get fresh reassurance

I was hosting a New Year's lunch party on 1 January 2005 in my house when I got a call from the PMO on the RAX. I had sent the PM greetings for the new year. This call from the PMO was to thank me for the same and offer his own greetings for the new year. I was told how unfortunate it was to withhold the order in abeyance. I was assured that I would eventually be the next CRB. We also briefly discussed the direction the Railways would take to chart its path for its future growth. My personal view and suggestion on the subject was also sought. It was most unusual. I cannot of course describe my happiness then. I came back and continued with the lunch party, terribly pleased. I only told my wife, who could not believe it. I sent my own proposal regarding the course of development that the Indian Railways should embark upon. Many might not know but I had visualized that the Railways would come out of its rut once it thought out of the box. My proposals were eventually responsible for the much talked about turnaround of the Railways.

But as far as my promotion to the Board was concerned, it was stuck for the next four months. It was very frustrating. I found it very hard to explain how and why I had missed the bus.

ADVERSITY HAUNTS US

Adversity, however, continued to haunt me. The stampede at the New Delhi Railway Station on 13 November 2004 was one such incident. Diwali was on 12 November. Member Mechanical Mr Garg had called us the next day for lunch at his residence. Lalu ji had returned from Dubai on 13th morning—a Saturday. He was going back to Patna by train leaving New Delhi at 3.30 p.m.

We had finished lunch, when the chief medical director, Dr D. Sharma called me to report a serious case of stampede at the New Delhi Railway Station. He told me that some passengers were seriously injured and were being brought to the Railways' central hospital. I left immediately and dropped my wife off at our S.P. Marg residence on the way to the station. Details of the incident started coming on my cell phone as I was on way. It had occurred around 2.30 p.m. There was huge rush for the *Jansadharan Express*—a fast train to Patna, scheduled to leave at 3.30 p.m. It was a very popular train with only unreserved accommodation and was on Platform No. 3 for boarding. Passengers were going through the main foot overbridge to the platform. In the rush, one old lady slipped and fell down on the staircase. This led to some others tripping and falling over each other. Over fifteen persons had sustained grievous injuries. They were taken to the hospital where five of them, including a 14-year-old girl, had succumbed to the injuries.

The MR was in the Rail Bhawan. I informed the CRB who was also in his office. I told him to inform the minister and suggested that the MR should come to New Delhi station. The media had converged at the station in great strength. The MR had in any case planned to catch a train to Patna. But the CRB told me that it would be better if I talked to the MR directly. Normally, the CRB briefs the minister in such cases. When I called his office, I was told by his PS that the MR was sleeping. I asked him to wake up the MR because it was an emergency. After a few minutes, the MR came on the line. I briefed him about the mishap. I requested that he come down to the station. There was some mischievous leak in the media that the stampede was the result of confusion caused because there was a last-minute announcement to change the placement of the rake to Platform No.1 (its usual platform position is on Platform No. 3.) It was alleged that it was done to make it more convenient for the MR to board the train. This may be true but firstly, such changes are not uncommon due to operating necessity and secondly the platform was the adjoining one and there was enough time for passengers to cross over. I suggested that he could deal with the media more effectively and in any case, it was not advisable for him to go by train.

The minister was calm and collected when he came to the station. I had briefed him on the action taken by us to run a large number of special trains to clear the heavy rush, especially considering the three consecutive holidays for Diwali, Chhath and Eid—all in a span of a week. The tragedy was accidental. Immediate action was taken to look after the injured in the Railways' central hospital and Ram Manohar Lohia Hospital. An emergency meeting was called to streamline the heavy passenger rush with the help of the Delhi Police. The police commissioner and Lt Governor, Mr Joshi, visited the site and offered their help. Around 7.30 p.m. calm returned to the station.

Thankfully, we came out strong out of the tragedy and those who thought that it would turn out to lead to my obituary were proved wrong. I thank God for His help.

WORST NIGHTMARE OF A RAILWAYMAN—COLLISION OF TRAINS

The worst nightmare of any railwayman is certainly the collision of passenger trains. Well, such a terrible collision happened in broad daylight, on 14 December 2004, barely a month after the tragic incident at New Delhi station.

I had gone to Saharanpur and intended to visit Jagadhari Workshop after my inspection at Saharanpur station and my meeting with the local passenger association. I reached Saharanpur around 9 a.m. by the *Dehradun Shatabdi* in the company of my wife. I met the local traders and the association but in the meanwhile, my wife as the president of the NRWWO took stock of the activities of the division with Renu Chandra, the divisional president.

The chief safety commissioner, RPF, called me around 12.30 p.m. to report the serious accident—a collision in Jalanndhar-Pathankot section of Firozpur division. I held Mr Awasthi in high regard because he was usually the first to communicate such information to me. I had mentioned his intelligence network to others. It was a terrible shock. A little later, I got a full version of the accident. It really was the worst type of accident to occur during the tenure of a railwayman.

An unfortunate accident

The single line section of Jalandhar-Pathankot was being doubled. Construction activities in connection with the doubling of the section were in progress in the section. A construction machine had damaged the communication cable between the Bhangala and Mirthal stations the previous evening. Thus, there was a breakdown in block communication (the block instruments between the two stations were not working). This called for an introduction of train services on a paper 'line clear' system. Under this system, two ASMs had to verify the 'line clear aspect' manually before allowing trains to enter the block section. Drivers were also expected to drive at a low speed, sharply looking out for any obstruction. This system was working alright and it was decided by the section controller to let 9112 *Jammu Tawi-Ahmedabad Express*, starting from Jammu and waiting at Mirthal station to start first. The other train, 1 JMP DMU train, a local commuter train, had to wait at Banghala station to allow the express train to cross. But due to some confusion which could not be explained, both the ASMs gave 'paper line' clear to their respective trains; thus, both trains entered the single line block section simultaneously. Obviously, ASM Bhangala mistook it due to a grave human error and started the local train. Normally, in such a situation, the local train is given precedence. Just after Bhangala, there was a sharp S-curve due to a road overbridge. This might have restricted visibility to some extent. But whatever the case, the express train collided head-on with 1 JMP DMU train going to Jammu from Jalandhar in broad daylight around 11.45 a.m. The accident caused the death of thirty-eight persons while fifty-two were injured. The Parliament was in session, so everything that could go wrong actually went wrong.

I spoke to the CRB who had already been informed of the accident. The MR was also briefed and he decided to go to the site by a special plane after making a brief announcement, as customary, in the house. He was expected to land at Pathankot Air Force base by 4 p.m. I was taken by a special train from Saharanpur. My wife got down at Ambala station. The DRM had made arrangements for her to go back to Delhi. I reached the site around 7 p.m. The MR had already gone back to Delhi by then. After flying back to Delhi, he went away to Patna.

The police had not given the site clearance certificate when I arrived at the site. It was required in such cases before the restoration work could start. They were carrying out their own investigation. Most of the officers had gone to Pathankot to see off the MR. It is what usually happened whenever a VIP visited the site of a major mishap. It was the duty of the team leader and the VIP to ensure that the team was not disturbed. After my arrival, I took the matter under my command. I obtained the police clearance certificate after which the ART started the clearance work. I spent the whole night overseeing the restoration and treatment of the injured. Injured passengers were admitted in two or three hospitals of the Punjab state government. I was pleasantly surprised at the high standard of civil hospitals even in small towns. It was admirable!

I had to stand up

I returned to Delhi in the morning totally demoralized and tired. The entire team looked defeated. In my view, the time had come to make a stand. After all the Northern Railway had done very well. This blot could not take away everything the team had toiled for. I also knew that the worst was yet to come. This needed moral authority and courage. It was a litmus test for the courage of their leader.

The Parliament was in uproar because the minister had gone to Patna without making any statement in the house after having visited the site. He returned from Patna on 15 December 2004 in the evening. He had to make the statement in the Parliament the following day. The CRB called me around 9 p.m. He told me that the minister wanted three senior officers—senior DOM, senior DSTE and senior DSO to be suspended. He also wanted action to be taken against the DRM. I told him that the action was not warranted. It was clearly the fault of two ASMs. They were responsible for admitting both trains into the section. Even after discovering the mistake, they were quarrelling with each other over the VHF set (walkie-talkie) instead of warning the drivers. I told him that in any construction work of doubling, damage to the block cable was not uncommon. The maintenance man of the S&T department could not locate the fault during the night. It could be located around 7 in the morning. To repair and restore communication, the traffic block was required. It was decided to give the block after the express train had passed. There was clearly no point in taking action against senior officers in this case.

The CRB was however not impressed with my explanation. He told me patronizingly, 'Listen you are in a crucial stage of your career. Do not be rigid and accept what MR wants us to do.' I said, 'There is no point in overreacting. But if the intention is to play to the gallery, you may hang me instead. It will have a much louder impact'. He was upset and hung up. Soon after, the minister called me. He asked me how the accident had taken place. I explained but he curtly asked me to submit a written report. I assumed and believed that the CRB must have told the MR about my stubborn attitude. It was 11 at night.

I was simply disgusted. If some action had to be taken, they could have issued instructions to that effect. By the time I had marshalled my thoughts it was 11.30 p.m. I immediately asked V.K. Singh to have the office opened. All officers concerned were called and by midnight, I was in the office. The report had to describe the accident, including the context. There was loose and irresponsible talk in the media about how the Railways still stuck to using magneto phone in the modern days when cell phones were so effective and a powerful means of communication. This myth had to be blown away. The report had to be prepared in the night to ensure that the minister saw the report the first thing in the morning.

Amrit Mathur—an excellent and very knowledgeable person— was my chief safety officer. He also came to the office. The report was ready by 3.30 a.m. The protocol officer was asked to hand the report over to the APS of the minister at 6 in the morning. I had spoken to the APS at night. I requested him to give the report to the minister as soon as he came out for tea. He also told the minister that I would meet him at 8.30 a.m. The minister had already seen the report when I met him. I then very calmly explained what had happened.

I clarified that no procedure was flouted and it was a simple case of human error. I explained that action taken against senior officers could be counterproductive. Someone might ask for action against Board member next time around and even against the minister. A statutory inquiry under the Railway Act by the commissioner of railway safety (CRS) was to start next day. Those found responsible would be dealt with severely. The minister was convinced and asked me to have some tea. The MR was clever. He had sensed that if he talked about action against senior officers, his political detractors would call for his blood. The minister agreed that the rule of the land also demanded a proper inquiry to ascertain responsibility. The local police also held the two ASMs responsible. Both ASMs were absconding. The police were after them. In light of that, the MR was convinced that there was no justification to take action against senior officers as suggested by the CRB. That would come after the outcome of inquiry by the CRS.

Then I explained that there was no truth in the allegation about the rule being flouted. The 'paper line clear' did not mean any ordinary piece of paper. It was a document authorizing the movement under the general rules and block working manual. The use of block phone was also not old-fashioned, even in the days of mobile phone. The block instrument ensured secure communication between two station masters. A cell phone could be misleading because there was no certainty about who was speaking on the phone. Even a mobile phone failed at times. There had to be a procedure legally placed in position for such situations. I told the minister that he would appreciate this better if he saw the working of block instruments. Without 'paper line clear' authorization, all train movements would stop. Being an emergency operation, it called for strict discipline by all concerned. In this case, both ASMs had failed as individuals and as human beings.

The MR was totally convinced. He was a much stronger person and very sure of himself. He was calm and collected. He knew how to deal with MPs and the media. I complimented him for these stellar qualities which a minister should have. Then he asked the OSD to prepare the statement in line with my report and briefing. He had also liked my suggestion that there was no reason to be apologetic or defensive in this case because human error or failure could cause any mishap. He said that an FIR should be lodged against the two ASMs because of their criminal negligence. They had failed to inform the driver and instead had indulged in quarrelling with each other.

I take moral responsibility

I returned very satisfied with the response of the MR. I now listened to his statement in the Parliament on TV with rapt attention. He had spoken exactly along the lines briefed to him. For the first time after three days, I smiled. The CRB spoke to me on his way back to the Rail Bhawan. He said, 'After all, the minister has saved you, Jaruhar.' Then I politely told him that the statement which the MR had read was prepared by me. I narrated to him what had happened in the morning. There was complete silence on the other end.

I thanked God because he gave me the courage to go the length to stand up for those not responsible for the mishap. It was a moral victory, but I could not absolve myself from the moral responsibility for the incident. I wrote in my MCDO to the Board that while action would be taken against those responsible but I had no hesitation in holding myself morally responsible for the accident which had led to the death of thirty-eight persons. The Railways as a system was accountable and I could not shy away from this.

This was a bold statement. My COM, Mathew John, was very reluctant about this statement but I had insisted. I understand that the MR had liked it. He had told others that I had a lot of courage.

MORAL COURAGE RESTORED—LESSONS IN LEADERSHIP

There was despondency all around, and a pall of gloom had descended. It brought down the morale. We had heard of collisions—side ones, rear collision—a train coming from rear and hitting the train in the rear—these were more common. We had also known of head on collisions during the night in a station yard with a stationary train or one during a non-interlocking operation. But a head-on collision in the midsection in broad daylight with no problem of visibility must be the rarest of rare incidents. It was therefore the worst nightmare of any railwayman.

The worst nightmare for a railwayman

The shock was profound. It was essential that something be done to restore the sagging morale of the team. I asked the COM to call all the senior divisional operating managers, safety officers and all operating officers of the headquarters for a talk. I listened to them. One after another, the officers told me that they would have to be very strict and work according to the rules. Thus, there would be no room for innovation or a fresh initiative. It was bad for any organization. Then I told them the story I learnt as a probationer in 1969 in the Railway Staff College, Baroda. It was about a thoroughbred who did not require a whip nor did it weep if it lost a race.

They had heard about my efforts to stand up for them risking my own neck. I urged them to work as if nothing had happened. The lesson of a paper line clear operation was that it must be for the shortest possible time. I was very happy when all their faces slowly lit up with smiles. I was sure that this was a resolve of the determined team.

I am grateful to many who stood by me, but I cannot forget Nitish ji who spoke to R. K. Singh, CRB, on his own. He told him to do everything possible to protect me. I thank him and R. K. Singh, who in any case tried to help me in whatever way, he thought good. Thank you, Sir.

We come out of it—lessons for all

I am very thankful to Mathew John and Amrit Mathur who stood up for me. They had ensured that no negative energy was passed down to the team. In my opinion this was vital. Some important lessons for a leader in such a traumatic situation could be outlined as follows:

- The leader must put organizational interests over everything else. He should certainly not worry about himself.
- He should be calm. He must be able to think clearly about what course to take, and not worry about the consequence. He needs to be far-sighted, to come out of the crisis. Otherwise, he would be deprived of the perspective necessary to come out of the crisis.
- His superiors as well as subordinate team members look to him for encouragement. Both need support and a possible way out of the crisis. If the leader sought sympathy for himself, he will soon be reduced to a victim. It was much better to be truthful and honest and go down as a martyr rather than one who had succumbed to his own fears.
- There were things to be done slowly and in stages in such a situation. Winning small battles was more important in this stage rather than

trying to achieve too many things at once. Even culprits deserve to be honourably treated. There was no point in repeating that one would be hanged if such an offence recurred. The warning was already there. As a true member of the team, realization should have already sunk deeply in his psyche. There was no need to stress the point and offend his innate wisdom or conscience.

We submit to karmic philosophy

At that time, many had thought that my career as a railwayman was over. I could not blame them either. The history of the Indian Railways is replete with such examples. That I and even others came out unscathed was certainly God's grace.

It was, however, painful and it tormented us. It had not spared us. The famous belief that the karma does not get destroyed is truly valid. Karma transforms itself following the principle of conservation of energy. It is our destiny to be up on our feet and to carry on with our duties regardless of consequences. It is the Law of Nature. So we had to endure the pain in humility. This was the atonement for the pain our own action had caused them. That was the only release from the bondage of karma.

THE DEBATE ABOUT SAFETY AGAINST COLLISION

In India, the accident renewed talk of providing a device similar to the European Train Control System (ETCS) to eliminate the element of human error. The Konkan Railway Corporation had developed and introduced a system known as *raksha kawach*—an anti-collision device (ACD). This was under trial in NF Railway. It was an indigenously developed device based on the global positioning system (GPS). It detected an obstruction on the line like two trains moving on the same track.

Anti-collision device upsets world leaders

This device had upset many world technology leaders like the ETCS. There was fierce opposition and serious doubts about the safety and efficacy of ACDs developed indigenously in India. I did not know the game very clearly at that time. The *Voice of America* invited me for an interview by arranging a teleconference with a number of groups, including the listeners. There was a high functionary from the National Aeronautics and Space Administration (NASA) besides the additional director from the Indian Space Research Organisation (ISRO) on the line. They all questioned me about the efficacy of the ACD in detecting an obstruction a few metres away. According to the NASA and the

ISRO experts, the GPS did not have that kind of accuracy. They doubted how an obstruction could be detected by using this system.

But the principle involved in the ACD was on the basis of adding in analog or digital form the successive incremental angular deviation so commonly used for laying a curve on the ground with the help of theodolites. I had an in-depth conversation on this through teleconferencing. I was able to satisfy the experts from NASA and ISRO that the GPS could be fine-tuned to actually detect an obstruction a few metres away with a very high degree of accuracy.

THE NRWWO LENDS THEIR SUPPORT

The contribution of the NRWWO for the welfare of railwaymen and their family is memorable. Their help was valuable because official means had limitations. The NRWWO helped hospitals, railway schools, and sick family members, physically challenged persons and supported railway families in times of natural calamity like the tsunami in Tamil Nadu or floods in Ambala. It really did us proud. I did not know how women created organizational strength for undertaking welfare projects. The help, compassion and succour provided by the team were truly commendable. As the CEO of the Railways, I acknowledged their contribution with great pride. The president of the NRWWO, a very simple and unassuming lady and my wife, knew her job and responsibility. She did us all proud in the way she conducted herself with dignity and humility.

Annual fund-raising effort was always a difficult task for the NRWWO. She had very thoughtfully decided to organize a Rail Mela where all divisions would participate by putting up handicrafts and products of their area. They wanted to invite Nitish Kumar to inaugurate the fair in January 2004. He had some reservations about activities organized by any women's organization run by wives of railway officers. I hinted to my wife that he might not accept the invitation.

But she insisted and sought an appointment with him. It was neither given nor denied. There were only about ten days left. I did not want to speak to the MR about this. But she was not able to meet or speak to him. I, therefore, decided to mention this to Nitish Kumar while accompanying him for a function at the Hazrat Nizamuddin station one morning to flag off a new train.

After the brief function, he had to go to the airport to accompany George Fernandes for some ceremony in the Northeast region. While travelling in his car, I said, 'The president of NRWWO had sought an appointment with you to invite you for their annual function. There has been no response from your office. There is no time left now. She wants to know if you would be kind enough to grace their function. I have told her about your views about the activities of the Railways' welfare organizations run by wives of railway officers. She however insists on meeting you. You are likely to be out of Delhi for a long time. I have, therefore, no other alternative but to request you on behalf of the NRWWO.' He started laughing and said that he was sorry to have caused inconvenience to the ladies. He said, 'You are right that I do not have a very good opinion so far about the activities of women welfare organizations. But since Mrs Jaruhar is its president, I must make an exception. Please tell her that I accept her invitation. I will attend the annual function as the chief guest, as desired by her.'

My wife and the other women were of course very happy. Many were surprised because they knew the MR had not attended such functions in the past. I escorted him to the venue—the lawn of Baroda House. He was very impressed with the activities on display. He was particularly very happy with the cheque of ₹5 lakh given by the NRWWO to the Railway Minister Welfare Fund. He asked R.K. Singh why he had not organized such an event when he was GM, Northern Railway. He praised my wife and was truly impressed. He thanked me subsequently for erasing a wrong notion that he was carrying in his mind. He was particularly impressed with the idea of the Rail Mela because it provided an opportunity to all railwaymen and their families to join the function. The next year's function was equally impressive and was remembered for long for the spirit of collective participation that it provided.

THE JUSTICE BANERJEE INQUIRY COMMITTEE ON GODHRA

I mention this episode only by way of highlighting how the GM, Northern Railway gets involved in whatever happens in Delhi even if unconnected with the affairs of the Northern Railway.

On 27 February 2002, coach S6 of the *Sabarmati Express* was burnt in the morning when the train was about to leave Godhra station on the Western Railway. Fifty-nine passengers, mostly Hindu pilgrims (known as kar sevaks) returning from Ayodhya died. At that time, the report was that the coach had been torched from outside by a mob of Muslims. I was in the Railway Board at that time. This resulted in a great aftermath in Gujarat. I remember only one thing in particular. On 28 February, Yashwant Sinha, the finance minister, was presenting the Annual Budget in the Parliament at the usual time. I was in the visitors' gallery of the House. The Shiv Sena MPs started demonstrating before the speaker that there has been no action so far by the government on the Godhra incident. It happened for 10-15 minutes when Manohar Joshi, a senior Shiv Sena MP, persuaded the MPs to sit down so that the Budget speech could start. I clearly recollect that without going into the question of who was responsible for the carnage, no secular leader like Sonia Gandhi, Mulayam Singh Yadav, Lalu Prasad, Somnath Chatterjee rose to condemn the incident.

But let me come back to the subject. The railway ministry on 17 May 2004, soon after the UPA came to power, appointed a committee headed by U.C. Banerjee, retired judge of the Supreme Court, for conducting an inquiry into the cause of the accident. A separate judicial commission had already been appointed by the Gujarat government for the same. There was lot of debate and accusation as to why the Railways had not inquired into the incident. I recall that under the Railway Act, the commissioner of Railway Safety conducts suo motu inquiry and only when he is satisfied that the reasons for the accident are plainly obvious, can he dispense with inquiry. In this case, the reason was apparent, and the state government was already appointing a Judicial Commission under the Commissions of Inquiry Act, 1952 and hence, the Railways did not demand a separate inquiry. Well whatever be the case, an inquiry was conducted by Justice Banerjee in Delhi. He was allotted 1, Chelmsford Road as his residence and office for the inquiry. I had no role in this case except providing the accommodation, etc. because the case belonged to the Western Railway and the Railway Board was coordinating it. So, I was surprised when I got a call from Vinoo Mathur, secretary Railway Board, 'Sir, Justice Banerjee is not happy with the support team which has been provided. He has asked for change in member secretary also. He was telling that the GM Northern had also not met him. I know you were not required to do that but might I suggest that you meet him once for the sake of courtesy.' I laughed at it, but Vinoo is such a nice person that one would like to comply with his wish. So, I went to see Justice Banerjee.

He was warm and said that he was so glad that I came to see him. He just chatted and was not charitable in his comments about the MR and his men. He said he knew he was my boss and would therefore not ask for my opinion. I offered all my help for the inquiry but he said nothing really was required. He said something in jest and not charitable at all. I told Vinoo that everything was fine and that I believed he would not bother him (Mathur) anymore. It was more important that the GM, NR should also meet and I was glad to have helped in the Board's task in getting the inquiry report as quickly as desired by the MR. The report was finally submitted in March 2006 when I was ME. The MR wanted the report to be placed in the Parliament which was not allowed as the inquiry was not held under the Commission of Inquiry Act or according to its procedures. The Gujarat High Court also did not allow any action to be taken on this report because the Judicial Commission was already inquiring into the case. It had some purpose and the MR was happy of its outcome.

IT IS TIME TO LEAVE AND BID GOODBYE

It was February 2005. I heard the news that the orders for posting as member, Railway Board were being processed. I expected to be posted as member staff by reactivating the old order kept under abeyance. Well it was not to be. On 27 February 2005, a cricket match between the Railway Board and the Northern Railway was arranged. It was an annual affair.

After the match, the CRB informed me that my orders as member engineering were expected on the next day. I was a bit surprised. I immediately understood the ploy to deny me the benefit of continuity that the old order kept under abeyance would have provided. Well I could do nothing about that. The orders were issued in the evening of 28 February 2005. Mr Xavier, the PPS asked me in the evening if I would like to join as the ME on the 28th, after S.P.S. Jain retired. Well, there was no reason for any hurry and on 1 March 2005 I finally took over as member engineering, Railway Board.

Before I go on to describe my last post, I must say how indebted I was to my secretary, Vinay Kumar Singh. He was a pillar of strength. I just marvel as to how he was able to do so many things and do them all at the same time. I was a difficult person to deal with—a very demanding boss. But he ensured that I carried on very well. He saved me from many embarrassments. I was very particular when dealing with something that needed all my concentration. I would tell him to hold other appointments at bay while I was busy. He always managed that very effectively. In this context, I cannot help but mention an anecdote just to highlight how such an effective and intelligent secretary can help his boss.

Vinay had been telling me that a famous lady from a royal family in Moradabad was seeking an appointment with me. She was also a former Congress MP and therefore it could not be avoided. Well, I agreed to meet her. He had, of course, warned me that she had a captivating and attractive personality and had given no agenda or purpose for the meeting except to call it a courtesy visit.

She was ushered into my room and it was immediately filled with the aroma of a perfume. She told me that she belonged to a family of nawabs—a daughter-in-law. I remembered having passed by their royal bungalow or palace. Everything about her was really regal—her attire, her way of sitting and speaking, her mannerisms. I found that she had no purpose but wanted just to chat. She invited me to her palace and offered to send famous mangoes from their gardens. I was totally uncomfortable and was just wondering how to bring the meeting to an end. She was perfectly at ease and was in no hurry at all. The obvious purpose, so it seemed, was to display various facets of her charm at the cost of extreme discomfiture to me.

And in walked Vinay with a profoundly apologetic face, 'Sir, I am sorry to intrude but there is an urgent call for you from the MR. He has to meet someone and he wants you to meet him in the Rail Bhawan immediately.' I said, 'But, Vinay, how can I just go abruptly. I cannot leave Madam like that.' I thought the lady understood and told me, 'GM sahib, no worries. I can understand. I have also been an MP. Please go and I thank you very much. Actually, I also have another appointment.' And she was gone. Vinay stood in the doorframe with a mischievous smile. I did not ask him how he had devised such an excuse but he had my thanks!

He looked after my family's needs as well; thus, making me completely free to battle with the challenges of the Northern Railway. His wife, Pragya, is very talented and helpful. Together they have a reputation for helping others. The smile on their faces had tremendous positive energy. His associates, Mukesh and Mohammad Ali, the protocol officers, had been great help. Without D.P.S. Sandhu the CPRO who managed the media in the best possible manner, I would not have succeeded at all. He earned respect from them. Whenever Vinay was away, Sandhu also doubled as my secretary. It is said that behind every successful person there were persons who worked silently. For me it is Vinay, Sandhu, Mukesh and Mohammad Ali! Thank you!

15

THE LAST POST

I had joined the Railways on 12 December 1968. It had taken almost thirty-seven years for me to reach the last post—member engineering of the Railway Board on 1 March 2005. When I look back, I am undoubtedly certain that when I had joined the Railways, I had not imagined, even in my wildest dreams that I would eventually climb to the topmost rung of the hierarchy of the Indian Railway Service of Engineers.

A great and long journey

In the farewell meeting in B.I.T. Sindri, my head of the department had mentioned that those joining the Railways eventually rose to become chief engineer. They had no knowledge of the levels beyond that. For that matter, even I had no idea about what opportunities one could aspire for beyond the post of a chief engineer.

I had come from a humble background. I had never expected to reach great heights in my career. With the profound grace of God, I had made a niche for myself in the Railways. For many railwaymen, positions of importance like secretary Railway Board; advisor vigilance; GM, Northern Railway; member engineering and ex-officio secretary to the Government of India were a rare combination. That I occupied all of them was a matter of envy for some. It also spoke volumes of the efficacy and fairness of the democratic system. It had allowed a so-called village boy to reach such heights. After all, many in Delhi considered Patna, an ancient city, as a village only.

I join reluctantly

It was true that I was not enthusiastic or excited about this posting and the promotion. I should have been posted as the MS but my claim was brushed aside. The appointment committee of the Cabinet had posted me as member staff in October 2004 and then, in its own wisdom, had kept the order in abeyance for four months in administrative exigency! Justice demanded that this wait for four months due to administrative reasons should have been credited to me. This evidently was a case of bias and caprice to deny me my due.

But nevertheless, I came to the Board, considering it as my destiny. I reached Rail Bhawan around 11 a.m., after attending a sports function where the CRB was the chief guest. The Rail Bhawan was a familiar place. By the time I entered my room on the second floor, I had a grip over my emotions. I took over the charge of member engineering as the thirty-first incumbent of the post. When I looked at the Honor Board, there were illustrious predecessors like M.N. Berry, B.C. Ganguli, G.P. Warrior, V.C.A. Padmanabhan, K.C. Sood, Ramachandran, Balachandran, E. Sreedharan, Y.P. Anand and so many others. I was in awe.

The first day as usual, was consumed by persons coming in to congratulate me. I went to see the minister at his residence in the evening when he returned from Patna. He congratulated me and was apparently happy. I was to look after Northern Railway also as its GM, till a regular person was posted. This increased the work load immensely. I called on the Cabinet secretary also. He was sorry about the fiasco that I had to suffer in my posting. He said that he was helpless and that I had become an unnecessary victim of the compulsions of coalition politics. He was certain that this would not be repeated when the process would start for the post of chairman Railway Board. It was reassuring, but I could not be sure that three months later, the same thing or similar compulsions would not bog down the post. I went to meet Mr Nair, PPS to the PM also. He also expressed a similar confidence. Well, it sounded good.

GREAT EXPECTATIONS—REDEMPTION OF THE GLORY OF THE CADRE

Just a couple of days later, Vipin (V.C. Sharma, director UIC) came to see me. An old associate from the Brahmaputra Bridge days in Tezpur, he was my conscience keeper. He told me that I must do something to elevate the stature of the IRSE cadre which had a low morale and was looked down upon.

Declining glory of the cadre—real challenge and great expectations

In the history of the Indian Railways, this cadre had occupied a unique position of glory. In the time to come, the shine had faded. Although the largest cadre, it was not recognized as one, which had once shaped the destiny of the Indian Railways. But I asked Vipin what I should or could do to retrieve the old respect and glory of the cadre. He did not know how that could be done. He was however sure and confident that I was the only person who could do that.

Engineers were leaders—they eventually abdicated their rights

Well, it was a tall order. I knew that no one could buy respect or demand glory. It would come by becoming a rightful owner of it. That would mean that as in past, the IRSE must become a leader once again. When the first page of the history of the Indian Railways, or more precisely that of railways in India, was being written, engineers were at the forefront. Besides construction of railway lines in the country, they had also designed the financial model of the project. It was the first exercise in public-private partnership in British India. The British government undertook to guarantee a minimum dividend to be paid as annuity to the private investors. That was clearly the first chapter of Indian Railways, and engineers were clearly the leaders. They had assured that:

- The best suited technology and construction technique was chosen.
- The alignment and route selected were by far the most suitable and remunerative to fetch maximum commercial returns for the project. The alignment also met the strategic requirement of the colonial power of the British to monitor the British rule in India.
- Construction technology and management exploited the local building material and provided scope for import of suitable material and equipment.
- Very difficult and challenging construction was completed in a record time to provide maximum return for the capital investment.

An engineer had thus achieved the following:

1) He saw.
   He had vision. He saw that in a country like India, reliable and cheap bulk transport was required. He sold the idea of a rail transport. All stakeholders, including the government, were convinced of the project. So, the engineer recognized the needs and provided a vision to achieve the mission.
2) He provided a plan.
   He presented an alignment and engineering plan, cost estimate and financial model to realize the plan.
3) He executed and commissioned the plan.
   Once the plan was accepted, he executed the scheme and commissioned it in time. The need was served and the benefits of the investment were seen to accrue in full measure.
4) He ensured that he would always be needed and one could not do without him.

Nobody worshipped the discredited leader

The engineer made it imperative that he would not only be needed for future schemes, but also required to maintain the existing services to ensure that the assets continued to serve the needs in the most effective manner.

These, according to the principles of management, were the hallmarks of a true leader. The moment even one of these was abdicated, he would lose leadership qualities. *And no one worshipped or glorified a discredited leader.*

The clear-cut way out was to regain the lost ground by being a leader again. If a cadre wanted to be recognized as a leader, it must win wars for the organization. History was testimony to umpteen episodes of even a small charge winning a battle. Nobody knew of an outfit which only said 'No' when a challenge confronted an organization. They would worship one which said, 'Yes'. They had given volumes to the organization even though they got nothing in return.

GOALS AHEAD—DEFINITION AND BLUEPRINT

I did not worry much about such a task. It was essential for me to look at what the Indian Railways needed. Sudhir Kumar, OSD to the minister, had once told me before I joined as ME that they were eagerly looking forward to my joining the Board as ME. The IR was at crossroads, and it was imperative that something be done out of the box to put the Railways on the way to economic recovery.

The beginning of 2005 was the period when the economy had shown a certain surge in the growth, may be as a part of a worldwide phenomenon. The economic growth as indicated in the growing gross domestic product (GDP), meant that the transport sector must also grow at a rate higher than the GDP rate of growth to support various sectors like power, farming, manufacturing, etc. As the GM, I had sincerely believed that the IR, in particular, was actually unable to match the demand of the growing economy on the transport sector as a whole. The reason for the failure of the IR to carry additional traffic offerings was quite obvious. The system had neither adequate rolling stocks—railway engines or freight wagons—nor did it have the available line capacity to run additional freight trains. The IR was being choked systematically. A long-term solution, involving acquisitions of rolling stocks and creating additional line capacity along critical corridors would be time-consuming or a long-term activity. Besides, it called for immediate injection of a huge capital investment.

My philosophy was that all service providers had to find technical solutions to the problems faced by the organization. After joining as ME, it was clearly my duty as chief of service provider to find a way out of the present constraint. The government had very recently provided a lump sum grant of ₹17,000 crore as the Special Rail Safety Fund. This was done due to the faith reposed in the Indian Railways as a premier organization. The time had perhaps come to redeem its pledge. A matter of great expectation!

I called a meeting of my executive directors and additional members concerned on 4 March 2005. The idea was to evaluate the task before us. It was necessary to sound a wake-up call to the organization. As a rule of thumb, the growth in the transport sector had to be 2 to 3 per cent higher than the GDP growth. The IR had carried 602 million ton in 2004-05, up by 45 million ton (557 million ton) in 2003-04. That was around an 8.50 per cent growth. There was no reason why the IR could not carry more than sixty million ton in 2005-06. This would be about 10 per cent higher than 2004-05. The problem was that the additional traffic would be along the most saturated routes. It meant running at least sixty extra freight trains in the loaded direction every day and running of the same number of empty rakes. Taking a turnaround of an average of seven days, it called for an additional fleet of 450 freight wagons and freight engines. Mind-boggling logistics!

I did not believe in 'No' as an option. It would mean that we as engineers did not try enough. In very simple terms, the economic growth in the country was asking us to do the following:

- Complete line capacity works like gauge conversion, doubling, new lines, etc., on a war footing to create additional capacity as envisaged in the National Rail Vikas Yojana.
- Increase general speed of trains to augment throughput. Track renewals, bridge rehabilitation and yard remodelling should be taken up on fast track in order to cut down on traffic restrictions.
- As both of the above measures were likely to take time, it was imperative to find out ways to increase the freight carrying capacity of the existing trains. It was necessary to explore the possibility of introducing heavy haul trains. This was a short-term solution to overcome the constraint of inadequate rolling stocks, inadequate line capacity and inadequate running staff like drivers and guards.

We had to identify the goals and needs of the organization. We had to enlist the support of the members of the team. There had to be broad conviction in the minds of the team members about what the team leader thought. The meeting had underlined the responsibility of the service provider. There was a conviction that with 'No' not being an option, the team had to find a solution. The idea thus was shared by all, and in my view, this was the greatest achievement of the meeting I held.

CONCEPT OF HEAVY AXLE LOAD EMERGES

The proposal to introduce heavy haul on the Indian Railways would clearly mean increasing the axle load of freight wagons. At that time, the permissible load was the carrying capacity of the wagon plus two ton as loading margin. If the carrying capacity of each wagon was increased by ten tons, the axle load would be nearly twenty-three ton each. This had never been agreed to earlier.

If my memory served right, the idea to introduce heavier axle load was being mooted for the last twenty-five years or so. No ME had thought this to be safe. I was aware of the hazards associated with the mission. As secretary Railway Board, I had witnessed an uproarious scene in the Board meeting. The ME and MM had fought bitterly over the plying of WDG diesel locomotive with slightly higher axle load on the North Eastern Railway. I suggested to the ME that it seemed possible. He gave me a dirty look and threw the file back to the MM. So, I asked my executive directors to re-examine the issue. I wanted them to express their views in a free, unbiased but objective manner.

The ball had started to roll. Additional member civil engineering (AMCE) Mr Arvindan was very knowledgeable. Having been in the IRICEN for long, he knew the subject well. He told me that he was very impressed with my views in the meeting. He promised to lend his full support. He was also convinced of the feasibility of a heavy haul.

It was key 'to look at it in different manner' I believed that as the head of the department I had to adopt this approach. I believed in the principle that the Railway Board was a policymaking unit and it could not be bogged down by codes or procedures framed by the Board. I asked the AMCE not to examine a crucial proposal like this only in terms of available codes or laid down procedures. By making such a statement, I had succeeded in opening a door to let in some fresh ideas.

About a week later, the heavy haul proposition was put in the file. It was clear from the file that the case did not require any great effort. This subject had been dealt more than once in the past. The file had all the relevant material to arrive at the conclusion that a heavy axle load would cause rail stress in excess of permissible limits. The imposed stress was calculated as 44 kg/sq mm against 42 kg/sq mm allowed for 90 UTS rail.

LOOK AT THE CONCEPT IN A DIFFERENT WAY

The matter would have ended there. Nobody in the past had hitherto ventured to exceed the permissible stress value. That was the bottom line. But we had undertaken that we would examine the case 'in a different manner'. We were determined neither to be bound by nor become a prisoner of any manual or code.

Accordingly, we examined the case further. The following main points emerged:

(i) Rail Stress: Track modulus is a term which broadly indicates the strength of the track structure to withstand pressure exerted by a train. This is a function of all that a track structure consists of, such as rail, sleeper, sleeper density, depth of ballast cushion, etc. With a known value of the track modulus, stress of the rail can be calculated for a particular axle load of a train. Greater is track modulus less is rail stress and vice versa. The value of track modulus used in the calculation was derived for 90 lb 72 UTS rail, 150 mm ballast cushion and CST 9 sleepers with N + 4 (1,300 sleepers per km), sleeper density and fish plated joints. We were presently blessed with 60 kg 90 UTS welded rail on 250 mm ballast cushion with mono block concrete sleepers of more than 1,660 sleepers per km. This should have a much higher track modulus, which would have caused much lower rail stress. I was told that although they agreed with me, the value of the track modulus for current modern track structure was not available. So, the old value of track modulus continued to be used.

It was incomprehensible that the value of the track modulus had never been updated. To the questions of why it hadn't, there was no answer. There was only an injured look. It only conveyed that hitherto its necessity was not felt and nobody had asked why. It had obviously served the purpose quite well.

(ii) Combination of stresses in rail in series: Certain factors like thermal stresses and creep were taken into account. There were nine such factors. Their effects were added in an algebraic sum. The overall permissible stress was reduced to that extent. The additional rail stress that the rail could carry was worked out on the basis of the reduced permissible stresses. To illustrate this with an example, we can assume that the overall permissible rail stress is 42 kg/ mm^2; the thermal stresses, etc., 35 kg/ mm^2; then available stress margin in rail was 7 (42-35) kg/mm^2. If the rail stress caused by the additional axle load was less than 7 kg/mm^2; it was fine, otherwise not safe.

Why were effects like thermal and other factors added in the series? They never occurred simultaneously in nature. It was therefore a 'deterministic reduction' in permissible stresses—an unfair and unnatural assumption. Obviously, with such a gross incorrect assumption, it could not carry a higher axle load.

(iii) High stresses in bridges, incompatible with physical condition: The stresses calculated on bridges particularly small arch bridges were found to be much higher. On average, the calculation showed 200 per cent overstress in bridges. The bridge could not be subjected to higher axle load. Even without a high axle load, the overstress was around 140 per cent.

Abutments, according to calculations, were overstressed. It was largely because of the higher horizontal longitudinal forces, which were caused by higher tractive or breaking forces. The calculated high overstress of 140 per cent, even without proposed high axle load should have certainly caused physical distress in the bridge. This had to be examined and corroborated by the actual physical condition of the bridge. Chief engineers were asked to personally inspect one such bridge to identify if there were any physical evidence of overstress in the bridge. They found the bridge to be apparently in a fine condition. One or two locations, reported cracks. I saw them myself. I found that the mortar had leeched out in such locations, which led to an obvious gap in the joints. This was incorrectly construed as a crack.

Thus, the calculated overstress of 140 per cent even without high axle load did not result in any noticeable physical distress in the structure. There could only be two possible alternative explanations. Either the calculation had been done on an incorrect premise or the bridge was not actually subjected to so much of longitudinal forces to cause tensions.

Some possible factors which could have resulted in smaller longitudinal forces could be listed as follows:

- The earth that had been filled behind the abutments was no longer granular material obeying Coulomb's or Rankine's theory. Thus, horizontal earth pressure was lower. In some cases, the earth pressure had to be calculated by also taking cohesion into account.
- The longitudinal forces from tractive or braking forces were not being transferred completely to the structure from the rail table due to ample play between fastenings, which absorbed the forces.
- According to Bridge Rules, the wind load stipulated was too high. Such high wind pressure on an empty stock would cause the offloading of wheels. This was unrealistic.

- The effect of hydrodynamic pressure was on the higher side. In a flowing river, water was not stored around the pier unlike the case of a dam. Thus, the concept of mass of water acting along the pier and exerting a hydrodynamic effect was doubtful and in a probabilistic theory, this could be safely discounted.

The Bridge Rules and other codes had been revised in recent times. According to the revised codes, higher loads and forces were to be taken for the design. The capacity of old structures was being evaluated on the basis of the new codes. Structures built on the basis of earlier codes had not shown any physical distress. These structures were actually physically safe although on theoretical calculations on the basis of new codes these bridges were unsafe. So, there was a basic question about the need to reassess the structural safety of these structures afresh.

Higher axle load is apparently feasible

The analysis convinced us that there was reasonable and good grounds to test heavy axle loads on the existing system. But a decision of this type could not be taken in view of past decisions made by my predecessors. This issue had been examined by the Board for the last twenty-five years at least. There was a note recorded by one ME that said 'not a single ounce could further be added'.

Issues that were in the way of the implementation of the proposal to run heavy axle load wagons were:

- The track stresses calculated on the basis of existing procedures were higher than permissible.
- Existing bridges particularly arch bridges showed an overstress in excess of 200 per cent of the permissible values.
- Some track structures were of 52 kg 72 UTS rail with isolated patches on 90lb rail.
- Existing codes and manuals were the basis of design and evaluation of carrying capacity of existing structures. Unless changed, any other procedure would be arbitrary and unacceptable.
- The CRS—the custodian of rail safety under the Railway Act, 1989 could not permit the running of heavy axle load trains in absence of a safety certificate issued by the CE and chief bridge engineer of the Railways. Unless the extant procedures were dispensed with, safety certificate could not be issued. This was important for safety because all routes on the Indian Railways carried mixed traffic—passenger as well as freight.
- This issue had been examined in the Board earlier—for at least the last

twenty-five years and none of my predecessors had approved the plying of heavy axle freight wagons.

These were serious bottlenecks. Even though heavy haul operation on similar track structure was under operation worldwide, it was not found feasible for the Indian Railways!

A great deal of pressure was being built in the MR's cell on the subject. Sudhir Kumar would often send a note attaching technical literature from abroad. I had to tell the minister very bluntly, 'Sir, it is not possible to run heavy haul train on the basis of some technical literature being put up by your OSD. According to all available codes, procedures and manual, the operation is unsafe. It will not be approved by CRS either. Without this, action would be illegal. In case of an accident, you will find it difficult to deal with it in the Parliament. I would, of course, face prosecution for culpable homicide, not amounting to murder. There is no point in pressurizing me. I have got to find out a way which meets the legal requirement'. Lalu ji started laughing. He appreciated my concern. 'Please ignore, Sudhir ji, and proceed as you deem fit. I would not like an action which was unauthorized', he said.

INTRODUCTION OF HEAVY HAUL—THE PILOT PROJECT

It was thus clear that the operation of heavy haul could not be permitted on the basis of extant rules, code or procedures. It was essential to demonstrate that actual stresses on account of a heavy axle load were actually lower. This called for trial runs. Scientific measurements that could prove that the induced stresses were within safe limits were required.

Recourse to pilot project studies

Apart from instrumentation, the impact of a higher axle load on the physical condition of rails and bridges had to be observed. It was particularly important to observe the behaviour of overstressed bridges. The instrumentation had to be entrusted to renowned institutes like IIT, SERC Chennai and some global ones with a proven record. This would establish the credibility of the test results. I was keen that the idea be accepted by all on its merit. The success of the proposal depended upon the supportive participation of those running heavy haul trains.

The Indian Railways had set up a chair in Roorkee—now IIT for undertaking various studies relating to the Railways. The Railway Board periodically reviewed the projects with them. I told director IIT, Roorkee that the IR was besieged by the problem of calculating rail stresses and evaluating quantum of longitudinal forces actually being transferred to the bridge structure. He fully agreed with my concept and agreed to take up the project. It provided a great deal of support for the heavy haul project.

Decision in principle for higher axle load operation

The 'Rules for Opening of Railways'—framed by the Railway Board under the authority of the Railway Act, 1989—had a provision to allow a trial on a pilot project basis. The Board had the authority to take up the pilot project, and member engineering is the competent authority under the Rules. But it was necessary that the trial should look like a genuine trial. There was, of course, no doubt about the actual intention.

Before the actual decision, the traffic department was asked to identify routes for such trials. As a matter of abundant precaution, heavy haul operation was planned on predominantly freight intensive routes. Heavy density passenger routes were not selected. The member traffic was interested in introducing a heavy haul on iron ore routes as that would fetch maximum revenue earnings. It was interesting to note to achieve the full carrying capacity in an open BOXN wagon; only minerals like iron and manganese ore, which have high density, could be loaded. CC + 10 loading meant 90 plus tonne. On this basis, routes were identified. A detailed survey was done of these routes to quickly assess track structures including bridges. Chief engineers were taken into confidence. Their involvement was therefore complete.

Cardinal decisions in heavy axle load operation

Thus, we had taken the following decision in respect of heavy haul operation on the Indian Railways:

1. Heavy axle load of 23 ton which in effect was approximately CC+10 loading would be introduced on selected routes of the IR on the existing track with the existing rolling stocks with a maximum speed of 70 kmph as a 'pilot project'.
2. During the trial, instrumentation would be carried out on suspect bridges to actually measure stresses to validate the assumption that bridges were safe for heavy haul operation.
3. The RDSO would measure rail stress on track with WILD instrument. With actual rail stress measured, it would be possible to work out track modulus through the extrapolation principle. With the revised track modulus, the calculation procedure of rail stress could be revised.
4. During the period of trial, there would be intensive supervision of

track, rolling stocks and bridges to detect any undue or unfavourable behaviour of the track or bridges. Extensive test by ultrasonic flaw detector would be carried out at close frequency to detect any tendency of rail fracture.
5. The pilot project would earn huge revenue because the freight would be charged on the basis of higher carrying capacity of wagons.
6. It was also decided that there would be a seminar to review the results of the trial after three months to evaluate the effect of heavy haul operation. The idea was that in the unlikely event of setting in of a distressed condition, the project could be reviewed and halted.

Board is briefed—concerns of members addressed

Before notifying them about the decision, I brought the subject before the Board. I was keen that the full Board be taken into confidence about the plan. Mr Varshney, MS, had been the executive director (standards) in the RDSO for a long time. He cautioned me against the dangerous proposal. According to him, bridges would be the worst victim. He feared plastic failure in rails. Ms Vijaya Lakshmi, the financial commissioner, was concerned about the likely premature rail renewal due to overstressing which would increase the burden on the Depreciation Reserve Fund.

All other members complimented me for this unprecedented decision. I assured the members by saying, 'If bridges had crumbled after the running of the first train, I would agree that the decision was foolhardy. But it was not so. According to calculations, the bridge had already been overstressed two times over. But they are in service without any problem. There was no evidence of any overstress. Likewise, the rail stress calculation was itself faulty. We have moved away from the "deterministic model" to a more scientific model known as the "probabilistic model". It was true that the rail would carry heavier loads. It might reach fatigue level earlier than that in the conventional approach. This could call for early renewal. But the revenue earning from the heavy haul operation would be quite high—upward of ₹5,000 crore annually—and I may have to spend about ₹200 crore additionally. That, such an eventuality would actually happen, is also not certain. Overall, it would undoubtedly make for a sound business approach.' There was no further dissent and the Board took note of the proposal.

The pilot project notified and introduced

Thereafter the proposal was notified on 5 May 2005—approximately two months after we had initially discussed it in the Board on 4 March. By any standard, this was a momentous decision. It took everyone by storm. In less than two months, we had crossed the highest peak in the history of the Indian Railways. A feat which had defied a solution for over twenty-five years had been achieved for the good of the IR. This had been done in a systematic manner. Everyone thought that this decision was long overdue. But unfortunately, those entrusted with the decision-making process were stumped by the extant codal provisions.

Probabilistic model in place of a deterministic one

We in the team had decided to challenge those assumptions and had successfully steered out of the classical mould of 'deterministic approach'. It was a paradigm shift. We had given up the philosophy of 'go-no go' as contained in a deterministic model. Instead we had reiterated that maximum stress had a range rather than a definite value. There was thus no need to add the effect of all the factors in an algebraic sum. This was not an arbitrary approach but was an accepted philosophy in dealing with wind and earthquake forces. There were some other considerations also. The test results on the rails supplied by SAIL had revealed that tested UTS of rail was never less than 95 kg/mm^2 instead of the stipulated 90 kg/mm^2. This was an available bonus.

It was essential for us to remember that we were in a commercial venture. From that point of view, there was nothing wrong if we had shown our keen business acumen and exploited the value of an asset without entering into a risky area. This was certainly an entrepreneurial exercise. We were definitely guided by good engineering practice. We were keen observers who noted the physical evidence of safe and sound behaviour of structures. We were not guided merely by theoretical calculations.

The traffic department was quite eager to introduce the project in some other sections as well, but I asked them to have patience and exercise caution. Many engineering friends were quite sceptical. They called this a Himalayan blunder. I am glad that my advice of caution was accepted. I cannot forget an instance of dedication of a mechanical engineer of the South Western Railway. On an inspection, he suspected a case of overloading in a particular CC+10 freight train. He chased the train by road and got it stopped in the territory of South-Central Railway. He got the overloaded wagon detached. Apart from the heroics, it showed commitment as the train was stopped in another adjoining railway. This was an event previously unheard of. It showed the measure of respect an engineer was able to command. I had taken up the case of some overloading in the South Eastern Railway. I was very happy that not only the member traffic but also the MR personally wrote to all the GMs to ensure utmost care and to personally monitor the trains.

A strong action to send positive intent of the Railway Board

In this context, I must relate an incident which though looked ordinary to me, was important to uphold all those who were committed to lend their wholehearted support to the introduction of heavy haul operation.

I was told by Mr Sharma, principal chief engineer (PCE) of NWR on a Sunday about how an AEN was suspended by the GM on instructions from the CRB due to a derailment caused by a rail fracture. I was surprised because I was not consulted and even the PCE did not tell me earlier. He told me that this section was renewed only four months ago and new 60 kg rail was provided. Now any new rail before being put is tested by ultrasonic flaw detector (USFD) by the steel plant as well as by the RITES who are the inspecting authority of rails supplied by SAIL. It was, therefore, very unlikely that a fracture would take place unless there was any inherent flaw in the rail steel at the stage of manufacturing. In any case, the AEN could not be held responsible. Although this section was not on a heavy haul route, such an action could easily send a wrong message to so many involved in the operation. This had to be prevented at all costs. As soon as I had arrived in the office on Monday, I sent a strong note to the MR explaining the position and I requested that the action taken against the AEN should be revoked by the end of the day. I stated that otherwise I would have to withdraw the heavy haul operation because I would have failed to protect my men from punitive action. Xavier was little hesitant and advised me to reconsider but I told him to send the note. I called Satish Agnihotri to go and tell the OSD, Sudhir Kumar, about how upset I was. He told Agnihotri that he would get the revocation done as soon as possible. I then called Vinay Agarwal, MD RITES, and Roongata, CMD SAIL and told them to thoroughly investigate it. They took immediate action and in the next 3-4 days confirmed that there was indeed a flaw that had escaped notice. The suspension order of the AEN was revoked by the afternoon. This was a positive message which was very important for the project on which the fortunes of the IR rested.

Review of the project under the IIPWE

After three months of operation, the first review was held in August 2005 under the aegis of Indian Institution of Permanent Way Engineers (IIPWE) where all the disciplines—engineering, mechanical, electrical, S&T and the traffic department of all railways where the pilot project had been tested—participated. Each railway—ER, SER, East Coast, SWR, SCR and SR—presented the results of their test and the physical behaviour of rails, bridges, rolling stocks and their effects on braking distances. The RDSO also presented their observations. There was no adverse report except for an initial increase in number of rail fractures. It was obviously due to comprehensive reporting. Consequently, there was no indication either during the physical observation or by the USFD testing of any abnormal increase in rail fractures. The test done by the RDSO with the help of WILD also showed as expected much higher value of track modulus.

The bridges had no adverse feature although more testing was in progress. Even retired engineers complimented us and agreed that the initial trial results were quite encouraging. The review led to the safe conclusion that the assumptions made during the introduction of heavy haul were established and validated. But as a measure of abundant precautions, the need to continue the trials and to complete ongoing tests was stressed. This would also give them a better idea of rail behaviour in the beginning of winter in November 2005 when the rails were more prone to fracture. We accordingly called for another review in December 2005.

Chief commissioner of railway safety—his concerns addressed

Chief Commissioner of Railway Safety G.P. Garg was however upset. He felt that the Board should have obtained the Commission's clearance for the trial. I called him for a meeting at the Board. The entire modality of the pilot project was explained to him. He was also briefed about the test results. The Railway Board had the authority to conduct pilot projects under the 'Rules for opening of Railways'. There was no breach in procedure as the ME was vested with the full power under the Railway Act. He however advised that the consent of commissioners of rail safety was desirable. The Board agreed to approach the CRS for sanctions. It was obtained without any difficulty for regular operation in view of favourable test results.

The IR joins world's heavy haul club

The stand on heavy haul was thus formally vindicated. It was a red-letter day for the IR because it had finally joined the club of heavy haul operators in world railways. In effect, the following broad objectives were achieved with regard to the heavy haul pilot project:

- Carrying capacity of 8-wheeler covered wagons (BCN) was increased by 6 tons (CC + 6) for all seasons.
- The carrying capacity of BOXN wagons was raised by 10 tons (CC +10) on iron ore routes. This effectively increased the axle load to 23 ton approximately. This was done for the first time.

- The carrying capacity of the container flat wagons was raised by about 8 tons. This increased the axle load to 20 ton approximately.

THE PRIDE AND GLORY OF ENGINEERS REDEEMED

The minister records appreciation of the historic event

A note was sent to the MR, highlighting the achievement in a routine report. I found a note from him which I could find time to see only at the end of the day when I was about to leave my office for the day. I was surprised to read it. I passed it on to Satish Agnihotri, my OSD.

> I must put on record my appreciation for the bold decisions taken by ME, Shri R.R. Jaruhar and his team of officers. Shri Jaruhar has achieved in [a] few months what Indian Railways were trying to achieve over 20-25 years. I hope we would see many more such innovative initiatives in the days to come.
>
> Sd. Lalu Prasad
> 01.08.05
> Minister of Railways

More important than appreciation was the acknowledgement by the minister, confirming that we had a new page in the history of the Indian Railways. It was a historic event and could be rightly called the third chapter in the history of the Indian Railways. The IR had emerged out of its own shadow to bring not only laurels for itself but it also played a role in the turnaround of the Indian economy. It was my proud privilege to be a leader of the team which had ushered the Railways into a position of glory and strength.

There was no looking back from there. The next review held in November 2005 only confirmed the earlier findings. The pilot project was however further extended up to July 2006 in order to conclude instrumentation work. But the heavy haul was extended to other railways also. From an ordinary train load of 3,700 ton the heavy haul train would carry 5,300 ton and plus. The profit that went to the Railways was high. The unit cost of transportation had gone down. Thus, the yield in crores of rupees per million ton was much higher. It solved the problem of a shortage of rolling stocks—freight wagons and locomotives, availability of paths on the busy traffic corridors and shortage of running staff like drivers and guards.

We look ahead—introduce 25-ton axle load

Encouraged by the success of 23-ton axle load operation, we announced our intention to run 25-ton axle load on the selected iron ore route of Dallirajhara to Bhilai Steel Plant on the South East Central Railway. This was for transporting iron ore to the steel plant at Bhilai. Some repair and the ongoing track renewal work had to be completed. One major bridge had to be tested. The special dedicated hopper rakes had to be strengthened and modified from vacuum brakes to air brake system. It took about eight months. But it was really satisfying when we finished making all the groundwork for 25-ton axle load operation. The Heavy Haul Club in the world railways had a minimum of 23-ton axle load operation. We were keen to go ahead. Although many railway systems had axle load upwards of 29 ton to 32.50 ton, these were all dedicated rail system for freight operation unlike the mixed traffic system of the Indian Railways. The introduction of the 23-ton axle load was thus commended by all as the most innovative initiative.

The Parliament applauds contribution of engineers

When the Rail Budget for 2006-07 was being prepared, the MR asked me if I wished to add something about the Railways' performance during 2005-06. I requested that he make a special mention of it in his Budget speech. He readily agreed and asked me to send a draft para accordingly. I would like to quote from his speech.

The excerpts from the Budget Speech of Lalu Prasad, MR, in the Lok Sabha while presenting the Rail Budget 2006-07:

> Record Breaking Output in Freight Business
>
> (21) In the current year, we are fast moving towards establishing a new record of loading 668 million tonnes, with a historic growth of 11%. This is the second consecutive year when we have increased our market share with growth rate higher than the growth rate of economy. This record-breaking performance has been possible through reduction in wagon turnaround time and through additional loading of 4 to 8 tonnes per wagon. This has enabled an increase of 100 million tonnes in our loading capacity and the generation of over ₹5000 crores in freight revenues. This is the foundation of our financial turnaround.
>
> (22) With the increase of just 1 tonne in the loading capacity of a wagon, our annual loading capacity is up by about 1 crore tonnes. In the last two years, we have increased the loading capacity of key wagons by 4 tonnes per wagon enhancing the Railways' annual loading capacity by 4

crore tonnes. Further, by starting 23 tonne axle load BOXN freight trains on identified routes, we have made our presence amongst the few countries which run heavy axle load trains. I would like to congratulate the entire railway family and particularly the civil and mechanical engineers for their historic achievement. Sir, due to these historic policy decisions, the unit cost of our freight traffic in the current year is lower than in 2001 not only on constant but also on current prices. Despite a heavy increase in diesel prices and additional burden of thousands of crores of rupees on account of salaries and pension, Railways have managed to reduce their unit cost, which is a historic achievement. In a competitive environment, one can be successful only by sharing the benefits of reduction in per unit cost with customers. This is what we have done.

(23) Sir, I am happy to inform the House that it has been decided to run 25 tonne axle load trains on two routes, for the first time in the Indian sub-continent, in the coming year, as a pilot project. These primarily non-passenger routes are Dallirajhara to Bhillai and Daitari to Banspani. Next year after taking stock, 23 and 22.3 tonne axle load trains will be introduced on important traffic routes, in a phased manner. Simultaneously, over the next five years, the feeder routes to the new freight corridors will be strengthened to make them fit for 25 tonne axle loads.

I was listening to the speech sitting in official gallery of the Parliament. Lalu ji, while reading this part of the speech, looked towards me. At that moment the entire House thumped the desk to accord their approval. That was the moment we had been waiting for!

I redeem my pledge—lead to earn back the pristine glory for engineers

While speaking to the IRSE forum at IRICEN in Pune later, I told the engineers about what V.C. Sharma had asked me to do to redeem the pride of the engineers. Not only the MR, but the entire House had acknowledged the contributions of the engineers towards the IR's turnaround. All the engineers should be justly proud of the appreciation and honour bestowed upon them by the nation. That must be the crowning glory of the engineering fraternity. It was redemption. But it had to be accepted with humility. We should re-dedicate our commitment to the IR, which has given us our place of pride. I was happy to lead the team with passion and commitment and a sense of fulfilment; I was happy to fulfil his wish and thus redeem the faith reposed on me. Thank you, Vipin!

RUNNING OF INDIA'S FIRST HIGH SPEED TRAIN

Another project in my mind was the running of a high-speed passenger train between Delhi and Agra at a speed of 150 kmph. I was associated with this project from the time I was chief engineer (TMC), Northern Railway. It was then decided to run this train between Kanpur and Delhi.

It was subsequently decided that the project be taken up between New Delhi and Agra. Nitish Kumar had announced the project in the 2004 Rail Budget. I was the project leader as GM, Northern Railway. Field trials were completed by February 2005. The CCRS had however expressed some serious concerns. He insisted upon fencing of railway tracks on both sides to prevent trespassing particularly by cattle. A large number of cases of trespassing by wild neel cows were reported in some stretches. We had considered this aspect but we could not overlook the problems villagers would have to face if both sides of the tracks were to be fenced. There was habitation on both sides of the track and villagers had to cross the track routinely. But we agreed to fence a selected location which had evidence on record of more rampant trespassing.

We carried out the final full-scale trials on 2 March 2005 at a speed of 160 kmph the day after I joined as ME. On the ABB locomotive cab, we felt the running was smooth at 160 kmph. It was not possible to feel the speed of the train except by the sight of the trees zooming past. Quite clearly, for speeds beyond 200 kmph, train control based on human faculty alone is not safe. It required specific routes to be fitted with automatic train control like the ETCS.

We were, however, keen that the Indian Railways broke the barrier of 150 kmph and could be counted in the group of high-speed passenger operating railways in the world. We had cleared the proposal, but the CRB, R. K. Singh, held up the file. He had no role in this. The file was put up for his information only. The European companies were advocating for ETCS in the Indian Railways. They had warned that high speed operation without the ETCS was hazardous. He collected adverse reports from the UIC who advised that the project be shelved. I was surprised because he had been fully involved in the decision-making process. However, I did not want to force the issue. Although it was only symbolic, the high-speed train was important from the IR's point of view.

After successful introduction of heavy haul, I pursued the subject afresh. Accordingly, the high-speed train was formally flagged off from New Delhi station on 15 February 2006. The train 2002/2001 New Delhi-Bhopal *Shatabdi Express*, with improved LHB coaches covered a distance of 196 km between Delhi and Agra in one hour and fifty-four minutes. The train ran at the maximum speed of 150 kmph. The minister mentioned this in his budget speech. The project was implemented by relying upon available resources and appropriately harnessing the existing skill and technology. This made engineers confident.

CHAIRMAN RAILWAY BOARD—JUSTICE DENIED

The time was coming to find a suitable replacement for R.K. Singh after his retirement on 31 July 2005. From the standpoint of extant rules, I was the most suitable and eligible candidate.

Minister said, 'Please keep in touch'

R.K. Singh told me that the MR seemed to be well disposed towards me and he saw no problem this time around. After a meeting at his residence, the MR told me that he regretted all that had happened the last time. He was impressed with my ability. He wanted me as the CRB after R.K. Singh retired. He said, 'Please keep in touch.' I failed to appreciate the import of his remark and foolishly replied, 'Sir, of course. I am your *secretary* in the ministry. I therefore normally meet you every day when you are in Delhi.' I believed all along that according to the rules, I would be posted as the next chairman. I was also reassured by the Cabinet secretary and the PMO. All the RJD MPs wished to see me as the first chairman from Bihar.

So, I did not do anything extraordinary during the period to promote my case. I was totally engrossed in implementing heavy haul operation on the IR till May 2005 and thereafter, battling and defending the decision. R.S. Varshney once mentioned that the MR had reassured him that he would be the next chairman. That was sometime in late June 2005. The minister had openly stated so many times that he was unhappy with Mr Varshney. Once, the MR had also told me about it. I asked R.K. Singh, about it. He however confirmed that Varshney had succeeded in persuading the MR to appoint him as the CRB. I was simply disgusted.

Varshney was so confident of his appointment that he went away to the US for a holiday, for fifteen days. According to him, he had spoken to the MR on phone as late as 15 July 2005 and the MR had told him that he saw no problem. As for me, I was chucked out simply because I did not 'keep in touch' with the minister!

What a travesty of justice!

But something more was to happen. J.P. Batra was also in the fray, in the absence of Varshney. Batra was GM, East Central Railway, Hajipur. According to R.K. Singh, it was disgusting the way Batra had applied pressure through the wife of the MR. I suggested that he should put forward the case with all the rules, position according to which I was the most eligible. He started laughing and said that nobody talked of any rule before the MR. The only argument advanced by Batra was that his case was similar to that of R.K. Singh. Both had a tenure of two years. There was no mention that a serving member with more than one year of residual service as the CRB was the first choice according to the Government Resolution 1987. What a travesty of justice!

The proposal was sent to the Cabinet secretary on 10 July. I was hopeful that the Cabinet secretary would certainly put his foot down. A close friend had offered to take me to the highest level in the government. I told him that even if I succeeded with his help, it would not be possible for me to work under a minister whose confidence I did not enjoy. So, I went away to South Central Railway (SCR), Secunderabad. In the evening of 15 July 2005, as I was getting ready to attend a cultural programme in the Railway Club, I got a call that the Cabinet secretary had cleared the proposal of J.P. Batra as proposed by the Ministry of Railways without raising a query or objection about my claim. It was curtains!

I could not beg—Batra posted as chairman

I walked out of my room in the officers' rest house to join the function. I enjoyed the evening thoroughly; it was as if nothing had happened at all. I mentioned it to Satish Agnihotri much later. He was deeply distressed and disappointed. *I had the good fortune of perception* to realize that I should not ask for something from someone who continuously sought favour from others. I should not be begging. I could not ask this from God who had already given me so much. I was in dire need of His blessings for my family. It would have been a selfish act if I asked more for myself. In any case, He must have known my wish. If He had decided against it then it had to have divine justification and it must be for my ultimate good!

In due course, J.P. Batra was posted as the chairman after R.K. Singh retired on 31 July 2005. Batra very kindly came to my room to seek my guidance and support. He was very emotional. He told me how everything had happened however, I had no regrets. I very honestly reassured him that he would receive my fullest support. I had kept my promise. To be fair he had reciprocated in full measure. He gave me the regard and respect for which I am very thankful to him.

I follow my destiny

I distinctly recall how upset my wife was. Normally she never said anything about my official business and she said nothing now. It was understandable. I might have looked for some sympathy but only momentarily. But nobody came to offer his shoulder for me to cry on either. I could fortunately overcome my frustration in a short time. I briskly moved forward in my mission. The two of us also decided that we need not be part of any social activity. We withdrew from them without regrets. Except for personal invitations for weddings and similar occasions my wife and I did not participate in railway functions. It in no way affected my official functioning.

GO FOR THE MISSION AHEAD

It was essential for the Indian Railways to analyse its weakness and accordingly list its priorities. The introduction of heavy haul was a temporary reprieve. It allowed the IR to load additional traffic in the existing train formation. This had given them the advantage of augmenting its productivity by lowering the unit cost of transportation. It had also allowed additional path to carry more trains. But in order to sustain the growth rate, it had to expand and strengthen its network—particularly the Golden Quadrilateral and Diagonals.

Bigger mission—evolving a long-term strategy

We proposed the following step-by-step measures to achieve this objective:

- Remove traffic bottlenecks
  Some yard layouts impeded free traffic movement. Such impediments had to be identified and had to be removed under 'Traffic Facilities' which had been planned ahead to be completed in two years' time. This would improve wagon turnaround immediately by cutting down terminal handlings.
- Remove speed restrictions
  Temporary speed restrictions regarding force were reviewed route wise. The idea was to rationalize restrictions in proper sequence to provide adequate stretch of restriction free track for the train to be able to pick up sectional speed. It was also ensured that after removal of restrictions, the normal saving in time should result in reduction in running time. The MT bravely agreed for zero-based time tabling. It was a concept based on a realistic record of the time taken by a train to cover a section.

  Permanent restrictions in force were also reviewed. Budget was provided to remove infirmities wherever possible. Removal of permanent restrictions was a heroic decision to improve sectional capacity.
- Identify alternative routes

The gauge conversion and doubling work improved route sectional capacity. Through a scientific study alternative traffic routes were identified. This called for the gauge conversion of selected routes and to connect new lines. Gauge conversion of Bhildi Samdi in the NWR is an example. It opened an alternative route to Kandla Port from Punjab and Northern India. The Railways' Capital Fund was resurrected for this purpose. The Capital Fund was credited from the large revenue surplus earned during 2005-06.

Likewise, doubling work was also identified along with electrification to remove bottlenecks caused by change of traction. Doubling along with the electrification of Mughalsarai-Lucknow-Moradabad-Ludhiana section is an example. Under this initiative, a third line or proposal for quadrupling was also taken up in order to strengthen the existing routes. Haldia Kharagpur third line was such a proposal.

- Create core infrastructure by expanding the network

The IR had to eventually move away from mixed traffic routes to dedicated freight corridors. That is how the concept of a dedicated freight corridor was evolved. As a nascent idea, it was talked about for long. Its time had perhaps come now. The idea was rapidly converted in to a bold initiative by sheer accident!

EMERGENCE OF A DEDICATED FREIGHT CORRIDOR

Sometime in early July 2005, a meeting was called by Mr Nair, PPS to the PM, to discuss an investment proposal in the wake of an ensuing visit by the Japanese prime minister to Delhi. The buzz was that Japan was keen to invest in India in a big way. I was asked to attend the meeting from the Ministry of Railways.

The meeting was called at a short notice. In our internal discussion, the Board had decided to emphasize freight business in light of the large-scale emerging growth in the Indian economy. Particularly the core industrial sectors like power, cement, steel and fertilizer were in a phenomenal growth mode. The Indian Railways had to construct a dedicated freight corridor to move away from the regime of being a mixed traffic route. We thought that it was an opportune moment to undertake a large investment in two freight corridors—the Western Corridor comprising Jawaharlal Nehru Port Trust (JNPT) near Mumbai and Delhi via Surat, Vadodara and the Eastern Corridor comprising Sonenagar-Mughalsarai-Allahabad-Khurja-Ludhiana. For the meeting, we worked out a rough cost of approximately ₹30,000 crore for the two sectors. I took a small one-page note to the meeting.

Mr Nair in his talk outlined the Japanese interest in a large infrastructural project calling for an investment of the order of ₹20,000 to ₹30,000 crore. No department came forward to avail the opportunity. The Ministry of Finance had serious reservations regarding the STEP (special terms of economic participation) loan proposed by the Japanese. They said that such terms had not been accepted earlier from Germany and other countries and thus it would set dangerous precedence. Mr Nair told the joint secretary (East) in the Ministry of External Affairs that the Japanese offer had apparently no takers and he must convey this to the Japanese delegation accordingly. I had kept quiet till then. I then talked of the need for dedicated freight corridors for the IR. I outlined the concept and explained how the project could take the IR on a path of high growth. I passed on the note to Mr Nair. He was immensely interested. It was something that they had been looking forward to. He asked JS (East) Ashok Kanth to take up the proposal with the Japanese delegation.

Japanese accept the scheme for funding

Ashok Kantha, JS (East), informed me in the evening that the Japanese delegation had accepted the proposal for funding. The proposal caught everyone's attention. The PM, in his address to the nation on 15 August 2005, from ramparts of the Red Fort announced that the project would be taken up with Japanese aid.

DFC PROJECT ANNOUNCED

The project started as a concept purely on an estimate. But we had a far-sighted vision for growth of the Indian Railways. It had come as fast as a bolt.

The ME is in charge of all projects from the stage of planning. I had therefore, taken it up with passion. Ghosh Dastidar, MT, was passionate about the scheme. It has been his dream as a young traffic officer to build an exclusive freight corridor. Thus, there was great urgency. Buoyed by the sterling performance of the IR, everyone was keen to support the Railways in this direction.

The following were required for the formal sanction of the project for each corridor:

- Detailed Project Report: This required preliminary engineering and traffic survey, based on which the final alignment was to be selected. Based on this, traffic projections, return on investment and project cost had to be worked out.
- The Financing Model: Design of a suitable financing model to execute the

project The Japanese aid was limited to around ₹11,000 crore. Thus, the gap between the project cost and the Japanese aid had to be bridged. The funding model had to be designed accordingly.
- Executing Mode: A special purpose vehicle (SPV) to execute the project. The structure and source of revenue had to be identified to discharge debts.

GETTING INTO SPECIFICS OF THE PROJECT

It was a stupendous task but we started speedily. A quick engineering field survey to fix the alignment was essential. The cost could be worked out on the basis of preliminary survey report. After the PM's announcement, we had only five months to place the proposal before the Parliament in the Railway Budget 2006.

The DFC approved by the Cabinet

The Cabinet note for the proposal had to be brought before CCEA, latest by 15 February 2006. The proposal had to be included in the Railway Budget to be placed in the Parliament on 24 February 2006. The project was estimated to cost ₹30,000 crore. According to the broad financing outline, ₹15,000 crore could be raised in the course of the project period of five years from the Railways' internal resources, which could easily yield ₹3,000 crore per annum. The balance could be raised by market borrowing. The mechanics and quantum of Japanese aid was yet to be finalized. The aid as and when finalized could become part of market borrowings. According to discussions with the Japanese delegation, ₹10,000 crore might come from Japan. The balance could be easily raised from the market since the project was financially viable.

This was considered a satisfactory financing model. The internal annual generation of the IR was around ₹12,000 crore. There was no doubt about the capacity of the IR to manage the finances for such a prestigious project. A SPV was planned—'Dedicated Freight Corridor Company, a PSU under the Ministry of Railways'. The CCEA approved the proposal in its special sitting on 21 February 2006. The project was included in the Pink Book of the budget proposal. It was placed in the Parliament with a token provision of ₹60 crore. This was duly passed by the Parliament but not before an uproarious scene was created by the Left Front MP from West Bengal. They wanted the Eastern Corridor to come to Howrah.

Concern of the Left Front MP addressed

P. Chidambaram, the then finance minister, was worried due to the possible repercussion of this incident in his budget due in three days. I explained to the MPs that Howrah had never been a freight terminal and hence the DFC could not go to Howrah. They saw the point. Both Kolkata and Haldia ports had limited capacity. To assuage the feelings of West Bengal particularly the Left MPs who were part of the UPA, the Central government agreed to develop either Haldia or a new port near Kolkata under the 'Look East Policy' of the government. This would be connected to Dankuni which was the freight terminal.

Basic philosophy and the technical model

Freight corridors were basically planned to collect traffic from feeder routes joining two ends of the respective corridor. For instance, the Eastern Corridor would receive traffic from Patratu-Garhwa, Asansol-Dhanbad section and Garhwa-Renukoot belts as the principal feeder routes converging at Sonenagar. That was why Sonenagar was the starting point of the corridor.

The feeder routes were important but were not exclusively for freight traffic. They had to be upgraded for 25-ton axle load operation, which could be safely carried out on the track structure consisting of 60 kg 90 UTS rail on mono block pre-stressed concrete sleepers of 1,670 per km and 250 mm ballast cushion. I had insisted in the Board meeting that it was high time that the new generation of freight wagons with a higher pay load should be developed. It would then be possible to reduce the axle load to not more than 30 ton.

PROMISE OF LEADING DFC

I am asked to lead DFC

When things moved forward, the minister called me to his room where the CRB was also present. He told me, 'Jaruhar Sahib, you have done so much and I am convinced that without you the DFC project cannot be completed. You should take full charge and when you retire you will head the DFC Company, which is being set up for this purpose.'

Sudhir Kumar said that they had consulted others also and the MR was fully convinced that there could not be any other person more suitable than I to head this project.

He told the MR, 'Sir, all say that Mr Jaruhar can do better than Sreedharan,

MD of the Delhi Metro. Sir, I will request that Jaruhar Sahib should be given all powers and a completely free hand so that he can deliver the project in five years' time.

Lalu ji nodded in complete agreement and said, 'I know you can do much better than Sreedharan. You should start immediately and see that everything is done at a fast pace.'

I replied, 'Thank you, Sir, for placing your full confidence in me. But I have one small suggestion, I should be appointed as the CMD (chairman and managing director) of the company which is as per the guidelines of the Bureau of Public Enterprise (BPE). I am a very senior person. As you know, all the chairmen Railway Board will be much junior to me.'

He immediately agreed. I said that I could now proceed to form my own team. As ME was part of the Board I could organize a team easily. I decided to set up a core group, which would start working immediately under my guidance till my retirement, seven months later. When the company was finally formed, the core group would merge with the company. J.P. Batra and I came out of the room. I told him that I would deal with the entire case as decided by the minister. He nodded but looked very grave. I could not interpret his demeanour immediately and was puzzled. Well, I could not understand or explain it at the time.

Intentions were however different

But it soon became clear that the actual intention was unlike what I had expected despite the MR telling me to lead the DFC. Gradually the files stopped coming to me. I was not consulted on vital issues of financing, project clearance or even on the SPV formation. I asked the CRB about it. He smiled and told me that the MR was having second thoughts. Even Sudhir Kumar looked embarrassed. Evidently, a lobby was in operation against me.

According to my nature, I thought it wise to be aloof. I however told the minister, 'You had asked me to be the CMD of DFC Company, but unfortunately I am not being consulted anymore.' He said that he was very unhappy and abused all the people concerned including the CRB. He told me that this work was to be done by me. But that was the end of it. No further communication took place on this subject. It was the classic manner in which one disposed of a person. The hint was obvious.

Railways' case before a GoM

Soon a group of ministers (GoM) headed by the finance minister was constituted to decide the final financial structure of the SPV for the Cabinet's approval. A big group advocated a public-private participation (PPP) model for the project. The meeting was called on 9 August 2006. Shrimant was going away to the US for his graduation on the 8th. I had taken a day's casual leave to be with him. The CRB called me late in the evening about the GoM meeting. He desperately wanted me to present the Railways' case before the GoM. I was annoyed because I had not been taken into confidence about the meeting. I however agreed to come for the meeting. In our internal meeting, I spoke about my displeasure to Batra.

During the GoM's meeting, Deputy Chairman Planning Commission Montek Singh Ahluwalia strongly advocated for the adoption of the PPP model for the DFC. The entire discussion took that direction. The discussion seemed to be drifting elsewhere when I spoke with the permission of the chair. I explained that the IR was able to carry the present growth in traffic only because of the recently introduced heavy haul operation. This was a short-term measure which would take care of the Indian economy till 2007-08. Beyond this, the IR was bound to hit a plateau unless additional line capacity was urgently created. The PPP route was bound to take much more time to reach financial closure. The DFC should be immediately in position to build additional lines. According to current projections, an additional traffic demand of 60 million ton would accrue annually beyond 2009, which the IR would not be in a position to carry. Taking an average yield of ₹55 crore per million ton, the loss of opportunity cost to the Railways would be roughly ₹3,300 crore annually. More importantly, in the PPP model, the IR would have to share its revenue earnings from its most profitable route. This would seriously impact the financial health of the IR. The short brief went very well. The finance minister, who was in the chair, observed that the IR should clearly go ahead with the work by gathering its own resources, as well as by market borrowing as extra budgetary resource.

I am dumped—no room for me

The railway ministry was asked to rework its proposal for the next GoM to be held after a week. Everyone had appreciated my presentation. Lalu ji was particularly happy. But the revised proposal never came to me. I was not even invited to the GoM. When asked, the CRB, very sheepishly, told me that the meeting was being held in the minister's room. Many others had been invited from different ministries. For lack of space, it was decided that only the CRB and the FC should attend this meeting. How preposterous was that? There was no space in the minister's room for a secretary of the Government of India! It was insolent by any standard. Till date, the lack of space has remained as a great enigma.

There was no further association with the project. Soon after I retired, there was an advertisement for the post of managing director. My friends asked me to apply for it but I declined. That was the end of the DFC for me. Today when I see that the project has still not started, I feel sorry for the Indian Railways.

CADRE REVIEW AND RESTRUCTURING

There were two important issues affecting the cadre of the engineering department. One was related to the engineering gangs and another, related to its officers.

New gang strength formula

A new formula to determine a gang's strength by the Gopalakrishnan Committee was kept on hold for a long time. The old formula had to be revised in view of large-scale mechanization of track maintenance. The Railway Board had set up a committee of experts in 1996 to recommend a new formula. After long deliberations of over eight years, the committee had finally submitted its report for acceptance to the Board.

For more than two years, the report travelled from one desk to another in the Railway Board without any decision being taken. My predecessor, S.P.S. Jain, had tried his best but according to him the FC was adamant in her views.

I went to Vijaya Lakshmi, FC. She told me that my predecessor was not prepared to listen. There was no meeting ground. I told her, 'Look Vijaya Lakshmi, this report has been prepared by some excellent civil engineers and finance officers. I respect them for their knowledge and experience. You will also agree with me in this respect. It will be grossly unfair if we decide to change the entire report. Yes, some minor adjustments and modifications suggested by you, have merit. You and I are the highest levels of decision-making authority in the Railways. It is our job and responsibility to finally decide on an issue. We cannot pass the buck further.' She smiled and said, 'You have said it. We have to decide and there is no other way. You have made the difference by admitting that some suggestions could be re-examined at your level. I agree and accept that whatever you decide on the technical matter I will go by that.' That was it.

EDCE (G) Promod Kumar and ED Finance Anup Prasad (he rose to be FC) examined the suggestions that have merit. Their effect was marginal. Both were pragmatic and methodical. The FC's suggestions were incorporated into the formula. The new gang strength formula that had been hanging in suspension for more than ten years was approved in two months' time. The FC cleared it just before she retired. I was called in, to her farewell meeting. She paid an eloquent tribute to me and mentioned how different I was in my approach.

Modern protective uniform for gangmen

The engineering gangmen needed modern protective gear and equipment for duty. This called for a change in the standard dress regulation. This issue had remained unresolved for long. The protective gear and outfit of the gangmen was inadequate. The new outfit would have cost ₹4 crore more. The IR had earned a record surplus. We owed it to the gangmen who had discharged the most arduous duty under all climatic conditions.

I once travelled with the MR from Patna to Barauni while conducting a window trailing inspection. It was a very hot afternoon. Gangmen were out for hot weather patrolling. I explained to the minister what the gang was doing. I told him about their difficult and demanding job. Its importance was immense for the safety. They were engaged in doing their rounds of cold weather patrolling and monsoon patrolling as well. The minister was very impressed. I told him that I wanted them to be properly equipped. This would cost ₹4 crore more but the Board Finance had some reservations about it. He said that he fully agreed with me.

He called some gangmen to the Rail Bhawan on his return. He saw their dress and personally enquired if they were comfortable. He immediately agreed with my suggestion to form a committee to suggest revised norms and standard of equipment. The whole thing was decided in a month's time.

I quote from the Budget speech of Lalu Prasad ji on 24 February 2006 in the Parliament, where he announced these staff welfare measures: 'Sir, gangmen and keymen maintain track in difficult conditions. I myself have seen them working in adverse conditions like severe summer and biting cold. Therefore, for about one lakh such employees, I have decided to make available quality shoes, socks, gloves, summer/winter uniforms and necessary implements.'

There was loud applause from all sections of the house on hearing his announcement. It brought a great deal of satisfaction amongst the gangmen and the union. The MR was very enthusiastic and whenever he went out, he made it a point to check if proper uniforms were being issued to the gangs.

Cadre restructuring of the IRSE

The cadre restructuring of Civil Engineering in the wake of the Fifth Pay Commission recommendations, was another issue that had affected the career prospects of officers. The government had decided to review the cadre structure with a view to minimize inter-service disparity in promotion, which had affected the morale of the officers.

The general idea was to make advancement uniform across all levels. A person having joined a particular cadre should expect to reach the level of joint secretary (JS) in 18-20 years. He should reach the level of additional secretary (AS) in 24-26 years of service. This was however not uniform and the time differential from cadre to cadre caused jealousy and frustration. I remember that the exercise was started in 2002 when I was secretary Railway Board.

IRSE was totally out

The exercise was still on in 2005-06. Proposals of some departments, like the IRTS and IRSME had already been approved when I came to the Board. The IRSE proposal had already been discussed with secretary DoP&T, and the expenditure secretary. They found no justification for any JS or AS level posts for the IRSE. The situation was gloomy. Many engineering officers were disappointed and requested that I do something.

I examined the proposal sent by the Railway Board in detail. According to the minutes of the meeting, the IRSE already had occupied many JS and AS level posts. No adjustment in the cadre was therefore called for. This argument was specious and should have been contested. The subject was to be discussed in the Committee of Secretaries, headed by the Cabinet secretary. That was the only way out, but chances were thin, as during the meeting with the secretary, DOP&T and expenditure secretary this was not adequately contested and my predecessor had not even recorded any note of dissent.

The note prepared by the DoP&T had some factually incorrect data. For instance, the note mentioned that out of eleven posts of AGM, four were held by IRSE officers. This was not correct. There were only nine AGM posts and only two were from the IRSE. Likewise, posts of MDs of the PSU were not in the cadre of the IRSE. The selection of the MD was done by the Public Service Enterprise Board (PSEB). It was open to all cadres. There was undoubtedly a strong lobby against the IRSE, which succeeded in creating a bias against the IRSE.

The Fifth Pay Commission recommended allotments of higher-grade posts on a percentage basis. I had, however, suggested that functional necessity should be the basis for reorganization. This was more appropriate and relevant. The civil engineering department in zonal headquarters had functions like CE in JS grade (senior administrative grades). The coordination among all these functions was done by the PCE in AS grade (higher administrative grade). This system was prevalent prior to the reorganization of the new zones. There were now seven additional zones. Thus, there was a need to have seven AS level posts and matching JS level posts for the new zones. After making adjustments with the available posts, five AS level and twenty-four JS level posts were still required.

Revised proposal had the expenditure secretary nodding

Before sending the revised proposal to DoP&T, I decided to discuss it with the secretary, DOP&T and the expenditure secretary. The secretary, DoP&T was in no mood to listen. He said that the subject could not be reopened as my predecessor had already agreed to the decision. Adarsh Kishore was the expenditure secretary. We knew each other well. He was aware of the injustice done to me in the case of the appointment of the CRB. There was no doubt in the minds of engineers that it was a lost battle. Just when I was leaving the Rail Bhawan for the appointment, I asked Satish Agnihotri, OSD, to accompany me to the meeting. I said laughingly, 'You should witness attempts made by me to retrieve a bad case.'

I requested Adarsh Kishore for his help. The cadre readjustment for the IRSE had a genuine justification but it had unfortunately been rejected earlier for want of proper appreciation. I said, 'I am the head of this cadre. If I do not succeed in getting a justified deal, officers of the cadre would definitely say that I could not have succeeded anyway. According to them, if I cannot look after myself, how I was expected to look after them. I do not like to go down in the history with that kind of stigma. I am sure you will appreciate my concern. Please, therefore, listen to my submission with an open mind.'

The expenditure secretary responded with great warmth. I presented the proposal based on functional necessity. He immediately agreed that it was the correct course to be taken. He promised to support me in the COS. The meeting was over in twenty minutes. Adarsh Kishore told me that he was very impressed with the way I had prepared the case. He had often admired me for the way I presented my case in various meetings either at the level of the Cabinet secretary or the PM.

The meeting of the COS was convened soon. The secretary, DOP&T started with vehement opposition to my proposal. He quoted the wrong data about the AGM. The Cabinet secretary asked me why a wrong figure had been given by the Board. I told him that it was not wrong when it had been given in 2003. In three years, the position had changed. I stated that according to the DoP&T, the IRSE cadre did not deserve any higher-grade post. It was unfortunate and could be considered a serious mistake. Otherwise, how could the largest cadre of the IR be denied any share of higher-grade posts out of cadre restructuring? There were 1,700 posts upward of senior scale in the IRSE as compared to about 700 to 800 in the IRTS or the IRSME. Both these cadres were given five posts in the AS. The justification was that the IRSE officers occupied posts of the MD of PSU. As a matter of record, for the last five years, the MD for RITES or IRCON had come from the IRSME. It was only now that an IRSE had been appointed through the PSEB. Posts of the PSU were never taken as part of the cadre before. The MD of the PSU was appointed through open selection and could not be part of any cadre.

The Cabinet secretary immediately agreed with me. He told the secretary DoP&T that their stand was not correct. He could not himself imagine that a cadre of 1,700 officers did not deserve a single post in either JS or AS level. The secretary DoP&T said that they had a large number of posts of CAO (HAG/AS) and CE construction (SAG/JS). I said that it was work-charged establishment to look after the projects. It had to be done according to the actual requirements of the work. It was not a regular establishment. Why should a cadre be penalized for being entrusted with project work?

Then, I went on to remove the misconception of the time differential in promotion prospects between the cadres. I said that during 1969-74, the IRSE had a total of twenty-two intakes. On the other hand, the IRSME alone, in one year had twenty-two officers. The large intakes coupled with a smaller cadre were bound to create congestion. During 1978-80, even the IRSE had heavy recruitments and by 2008-09 congestion would certainly occur. I said, 'I am pleading for posts on functional necessity. I am not looking to balance the cadre.' The argument was irrefutable. The Cabinet secretary looked at the expenditure secretary and said, 'We have to do something. We cannot deny the biggest cadre completely. The member engineering's argument has a lot of merit'. Adarsh Kishore told him that the ME had already discussed the case with him. He said, 'His needs are justified. We should agree to allot five AS level posts and eighteen JS level posts. The Cabinet secretary agreed with Adarsh Kishore. The secretary, DoP&T was however very upset but had to concede.

IRSE officers are jubilant

The development was overwhelming and it had surpassed anyone's expectations. The Cabinet secretary directed that a Cabinet note be prepared accordingly. He also directed that another cadre review should be undertaken in 2009-2010 to address the problem of congestion in the cadre, as pointed out by the ME. I thanked Adarsh Kishore profusely. He promptly said that I deserved it.

The news travelled like wild fire. I received compliments from the IRSE officers. Satish must have told the others how the dead case had been retrieved and resurrected. Next day, many officers came to thank me. Satish also told me that the IRSE officers had decided to felicitate me. I was content and truly grateful to God, who allowed me to do the task that had seemed impossible at one point of time!

The Cabinet note was prepared in time. When the subject came up for the Cabinet meeting, I personally spoke to Kamal Nath, the then commerce minister and our own minister. This was just to take precautions against the subject being deflected in the Cabinet because of an adverse lobby. Fortunately, nothing of the sort happened. The Cabinet approved it without any demurring.

RAIL MANUFACTURING TECHNOLOGY—BITTER STRUGGLE

Satish Agnihotri had told me about a proposal to procure rails from private suppliers. He said that there was lot of pressure from the MR cell on the subject. It was his brief when I joined the Board.

I knew of the background of rail supply as secretary Railway Board. The minister had decided to procure rail through SAIL. But the rail from SAIL had higher hydrogen content and was not considered suitable. The Justice Khanna Committee on Rail Safety had also recommended that rail steel should have lower hydrogen content (2-3 per cent) as per global practice. Hydrogen content (4-6 per cent) in rail steel was permitted by the IR. Hydrogen in rail mass formed tiny bubbles, which made the rail prone to premature failure. SAIL used a hydrogen vacuum tank process to remove hydrogen from the molten steel for casting rail. This process due to its inherent limitation could not ensure a uniform hydrogen content of 2-3 per cent in the entire steel mass. This process was more suitable for smaller productions. For larger production, like in our case, a hydrogen degasser plant was more suitable and was used worldwide. SAIL would have to install this plant. But installing the modern hydrogen degasser plant called for heavy investment which SAIL was unwilling to undertake.

Nitish Kumar ji took a lot of initiative. After meeting with the steel minister, it was jointly decided that SAIL would install a hydrogen degasser plant and introduce other quality control programmes with investment of over ₹300 crore to produce quality rail. According to the joint MoU, IR would buy rail from SAIL only. The rail price would be fixed mutually by a standing committee of the Railways and SAIL. The current production capacity of SAIL was one million ton annually with a provision to enhance it to 1.5 million ton. IR at that time required less than one million tonne. Thus, the capacity available with SAIL was adequate for IR. The joint MoU was presented by the MR to the Parliament, along with the action taken based on the report by the Khanna Committee Report in 2003.

According to the MoU, the Railways need not procure rail from private suppliers. Jindal Steel had actively pursued their case to supply rail from their Raipur plant. I was also told that my predecessor had sent a strong note against the proposal. This was supported by the CRB. I had therefore felt quite at ease.

There is a noose around my neck

However, I was a bit rattled when I was called into the MR's room one day and was told that the rail supply from Jindal Steel had to be expedited. The RDSO was asked to inspect and study the manufacturing and quality control system of Jindal's Raipur plant. I was not aware of this. The RDSO had cleared the plant and had submitted a favourable report. I called for the file. In spite of a strong note from the ED, the ME wanted that the IR procure rail from JSW in order to kill the monopoly enjoyed by SAIL. This was endorsed by the CRB. I immediately knew that the noose was around my neck.

There was nothing adverse about steel produced by JSW as reported by the RDSO. From the presentation and the literature, I found that the JSW used vacuum tank process to remove hydrogen. Experts, although did not find any major difference between the two processes, but for bulk production they considered hydrogen degasser a superior process, which ensured the uniform removal of hydrogen in the entire cross section of the ladle carrying molten steel. This was a crucial and important aspect.

I stand up to defend the MoU

I called the CMD, SAIL, Mr Roongta, for a meeting before I visited Bhilai steel plant. I told him that according to JSW's report, rail produced by SAIL was inferior in quality with regard to six quality control parameters. I requested for an independent technical audit by an institution of repute in the world. He got the hint. He went ahead with the complete audit to bring a status report and quality assurance programme.

I thanked Mr Roongta for his swift response. My inspection at Bhilai was revealing. I was convinced that the rail produced by a hydrogen degasser plant was much superior. SAIL confirmed that their present production capacity of 1.2 million ton could be raised to 1.5 million ton. The IR's requirement was 0.80 million ton; thus, capacity was not a constraint at all.

The rail pricing, according to the MoU signed between the IR and SAIL had been pending. I took this opportunity to finalize it. We were able to secure a cut in the price of ₹500 per metric ton.

In the final analysis regarding the procurement of rails from JSW, I asked the following questions:

(i) The IR had signed a MoU with SAIL in 2003, which had been placed before the Parliament. According to this, the IR would buy rails from

SAIL—a Central PSU capable of meeting the requirements of IR. What then would be the justification to procure rail from a private supplier?
(ii) With large investment, SAIL had replaced the vacuum tank hydrogen plant by a modern hydrogen degasser at the instance of the IR. Now the IR proposed to buy steel from a private supplier, which used old vacuum tank process. Why should the IR now opt for rail produced by vacuum tank process?
(iii) The available literature and my own examination had shown hydrogen degasser to be a far superior process for bulk production. This was also the view expressed in the Justice Khanna Committee report, which was accepted by the government in 2003. What was the justification now in going back to the vacuum tank process by ignoring the acknowledged superior process of hydrogen degassing?
(iv) Normally for procurement from private sources, a notice of intent inviting all interested parties is issued. This was not followed in case of the JSW. Why?

There was no reply. My officer on the Board and those from the RDSO reported of a terrific pressure to submit a favourable report. I told the MR that in case I agreed with him I would end up in a vigilance case. He would also find it very difficult to defend the action, either in the media or the Parliament. The file remained with him for more than three months, and was returned approving my stand.

Weathering the storm

A severe diatribe was let loose against me in the media, as well as in the Standing Committee of the Parliament for the Railways. Although the chairman of the Standing Committee, Basudeb Acharya, had appreciated my views, he had to allow such a discussion because of a notice issued by many members. More than fifty MPs also wrote to the MR. A reply with a full account was put forward to the MR. Such references from a MP is known as a CA3 reference and according to the procedure laid down, such references are first verified by the MP concerned, if it has been actually issued by him. One of the references was from P. Chidambaram, the then finance minister. He asked me why I was checking with him and what the matter was about. I explained it to him. He then nodded and winked at me saying that he did not remember having sent a reference like that! A note was also submitted to the Standing Committee. There was no more discussion after that in the committee.

A close relative of mine spoke to me about the futility of waging such a personal war, as the JSW had a lot of clout that could work against me. I had fought a principled battle, which had proven very costly. I politely told Naveen Jindal, 'Sir, I respect you as an MP but try to appreciate how, with the given background, if we agree to buy rail from JSW—the decision will be defenceless.' I have no regrets because of my conviction. The only other person who patted me, was Mr Roongta, the CMD, SAIL.

PAMBAN BRIDGE—ITS RETROFITTING FOR BROAD GAUGE

President A.P.J. Kalam was the chief guest at an RPF function in Delhi. During tea, he mentioned that he was disappointed to know that the broad gauge line could not go to Rameshwaram. The broad gauge line was to terminate at Mandapam because a meter gauge bridge known as Pamban across the Strait of Rameshwaram could not be converted by retrofitting it to allow broad gauge loading.

Dr Kalam was from Rameshwaram. The government had decided to convert the meter gauge section of Madurai-Rameshwaram on his request. Rameshwaram a holy Hindu shrine—a jyotirlinga—which is an important destination of all devotees of Lord Shiva. The Board had decided to retain the Pamban rail bridge as a heritage structure. A new broad gauge bridge would be a mammoth project. The Board agreed to construct a carriage and wagon maintenance facility at Mandapam at a cost of ₹45 crore. I had not studied the problem till then. I told the president that I would try to find out a solution.

It was September 2005. I asked the CAO, Southern Railway for a brief. He informed me that the main navigational span known as Scherzer span of 289 feet posed an insurmountable problem. I spoke to D.C. Mitra, the PCE that it was my intention to re-examine the issue. He had studied the problem some time before. I was then very busy with the heavy axle load project. I visited the Pamban Bridge in October 2005. Mitra had already prepared the background material on the subject.

Located in the Gulf of Mannar, the Pamban Bridge commissioned on 24 February 1914 connected the last station on the mainland of Indian Peninsula— Mandapam to the Rameshwaram islands. The decision to construct the Pamban Bridge over Palk Strait was taken in a meeting held in Dhanushkodi on 25 November 1908 as a measure to connect Sri Lanka by a meter gauge railway line. The proposal included a Scherzer Rolling Lift Navigational span of 289 feet designed by the Scherzer Rolling Lift Bridge Company, Chicago. The bridge of 2,050 metre length comprised 143 spans of 40 feet and two spans of 13.2 metre besides the 289 feet Scherzer span. The work on the bridge was started in June 1911 and completed by June 1913 except the Scherzer span, which was completed in December 1913.

Only the Scherzer Navigational span had major issues when being converted into a broad gauge line. The foundations and all 40-feet span of the Pamban Bridge posed no problem. The problem consisted of the following:

(i) The bridge did not have dynamic dimensional clearance for broad gauge schedules of dimensions.
(ii) The stresses induced by standard MBG loading were too high for the members of the truss.
(iii) The additional dead load on the bridge upset the static equilibrium of the span when lifted. This called for additional anchorage. Because of space constraints, extra kentledge weight could not be provided.
(iv) The existing bridge could be lifted by operating a winch by two persons with ease. A heavier structure would rob it of such ease.

Because of the insurmountable problems, the conversion of the Pamban Bridge for a broad gauge was given up.

I told my engineers that quite clearly the structure was unsafe due to MBG loading. Hence there was no point in pursuing it. The president while discussing the subject had wished that Hindu devotees should be able to visit Rameshwaram Temple by train. I said, 'So let us see if a passenger train with ordinary passenger coaches, AC sleeper class, AC 3 tier coach (this had the heaviest axle load in coaching rolling stock) plus diesel loco can run safely on the bridge. If this was feasible, the main purpose would be served. This is the functional need.'

This was the basic change in the paradigm. Instead of automatically or routinely following standard loadings according to the bridge rules, we proposed to test the bridge on basis of the load required for the functional need that bridge must carry. This was a simple exercise. It was quickly checked on the spot. There was no problem in this. By changing the floor and depth of the cross girder, the vertical clearance could also be provided. After checking for passenger train loading, we also checked the bridge for cement, coal, foodgrain loading as they were commonly needed by people. The mineral loading caused a problem but no mineral like limestone or iron ore would be needed in Rameshwaram. So, for all practical purposes, the retrofitted bridge would serve all the functional needs of the local population.

It was feasible based on the prima facie evidence to make the meter gauge bridge suitable for a broad gauge passenger train after suitable alteration and modification. Static equilibrium of the lifting span was also possible by adjusting the kentledge weight within the available space. Use of heavier cast iron blocks instead of concrete blocks could provide the additional counter balancing moment.

As ME, I could permit the bridge design with a non-standard loading departing from the prescribed loading in Bridge Rules. Since it was a crucial decision, the SERC (Structural Engineering Research Centre) Chennai and IIT Chennai were requested to check the design. Besides the theoretical design, we insisted upon extensive instrumentation to demonstrate that after broad gauge loading, the bridge had no overstress. The project was assigned to chief bridge engineer, A.K. Sinha.

I visited the temple of Lord Shiva at Rameshwaram in the evening to seek blessings from the Lord. The chief priest received me and performed the pooja. He was very happy to know that the Railways had decided to convert the bridge to broad gauge. 'All pilgrims visiting Rameshwaram will thank you,' he said. Overwhelmed, I wondered how they knew of a decision that had been taken barely a couple of hours ago.

The work was started departmentally in April 2006 with the help of Arakkonam Bridge workshop of the Southern Railway. Before starting of work on Scherzer Span, I decided to brief the president. The president had called eminent scientists, including one expert on corrosion. Dr Kalam was a very keen observer and he critically examined and satisfied himself. He gave some valuable suggestions. The presentation continued for almost an hour and half in the 'Hall of Intellectuals'. The hall was used for discussion with top scientists and intellectuals. We were no intellectuals hence it was a great honour for us. I was subjected to keen questioning and I was happy that our decision to entrust the design to the SERC and IIT Chennai proved to be very satisfactory. Most searching questions were asked on corrosion affecting the bridge. A detailed study was made on this and on the advice of IIT Chennai special measures in the design were adopted. The president's expert on corrosion was fully satisfied with the study made by IIT. The president was personally satisfied by our technical concept and decision. After the presentation, the president took us to his famous Mughal Gardens. He entertained us with tea and snacks. I was deeply touched. He asked me when the retrofitting of the bridge would be completed, particularly taking into consideration my retirement in January 2007. I promised that the major modification works would be completed before my retirement.

On 23 January 2007, I visited the Pamban Bridge when the structural work was completed. I travelled with Mr Velu, minister of state for railways (also from Chennai) on a broad gauge motor trolley across the bridge. There was a big celebration in Rameshwaram. A large press conference was held. The media and the minister paid rich tribute to our innovative approach, which saved more than Rs 500 crore. The head priest again welcomed me in the temple when I went to seek Lord's blessings for our effort. I wrote to Shankar, the president's secretary about completing the work. I, of course, could not meet the president as he was away from Delhi.

The inauguration of the bridge took place in July 2007 by Sonia Gandhi, the Congress president and the chairperson of the UPA. Many had expected Dr Kalam to inaugurate the bridge. After my retirement, the Board was kind to sponsor my visit to this bridge. I thanked them. I went to have a look at the operational bridge. I gave some more suggestions for its improvement. I sought the blessings of Lord Shiva once again with a great sense of fulfilment.

I recall that when I was in Chennai to attend a seminar of the IPWE, M.N. Prasad, former ME and the CRB, had come to attend the seminar. He was very critical of my decision to retrofit the existing Pamban Bridge to suit broad gauge loading. He had also criticized my decision to introduce heavy haul operation with 23-ton axle load. 'I had examined the Pamban Bridge myself and it could never take broad gauge load. Apart from heavier loads, the bridge was subjected to acute corrosion', he said. Regarding the heavy haul he said, 'As ME, I had examined the heavy axle load twice and, on both occasions, I had ruled against the proposal. I am very concerned about you, Jaruhar. Should there be a judicial commission to examine your decision, you will be in an extremely difficult position to defend your action.'

I have always held Mr Prasad in high esteem and I knew how he felt about me. So, with all the humility at my command, I assured him that the decisions in both cases were correct There was one basic difference in our approach—instead of standard MBG loading according to the prescribed Bridge Rules; we had tested the bridge for the functional load it had to actually carry. The concern on corrosion was also fully addressed by experts. My decision on heavy haul was based on transformed paradigm of probabilistic model instead of deterministic model. We did not have time for more detailed discussion and one thing which I wanted him to appreciate was that once I was looking at a particular functional requirement of a structure and good engineering practices, it freed me to think afresh. I was no longer required to be guided by dictates of standard Rules and Procedures. I know he was far from being convinced but for the mind to be free, you have to open it to new ideas.

RECHECKING OF OTHER MEGA BRIDGE

I applied the same principle while reviewing the design of mega bridges like the one on the Ganga near Patna. Rajeev Bhargava, CAO, when asked, informed me that the depth of the foundation according to the RITES' design was 210 feet. I was alarmed!

All the bridges built on the Ganga from Hardwar to Paksi in Bangladesh had foundation depth varying from 160-180 feet only. Well, foundations of these bridges were constructed more than 130 years ago with plain concrete. Most of them had bond bars only in well steining. None of them had shown any distress under heavy loading, even in carrying today's heavy loads. In fact, two bridges on the Ganga near Patna—a road bridge in Patna constructed in 1980 and another near Mokameh a rail-cum-road bridge about 150 km downstream—had no problem with its foundation. They were completely sound. They had seen adverse factors like flood, earthquake and heavier loads. 'Why on earth, should the depth of the foundation of this bridge be more?' I asked Bhargava.

There was no logic but I was told that the RITES had made a design on the basis of a technical paper. Where was the need to depart from the established procedure and engineering practice? There was no answer. At one stage, I threatened the RITES for its unprofessional approach. Even the TAG headed by an eminent scholar from IIT Roorkee, Prof. Arya supported my contention. I asked the RITES to design according to the technical instructions that had been issued by me. They were in consonance with past engineering practices and Railway Bridge Codes. I am thankful to Bhargava. He spearheaded the campaign against this sort of uncalled for and expensive design. As a result, the design of the rail bridge in Patna became sleek and competitive.

An interesting event took place with regard to the rail bridge. The superstructure of the road bridge on the Ganga in Patna named Mahatma Gandhi Setu was damaged and experts declared it unsafe. Nitish Kumar, CM, mentioned it once because the vital link to north Bihar was being disrupted. I said that if he liked, we could convert this rail bridge to a rail-cum-road bridge—the additional cost would have to be shared by the state government. He was happy and wrote to the PM. In course of some meeting, the PM asked me if we could help Bihar CM. I said that it was possible and the PM could confirm it. This was done and Nitish Kumar was very happy indeed. This saved a lot of public money of over ₹700 crore.

The Kosi and Ganga bridges near Monghyr were also accordingly reviewed to achieve considerable savings by applying sound engineering practices. Here the basic principle was to consider and appreciate the sound health of an existing structure. They clearly established the adequacy of existing design over a long period of time (over a hundred years). My philosophy was that a new procedure should improve a structure in terms of economy and safety. In case an old structure that was designed on old principles had served its purpose for well over a century, a new procedure that made the structure heavier and more expensive without any advantage could not be justified.

BRIDGE TALK

I wrote eight technical papers providing the guidelines for the design and inspection of old structures. I inspected some bridges referred to by the Railways. One such bridge was in Lucknow, NR, referred to by the CE. In his view, the arch bridge was distressed and had to be rebuilt. I found that some bricks from the intrados (bottom of the arch) of the arch masonry had become loose thus the joint was opened. I started laughing when I saw it. I told them to recall the basic structural behaviour of an arch. It had only compressive forces. 'Hence how is it possible that the brick is loose?' I asked. There was no answer. They were still looking at the opened joint and wanted to know if it was not distressed, what could be the reason. I said, 'It only indicates that the arch is not fully stressed. There is not enough compressive force to press the brick to be held in its position. The brick is falling since mortar from the joint has leached in course of time.' They asked me how I knew. I then laughed and said, 'The bridge talks to me.' People realized that I had made a simple but correct statement. I subsequently issued a technical note on arch bridges. Consequent to this, many rebuilding proposals were withdrawn.

I must describe the inspection of Jubilee Bridge near Kolkata on Naihati-Bandel section of the Eastern Railway.

The bridge across the Hooghly had a problem with its pendulum bearings. The one on the downstream side was fine but the other one had cracked. Mr Khare, PCE Eastern Railway, had talked to me about this. I had gone to Kolkata with Lalu ji in connection with inauguration of the airport metro line. I had to go to inspect the Kosi Bridge from there and the MR was also to go there. I decided to inspect this bridge and went there with all the officers. I was silent while approaching the bridge. This was a pendulum type of bearing which was unique. It was obvious that the bridge girder was being obstructed and not being allowed to breathe freely (meaning expand or contract). This had exerted undue forces on the bearing for which it hadn't been designed. Everyone started looking at each other when I said this. I started walking towards the central pier because this observation had to be established. The bearing on the downstream side had not shown any distress. This was a 150-metre span. The chief bridge engineer, L. M. Jha, vehemently asserted that this aspect had already been examined. But I kept on walking without saying anything. I reached the expansion joint of the adjoining span. True to my assumption, the joint had been jammed, not allowing any longitudinal movement. The huge extra force was thus passed on to the pendulum bearing at the abutment. On the downstream of the girder, the joint was free. It allowed axial movement as per the structural design of the bridge.

Satish Agnihotri was with me. He was intently looking at the joint in disbelief. He was the first to speak. Very slowly, he said to the CBE, 'You were very confident, saying that you had seen this aspect. But the ME-sir came to this point straightaway.' There was a total disbelief. In my opinion, it is essential to apply the basics of structural engineering. Unless this is established, one can never find a correct technical solution.

When I returned to my inspection carriage in Howrah, the CAO, South Eastern Railway, A.K. Ganguli (God bless his soul because he passed away soon thereafter because of a massive heart stroke. He was the son of the legendary B.C. Ganguli. His elder brother was Ashok Ganguli, who was my DEN in Tori Kumandih doubling) asked me how I had reached to the expansion joint directly. 'Is it another case of the bridge talking to you?' he asked. I said, 'When I say the bridge talks to me, I mean that the bridge exhibits its health, which can be observed by looking at some key locations. A look at the bearing of a simply supported girder will tell its own story. If there is any sign of movement it is good. A distressed bridge by its physical appearance will indicate the discomfort the bridge is undergoing. It is fortunate that the bridge does not lie or feign illness as a human being often does. A man when actually sick might say that he was fine. When he is fine, he might say that he is very ill indeed. It is much easier to find out about the health of a bridge. A design engineer might say, on the basis of his calculation, that the bridge had an overstress of over 200 per cent. When you actually see it, it may not exhibit any sign of overstress. It is actually saying that I am fine, do not worry about me. It is a signal to the revisit design calculations, basic ground conditions and preponderance of design load actually imposed on the structure. That is what the bridge talks to me about.'

As a good doctor, one has to develop a clinical sense. This comes from a continuous application of knowledge derived from observation. According to reports, Dr B.C. Roy (apart from being a a close associate of Mahatma Gandhi and Jawaharlal Nehru, he was the chief minister of West Bengal) was a celebrated physician. He could diagnose diseases by smell. He practised in England. His extraordinary clinical sense was considered very intriguing. English doctors decided to test his faculty. According to the story, he was blindfolded and taken to a ward with a smallpox patient. As soon as he had entered the ward, he said, 'Oh, it is a case of smallpox'. By the smell that the sick person had emitted he could accurately diagnose the disease! Such development of faculty can be seen in every field—be it in the case of a car mechanic or simply a cook, who just picks up a grain of rice to say whether it has been cooked.

EXPERIENCE OF DELHI METRO

Being member engineering, I was on the Board of the Delhi Metro Rail Corporation (DMRC). This was a SPV formed by the Delhi government and Government of India. The Ministry of Urban Development is the nodal ministry and its secretary is the chairman of the Board. Since the very beginning, this project attracted controversy. The Indian Railways in its wisdom had decided not to execute this project. It was unfair indeed!

According to the IR, the urban transport project was always very expensive and completely unviable. The IR had already burnt its hands by carrying a bulk of suburban transport by rail in Mumbai, Kolkata and Chennai, and partly in Delhi. The operational cost of transport was quite heavy. Without any support from the Central or state governments, it was a serious drag on the finances of the IR. Thus, the Railways firmly refused to execute the Delhi Metro without full financial support from the urban development ministry. Urban transport is linked with state road transport. Although the argument had force, rail-based metro services could not be run by any other agency. The IR administered the Railway Act regulating rail based public transport. In my assessment, this was a wrong decision. The IR could not abdicate its public responsibility in this respect. Nitish ji was also against this decision taken by the Board. He had strongly expressed his views. As secretary Railway Board, I had also supported his view.

The Central government, however, did not support the IR in matter of financing the project. The IR also had problems with its own finances at that time. This project was undertaken with the help of Japanese financing. Sreedharan, former ME, was appointed as MD of the DMRC.

DMRC adopts broad gauge after a long debate

The project required many experienced engineers. The IR lent their services on deputation. The Delhi Metro was subjected to control by the Railway Act. The basic statutory control in supervision and certification was therefore by the IR. Sreedharan decided to introduce standard gauge (4 feet 8 1/2 inches—1435 mm) instead of broad gauge (5 feet 6.00 inches -1676 mm) the standard of IR. The Delhi Metro was a standalone system. According to him, modern SG rolling stock was a proven system in the world. This could be straightaway introduced here. The IR raised serious objections. The government had decided to have uni-gauge policy not very long ago and in view of this any other gauge would be repugnant. The subject was debated at length. This was finally decided in GoM meeting headed by L.K. Advani. The GoM accepting the advice of the IR, the technical ministry, decided for DMRC to adopt the BG.

This policy decision did not suit the DMRC. Possibly a strong lobby supported standard gauge and it did not like it either. Sreedharan had already constructed bridges and tunnels with standard gauge specification. He requested ME to permit coaches with SG dimensions on BG under frame. For a very strange reason, ME R.N. Malhotra approved this. For all time to come, this completely killed the capacity provided by a broad gauge coach. It went against the spirit of the decision of the GoM. It was a travesty of justice. Clearance or approval given once was made universally applicable. I have not seen a bigger joke than this on a credulous public!

During the inauguration of the DMRC in 2002, there was a serious issue because of umpteen infringements in coaches. The MM was not at all inclined to oblige Sreedharan. Without his technical approval, CCRS could not approve the operation of the Metro. It created a serious impasse just before the inauguration of the train by the PM. Nitish ji asked the Board to find a solution. As an interim measure, the Board authorized an independent International Inspecting Organization to issue a safety certificate. The DMRC was directed to comply with all the objections raised by the RDSO before the next run. This was to avoid serious embarrassment. That was the last time Sreedharan ever came to the Board.

The only time that the DMRC approached me was for post facto approval for rail. The DMRC had used imported 60 kg rail. During the CRS inspection, it was found to have a higher hydrogen content than what had been prescribed by the IRS specifications. The DMRC was asked to seek dispensation from the Railway Board for rails having 6 per cent hydrogen content. I had received a casual letter from the DMRC, without explaining the reason for not adhering to the specifications. There was no response from them when asked about the specifications. Once secretary, MOUD (Ministry of Urban Development) Anil Baijal spoke to me to clear the proposal. I told him that I had asked the DMRC to explain the reason for not following the IRS specification.

He agreed with me but told me, 'Jaruhar Sahib, Sreedharan is an institution by himself and he does not listen to anyone. But I will tell him to comply with your query.' I received a long letter saying that the Railways had all along used rails with more than 6 per cent hydrogen content. The Delhi Metro had much lighter traffic. It should be safe to have rail with larger hydrogen content. I found this to be very offensive. I knew that Delhi Metro used 60 kg head hardened imported rail at a very high cost. It had specifically wanted head hardened rail because SAIL did not roll it. For its lighter traffic (14 ton axle load), 52 kg rail was good enough. Why did the DMRC use rail with 6 per cent hydrogen content when the quality of imported rail was known to be good? The IR used higher hydrogen content (> 3%) before 2003. It had since revised the IRS specifications following the Khanna Committee Report. Higher hydrogen content was known to cause fracture in the rail. It had nothing to do with axle load. It was a metallurgical phenomenon. Use of 52 kg rail could have caused them to save over 15 per cent—quite a substantial amount. I said that the Board had noted the fact that the Metro used rails not meeting the IRS' specification. Surely it must have hurt the DMRC but I only regret that he had provoked a reaction!

The bogey of standard gauge resurfaces

The question of gauge was once again raised for metro rail—this time by the Mumbai Metro, the rail organization set up by the state government. Quite interestingly, this was recommended by the DMRC—their consultant.

The chief secretary of Maharashtra wrote to the Railway Board on the subject. I replied that the issue had already been settled by the government. The secretary, MOUD, however, told me that the DMRC had obtained an opinion from Attorney General Banerjee that the metro in a municipal limit could be considered similar to a tramway. Accordingly, it could be considered under the Tram Way Act which was administered by the state government. The objective of the exercise was to take away the subject of the Metro from the scope of the Railway Act. This would knock out the Indian Railways from this metro business. This was due to intense hostility against the IR. The resident commissioner of Karnataka had once bluntly said that they would prefer to be away from the Rail Bhawan. Indian Railways' officers were so swollen-headed that one could not even talk to them!

I took up the issue with the secretary, MOUD. I asked him how such an issue was referred to the AG without consulting MR. The earlier decision was taken in consultation with law ministry. In our view, the AG had not been briefed properly. Tram and rail could not be compared. The Railways had an exclusive right of way whereas tram shared it with other modes of transport like cars, buses, etc. The Maharashtra CM also visited the MR. In the meeting, I explained the advantage of a BG system. In India, in the long run, a BG operation was bound to be more economical because of its 16 per cent higher capacity.

Strangely, a GoM was again constituted to consider this aspect. I had met Sharad Pawar the then agricultural minister who headed the GoM. I also met

Jaipal Reddy the then minister of urban development. Both of them were convinced by our presentation. Before the GoM, many issues were raised. There was no satisfactory defence against the argument. The GoM, however, decided that the gauge should be a techno-economic consideration. It should be left with the Administrative Department executing the project. The same government which had once decided on the uni-gauge policy had now decided to leave the choice of gauge as an open optional parameter. During the GoM, we submitted that Lord Dalhousie in his wisdom had selected a wider gauge of 5'6" mostly on consideration of capacity and safety. The earlier GoM had thought it fit to have BG for the Delhi metro.

In my assessment, the Delhi Metro would be saturated soon. A BG metro with 8 or 12 coaches could easily serve the population for the next fifty years.

The decision would open gates of unrestricted import of standard gauge rolling stocks from the western market. It was not difficult to spot the greater beneficiary. There was no wonder therefore when such foreign governments were quite willing to felicitate Indian architects of Metro rails.

Delhi Metro has a different gauge—standard gauge

Following this decision, the Delhi Metro proposed to construct an airport line on the standard gauge. This issue had already been discussed in the committee of secretaries (CoS) by the Cabinet secretary. The subject was brought to the DMRC Board for discussion after the CoS. I pointed this out to the chairman— Mr Baijal, secretary, MOUD. I insisted that this fact should be recorded. Very reluctantly, it was conceded that it was done due to urgency. The Cabinet secretary had fixed the CoS meeting before the DMRC Board could discuss it. The proposal was for the standard gauge because it would run at a speed of 120 kmph. It had the following shortcomings:

(i) The stretch was less than sixteen km with four stations in between. It was therefore impossible to attain a speed of 120 kmph.
(ii) The connectivity with other sections/routes of the Delhi Metro to the airport would be deprived because of the different gauge.
(iii) Maintenance would be quite difficult because it would require coaching facilities exclusively for standard gauge stocks. This would add to the cost of the system.

There was a loud protest from all members in the Board. The draft of the minutes however did not include my remarks in the meeting. I protested. With the support of the chairman, this was rectified. The Cabinet note was prepared. Nobody supported it—MOF, MOUD and even the PMO. I have not seen a

Cabinet note prepared by a ministry in which it did not endorse the proposal. This note was seeking approval from the Cabinet not to construct the S.G. line!

This note was taken to the GoM meeting chaired by the minister of external affairs. I explained how this standalone system would not be in the overall interest. This was agreed to by everyone. Even Mr Baijal supported me. The committee agreed that it should not be on standard gauge as the Cabinet note had said. I came out of the meeting and was waiting for my car in the portico of the South Block. The finance minister came and said that I had spoken well and patted me before getting into the car. But there was strong support in the Cabinet. I do not know how but when the minutes of the meeting were issued, it said that the proposal had been approved! Hats off!

The development of metro in India had not been done based on good techno-economic considerations. V.K.J. Rane former MD, IRCON had spearheaded a campaign in this direction. I believed that there was an urgency about it. All technical persons concerned should sit down once again and do some course correction. The country's political system was guided by the advice of experts. They should think about the country and its people first. They should come up with sound advice. I could not imagine the cost of the metro rail as was being proposed at the time. As ME, I was involved with Kolkata and Chennai metros. This cost about ₹60-80 crore per km (2005-06). Now the proposed cost was over ₹200 crore per km. The comparison was offensive. At some point in time, posterity is sure to ask uncomfortable questions.

EXPERIENCES WITH THE PUBLIC SECTOR UNDERTAKINGS— KONKAN AND RVNL

The Indian Railways has ten public sector undertakings. The Rail Land Development Authority (RLDA) was also created by an Act of Parliament in 2006. The ME is chairman of the Konkan Railway Corporation (KRC), with its office at New Mumbai. The ME is also the chairman of the RLDA. The RLDA was set up towards the end of my service. Its main objective was to deal with the surplus railway land. The subject was very controversial. I had remarked to Lalu ji that the land deal would definitely lead to a vigilance inquiry. Anyway, there was not a lot of activity, even after I retired.

Konkan Railway Corporation

The 760-km long Konkan Railway Project, was commissioned in 1998 on BOT (build, operate, transfer) basis with four states—Maharashtra, Kerala, Goa and Karnataka and the Ministry of Railways. This project had two illustrious managing directors—Mr Sreedharan and Mr Rajaram. They were visionaries and provided tremendous thrust to the KRC. However, the KRC did not fetch the returns that had attracted the BOT participants. As a result of poor financial return, the Konkan Railway largely operated out of the grant provided by the MR. The Railways did not have the wherewithal to undertake routine maintenance. The KRC had won a lot of prestigious engineering projects—one was part of a new Jammu and Kashmir line between Katra to Laole.

Unless the rail traffic was routed through this line, there was no chance of the KRC turning around. I was convinced that it would solve the crux of the problem. The Indian Railways was extremely reluctant to part with the traffic. We had a good director (operations) in Anurag Mishra. He was EDTT in the Railway Board and also DRM, Nagpur in the Central Railway. Fortunately, the Railways was also doing well. With the help of MT, Ghosh Dastidar, my good friend, it was possible to divert some traffic through the KRC. This immediately improved its operating ratio.

I also prevailed upon the FC, Ms Vijaya Lakshmi, to delegate financial powers to the KRC so that they could do important traffic facility work. Since the KRC was making a loss, there was extreme reluctance and it was not easy to obtain it for them. But I enjoyed the confidence of all in the Board and my advice was accepted. I had told the Board that after all, it was a useful asset for the Indian Railways. It was also a fact that many zonal railways in the IR were making a loss but still important activities were allowed in those railways. We could not place the KRC on a different scale in this respect. I had argued powerfully and thanks to the MT and the FC specifically, who supported me.

There was a large cost overrun in the project and it was necessary for all the stakeholders to suitably increase their equity participation to enable the KRC to discharge its debt liability. But the stakeholders were not willing to increase their equity. A dialogue was therefore initiated in the Ministry of Finance to bail the KRC out through suitable financial restructuring. The liability of the SPV could thereafter be converted as a grant from the Central government to bring about financial closure. Because of the traffic diverted by the IR, the productivity of the KRC had improved. The organization had started to look up.

Pilot Project—Sky Bus

The KRC had started two projects. Both were unfortunately languishing. One of them was Sky Bus. An elevated rail car, it had a good potential for urban transport. This was started as a pilot project in Goa with the enthusiastic approval of Prime Minister Atal Bihari Vajpayee. Unfortunately, there was an accident during the trial run. Lots of questions were raised about the safety of its operation. A committee was set up under the chairmanship of Dr Indiresen former director, IIT Madras and an eminent scientist. The committee made very useful suggestions in its report. In the committee's view, the project had a good potential regarding the urban mass transport. It recommended that it be taken up as a research project.

The KRC had no resources to undertake the research project. The KRC did not have the money to run the prototype trial. There were vested interests to kill the initiative conceived by Raja Ram. I was convinced that if the KRC was given proper support, this project could become viable. There was a trade enquiry about it from other countries as well. I requested Shivadasan, FC, to give them about ₹5 crore as a research grant. It was accordingly provided as a budget grant. In my view, it was a good initiative. The research project would certainly remove all doubts about its efficacy. I was about to retire and so I could not pursue it further.

Anti-collision device—a major safety initiative

Likewise, the ACD was a novel apparatus to prevent collision of trains. An indigenous device, it had challenged the much talked about ETCS. So, there was a great deal of hostility against its use. This was again a development of Raja Ram. Nitish ji had supported this scheme and had announced it in the Parliament as a major initiative in safety. This was launched on the KRC on 20 January, 2004. It was christened 'Raksha Kawach' by Nitish Kumar.

Because of the hostility and reluctance against the introduction of the ACD, it had to suffer delays at all levels. A decision was taken to run a field trial in NF Railway before its formal induction into the Railways. Raja Ram was reportedly under intense pressure to sell the patent to some foreign countries. It was alleged that Raja Ram was told that if it was not accepted, the ACD might not see the light of the day. The S&T department had serious technical reservations about its efficacy. All these issues were tested during the field trial. Some corrections were called for and the software was accordingly updated. The full Board saw the presentation from the NF Railway, the RDSO and the KRC. After a great deal of discussion, the Board finally approved the scheme for prototype adoption in the IR.

Someone told Lalu ji that the scheme was a fraud. I had a chance to speak to the MR about the motive behind such slander against the ACD. Competitors outside were against its introduction. I requested him to watch demonstration of the device in Goa where he had to attend a meeting of Rajbhasha.

He saw the demonstration of the ACD on the Konkan Railway. He was very happy and fully satisfied with its performance. He told me on his return that this was an open case of intrigue. He ordered that the device be pushed ahead and cleared for use in the IR. Vested interests had obviously succeeded in stalling the use of the ACD even after the Board had unanimously approved the scheme. Although Indian patent and South African patent had been received, the global patent was awaited.

Rail Vikas Nigam Limited

Rail Vikas Nigam Limited (RVNL) is another PSU under the Ministry of Railways. It was set up to execute projects for strengthening the golden quadrilateral and its diagonals and to augment port connectivity under the National Rail Vikas Yojana launched by the Government of India. The CRB was its part-time chairman.

The RVNL however was besieged by many teething problems. It faced criticisms galore—the most serious and general being the lack of cohesiveness in its team. I was thus surprised and intrigued to receive an order in April 2005 from the MR, appointing me as chairman. The intrigue was complete soon thereafter. The annual performance report of the RVNL was put up to MR in March in a routine manner. The minister had observed, 'If the performance of the RVNL does not improve, it should be closed down by June 2005.' With those observations of the MR, the file was sent to me, as I was new chairman of the company.

I was angry and upset. I told R.K. Singh, 'It was unfair of you to propose my appointment as chairman of the RVNL after it has been abandoned and condemned by all as a sinking ship. You have conveniently passed on its rudder to me after having been in charge of the RVNL for the last two years.' But there was no way but to hold the baby!

I called the MD and the top functionaries of the RVNL for a review in the Board. They had planned a PowerPoint presentation for me. I curtly told the MD, J.P. Shukla, 'I am not interested in any presentation. The MR has recorded that the RVNL should be closed by June 2005 if its performance does not improve. If you wish to redeem yourself, you must complete a major project in a record time. The Delhi-Rewari gauge conversion is more than 100 km long. This must be completed by December 2006. That is your only chance.'

There was complete silence. I asked them to go ahead from that very day. I said, 'On the other hand, if it is not possible, then all of you should go home. I will tell the MR that nothing can be done with the RVNL.' After saying this, I just walked out of the meeting room. This took exactly fifteen minutes. I was blunt and rude. I had no time for pleasantries. I wanted to shake them up so that they take the work seriously.

After three months, the MR told me, 'I do not know what you have done but I find a lot of activities in the RVNL. It appears there has been a real resurgence. Please keep it up.' I had pushed the paddle really hard. I had refused to attend any dinners organized by the RVNL. Thus, I was trying to send a signal that retrieving its glory and setting high standards was of greater priority. I was determined that the RVNL achieve it.

The Board of the RVNL was a divided lot. Most of the independent directors did not trust the MD or other directors. I interacted with them separately. I started addressing their concerns. I enlisted their support to achieve the targets given to the RVNL. Shortly, mutual trust was developed. This was the key.

Leaving behind the reputation of non-performers of previous years, the RVNL during 2005-06 completed 114 km of doubling, 430 km of gauge conversion and 458 km of railway electrification. I presented the whole team before Lalu ji. He complimented them profusely. For once, J.P. Shukla was happy. I was glad that he had kept up the pace after faltering initially.

J.P. Shukla was supposed to retire in May 2006. There was an urgency to select a successor. Many were lobbying for the post. Some of the contenders frightened me. I did not want the RVNL to slip back to its original position. All our efforts to build a sound work culture would be lost. Good leadership by a dynamic MD was the key. None of the contenders for the post gave me any confidence in this respect. I had asked D.C. Mitra, PCE, Southern Railway, to apply for the post. He was a tough guy and a person with great initiative. But I could not do much about the selection done by the Public Enterprise Selection Board (PESB). The chairman Railway Board was normally detailed to assist the PESB in the selection of the MD. Likewise, the selection of the MD, IRCON was also on the cards. For this also similar lobbying was going on. The outgoing MD, IRCON, B.S. Kapoor, had come to me for help so that a suitable successor could be selected.

I was with the MR in his room one late afternoon. I told him that the selection of the MD, RVNL was being held on the following day. Selection for MD, IRCON was also to be held a week later. 'Sir, you know how important it is to have the right person as the MD. We have had so much of a problem with the RVNL because of poor leadership. The RVNL is back on the rails after a lot of effort. I hear that some contenders are openly lobbying to be selected. I am disturbed because they claim to be moving with their bags full! A wrong choice will only make your and my work more difficult,' I said. He reacted sharply and asked me who was spreading this rumour. I said that the candidates themselves were talking about it. I knew it was improper to be specific about what the contenders claimed. But the fact was that I was concerned about the

RVNL, and I thought that I must tell Lalu ji about what was being talked. It was about 6 p.m. when I came out of his room and certainly, both of us were annoyed—he with me and I with myself!

The CRB called me around 7 p.m. and said, 'MR is very upset. He has asked me that the ME must go to the PESB selection the next day. He has insisted that the ME should be given a free hand in both for selection of MD, RVNL and IRCON. They should be appointed with the ME's recommendation'.

I was stunned.

'But I cannot go to the PESB without the specific approval of the MR. The PESB has also to be informed accordingly,' I told him. He had already obtained the MR's approval and had also informed the chairman, PESB. The file came to me around 7.30 p.m. The interview was fixed for 10.30 a.m. the following day.

R.K. Singh had been a member of the PSEB after his retirement. He called me up to know if I had seen the selection file. He had come to know that the MR had deputed me to assist the PSEB. He asked me if the MR had indicated any preference; in that case, he would support me.

I told him, 'I have not asked the MR, but I have been given a free hand. I will act accordingly. I have yet to see the file. I will make up my mind after that.'

He said, 'Oh! That is very good. Then if you tell me your choice, I will fully support you.'

I did not want to give him an inkling on phone. It would have been too dangerous. I was going out for a meeting with the PM at Race Course just then. I reached home only after 10 p.m. There was another call from him. I had to tell him I could not see the file, but I would tell him when I reached the PSEB for the interview. By the time I reached the PSEB, the interview had already been called. But I told him of my preference as we moved to the boardroom.

There were six candidates for the interview. They were well-informed but their profile and work experience did not instil confidence in me. The chairman signalled his choice of a candidate after the interview. He had done very well. He proposed him as the number one choice. Then he sought my opinion about the choice. I held my head in both hands.

I slowly said, 'I respect your choice. But I am looking at the scene on his appointment. I have known him for over thirty years. I have doubts about his delivery. Of course, he is excellent in oral presentation. He can defend his organization. But he lacks the thrust that the organization needs. As the ME, I will have some struggle ahead.'

Then I described how the RVNL had been practically dumped and condemned. It was only because of my herculean efforts that this had started showing results.

Fortunately, the PESB knew my reputation. They had great regard for me. The chairman said, 'No, no, Mr Jaruhar, we are aware of your vital role for this organization. We are certainly concerned about its performance. Please tell me who you would like to select?'

I said that my preference was D.C. Mitra.

'But he has performed poorly. He has not answered many questions on company affairs,' the chairman said. 'It is true that he did not answer questions on balance sheet and debt equity ratio, etc. But these things he can master in a fortnight. He has to be conversant with these terms. What cannot be acquired is a person's ability to complete a project. To his credit, he has completed many projects in difficult circumstances. The experience is invaluable. You have to decide what attribute has greater premium?' I remarked. There was complete silence. Then the chairman nodded and said that he was in complete agreement with me. He said that if others agreed, the PESB would place Mr Mitra as the number one choice. Everyone agreed.

When Mitra met me in my office, and I virtually fired him for not having prepared himself for the interview. He said that the other contenders were giants in comparison. He said, 'I knew that I had no chance. I had only come for the interview because you had asked me to attend it. There was no point in wasting hours in preparation.' What an answer! I could not blame him really. By the evening, the news was out. Mitra asked me if he was selected after all. He could not believe that because I had pulled him up for his poor performance. I knew from where the information had leaked. That member also credited himself with the result! Good, I thought, but Mitra proved to be a worthy MD, and the RVNL turned around. A little later, the MD of IRCON was selected without any hiccups.

TURNAROUND OF THE INDIAN RAILWAYS—AN ANALYSIS

Towards the end of 2005-06, there was talk of a massive turnaround of the Indian Railways. While delivering the Rail Budget 2006-07 speech in the Parliament, the MR spoke of the record-breaking turnaround of the Indian Railways on the basis of performance of the IR for the first nine months of 2005-06. The growth in freight loading was recorded as 10 per cent and that for the freight revenue was over 18 per cent.

It would be interesting to analyse the growth in freight loading. This had determined the financial performance of the IR. I have selected the period from 2001-02 to 2008-09. This will serve as the backdrop of the analysis of the IR's turnaround. It has been a subject of raging discussion by all. Premier management institutions like the IIM Ahmedabad; Indian School of Business, Hyderabad; Harvard Business School and the World Bank and several other experts have examined the subject critically.

Year	Freight loading in MT	Incremental loading over the previous year in MT	% increase over the previous year
2001-02	492.50	-	-
2002-03	518.74	26.24	5.32%
2003-04	557.39	38.65	7.45%
2004-05	602.10	44.71	7.43%
2005-06	666.51	64.40	10.70%
2006-07	728.00	61.49	9.23%
2007-08	790.00	62.00	8.52%
2008-09	833.00	43.00	5.44%

Source: Collated by the author from various sources.

Likewise, it will be interesting to analyse the financial performance of the IR for the period 2005-06 to 2008-09. This period is claimed to be the golden period of the IR. This period is marked by sustained growth and excellent financial results. The political reins of the railway ministry during this period were with Lalu ji. I was an important member of the Board during these two crucial years (2005-06 and 2006-07).

FINANCIAL RESULTS (figures in crore)

Particulars/ Year	2005-06	2006-07	2007-08	2008-09
Passenger Earning	15126	17224	19844	21931
Freight Earning	36287	41716	47434	53433
Other Coaching Earning	1153	1717	1800	1971
Sundry Earning	1839	1711	2565	2500
Gross Traffic Receipts	54491	62370	71720	79861
Ordinary Working Expenses	35030	37432	41033	54349
Operating Ratio	83.72%	76.30%	75.94%	90.46%
Internal Resources before dividend	12966	14427	18334	9174
Fund Balance	11280	10206	13431	4456

Source: Collated by the author from various sources.

The financial results are quite revealing. The internal revenue before dividend in 2001-02 was ₹4,790 crore and that after dividend payment was ₹4,204 crore. For

2004-05, the internal generation of revenue before dividend was ₹5,270 crore and that after dividend payment was ₹2,074 crore. The operating ratio in 2001–02 was 98 per cent and that in 2004–05 was 90.98 per cent.

Financial performance showed a massive turnaround

In plain words, the fortune of the IR had boomed between 2005 and 2008. It was therefore appropriately being called the golden period of the Indian Railways. The Internal Resources before dividend had increased from ₹4,790 crore in 2001-02 to ₹12,966 crore in 2005–06. It had shot up from the figure of ₹5,270 crore in 2004-05 to ₹12, 966 crore in 2005–06. This was an outstanding performance. According to records, it was sustained during the best part of the tenure of Lalu ji, as the MR, up to 2007-08.

This was heralded as the biggest turnaround of the IR particularly in the backdrop of the report of the committee, set up in the mid-90s, headed by Rakesh Mohan. The report submitted in 2001, inter alia said, 'The Indian Railways is on the verge of a financial crisis'. It was rapidly moving towards fatal bankruptcy and would be saddled with an additional financial liability of over ₹61,000 crore in sixteen years. 'It is in a terminal debt trap,' the report had concluded.

Large gain in internally generated revenue in 2005-06, 2006-07 and 2007-08 had been in the order of ₹6,000 crore, ₹8,000 crore and ₹10,000 crore, respectively. Introduction of heavy axle load must be regarded as the single largest contributor to the generation of revenue. This has been accepted by various reports by IIM Ahmedabad and others. It has been dealt with in greater detail in the book *Changing Tracks—Reinventing the Spirit of Indian Railways* by Dr V. Nilakant of the University of New Zealand and Dr S. Ramnarayan of the Indian School of Business, Hyderabad.

The subject of the financial turnaround of the Indian Railways provoked intense debate. A large section of the intelligentsia in the country and also abroad was reluctant to accept Lalu ji as some kind of 'management guru'. A large group of students and faculty members from the world's best business schools like Harvard, Kellogg and Wharton interacted with Lalu ji in an open session in Delhi. IIM Ahmedabad was engaged to conduct research on the subject. After the report, there was an open session at the IIM also. Others questioned the claims of the IR, claiming that the spectacular financial results by an organization were discredited and the IR's were recommended for a complete overhaul as a corporate business entity.

FREQUENTLY ASKED QUESTIONS ON THE TURNAROUND OF THE IR

I had the opportunity to defend the claim regarding the turnaround of the IR in various forums. I wish to present an objective analysis of the criticism brieflyfor proper appreciation.

1. Was the Indian Railways actually bankrupt and heading towards terminal debt?

I do not agree with this statement. It was, however, used by Lalu ji to highlight the performance of the IR under his regime. An organization with internally generated resource of ₹4,790 crore in 2001-02 could nowhere in the world be called a bankrupt organization.

The criticism probably stemmed from the fact that the IR could not pay dividends fully. It is not an isolated phenomenon with any organization. It was saddled with grave liability accrued out of the Fifth Pay Commission awards. It was a passing phase. The statement made in the report of Dr Rakesh Mohan was thus not warranted. No organization was known to be bankrupt for not having paid dividends for a couple of years.

2. Was the growth a sudden affair and did it reflect ineffective handling by the previous government?

Again, the answer is 'No'. The pattern of growth in freight traffic clearly showed annual growth of 5.3 to 7.45 per cent. This was in consonance with general growth in the national economy with GDP growth rate of 5 per cent. The economy was picking up from 2002 onwards. It was over 7 per cent in 2005-06. The previous regime also registered growth rate. It had taken many initiatives of far-reaching consequences. They had an important bearing on IR's performance. The injection of the Special Railway Safety Fund of ₹17,000 crore in 2001 to completely replace the outmoded and obsolete assets with improved specifications had set the platform for the introduction of heavy haul operation in the IR. Likewise, the introduction of the National Rail Vikas Yojana with a central funding of ₹15,000 crore was to target capacity building on core routes of the IR apart from providing port connectivity and construction of mega bridges. These were visionary and pathbreaking initiatives of the previous government and special tribute must be paid to Atal Bihari Vajpayee, PM; Yashwant Sinha, FM; and Nitish Kumar, MR, for these far-sighted and visionary initiatives. The growth registered beyond 2005-06 picked up on two counts. One was the surge in Indian economy in 2005-06 (7 per cent plus GDP growth) and secondly, measures like heavy haul operation and rationalization of freight tariff brought large freight revenue. Clearly, the sudden spurt had little to do with Lalu ji's regime.

3. Was there a turnaround after all? Or was it only a juggling of figures?

If we consider the growth or financial attainment, it was certainly spectacular. The IR not only paid its dividends but also the arrears accrued in the deferred dividends. From this standpoint, this could be considered a turnaround in fortunes for the Indian Railways.

The criticism about accounting jugglery is not correct. There were two aspects to it. First, there is an allegation about the accounting system being tinkered with. Actually, the necessary changes were made to show lease charges as capital expenditure in accordance with the suggestion made by the CAG to show more transparency as modern accounting system. Accordingly, in his Budget speech presenting the Rail Budget for 2006-07, the MR reported that ₹1,616 crore were reduced from operating expenses. This was done with the approval of the CAG and there was no jugglery at all.

Second, there is a criticism about reporting a profit of ₹25,000 crore during 2007-08 by the MR in his budget speech of 2008-09 and also about his claim to have earned a profit of ₹90,000 crore in his entire tenure. At the very outset, there is no concept of profit in the Railways. It is only revenue surplus (or more precisely excess of receipt over expenditure, as mentioned in the Budget documents). This could be used for investment for creation of assets by appropriating it to the Development Fund and the Capital Fund. This figure for 2007-08 was shown as ₹13, 534 crore. But the figure of cash surplus shown in the 'Statement of cash and investible surplus (Explanatory Memorandum on the Railway Budget)' was ₹25, 065 crore shown as cash surplus before dividend. From this, the following had to be deducted to reflect the true surplus:

S. No.	Items or Head	Amount in Crore
1	Interest on fund balance	1300.36
2	Safety surcharge on passenger fare merged with earnings	1000.00
3	Capital recovery component on leased assets of the IRFC	1810.00
4	Operating subsidy to compensate on loss to NF Railway as part of sundry earnings	580.00
5	Contribution to the DRF as operating expenses	7000.00
6	Total deductions	11690.00

Source: Compiled by the author from various rail budget documents.

When deducted from cash surplus, this would come to (₹ 25,065—11,690) ₹13,375 crore. Thus, at best, the statement could be called hyperbolical, but it nevertheless underlined the superlative achievement. There was no need to take away the credit for this achievement from the Indian Railways.

4. Was Lalu ji a management guru who turned around the Indian Railways just after assuming charge of the railway ministry in May 2004?

First of all, it must be accepted that the Indian economy was surging as never before. The surge was already noticeable from 2003-04 onwards. Of course, it gathered momentum by 2005. Transport per se is not an activity which created economic growth. But without adequate transport capacity, economic growth would be stifled. The growth of the Indian economy was also a result of global boom. It created a challenge for all transport segments, including the Railways. In my opinion the greatest challenge before the IR in 2005 was to pick up growth at 7 per cent or above in face of factors like inadequate line capacity, rolling stock and dearth of key operating personnel like drivers, guards, carriage and wagon staff, etc. That IR accepted the challenge, and actually delivered results through pure innovation and dedication must be considered as the most outstanding performance.

It is true that only the economic growth driver could not have brought spectacular success. Without doubt, it was superb teamwork and a most motivated Board which came together to bring about revolutionary changes in the work. I give full credit to J.P. Batra, CRB; S. Ghosh Dastidar, member traffic; R.R. Bhandari, member mechanical and the team of Shivadasan and Balachandran financial commissioner and additional member (budget), respectively. I provided the support in the crucial area of heavy haul, which turned out to carry the bulk of incremental gain for the IR.

In a team like this, there was no doubt that Minister of Railways Lalu Prasad with his able lieutenant Sudhir Kumar, OSD, provided full support to the Board. In my perception, being the leader of the team, it would be harsh and a matter of ingratitude to take away the credit for the achievement from Lalu ji. After all, had he failed, people would not have spared him for ruining the IR after whatever had happened to Bihar. As a winning captain of the team, he deserved the accolade. The fact is that nothing succeeds like success. If someone called him management guru and academicians from the likes of IIM, Harvard, Kellogg, Wharton and many other institutions were willing to listen to him and learn from him, nobody should find fault with him on this score. Actually the phrase 'management guru' was the handiwork of the media, which nobody objected to!

5. Did the Railways take the easy way out and capitalize on the initiatives already taken by the previous regime? Would the turnaround be sustainable?

There was no doubt that the Railways took advantage of the initiatives taken by the earlier regime. The SRSF was an initiative which was great. It took care of the defunct assets and provided good infrastructure to usher in heavy haul operation. Rationalizing the tariff schedule was also very welcome. This was already initiated by the previous regime. It was further consolidated during the next regime. But to be fair, this has to be a continuous process. It was difficult to achieve everything in a spell of five years.

But to say that it took the easy way out is not justified. Introduction of heavy haul or higher axle load operation has been a revolutionary concept or initiative. Unless the principle of Probabilistic Model was accepted it was impossible to establish safe and acceptable stress level due to higher axle load. It would not have been possible to justify it on the basis of 'deterministic model'. This could not be done for the last twenty-five years. It could not be granted a safety certificate on the basis of extant provisions in the codes. No chief engineer or chief bridge engineer could be forced to sign the safety certificate unless the results of the pilot project and instrumentation had established the safety of operation.

Whatever was done was an interim measure. This could serve the purpose for the next three years. Many measures in capacity building like dedicated freight corridor were initiated. The measures to remove bottlenecks in yards and other works related to operating improvements were also initiated to remove lethal delays. The turnaround can therefore be sustained if follow-up actions are pursued with equal swiftness.

SOME DISASTERS—LESSONS AND EXPERIENCE

Bomb blast in Mumbai suburban trains in July 2006

The Indian Railways is a dynamic organization, working around the clock, catering to a vast population. So it is hardly surprising that unpleasant and untoward incidents happen. Sometimes the event has something to do with the Railways and at other times, the Railways have no role, but regardless, must bear the brunt. The bomb blast in on the suburban train on 11 July 2006 in the Western Railway Mumbai affected the entire nation. A series of blasts took place around 6.30 p.m., a peak travel time, killing about two hundred persons and injuring more than seven hundred. It was a gruesome attack by terrorists.

Traditionally, trains have been a soft target. The Railways rallied splendidly to normalize its services in several incidents of natural calamity in the past. But this incident had different overtones. The entire international community was watching it with a lot of concern. It was a matter of great pride that the train services were normalized by six in the morning under the dynamic leadership of Vivek Sahai the AGM of the Western Railway. The entire operation was a testimony of Indian Railways' capacity to bounce back in state of emergency. This was particularly a laudable effort because Mumbai's suburban train services are the lifeline of the city and by starting to function in the soonest possible time, it reassured the public of normalcy. This was the best countermeasure against the terrorist attack for they sought to create panic and upset peace. When trains started running normally, nerves were calmed.

There was an extreme pressure on the Railway Board to look after the security of the Railways. This was seriously debated in the Board. Law and order was not the responsibility of the IR. This point was forcibly put across the home ministry. It constitutionally belonged to the state government. The MR had strongly told the Union home minister that the constitutional responsibility could not be passed on to the Railways. The RPF could not deal with general law and order. It was not trained in tackling subversive and terrorist activities. In this connection, I recall that home ministry proposed elevation of DG RPF as member (security) of the Railway Board. The suggestion was unacceptable and the Board in its resolution rejected it outright.

Bhagalpur tragedy—a freak accident

Another freak accident at Bhagalpur (Eastern Railway) shows how top management react while dealing with the aftereffects of a tragedy. An old masonry road overbridge across Bhagalpur station yard had served for more than hundred years. A new bridge was already constructed to replace this old three span arch bridge and it had to be dismantled, to clear the yard. Quite clearly, someone did not appreciate that it was necessary to secure the side span first before the central arch span could be dismantled. This had made the side span unsupported and hence unstable. In the morning of 2 December 2006, when the *Jamalpur Howrah Express* was passing under the bridge, the unsupported side span collapsed under the vibration of the passing train. The accident caused death of thirty-five passengers and injuries to seventeen persons. It was a freak and unfortunate accident, which totally rattled us.

Mr Gangopadhyay, CAO of Eastern Railway, informed me of it around 7.30 a.m. He was obviously too shocked to be coherent on the phone. He was not sure but said that some passengers must have died. It was a Saturday. I rushed and reached Bhagalpur by evening to witness utter chaos at the site. Over five hundred onlookers thronged the place, making the rescue operation extremely hazardous. Lalu ji was touring the area for some by-election. He came to the site at 9 p.m.

I briefed the minister about the accident. People jostled us and, in the melee, I was pushed down and fell on my head, just missing the rail. The MR went to the hospital to see the injured. The site engineers had clearly not taken elementary precautions. This was a freak incident. I returned to Delhi via Kolkata. The MR came back to Delhi around 5 p.m. There was an emergency meeting to review the situation. It was a Sunday and the Parliament was in session. The minister had to make a statement in the Parliament on Monday morning. Everyone in the meeting advocated strong action against the top engineers. I found that unfair and unwarranted. After everyone had spoken, I told the minister, 'Sir, we are very senior persons and therefore we are expected to respond to a situation in a careful manner. The accident was a freak one. It was a little like a tree being cut, which fell upon the road, killing someone. Can the topmost person like a district magistrate be suspended for the accident? Why are we asking for action against the CE or the CAO? Persons directly involved have already been suspended. The local police have registered a case of criminal neglect against them. Is the action proposed meant to dramatize the situation or show toughness? In that case, I am prepared to go home. It will have a much bigger impact. In any case, I am the setting sun. Let me carry this responsibility with me. But please bear in mind that if we overreact, they will next ask for action against the minister.' The MR looked upset and firmly said that there was no question of my going. He accepted my arguments. After everyone left his room, Lalu ji spoke to me, 'Jaruhar Sahib, I am touched by your gesture. I cannot forget what you have done for the Railways. I can see and appreciate your courage in trying to stand up for your people. Please do not worry, we will overcome the tragedy.'

The spectre of political vendetta looms large

This case raked up political vendetta between Nitish ji and Lalu ji. In the period between the Rajdhani accident in October 2001 and the Bhagalpur accident in December 2006, the role of two political rivals had reversed. Lalu ji was the de facto chief minister of Bihar (although his wife Rabri Devi was the CM but it was well known that Lalu ji ran Bihar) in October 2001 and Nitish ji was the rail minister. Lalu ji had not left any stone unturned to embarrass Nitish ji then. He had even rejected the clear evidence of sabotage for the Rajdhani accident. Now in December 2006, Nitish ji was the CM and Lalu ji the MR.

Now it was the turn of Nitish ji to persecute Lalu ji. I learnt that IG

Bhagalpur Range was directed to arrest senior officers of the Railways for this criminal neglect. I sent a message to Nitish ji requesting him not to make this a political issue. I gave details of the accident and explained that it was a freak accident. The CRS inquiry was on and we could wait for the outcome before taking police action. He asked me how he could forget the way Lalu ji had acted in the case of the Rajdhani accident. But he was quite concerned. The police acted reasonably and I learnt that Nitish ji called off his visit to Bhagalpur lest it should affect ongoing inquiry.

Lalu ji was of course upset. He told me that the local media in Bihar had unleashed severe campaign against him. I reminded him of an identical action taken in Bihar in case of the Rajdhani accident, and I told him that it was expected. He smiled meaningfully. It was what politics was all about.

It was time for me to retire in January 2007. We had succeeded in retaining the honour the department had earned by its long year of service to the Indian Railways. Rakesh Chopra, additional member civil engineering and Satish Agnihotri knew the background development of this case. He must have told others how it was achieved. Once Gangopadhyay told me that he owed his honour to me. Without the tough stand, sanity would not have prevailed.

THE EPISODE CONCERNING DG (OPERATION)—DIVIDE IN BODY FABRIC OF THE IR

December 2006 was coming to an end. Apart from the end, I was also approaching the final destination of my career in the Indian Railways. This was the time when four posts of director general (DG) operation were created by the traffic department. The development took us all completely by surprise. The MT, CRB and MS (incidentally all belonged to the IRTS) had mooted the proposal for creating one DG for each metro in grade of DG (Health & RPF). The DG would be higher in status than the GM. He would take over the control of rail operation in the region. The COM of the Railways would directly report to the DG.

A Cabinet note, duly approved by the MR, was sent to the Cabinet. Since the Railways was doing so well, the Cabinet had no difficulty in approving the creation of these posts. I had heard about it as a gossip and I did not believe it. This would cause a sweeping change in the hierarchy of the Indian Railways. I, therefore, trusted that such a proposal would have been certainly discussed in the Board. Besides, I enjoyed respect and trust of the MT and the CRB. They would have certainly taken me into confidence. The proposal would make the GM defunct. A superior person would oversee the rail operation. This was the statutory duty of open line GM under the Railway Act. The position would become incongruous. It affected all departments. The proposal should have been discussed in the Board before taking it to the Cabinet.

There is sharp reaction to creation of the post of the DG

I first came to know about it while attending a meeting with the MR in his room. K.P. Yadav (the EDPG to MR and an IRTS officer), mentioned the creation of the post of the DG by the Cabinet. My antennae were up. After returning to my room, I told Rakesh Chopra, AMCE, about what I had heard. He confirmed that the Cabinet had already approved the proposal. Then I asked the CRB about the creation of the posts of DG operation. I requested him to send the file to me. He was very nice and asked secretary Railway Board to show me the file. Mathew John, the secretary had been my COM in the Northern Railway. He brought the file to me. He said that whatever had happened was not good for the Indian Railways.

I was shocked to read the file and the Cabinet note. I called my other colleague members—Ramesh Chandra, member electrical and A.K. Rao, member mechanical. They were equally shocked. We decided to send the file to the minister with our comments. I requested the MR to hold back the operation of the decision as it had serious ramifications. It had already evoked severe reactions from all sides. The Federation of Railway Officers had taken up the matter with the MR. Many MPs had also spoken to him in this regard. The file reached the MR with sharp comments from three Board members. The MR's cell was unnerved. Sudhir Kumar told me that he had not appreciated the implication of the decision fully. Now he was convinced that it was going to cause permanent damage to the fabric of the IR. I told him to request the MR to hold a meeting of all the Board members to know the full implication of the decision. Sudhir assured me that this would not be implemented. But he requested that I play a role in repairing the damage.

The minister responds to the reaction—damage control

All the Board members were present at the meeting, in the MR's room. He asked me to brief him about the issue because he was deeply concerned. I stood up to speak. The MR asked me to be seated while I spoke. I said, 'Sir, I will have to stand up and say what I have to. We have outlined our apprehension and anguish in the file on the decision to create the DG (operation) posts. I will request you to hear me and my colleagues out. After listening to us, you need to decide. Whether I should stand or sit down before all of you will depend upon your decision. In case you decide to pursue with the Cabinet decision, I cannot sit with my IRTS friends because they are the breadwinners as described in the Cabinet note. They will be masters now, after what the Cabinet has decided. I will forfeit my rights to be an equal partner in the Board. I cannot sit along with them because my position would be on the floor.'

There was a strong protest from Mr Jena, MS. He said that it was never meant in that manner. I said, 'But the Cabinet note begins by saying that IRTS is "the Breadwinner" of the Indian Railways. It is an offensive statement. Sir, unfortunately my English is not so good. You may have the same problem. It should therefore be referred to a knowledgeable person like Sudhir Kumar, a seasoned IAS officer. He can definitely confirm what the term "breadwinners" means.' Sudhir Kumar nodded. According to him, he also did not notice it when the Cabinet note had come to him for the approval of the MR.

MM and ML were requested to explain this further. Engineering, Mechanical, Electrical and Signalling departments actually provided the basic infrastructure to run the railways. Without their efforts, it would have been impossible to run any train. 'A train can be run without an IRTS officer but it cannot be run without an active association of these technical departments,' ML said. I said that during the last year and a half, we strove to bring laurels to the IR by creating a homogeneous bond across the entire fabric of the IR. Unfortunately, this single decision would completely destroy it.

The minister did not take much time in appreciating the sensitivity of the issue. This would destroy everything he had achieved. He said, 'I am very sorry to hear about your pain which is fully justified. I know it is a bad decision. It was taken without fully appreciating its implication. I was not aware that it was not discussed in the Board. I have decided to withdraw this forthwith.' I said, 'Sir, we thank you, but this decision has upset many people. I request you to call representatives of the FROA. Please assuage their hurt feelings by announcing the cancellation of the order before them.' He immediately agreed. The FROA was called in. The MR told them that a wrong decision had been taken. He said that he would get the order withdrawn.

There was great relief and rejoicing everywhere. Sudhir Kumar thanked me for the way the whole affair had been conducted. It also brought much praise to the MR. This dangerous, divisive and flippant move to have a short-term gain was undone in the best interest of the Indian Railways. That it happened in the last few days of my service made me sad. I had to speak harshly against my very good friends. I had honestly believed that operations was the most crucial function of the IR, but I had not dreamt that it would be construed to have a sense of superiority over others. That had left a bad taste in my mouth. I was also hurt by the secretive manner in which it had been executed. It belied the basic trust amongst colleagues of long years. But that is part of human failings. The IR must move forward with a new resolve by burying the episode for good!

SAND IN THE HOURGLASS RUNS OUT FOR ME

The sand in the hourglass of my service days was fast slipping away. I had reached the juncture when only fifteen more days were left for me to move to the vanaprastha stage of my life. These were the days when we had to accept greetings of farewell from many quarters. I had decided to go to Kolkata because I had started my railway journey from the Eastern Railway. I also went to Kanchrapara. I visited the old quarters where I had stayed as AEN—my first work post. I had got married here. It was an emotional experience. I was sorry to see the pitiable upkeep of the house which had once boasted of a beautiful garden and a fine ambience.

I also travelled to Mumbai with my wife mainly because of my good friend V.K. Kaul, GM, Central Railway. Subodh Jain, PCE Central, was my conscious keeper in many ways. I loved Goyal, PCE Western, because of my old association from the NF Railway. I must also thank Vats, CAO/CR, and Uttamchand, CAO/WR, who also joined in the function. The Western and Central Railways' officers had organized a combined farewell. I also attended the last Board meeting of the Konkan Railway Corporation. As is usual, tributes and words of praise and good wishes were expressed to me and my wife. When we came to Mumbai Central station to catch the *Rajdhani Express*, I was shocked to see the whole coach decorated with flowers as if it were a bridal coach. Feeling extremely embarrassed—as all the passengers were looking at us we were at the same time, deeply touched by the show of love and affection.

I also travelled to the Pamban Bridge site as I had already described elsewhere to fulfil the promise, I had made to Dr A.P.J. Kalam. We also went to Gorakhpur mainly because of a very compelling invitation from Sukhbir Singh, GM, North Eastern Railway. We had spent an important phase of our life there. I also went to Lucknow on the invitation of DRM, Northern Railway. I always considered Lucknow as a cultural centre. The musical evening staged by the artist group led by Mithilesh has been unforgettable, where they sang all of my favourite old songs.

THE GOODBYE AND BEFORE IT

In the meantime, we were seriously concerned about a place to stay after I retired. I did not own a house. In desperation, I rented a house in Gurgaon.

But my old boss Kanwarjit Singh, who had settled down in Gurgaon, in the phase II pocket of the IRWO housing society, insisted that I procure one in that colony. It was largely because of his initiative that we got this house on 27 January 2007. I must thank Satish Agnihotri who did all the legwork and necessary documentations for the house for which I had no money. Luckily, the bank loan was arranged in the name of Shreya, my daughter, who was working with the Standard Chartered Bank. Branch Manager of Canara Bank Mr Mittal was particularly considerate. The keys were passed on to Shreya eventually on 22 February 2007 after I had retired. There was no doubt that things had been largely facilitated because of the post I had occupied.

So on 31 January 2007, I walked to the Rail Bhawan for the last time. As I entered through Gate Number 4, I was weighed down by a sense of great humility. I thanked God that He had been kind to allow me to serve a mammoth organization like the Indian Railways. There was the usual Board meeting, where the members thanked and wished me well and we had a customary sit-in lunch. The evening was dedicated to the formal farewell in the conference hall of the Rail Bhawan. My retirement dues were formally paid, and then, with the final words of love and good wishes, I returned to my room to collect my belongings before I left the Railways for good.

On the day I had joined as ME, I had started to keep a score book detailing number of days left before I retired. I sat down and struck the last day to signal the end of my career as a railwayman—a name with which every railwayman wanted to be associated. Each of them would say with just pride, 'Once a railwayman, always a railwayman'.

My personal staff came to wish me. I gave them a small souvenir as a token of gratitude for their help and cooperation. I was keenly aware that it had been a demanding time for them. They must have suffered a great deal on my account. I am grateful to V.T. Xavier. He is an excellent officer and he has never let me down. An upright person, he had served fifteen MEs before me. He bailed me out of many tough situations. His advice was extremely valuable. V. Kumar was another senior PS. He looked after my personal appointments. Satish Agnihotri, my OSD, was my conscience keeper and spiritual brother. He carried out tricky and complicated assignments for me. He was a great plank between me and the MR cell above, as well as my younger colleagues who looked up to the ME for help in their personal and service life. I feel very grateful to them. I also thanked my peon Babulal and others and other supporting staff including my staff car driver.

It was 7 p.m. and time for me to leave the Rail Bhawan. I walked out with a heavy heart but with a profound sense of satisfaction that I had discharged my duties as I had promised my mother. I was grateful to the organization which had looked after me and my family. It was a protective umbrella that had allowed me to grow both in personal and professional spheres. It had been a great journey. I had reached great heights by putting my heart and soul into what I did. This was the height many wished to reach, but few actually did. That I could walk out of the Rail Bhawan for the last time with my head held high was the greatest of blessings. Thank you, Indian Railways!

I reached home and was received by my wife who welcomed me as always. And both of us walked together in contentment. It is with an immense feeling of gratitude that I end my story here.

EPILOGUE

I have decided to write the epilogue in order to conclude the account of memories of a railway engineer.

I MISSED LALU JI DURING MY FAREWELL

It is a well-established practice in the Railway Board for the railway minister to preside over the farewell function of the retiring member of the Railway Board. The function is held in the conference hall of the Rail Bhawan at five in the evening on the last day of the month. This date is known in advance, I have known railway ministers to adjust their engagements accordingly. Thus, I was expecting Lalu ji to preside over the function. I was disappointed when he was out of Delhi. I missed him particularly.

He returned late in the night of 31 January. I went to see him at his residence the next morning. He was very apologetic, of course. While taking leave of him, I reminded him of his promise to withdraw the Cabinet note on creation of four posts of DG (operations). My information was that the IRTS lobby was keeping the file to let the suspense grow. They wanted to wait till I retired. Lalu ji spoke to Sudhir immediately. I have been told that the decision has been ultimately withdrawn. Here, I also met S.K. Vij who succeeded me as ME. He had also come to meet the MR with sweets.

I ATTENDED A COLOURFUL FAREWELL PARTY AT THE CLUB

I must also mention the colourful farewell party at the Railway Club, S.P. Marg. It was as usual a very emotional experience and Rakesh Chopra was eloquent in appraising me. Krishna Chander, the oldest ME present, jokingly asked me not to believe them. I think he was absolutely correct.

RECOMMENDATION FOR PADMA SHRI

Sudhir, OSD to MR, usually praised me for my contributions towards the turnaround of the Railways. He also regretted that because of petty considerations, I was not allowed my due in the Railways. He mentioned that Lalu ji had agreed to recommend my case for the Padma Shri award in 2008-09. He requested that I send a draft citation, which I did. It was sent to the government on 30 September 2008. I was very busy with the wedding of Shreya which was to take place on 14 October 2008. S.B. Ghoshdastidar, former MT, was also recommended. I was asked to lobby for it. It was not possible for me to do so. Thus, despite my outstanding achievements, I was bypassed. But my good friend Ghoshdastidar was approved. He called on me. I was very happy. Evidently, honour and laurels are destined by the Lord.

Expert Group on the Kashmir Project

The Jammu and Kashmir project was put under abeyance by the Board in October 2008, citing technical problems in the alignment. It was felt by the ME that an alternative alignment might be more durable and maintainable. The decision became controversial. I was asked to chair a brainstorming session in the Northern Railway in August 2008. We unanimously opined that the present alignment between Kazigund-Katra was correct and the only changes required were some local adjustments. But stopping the work had extensive international ramifications. Another expert committee was constituted by the Board. Mr Ravindra, past ME and CRB, was the chairman. I was also a member. During deliberations, many currents with vested interests were visible. I had to steer the discussion back to the course at times by becoming unpleasant. Mr Ravindra is an extremely intelligent and knowledgeable person. He could be very firm. I think because of his rich experience and my knowledge of the terrain, we were able to resolve the issue by retaining the old alignment with minor adjustments. The project was revived based on our reports. I am satisfied that subsequent tests and studies corroborated our assessment in the report. In any case, I had never imagined that I would play any further role in this project after my retirement.

MEETING DR A.P.J. KALAM—FORMER PRESIDENT

I called on Dr Kalam at his residence in Delhi on 26 February 10. He was very pleasant and received me with lot of warmth. He recalled my contribution for the Pamban Bridge. He was a simple person. He made me believe that all those who visit Rameshwaram would remember me. It was his magnanimity. I wished to meet him because he had inspired me to take up this work. I reminded him that the idea had begun from his statement, 'At least a passenger train could go!' I was touched by his simplicity and warmth. I salute the spirit of service, which he championed. May his soul rest in peace. I wrote a tribute to commemorate him.

BOOKS AND STUDIES ON THE TURNAROUND OF THE INDIAN RAILWAYS

A number of agencies have studied the turnaround of the IR. The World Bank team made an incisive study. They had a number of interactions with me. I was subsequently informed by Atul Agarwal that no report was published in the end.

The Harvard School of Business (HBS) also carried out a study. I helped them in their study. Rachna Tahilyani, research associate, HBS, informed me in her letter dated 15 October 2009 that HBS had published a case study 'Indian Railways: Building a Permanent Legacy'. They duly acknowledged my contribution in the case. This would be taught to second-year MBA students in the fall of 2010 under 'Doing Business under Emerging Markets'.

Professor S. Ramnarayan of the Indian School of Business, Hyderabad, and Prof. V. Nilakant from the University of New Zealand worked with me for over two years to write a book on the turnaround of the Indian Railways. The book *Changing Tracks—Reinventing the Spirit of Indian Railways* was launched on 26 March 2010 in an impressive ceremony in Delhi. The book deals with the major contributions to the turnaround and the authors graciously called me a champion of the exercise. Dr Ramnarayan incidentally also encouraged me to write this memoir.

MY TRIBUTES

In my journey spanning over thirty-nine years in the Indian Railways, I had the benefit of counselling, advice and help from a large number of illustrious persons. Regretfully, some of them are no more when this report on my reminiscences is ready. My tributes to the following who mentored or guided me to be the railwayman, I am today:

1. B.C. Ganguli 2. V.C.A. Padmanabhan 3. K. Balachandran 4. Ashok Saikia 5. T.N. Joshi 6. H.D. Bhowmick 7. S.N. Sachdev 8. V.K.J. Rane 9. M.N. Prasad 10. R.K. Singh 11. T.N. Ramachandran 12. R. K. Banerjee 13. Massihuzamman.

ACKNOWLEDGEMENTS

First of all, I acknowledge the divine grace of Shiv Baba for helping me to write this memoir. Without His help and continuous support, it would have never been possible to start and finish the book!

It was Ajay Shukla, the former chief safety officer of the Northern Railway, who first encouraged me to write about my long experience with the Railways. Given my hectic schedule, I could not do so while in service, so when I retired I commenced the exercise much due to Ajay's coaxing. So, I thank him for his support in all earnestness. Like him, there had been many others nudging me to pen down my thoughts about my many years in service with the Railways. I am unable to name them all, but I gratefully acknowledge their support and belief in me.

It was my son, Shrimant, who kindly provided me with a laptop to key in my thoughts. He was then doing his Master's in Penn State University in the US. The first draft of my memoir was reviewed by him and subsequently he and his friend Nayantara Abraham reviewed several drafts even when he was busy as project manager in Northwestern Memorial Hospital, Chicago. Both had been very encouraging and appreciative while going through the various drafts. I thank both of them.

Anubha, my wife; Shravani, my eldest daughter; Shreya, my second daughter, and her husband Manav offered many useful suggestions. I am particularly grateful to Anubha for her constant checks to ensure that I do not get carried away while writing about my rather eventful tenure with the Indian Railways. I cannot thank them enough.

Vinay Kumar Singh my erstwhile secretary and now managing director of the National Capital Region Transport Corporation (NCRTC), Satish Agnihotri my OSD and now retired as chairman and managing director (CMD) of the Rail Vikas Nigam Ltd (RVNL) were a constant source of encouragement. Mukesh Sharma, the protocol officer of the Northern Railway provided a lot of support. Amrit Mathur my erstwhile chief safety officer and presently celebrated columnist with the *Hindustan Times* as well as a cricket administrator also encouraged me a great deal. My deep gratitude to all of them for their support.

I am also grateful to Sarvesh Chaube and Rajesh Agarwal, the present members of the Railway Board and Vinod Yadav, the chairman Railway Board for their good wishes. I had the good fortune to have a long association with them when I served, and I therefore very fondly and gratefully acknowledge their good wishes.

Many of my former colleagues who had made my work simple and successful have also lent a lot of support in writing this book. I would especially like to mention and thank Vipin Sharma, Shashank Vaidya, Pankaj Jain, Aditya Mittal, R.G. Singh, H. K. Singh, J.P. Das, Rakesh Chopra, B. D. Garg, Anurag Sharma, Subodh Jain, A. P. Mishra, J.P. Shukla and D.C. Mitra (CMD, RVNL) and Satish Kumar.

Amber, my nephew and Mukul, my son-law, have provided immense emotional and logistical support while I was writing this book. I cannot thank them enough!

Lastly, Dibakar Ghosh and the editorial team of Rupa Publications deserve all the thanks for enriching this book with their invaluable suggestions.